# ANIMALS AND THE LAW

Other books in the *Essentials of Canadian Law* Series

Immigration Law

International Trade Law

Family Law

Copyright Law

The Law of Equitable Remedies

The Law of Sentencing

Administrative Law

Ethics and Canadian Criminal Law

Securities Law

Computer Law 2/e

Maritime Law

Insurance Law

International Human Rights Law

The Law of Trusts 2/e

Franchise Law

Personal Property Security Law

The Law of Contracts

Pension Law

Constitutional Law 3/e

Legal Ethics and Professional Responsibility 2/e

Refugee Law

Mergers, Acquisitions, and Other Changes of Corporate Control

Bank and Customer Law in Canada

Statutory Interpretation 2/e

National Security Law: Canadian Practice in International Perspective

Remedies: The Law of Damages 2/e

Public International Law 2/e

Criminal Procedure

Individual Employment Law 2/e

Environmental Law 3/e

Bankruptcy and Insolvency Law

Criminal Law 4/e

The Law of Partnerships and Corporations 3/e

The Charter of Rights and Freedoms 4/e

Youth Criminal Justice Law 2/e

Civil Litigation

International and Transnational Criminal Law

Conflict of Laws

Detention and Arrest

Canadian Telecommunications Law

The Law of Torts 4/e

Intellectual Property Law 2/e

The Law of Evidence 6/e

Income Tax Law 2/e

ESSENTIALS OF
CANADIAN LAW

# ANIMALS AND THE LAW

**LESLI BISGOULD**

Adjunct Professor, Faculty of Law,
University of Toronto, 2011–12
Barrister, Legal Aid Ontario Clinic Resource Office

IRWIN
LAW

Animals and the Law
© Irwin Law Inc., 2011

Published in 2011 by

Irwin Law Inc.
14 Duncan Street
Suite 206
Toronto, ON
M5H 3G8

www.irwinlaw.com

ISBN: 978-1-55221-231-8
e-book ISBN: 978-1-55221-232-5

**Library and Archives Canada Cataloguing in Publication**

Bisgould, Lesli
    Animals and the law / Lesli Bisgould.

(Essentials of Canadian law)
Includes bibliographical references and index.
Also issued in electronic format.
ISBN 978-1-55221-231-8

    1. Animals--Law and legislation--Canada.  2. Animal welfare--Law and legislation--Canada.  I. Title.  II. Series: Essentials of Canadian law

KE452.A5B58 2011     344.7104'9     C2011-907526-1
KF3841.B58 2011

The publisher acknowledges the financial support of the Government of Canada through the Canada Book Fund for its publishing activities.

We acknowledge the assistance of the OMDC Book Fund, an initiative of Ontario Media Development Corporation.

Printed and bound in Canada.

1 2 3 4 5   15 14 13 12 11

# SUMMARY
# TABLE OF CONTENTS

# DETAILED TABLE OF CONTENTS

# PART III: SPECIFIC USES OF ANIMAL THINGS    125

CHAPTER 7

# RESEARCH TOOLS   201

# FOREWORD

It is clear that we need to rethink our relationship with animals. Part of that task of necessity is to re-imagine how we conceive of them. Beyond a doubt, there has been an increasing sensitivity to animal welfare over recent decades, and good as that is, it is not sufficient if all that emerges from it are increased penalties which, theoretically, could be imposed on humans who engage in animal cruelty. The relationship is far more complex than that.

This book examines the unique role that animals play as living property in a legal system conceived by and for human beings. On the one hand, animals are things that we buy, eat, and use in experiments. On the other, they are beloved family companions in a bond that scarcely allows for separation between self and other. Our law does not handle this discord with much dexterity.

Indeed, it is this core ambiguity that provides the context for examining the history of — and the historical basis for — laws with respect to animals. The book traces these, from the animal trials which began in the thirteenth century in Europe, through the development of anti-cruelty laws, to the present struggle to cope with the conflicting implications of biotechnology and other industrial uses for animals, and indeed, artificially created living things. Throughout, the book critically evaluates the present legal status of animals and asks us to consider whether animals should be viewed as objects, as legal subjects, as legal persons, or as something else entirely.

Read on. You will remember this book.

*Clayton C Ruby*
Barrister and Solicitor
Toronto, Canada

# ACKNOWLEDGEMENTS

I must start by gratefully acknowledging Irwin Law's interest in publishing a book about animals and the law, and the decision that the subject is an essential one for its collection. Alisa Posesorski was keenly interested and was so easy to deal with that the process was enjoyable.

My colleagues at the Clinic Resource Office were very supportive of the effort to get this book written. Katryn Pereira did everything she could to get me the time I needed to write it, and many others helped me stay up-to-date on developments.

I am so grateful for the generous contributions of four women who were law students at the time we began to talk about animals. Maria Golarz, Camille Labchuk, Annalea Pippus, and Tina Sun each did research and drafting for a respective chapter, of which I made significant use in the final version. I am thankful, not only for the work they saved me, but for the inspiration I draw from the committed intellectual approach they took to the subject. Others helped me put the pieces together. Thank you to Mark Arnold and Kate Kempton for answering questions, and to Kathy Bocsi and Charlene Schafer for helping with some research.

I thank and admire Clayton Ruby, who has been such a generous mentor and who has represented the interests of animals, and the people who advocate for them, with the same determination and wholeheartedness with which he is known to fight for human rights.

I am motivated by many advocates for animals who work long hours in bleak subject matter, persevering to tell truths that some people would prefer not to be known. Too many individuals to name have inspired me and helped me find the information I needed over the years, and for this book. Thank you to Rebecca Aldworth, Stephanie Brown, Rob Laidlaw, Barry Kent MacKay, Debra Probert, Liz White, and Julie Woodyer for the work they persist in doing, and for the assistance they have given me in ensuring that what I say here is accurate. Norman Taylor shares all the news he can find about animal-legal issues, and I have relied on information he provided in several places in this book.

My deepest gratitude is for my family and particularly my parents, Elaine and Harvey Bisgould, who could not have been more supportive in this, or in any of my endeavours. My appreciation for honesty, integrity, speaking up for what is right, and for animals themselves, comes straight from my upbringing.

Albert Vila's pursuit of knowledge and clarity of thought enriches my own contemplations on all subjects, including this one. His support and encouragement helped me through difficult struggles in my mind and at the computer, and he never complained when I turned our home into my office while writing this book. He is my favourite animal of all.

# INTRODUCTION

Orwell was right. Some animals really are more equal than others.[1]

For present purposes, that statement has three connotations: first, as between animals themselves; second, as between humans themselves; and finally (and the ultimate subject of this book), between humans and all the other species that comprise the animal kingdom. Each of these is considered below, leading to an overview of the general nature of the problems facing animals in the legal system, or more precisely, facing the people who seek some sort of legal consideration of their interests.

## A. ANIMAL TO ANIMAL

There are some animals on whom Canadians spend billions of dollars buying the right food, designer clothing, and furniture; getting medical care, prescription drugs, and the expensive insurance policies to assure them; and arranging daycare, therapy, even yoga. These animals have cute names. We hire photographers to take their portraits. They are our friends and companions. They live in our homes and might even sleep in our beds.[2]

---

1   George Orwell, *Animal Farm* (New York: Signet Classics, 1986).
2   In 2007, approximately 7.9 million cats and 5.9 million dogs lived in Canadian homes; see John Sorenson, *About Canada: Animal Rights* (Winnipeg: Fernwood, 2010) at 9 [Sorenson].

There are other animals whom we profess to love too but do not usually live in our homes. They have names like Shamu and Dumbo, monikers which sometimes persist even as the individual animals behind them are dying, being replaced by others called Shamu and Dumbo, so that we do not notice. These animals live in cages or tanks or in the beast wagons in which they constantly travel, so that we can occasionally get close to them. The thrill of seeing these animals seems to sublimate any questions we might have about what life is like on the other side of the enclosure.

Other animals do not have personalized names. There are numbers tattooed on their skin or on tags punched through their ears or recorded on their charts. They live confined in stalls or cages or other small enclosures. Beyond ensuring their fitness for the purpose to which they are put, their well-being is largely irrelevant and every dollar spent on it diminishes the profit to be made from them.

There are also innumerable anonymous animals who do not come into captivity, but they are injured or killed, for food or for fun, or because they are bothering us in some way.

In an estimated 12,000–15,000 years of domestication, we have established a variety of contradictory relationships with animals both wild and captive, regarding them interchangeably as companions, family members, entertainers, servants, vermin, tools, models, specimens, units of production, modes of transportation, edible parts, fashionable parts, body parts factories, and most recently—once genetically modified—as our very own inventions.

In creating these relationships, we sometimes distinguish between species of animals: in Western culture, we happily eat cows and pigs, but not dogs or cats. Other times, we don't: dogs and cats are our companions but they are also the subjects of a wide variety of painful scientific procedures. The contradictions are so common as to go largely unnoticed, and they have existed right from the start.

In 1978, a 12,000-year-old grave was discovered in northern Israel, containing the skeletons of an elderly person and a five-month-old puppy. They were buried together, arranged such that the left hand of the person was resting on the puppy's shoulder.[3] This gesture reflects a deep emotional attachment, even then, between people and animals, especially dogs. The arrangement of the bodies suggests that even in death, animals comfort us. However, there is a more sinister aspect, in

---

3    Simon JM Davis & François R Valla, "Evidence for Domestication of the Dog 12,000 Years Ago in the Natufian of Israel" (1978) 276 Nature 608–10. Thank you to John Sorenson for bringing this to the author's attention.

that the puppy appears to have been killed in order to accompany the person to the grave. The puppy's life was ended in order to satisfy human emotional needs regarding death.[4]

More recently, a news story broke in early 2011 that over two days the previous April, Outdoor Adventures in Whistler had rounded up and shot or stabbed one hundred of its sled dogs because business was slow after the Vancouver Olympics. Public outrage was immediate and universal, but as some observers pointed out, many other animals are regularly shot or cut or otherwise brutalized—in recreational pastimes or industrial practices, with public funding or at least public support, and without any objection whatsoever.[5]

Since our views about animals are so confused, it should not be surprising that our laws are confused as well. On the one hand, federal and provincial anti-cruelty legislation across the country purports to prohibit causing "unnecessary pain and suffering" to animals, admitting as their premise that animals feel pain and suffering in the first place, and also that people care about that. This would seem to reflect public opinion: a 2010 Harris/Decima poll found that 95 percent of Canadians agree that animal pain and suffering should be reduced as much as possible.[6]

On the other hand, one need not be a legal expert to figure out that in prohibiting "unnecessary" pain and suffering, we create a corollary and thereby permit the causing of pain and suffering that is "necessary." Since we draft the laws and we interpret them, we have effectively written ourselves permission to hurt animals as we see fit.

This ultimately means that when it comes to the treatment of animals, there is no act, however violent or harmful, that is categorically illegal. In fact, the same act of hurting an animal might be seen to be abhorrent or admirable, depending on the circumstance. If a sadistic person with nothing better to do one day decides to restrain a dog and burn him with a blowtorch, she would likely be considered to have caused unnecessary pain and suffering to the dog; however, if the per-

---

4    Jim Mason, *An Unnatural Order: Why We Are Destroying the Planet and Each Other* (New York: Continuum, 1997) at 113.

5    Stephen Hume, "In the Time it Takes to Read This, Nearly 20,000 Farm Animals Will be Slaughtered" *Vancouver Sun* (3 February 2011); Maneesha Deckha, "Laws Must See Animals as More Than Property" *Victoria Times Colonist* (3 February 2011). Hume and Deckha respond to the scene in which dogs were shot and lingered in pain while other dogs watched, including one who had half of her face blown off, as well as others whose throats were slit and suffered such agony that the man who did it was treated for post-traumatic stress disorder.

6    Harris/Decima, *Humane Treatment of Animals* (3 December 2010).

son is a researcher who restrains and blowtorches a dog in a laboratory, in the course of his study of the effect, development, or treatment of burns, then the same act, which causes the same pain and suffering to the same dog, is now "necessary" and not only lawful but encouraged with public incentives, such as funding with tax dollars, grants, or charitable donations and the professional status that accompanies publication of the results.[7]

In business, the instrumental use of animals is extensive; many hundreds of millions of animals are killed every year. In the agriculture, fashion, research, entertainment, recreation, and pet industries—animals or their body parts are the central object of consumption, while a long list of spin-off industries relies on the by-product, so that animal bits are found in such things as windshield wiper fluid, compact discs, car and bicycle tires, plastic bags, vitamins, shampoos, and fabric softeners. Inasmuch as profit is considered as legitimate a necessity as any other, even the beloved animals can suffer miserably in the hands of the industries which breed, capture, and bring them to us. In the context of other industries, where animals are brought into existence for the specific purpose of being hurt, killed, and dismembered, what can "humane treatment" and "unnecessary suffering" really mean?

The anti-cruelty laws which encapsulate this perspective have a very flexible interpretation, depending on the kind of animal at issue and the use to which the animal is being put. They have proved to be a very limited tool in terms of protecting most animals from most of the pain and suffering that humans cause them. Necessity itself is a loaded concept. Its mere invocation is sufficient to demonstrate the categorical distinction which law makes between humans and animals.

## B. HUMAN TO HUMAN

Of course making distinctions is not unusual human behaviour. In *Animal Farm*, Orwell was using animals as a metaphor for humans because even in the human realm, we draw lines between groups. Distinguishing between "us" and "them" has always been a convenient way of excluding "them" from some privilege or advantage enjoyed by "us," and of rationalizing the harm we cause to others, directly or indirectly, for our own benefit. One need only consult the list of enumerated grounds of discrimination in any province's human rights legislation, or the

---

7    This example is given in Gary L Francione, *Introduction to Animal Rights: Your Child or the Dog* (Philadelphia: Temple University Press, 2000) at 4.

lengthy dockets of the tribunals empowered to adjudicate those claims, to be reminded of just the most obvious power imbalances which perpetuate in our own relations.

In an effort to check our discriminatory tendencies in respect of one another, we have developed a theory of equality. This is a legal concept. We are not really "equal" in our attributes or abilities. Some people are better at math than others. Some are better athletes, or artists. Some can compose operas, some can sing them. Some are nicer or funnier or taller. More pointedly, we have different genders, disabilities, or religious beliefs. Some of these differences are genetic, or at least biological, while others are acquired.

The legal notion of equality recognizes that while we differ in these many ways, the differences are not morally relevant when it comes to certain fundamentals in our treatment of one another. The legal notion of equality calls upon us to identify the morally relevant differences on which we base the distinctions we make, so as to justify differential treatment in a principled manner. Age might be a morally relevant factor when it comes to determining who can drive, vote, or see restricted movies, but it is not relevant when it comes to determining whether it is all right for someone to be injured or killed.

There is considerable controversy about how to achieve human equality, including, for example, whether there is a meaningful distinction between "equality" and "human rights" and whether "rights" are the best mechanism in the first place, and in particular, legal rights, which require the state to assert its power to protect the interest in question. Neither law in general, nor human rights nor equality law in particular, is a panacea, and their respective constraints are subjects unto themselves.

For present purposes, it suffices to consider that while we have not yet succeeded in assuring legal equality between all humans, we do, at least ostensibly, strive toward this goal. Memories of our own involvement in human slavery and detention centres, or of times when women could not vote or claim any interest in their husband's property, discomfit modern Canadians. In the legal system, however many of its flaws might be the subject of valid criticism elsewhere, we have a somewhat democratic forum where conflicts in our respective interests can be articulated and considered.

To that end, we do generally agree on at least this one fundamental principle: humans have an interest in their own lives and in not being treated exclusively as the resource of another, and the law should protect this interest. In fact, there are few circumstances where killing anybody, for any reason, can be justified and the justification is almost never based on membership in a particular group.[8] A good example of this fundamental principle is the persistent but elusive "necessity" defence, which exists in both civil and criminal law, according to which a person who harms another might be able to defend himself by proving that the harm he caused was not as bad as the harm he sought to prevent.

This defence is the highlight of *R v Dudley & Stephens*,[9] a 130-year-old British case which Canadian law students still study. Dudley, Stephens, Parker, and Brooks were the only survivors of a British shipwreck, which left them stranded at sea in a small lifeboat with only a few turnips, a thousand miles from land. When the turnips were gone and little hope of survival remained, Dudley and Stephens decided to kill Parker, without his consent, and sustain themselves with his flesh and blood. Days after doing so, they were found by a passing ship, taken to shore, and charged with murder.

At trial, they invoked the necessity defence — they had to kill Parker for the sake of their own survival. The jury did find that Parker was much weaker than the others, that he would have died first even if he had not been murdered, and that there was no reasonable prospect that the men would be saved. However, this defence was rejected. The concept of "necessity" could never justify killing another person so as to use him as a resource for one's own purpose, however important that purpose might be. In so deciding, the court asked, "Who is to be the judge of this sort of necessity? By what measure is the comparative value of lives to be measured?" — apposite questions in that context, as in this one.[10]

While the court had some sympathy for the predicament of Dudley and Stephens, its greater concern was for what allowing this defence would mean to the fundamental principle that a person may not be used as the means to another person's ends, however much or however many others might benefit by it.

To consider a more topical example, across the country there are long lists of people who are desperately waiting for organ donations.

---

8    Exceptional circumstances include war, which in modern times has to encompass more ill-defined wars, such as the "war on terror." The case can also be made that it practically extends to other political wars, including the "war on drugs" and the "war on crime" more generally.

9    *R v Dudley & Stephens* (1884), [1881–85] All ER 61 (QB); the significance of this case in this context is discussed in Gary L Francione, *Animals, Property and the Law* (Philadelphia: Temple University Press, 1995) at 21–23 and accompanying footnotes.

10    *Ibid* at 67, Lord Coleridge CJ.

Some individuals consent to donate their organs, in life or in death, to others in need, but the number of donors has not yet begun to match the number of people on the waiting list. Were one of those desperate, waiting people to capture a healthy-looking stranger, help herself to one of his kidneys and then claim it was necessary for her own survival, we know without a trial that she would have no defence. We just do not permit the word "necessary" in that context. Among legal equals, however qualified that assertion must be from time to time, and whoever is to be "the judge of this kind of necessity," there are limits. Yet, those limits do not persist beyond the species barrier.

# C. HUMAN TO ANIMAL

While modern society would just as readily reject the idea of necessary murder and cannibalism as did Victorian-era England, what we do permit ourselves to eat cannot be considered necessary in these modern times, in most Canadian places.[11] Necessity takes on another meaning entirely in the animal context, revealing the root of the problem for animals in Canadian law.

For a country that prides itself on its peaceful ways, Canadians cause a lot of animals a lot of pain and suffering. Most of it is not by way of the individual horrific acts of violence regularly in the news, but by institutionalized, often profitable practices which are daily routines and hardly ever news items. Often these practices can only be justified by reasons of habit, preference, convenience, and convention. However, animal interests are subordinated to human interests in this manner because animals have no legal status by which to assert any objection. Whether in the federal, provincial, or municipal context, humans have the right to *own* property (among other things), and enjoy all of the rights that accompany that status, whereas animals *are* property, with all the implications that designation suggests. Often this status is not even directly asserted or proved, it is the inevitable premise on which laws are made and interpreted.

To argue against human necessity in the context of a person's use of her animal is much like asking the court to weigh the interests of a person who wants to drive her car against the interests of the car in not being driven. The owner might have to fill up with gas, change the oil, and do repairs from time to time if she wants the car to run well, but in the end it is really up to her to decide. She is also free to neglect

---

11    For further discussion, see Chapter 6.

or destroy her car. That is the essence of property ownership, that one can do as she pleases with her property. The only real constraint on this freedom arises when it might cause harm (to third parties), but to suggest that property itself has its own interest in not being harmed is absurd.[12]

Animals are treated a little differently from cars in that there are no anti-cruelty laws governing the latter which require a consideration of whether an act causes a car unnecessary pain and suffering. To the extent that law has added an element of consideration that does not apply to other property, it has acknowledged that animals are unique in the category and that they do have their own interests. Anti-cruelty laws might be considered the first wave of animal protection in Canada.

However, anti-cruelty laws date from the nineteenth century and they are based on the knowledge and values of the time. As a result of the limitations mentioned, they provide only minimal protection to a small number of animals in limited circumstances. The necessity element severely constrains, or even predetermines, their ultimate effect.

Just like the necessity of blowtorching a dog depends on the context, other harm is similarly interpreted. Charges might arise from the slaughter of the Whistler sled dogs, given the brutality with which it was undertaken. But even if they do, these could only address the manner in which these animals were killed. Had one hundred dogs been killed in an orderly fashion at a veterinarian's office, there would have been no legal offence, even though they would still have been discarded for economic reasons.

However, people do not treat animals badly because animals are property, animals are classified as property so that people can treat them badly.[13] We can choose to classify them differently and to act accordingly. The moral imperative to do so arises in modern times with the transformation of our knowledge about animals through post-Darwinian science. We now know that animals are much different than what we claimed they were when we embarked upon determining their legal status and writing the rules of our relationship with them. The factual support for the simplistic, reductionist approach to animal life on which the current laws rest no longer exists. Evidence of our more

---

12   Even in the case of the unusual exceptions that do exist, such as when buildings are designated heritage sites, thereby limiting the renovations their owners can undertake, this is not because the property has its own interests worthy of protection, but rather because of a broader public interest in the aesthetic and historical value of the property, beyond that of the individual owner.

13   This is how Professor Wendy Adams states it in her article "Human Subjects and Animal Objects: Animals as 'Other' in Law" (2009) 3:1 J Animal L & Ethics 29.

fundamental biological kinship with other animals, and of their complex and sophisticated lives, has increased public attention and provides the basis for the growing ethical and legal interest in animals which is emerging in Canada.

"Because we can" is nowhere else a valid defence in ethics or law. Therefore, the second wave of legal attention to animals goes beyond the traditional limits of anti-cruelty legislation and recognizes the right of animals to have their own interests considered in law. In a variety of indirect ways, animals are already coming before the law and there is unprecedented pressure on the law and legislators to re-examine their property status and develop a new approach which more accurately reflects modern knowledge.

Orwell can only have gone to the trouble of so artfully portraying the dangers of ignorance and indifference as he did in Animal Farm with the hope that people might recognize them and do better. Animal rights legal theory emerges in the same spirit.

# D. ORGANIZATION OF THIS BOOK

The first chapter reviews the history of Western ideas about animals and traces their sometimes surprising development to modern times, showing how animals came to acquire their current status as legal things. Chapter 2 considers the unusual manner in which the law distinguishes lawful from unlawful behaviour in the context of animals, and it examines the assumptions on which the distinction rests. It considers the emergent animal rights legal theory which explains the limitations within that current status, and offers an alternative approach consistent with notions of legal personhood.

The third chapter begins to look at the legal landscape for animals by focusing on the federal laws of general application in the *Criminal Code* and reviewing the development of Canadian anti-cruelty legislation, the issues in interpretation, and the frustrated efforts to update the provisions. Chapter 4 turns to the provincial jurisdiction and reviews the general powers contained in the various provincial animal welfare statutes.

Chapters 5 through 8 look at specific, current manifestations of the "animal as thing" approach. Given that animals pervade so many realms of human existence, they are implicated in a wide variety of legal fields. One book cannot fully address them all, but it can identify where they arise and how they vary. For example, in the context of animal companions, traditional legal fields like family, estates, and housing law are now struggling with the enhanced importance being attached to animal interests. In other areas, such as agriculture and research, the nature of the issue is such that, beyond understanding the subtleties of the legal landscape in which the practices occur, there is not yet much jurisprudence to consider (although there is some).

What unites the developments in these different subject areas is that they are the result of increasing and informed attention to the interests of animals. As a legal thinker considers a legal problem involving animals, whatever the realm of law in which it arises, she can assess the possible solutions not only in terms of the traditional concerns of the field, but also with regard to the question of whether a proposed solution reinforces the old assumption about animal things, or replaces it with respect for the interests of animals themselves.

Finally, the closing thoughts note some of the initiatives undertaken in various jurisdictions in an effort to better protect animals and to enhance their status in law, including efforts to recognize legal personhood for animals.

## E. A WORD ABOUT TERMINOLOGY

Precision in language is important in law. It could therefore be inappropriate to speak of "humans" and "animals" as if they are distinct from one another. In doing so, one runs the risk of reinforcing the assumed categorical distinctions that are the subject of criticism in the chapters to come. The subtle effects of unspoken assumptions in language in this context cannot be overstated, inasmuch as they imply, without ever having to explain, that one is referring to a being of lesser status and import: we do not refer to individual people as "it," nor does any person like to be described as a rat, a pig, a dog, a weasel, a chicken, a mule, a snake, an ape, or a bird-brain. As sociologist John Sorenson puts it, who wants to be "treated like an animal"?[14]

Rather than perpetuate this kind of distinction, some people more accurately use the terms "human animal" and "nonhuman animal." In not doing so in this book, the intent is not to diminish the significance of that reminder. It is simply a recognition that this lengthy terminology can be cumbersome where it has to be so frequently repeated. As one proceeds through the book, the fact of human animality becomes an inherent part of the discussion; therefore in respect for the reader, the discussion proceeds with the shorter terms used in common parlance.

---

14   Sorenson, above note 2 at 20.

Language can also be used to diminish the apparent harm being done to an animal. Instead of using the word "kill" in reference to animals, words like "harvest," "cull," and "euthanize" are sometimes employed. Often, the use of such words is not only controversial but inaccurate: for example, *euthanasia* is a term properly applied when a life is ended in that individual's own interest, to bring an end to his pain and suffering, and not for somebody else's financial or other purposes; when fur is *harvested* from an animal, it does not grow back next year. In this regard, this book uses language that accurately describes the act in question.

# PART I

# WHAT IS AN ANIMAL?

# CHAPTER 1

# THE HISTORY OF WESTERN IDEAS ABOUT ANIMALS

Why do we treat animals, like animals?

— Dr. Doolittle[1]

The status of animals in Western legal thought seems to have developed on two ideological paths which, distinct though they are in some ways, have crossed and commingled on this subject just as they have on others: first is the biblical interpretation of the human-animal divide, according to which God gave dominion over all of the animals to humanity, and "dominion" means ownership and control;[2] second is a more or less secular philosophy that sees all animals as being categorically distinct from humans on the basis of one or more of their incapacities or inferiorities.[3]

At various points in history, biblical or secular philosophy has maintained that animals do not feel; or if they do feel, their feelings are of no concern to us because they do not reason; or, if their feelings are of concern to us, it is only because of the harm that hurting them does to our own character; or if hurting them does matter to them, we are the superior being, so our interests trump theirs in any event. As a result, when it came to formalizing the rules of the human-animal

---

1    *Dr. Doolittle*, 1967, DVD, directed by Richard Fleischer (Calabasas, CA: Twentieth Century Fox Home Entertainment, 2000).

2    Gen 1:20–28.

3    For further discussion see Gary L Francione, *Animals, Property and the Law* (Philadelphia: Temple University Press, 1995) at 36–37.

relationship, the interests of the latter were largely disregarded and animals have held the legal status of property from the moment general property law notions were conceived.

On the other hand, while the dominant perspective has always been some variation of that theme—animals matter less, if they matter at all—that has never been the only perspective apparent. Wherever one touches down in history, one can find an alternative voice bespeaking some sort of kinship with animals, or at least some animals, and seeking to improve our approach to them.[4]

That alternative voice becomes more audible in modern times but has yet to ameliorate the legal status of animals in any meaningful way. Despite developments in science and philosophy, we are stuck in a conflict between what we openly refer to as our "love" for animals and our often violent exploitation of them. But as knowledge about the similarities between humans and other animals continues to accumulate, the "alternative" voice becomes more popular. Increasingly, people turn to law to develop ways to reflect that new awareness and meaningfully protect animal interests.

This chapter and the next are a whirlwind tour through the history of these ideas. Chapter 1 begins with a glimpse at ancient Greece, where serious Western philosophical thought began, and then skips ahead to some of the influential thinkers from the Age of Reason through to the nineteenth century. Chapter 2 picks up in the twentieth century and considers where we are in this early stage of the twenty-first century in our understanding of what an animal is and what status animals have and ought to have in law. These chapters provide a backdrop for consideration in subsequent chapters of the legal issues that arise in modern times in the specific kinds of relationships we now have with animals.

## A. ANCIENT GREECE

Humans and animals had interacted for thousands of years, both before and after domestication, before the Greeks first gave serious intellectual attention to these relationships. While being cautious not to oversimplify the complexity of ancient philosophical thinking, it is fair to say in a general way that the Greeks took ideas seriously and understood that everything in the universe, human existence, and our role

---

4   An interesting read on this subject is Erika Ritter, *The Dog By the Cradle, the Serpent Beneath: Some Paradoxes of Human-Animal Relationships* (Toronto: Key Porter Books, 2009).

in it, included animals. Some of the most prominent philosophers of ancient Greece attributed profound significance to the lives of animals, often with great eloquence and colour.[5] Best known in this regard are Pythagoras and Plutarch.

Pythagoras (6 BCE) was well known for his broad interest in many subjects, such as mathematics, astronomy, music, healing, and politics. Pythagoreans, who followed and pursued his ideas, were progressives in their time, even including women in their secret society. Their belief in the sanctity of life, including animals, is well known. Pythagoreans believed in a fluid connection and kinship between all species which was exemplified by their belief in the transmigration of souls, according to which the souls of all animals, humans included, entered other animals after death. Pythagoreans were vegetarians who wore no animal skins and objected to cruelty to animals. The movement persisted in some form for hundreds of years; for centuries after Pythagoras' death, before the term "vegetarian" was coined, those who refrained from eating meat were referred to as Pythagoreans, and their diet as a Pythagorean diet.[6]

Plutarch (1 BCE) wrote about animal entitlements generally and vegetarianism in particular. His essays *On the Eating of Flesh* passionately defended Pythagorean vegetarianism against a variety of criticisms:

> Can you really ask what reason Pythagoras had for abstaining from flesh? For my part I rather wonder both by what accident and in what state of soul or mind the first man who did so, touched his mouth to gore and brought his lips to the flesh of a dead creature, he who set forth tables of dead, stale bodies and ventured to call food and nourishment the parts that had a little before bellowed and cried, moved and lived. How could his eyes endure the slaughter when throats were slit and hides flayed and limbs torn from limb? How could his nose endure the stench? How was it that the pollution did not turn away his taste, which made contact with the sores of others and sucked juices and serums from mortal wounds?[7]

---

5    Richard Sorabji, *Animal Minds and Human Morals: The Origins of the Western Debate* (Ithaca: Cornell University Press, 1993) at 178–79 and generally.

6    Angus Taylor, *Animals and Ethics: An Overview of the Philosophical Debate*, 3d ed (Peterborough, ON: Broadview Press, 2009) at 92. See, generally, Walter Burkert, *Lore and Science in Ancient Pythagoreanism* (Cambridge, MA: Harvard University Press, 1972).

7    Plutarch, "On the Eating of Flesh" in *Plutarch's Moralia*, vol XII (Cambridge, MA: Harvard University Press, 1957) at 541. Anyone who thinks that the animal rights activists of today are radical in their criticisms of the consumption of meat should read these two essays in their entirety.

He later bemoaned that "for the sake of a little flesh, we deprive [animals] of sun, of light, of the duration of life to which they are entitled by birth and being."[8] That animals suffer, have their own intelligence, and an interest in their own lives, were uncontroversial first principles to Plutarch and other neo-Platonists.

Aristotle (4 BCE) had a different perspective. Some argue that Aristotle offered a "rich body of thought" as to how we are related to other animals, that he loved animals (or at least the study of animals), and showed an understanding of "how continuous their abilities are with those of human beings in many cases."[9] It does seem clear that Aristotle granted that animals have sensations and desires which animate them and give them the ability to move. However, Aristotle's enduring observations are of animals as irrational, clearly subordinate to humans, and ultimately morally irrelevant.

His most noted and stark assertion is that animals were created for the sake of humans: tame animals were for our own use and for food; wild animals were for food and for clothing. For Aristotle, animals and human slaves both existed for their master's good, and neither had any share in happiness or in a life of free choice. "But neither is there friendship towards a horse or an ox, nor to a slave *qua* slave. For there is nothing common to the two parties; the slave is a living tool and the tool is a lifeless slave."[10]

As with so many other subjects, it was Aristotle's thoughts on animals that found their way into later religious doctrine. Thomas Aquinas (1225–1274), an immensely influential Catholic theologian, interpreted Aristotle, to whom he referred simply as "the Philosopher," for a medieval Europe that was really not acquainted with the ancient Greeks. Because "man" was made in the image of God, and possessed rationality and prudence, it was natural to see life as a hierarchy with man on top as master over the animals. Similar to Aristotle, Aquinas's animals were irrational and irrelevant, except to the extent that kindness to animals encouraged people to be kinder to one another, and also prevented harm to the interests people had in the animals they kept. As far as Aquinas was concerned, animals did not think for themselves and may have been possessed by Satan.[11]

---

8   *Ibid* at 550–52.

9   Martha C Nussbaum, "Animal Rights: The Need for a Theoretical Basis" (2001) 114 Harv L Rev 1506 at 1516–518.

10   Aristotle, "Nicomachean Ethics" in WD Ross, ed, *The Works of Aristotle*, vol IX (London: Oxford University Press, 1915) at 116a & 116b.

11   Edward P Evans, *The Criminal Prosecution and Capital Punishment of Animals* (1906; repr, London: Faber and Faber Limited, 1987) at 52 and 54; see also St

# B. THE AGE OF REASON THROUGH THE EIGHTEENTH CENTURY

Some of the philosophers who have had profound influence on matters distinctly human have also turned their minds to animals. The view of animals that would later be entrenched in law has been widely ascribed to René Descartes (1596–1650), most notably known as the founder of modern philosophy. Descartes' writings in mathematics, scholastic philosophy, and law were strongly influenced by the Catholic doctrine that preceded them, and in turn had a deep influence on much of Western thought that came after. Descartes attempted to apply the rational inductive methods of science, particularly of math, to philosophy. Rationalism was a system of thought based on reason alone, and truth had to be proved with a certainty equal to that which applied in mathematics. This idea succeeded and devalued the medieval reliance on the senses as the ultimate source of knowledge. As the pendulum swung away from sensationalism, it was by means of reason alone that universal self-evident truths could be discovered, and from these, which the remaining content of philosophy could be deductively derived.

If so vast a philosopher can be distilled to one thought, *cogito ergo sum* (I think, therefore I am) best represents Descartes' legacy as it pertains to animals, if not more broadly. It was this essence of the new rationalism that would usher in the modern age and solidify the human-animal divide for modern times. Reason required consciousness and for Descartes, consciousness was demonstrated by language. Since Descartes did not perceive that animals exhibited linguistic behaviour, he determined that they could not be regarded as conscious or sentient beings. Famously comparing animals to "automata" and "moving machines fabricated by human industry," he pronounced upon the differences between "men" and "brutes":

> For it is highly deserving of remark, that there are no men so dull and stupid, not even idiots, as to be incapable of joining together different words, and thereby constructing a declaration by which to make their thoughts understood; and that on the other hand, there is no other animal, however perfect or happily circumstanced, which can do the like . . . . And this proves not only that the brutes have less reason than man, but that they have none at all . . . .[12]

Thomas Aquinas, "Summa Theologica" in Fathers of the English Dominican Provience, *The Summa Theologica of St Thomas Aquinas* (New York: Benzinger Bros, 1918) Part 1, Questions 64.1 and 65.3.

12   René Descartes, *A Discourse on Method, Part V, Meditations and Principles Writing* (London: JM Dent and Sons, 1975) at 45, and, more generally, at 43–46.

Descartes and his contemporaries experimented on non-anaesthetized dogs and other animals, and he compared their cries to the noise of a malfunctioning machine. Over some public objections to those cries, he insisted that animals were unable to think, communicate, or feel pleasure or pain:

> What is worthy of remark is that though many animals manifest in some of their actions more skill than we do ourselves, those same animals, in some of their other actions, are found to show none at all. Thus their doing certain things better than we do is no proof of their being endowed with mind. For on that assumption they would have to possess more of it than any of us do, and ought to surpass us in all things. On the contrary, what it shows is that they are destitute of mind and that it is nature which acts in them according to the disposition of their organs, just as a clock, which is composed only of wheels and weights, can number the hours and measure time more exactly that we can with all our knowledge.[13]

Similarly, Descartes' student, Malebranche, expressed that "animals eat without pleasure, cry without pain, grow without knowing it; they desire nothing, fear nothing, know nothing."[14] Cartesian dualism thus essentially maintained that animals were no more than the sum of their parts; they were fundamentally different from and categorically inferior to humans. From this it has generally followed that humanity's only concern about animals was to whom they belonged, what purpose they served, and how human harm to animals would affect other humans.[15]

There are conflicting perspectives regarding Descartes' influence on our views about our relationship with animals. Some observe that Descartes did not invent the idea that animals are in a different order from humans, he merely formalized it in a new way, and that the notion that we have an obligation to animals themselves to treat them compassionately, as opposed to out of obligation to our own interests, is a recent, Western idea.[16]

---

13    *Ibid* at 46–47.
14    Peter Harrison, "Descartes on Animals" (1992) 42:167 The Philosophical Quarterly 219.
15    Francione, *Animals, Property and the Law*, above note 3 at 8–11.
16    Paraphrasing Professor O'Hearne, a fictional character in John Maxwell Coetzee, *The Lives of Animals* (Princeton: Princeton University Press, 1999) at 58–67. In a modern nod to the ancient Greek dialogues, Coetzee uses this literary structure as a device to present a very interesting and sophisticated discussion of animal rights through university lectures and the ensuing debate between the characters.

Others maintain that the discontinuity Descartes saw between animals and humans was simply the result of incomplete information. The science of Descartes' day had no acquaintance with animals in the way science can show them to us today, and Descartes had little cause to question the assumption that animals were incapable of thought. Nor did he have access to the fossil record that would reveal a graded continuum of anthropoid creatures stretching from the higher primates to *homo sapiens*, who were exterminated by humanity in the course of its rise to power.[17]

Both of these perspectives bear elements of truth, although they do not account for the fact that Pythagoras, Plutarch, and others who shared their view did not have modern scientific knowledge either. Nor were Descartes' views universally held even around his own time.

Guillaume-Hyacinthe Bougeant (1694–1743), known as le Père Bougeant, Jesuit priest and historian, wondered why, if animals are just machines, we do not pet our watches? On the other hand, while rejecting the notion of animal automata, Bougeant struggled with the conflict posed by his own observations. If animals did feel hope, fear, happiness, sadness, and other emotions that humans felt, did this not suggest a spiritual principle within them, which was not very different from the human soul? This conclusion was clearly not sustainable, since it involved the immortality of an animal's soul and necessitated some provision for its reward or punishment after death. If they are capable of right and wrong, if they are to receive reward or punishment, there must be a heaven and hell for them. "Beasts, in that case, would be a species of man or men a species of beast, both of which propositions are incompatible with the teachings of religion."[18]

Others were less restrained in their contemplation of human superiority. Montaigne (1533–1592), one of the most influential writers of the French Renaissance, considered to be the founder of modern skepticism, slightly preceded Descartes, but he anticipated the arguments Descartes would soon make, wondering "When I play with my cat, how do I know that she is not passing time with me, rather than I with her?" Montaigne rejected any notion of a hierarchy with humans at the top, finding it to be "clear that it is not upon any true ground of reason, but from a foolish arrogance and stubbornness, that we put ourselves before the other animals, and remove ourselves from their condition and fellowship."[19] .

---

17    *Ibid* at 61 (paraphrasing the character Elizabeth Costello).
18    Evans, above note 11 at 66–67.
19    Michel Eyquem de Montaigne, "Apology for Raymond Sebond" [c. 1592] in EJ Trechmann, *Essays of Montaigne* (1593; repr, London: Oxford University Press, 1927) at 464–80.

Voltaire's (1694–1778) criticism of the Cartesian perspective was still more emphatic:

> Hold then the same view of the dog which has lost his master, which has sought him in all the thoroughfares with cries of sorrow, which comes into the house troubled and restless, goes downstairs and goes upstairs; goes from room to room, finds at last in his study the master he loves, and betokens his gladness by soft whimpers, frisks and caresses.
>
> There are barbarians who seize this dog, who so greatly surpasses man in fidelity and friendship, and nail him down to a table and dissect him alive, to show you the mesaraic veins! You discover in him all the same organs of feeling as in yourself. Answer me, mechanist, has Nature arranged all the springs of feeling in this animal to the end that he might not feel?[20]

Whatever their source or their shortcomings, and despite these alternative observations, Descartes' views that animals are not rational and do not matter did take hold. Although few would later go so far as to claim that animals were actual machines, the treatment to which animals would be subjected did rest necessarily on or very near that assumption. Later, when animal sentience was more widely admitted, their status as irrational and irrelevant creatures was already entrenched.

For as Descartes opined about animal machines, other foundational ideas were taking hold in Western philosophy. Enter John Locke (1632–1704), the primary architect of Western theory of property rights. Locke's notion that a property right gives the owner exclusive use and control of an object is well known to be the cornerstone of modern property law. It is less often contemplated that the idea originated with Locke's need to find a way to ground a private entitlement to animals and other "natural resources."

Locke subscribed to the biblical view about creation of the universe and human supremacy. According to Genesis, God created the earth and all its resources for the common use of all people. But in that case, how could any one person use anything without infringing upon the corresponding entitlement that everybody else had too? How can a person take his firewood from a tree owned by all? Animals, too, were "produced by the spontaneous hand of nature," and surely God had given us dominion over them in order that they could be of some use, so it was necessary to appropriate them in some way.

---

20    Voltaire, "Bêtes" in *Dictionnaire Philosophique* (1764; repr, Paris: Garnier Frères, 1961) at 51.

Locke appreciated the importance of property rights being "natural" as social conventions change. His solution was to link but distinguish the physical and the metaphysical—if God created humanity in his image, then we belong to God; but our bodies belong to us, and therefore so does the labour our bodies perform. So we could acquire property by joining our labour to an object in nature. When a person attached her own labour to the communal tree, she earned its exclusive use. When a person took control over or killed a wild animal, it was his to keep.

As biblical doctrine had long maintained, and as Descartes had just confirmed, animals were inferior ranks of creatures to which we owed no moral obligation. Locke did not deny that animals felt pain, as Descartes had; rather, he denied that their pain mattered, in and of itself. Echoing Aquinas, Locke insisted that the right not to be harmed adhered to the animal's owner, or to a person being harmed by an animal, but not to an animal directly. Animal suffering only mattered to the extent that our act in causing it might have an undesirable effect on us. Locke thought children should be taught to be kind to animals; it was wrong to damage resources and moreover "tormenting and killing of beasts [would], by degrees, harden their minds even towards men," and he agreed with the practice of his time to prohibit butchers from sitting on juries in capital cases, on the assumption that their occupation could make them less compassionate.[21]

As it turns out, Locke was on to something. Recent studies show a correlation between violence to animals and people. Many serial killers and mass murderers began their killing sprees with animals, and it is not uncommon for domestic violence to begin with a family pet.[22] The perspective to which Locke and others have adhered admits of a tacit connection between the species, perhaps even a recognition of similarities along the lines, if not to the degree that Montaigne and Voltaire articulated more directly.

---

21  Francione, *Animals, Property and the Law*, above note 3 at 38–40.
22  Department of Justice Canada, *Crimes Against Animals: A Consultation Paper* (Ottawa: Department of Justice, 1998) at 1; "Relationship Between Animals (Pet) Abuse and Family Violence" in *Domestic Violence Handbook: for Police and Crown Prosecutors* (Edmonton: Alberta Justice Communications, 2008) at 149–50; Frank Ascione & Phil Arkow, eds, *Child Abuse, Domestic Violence and Animal Abuse: Linking the Circles of Compassion for Prevention and Intervention* (West Lafayette, IN: Purdue University Press, 1999); Dana Campbell, "Correlation Between Violence to Animals and Violence to Humans" in Martine Lachance, ed, *L'animal dans la spirale des besoins de l'humain* (Cowansville, QC: Yvon Blais, 2010) at 127–29; and Charlotte A Lacroix, *Another Weapon for Combating Family Violence: Prevention of Animal Abuse* (1998) 4 Animal L 1.

Yet, regardless of what Locke might have unintentionally admitted in his more *obiter*-like comments about animals, it is the fundamental property notions that he devised that have had a lasting influence on British common law. From the time Locke articulated these laws, animals have had the legal status of property. To date, they remain possessions, chattels, and things.[23]

Rousseau (1712–1778) followed Locke, similarly granting that animals feel pain, but Rousseau denied them any intelligence. He supported a fairly unimportant "kind of" obligation to them. He sought to

> put an end to the time-honoured disputes concerning the participation of animals in natural law: for it is clear that, being destitute of intelligence and liberty, they cannot recognize that law; as they partake, however, in some measure of our nature, in consequence of the sensibility with which they are endowed, they ought to partake of natural right, so that mankind is subjected to a kind of obligation even toward the brutes.[24]

Kant (1724–1804) propelled these ideas into the next century. He similarly accepted that animals were not machines, but were sentient and could suffer. Still, he found no moral obligations owed to them because they were not rational or self-aware. He believed that animals existed solely for human ends. Troubled as Locke was by the implications for people of cruel behaviour, Kant too worried that "he who is cruel to an animal will be hard also in his dealings with men."[25]

This general perspective allowed animal use to expand for many years without any concern that people might have any legal duties to animals themselves. Even as social pressure later developed to impose some constraints on the harms people could cause them, the lower moral standard justified by their lesser capacities was well accepted, and the legal duties that arose in early anti-cruelty legislation were responding largely, although not entirely, to the secondary concern

---

23   Jeremy Rifkin has an interesting discussion about how the very idea of property developed with the domestication and ownership of animals. He identifies the linguistic indicators, such as the fact that, in English, the word "cattle" has the same etymological root as "capital." In Latin, cattle is *pecus*, while money is *pecunia*; in Spanish, cattle is *ganado*, while property is *ganaderia*. In many European languages, the word for "cattle" is synonymous or very closely related to the words for "chattel" and "capital": Jeremy Rifkin, *Beyond Beef* (New York: Dutton Books, 1992) at 28.

24   Jean-Jacques Rousseau, *A Discourse on Inequality* (1754; repr, London: Penguin Books, 1984) at the preface.

25   Immanuel Kant, "Of Duties to Animals and Spirits" in *Lectures on Ethics* (Cambridge: Cambridge University Press, 1997) at 212–13.

shared by Locke, Rousseau, Kant, and others that in hurting animals, people were hurting themselves.

However, Jeremy Bentham (1748–1832) rejected the distinctions other philosophers were making, and not just on the subject of animals. Although he strongly advocated individual rights (for humans), he rejected the basic notion of natural rights on which Locke's conclusions were premised as "nonsense upon stilts."[26] Bentham was one of the founders of modern utilitarianism with progressive views on many subjects, including the separation of church and state, freedom of expression, abolition of slavery and the death penalty, and rights for women. He dismissed the idea that the absence of a characteristic such as language, self-awareness, or the ability to reason was a basis for excluding animals from the sphere of moral consideration. Reliance on these characteristics had degraded animals "to a class of things" with the result that their interests were being completely ignored.[27]

While Cartesians denied animals any thoughts or feelings, and while Lockians admitted animals had feelings but denied them any import, Bentham saw animal suffering as significant for its own sake. Sentience was the only characteristic necessary for a being to have moral significance. In a passage that has become the central tenet of the modern animal welfare movement—though it was just a footnote in a broader discussion in his *Introduction to the Principles of Morals and Legislation*—he observed:

> The day may come, when the rest of animal creation may acquire those rights which never could have been withholden from them but by the hand of tyranny. The French have already discovered that the blackness of the skin is no reason why a human being should be abandoned without redress to the caprice of a tormentor. It may come one day to be recognized, that the number of legs, the villosity of the skin, or the termination of the os sacrum, are reasons equally insufficient for abandoning a sensitive begin to the same fate. What else is it that should trace the insuperable line? Is it the faculty of reason, or, perhaps the faculty of discourse? But a full-grown horse or dog, is beyond comparison a more rational, as well as a more conversable animal, than any infant of a day, or a week, or even a month old.

---

26    Ross Harrison, "Jeremy Bentham" in Ted Honderich, ed, *The Oxford Companion to Philosophy* (Oxford: Oxford University Press, 1995) at 85–88.

27    Jeremy Bentham, *The Principles of Morals and Legislation* (1781; repr, Buffalo: Prometheus Books, 1988) at 310.

> But suppose it were otherwise, what would it avail? The question is not Can they *reason*? Nor, can they *talk*? but, Can they *suffer*?[28]

This concern for animal suffering by a prominent jurist was significant in its day. Animals would receive more attention in the ethical realm as the nineteenth century unfolded, but when Bentham wrote, far more prevalent was the perspective articulated by Reverend Sydney Smith. In a lecture he gave at the Royal Institution, Smith sought to offer some comfort to those who "look upon every compliment which is paid to the ape as high treason to the dignity of man":

> There may, perhaps, be more of rashness and ill-fated security in my opinion, than of magnanimity or liberality; but I confess I feel myself so much at ease about the superiority of mankind,—I have such a marked and decided contempt for the understanding of every baboon I have yet seen,—I feel so sure that the blue ape without a tail will never rival us in poetry, painting, and music,—that I see no reason whatever, why justice may not be done to the few fragments of the soul, and tatters of understanding, which they may really possess. I have sometimes, perhaps, felt a little uneasy at Exeter 'Change, from contrasting the monkeys with the 'prentice-boys who are teazing them; but a few pages of Locke, or a few lines of Milton, have always restored me to tranquility, and convinced me that the superiority of man had nothing to fear.[29]

About the same time, philosopher Thomas Taylor used an analogy to animals to dismiss the equally silly idea of rights for women. When Mary Wollstonecraft published her *A Vindication of the Rights of Woman* in 1792, Taylor responded with *A Vindication of the Rights of Brutes*. He combined Wollstonecraft's arguments with Thomas Paine's *Rights of Man* to show that the concept was so absurd it would just as well support an argument that even the brutes have intrinsic dignity.[30]

Bentham himself was no animal rights activist. He did not deny the property status of animals or the right of people to use animals as resources; his concern was directed at what he perceived to be gratuitous, unnecessary suffering. At times he opposed sports, like fox hunting

---

28    *Ibid* at 310–11, n 1.

29    Sydney Smith, Lecture XVII, "On the Faculties of Animals, as Compared With Those of Men" in *Elementary Sketches of Moral Philosophy: Delivered at the Royal Institution in the Years 1804, 1805 and 1806* (London: Spottiswoode and Shaw, 1849) at 238.

30    Thomas Taylor, "A Vindication of the Rights of Brutes, (1792)" in Adriana Craciun, ed, *Mary Wollstonecraft's A Vindication of the Rights of Woman: A Sourcebook* (New York: Routledge, 2002) at 40.

and sport fishing, but at other times he suggested they would be acceptable provided they cause the animal no more suffering than would death in the course of nature. Bentham agreed with his contemporaries that animals were not self-aware and that this was a qualitative distinction that justified according greater value to human lives and according authority to humans to use animals for their own purposes. It was the infliction of gratuitous suffering which he condemned.[31]

However, in terms of acknowledging the ability of animals to suffer and giving serious philosophical attention to the possibility that when humans cause such suffering, it raises ethical concerns with respect to animals themselves, Bentham was a bridge between ideological revolutions. He linked the French revolution and the lofty ideals it sought to import into all *human* relations to what might be called the "evolution revolution" that was instigated when Darwin implied that those ideals might have to be extended further still.

## C. BEFORE AND AFTER THE AGE OF REASON: EUROPE'S ANIMAL TRIALS

While these ideas were percolating in Western Europe, a strange but related phenomenon was playing out in the courtrooms of the same part of the continent and beyond: animals were being put on trial.

The events are well enough documented to be confirmed — Shakespeare refers to a wolf being hanged for killing a man in *The Merchant of Venice*[32] — yet they are little known and rarely discussed. The practice is most thoroughly described in a 1906 book called *The Criminal Prosecution and Capital Punishment of Animals* by American literary scholar EP Evans.[33] Full of tales of trespassing caterpillars, egg-laying roosters, and man-slaughtering pigs, it might just as well have been written by Jonathan Swift.

Evans analyzes the evidence of hundreds of documented animal trials. He believed these to be just the tip of the iceberg, since often only convictions were recorded and medieval records were not well preserved. Nevertheless, what remains for curiosity and contested an-

---

31  Nussbaum, above note 9 at 1525. See also Gary L Francione, *Introduction to Animal Rights: Your Child or the Dog* (Philadelphia: Temple University Press, 2000) at 130–34.

32  4.1.135. References are to act, scene, and line.

33  Evans, above note 11. The description of the practice in this section comes largely from this book, except where other references are made.

alysis is a thousand-year phenomenon that occurred from the ninth to the nineteenth century, mostly in Western Europe—France, Normandy, Switzerland, Italy, Germany, and Spain. The record also includes an undescribed event somewhere in Canada at the end of the seventeenth century concerning turtledoves, another in New Haven, Connecticut concerning two heifers, three sheep, and two sows, and one in Russia, concerning a male goat who was banished to Siberia.[34]

The trials can be roughly divided into two categories, secular and ecclesiastical, although it is difficult to entirely separate church-driven influence even from the former. Secular trials were generally of individual "beasts" who had hurt or killed people. From thirteenth-century France, they moved to Italy and Germany and beyond. Oxen, cows, horses, and dogs were tried, though pigs were the most commonly accused, particularly of killing babies. Ecclesiastical trials involved large groups of "vermin" including insects and small mammals that usually destroyed fields and crops, though eels and dolphins appear in the records as well. They began in Switzerland and spread first to surrounding areas, then much more widely.

A respected sixteenth-century French jurist, Bartholomew Chassenée, began his career by representing some rats who were on trial at Auton for feloniously eating the province's barley crops, and thereby destroying them. Rats, as Evans notes, were of bad reputation and notorious guilt, so Chassenée had to be creative when he was asked to defend them. When his clients failed to attend their first appearance, he claimed that they were dispersed over a large tract of land, and dwelt in many villages, so that the single summons that had been issued was insufficient.

When, after a second citation was issued and published in all parishes, they still did not appear, he submitted that the length and difficulty of the journey and the perils along the way—including cats—made it too dangerous for them to be expected to attend. Chassenée claimed that if an accused cannot come to a place cited in safety, he may exercise a right of refusal.[35] The defence was apparently successful.[36] Subsequent discussions of the case and of Chassenée's representation indicate that he brought to bear every available argument for his clients, and his plea was so eloquently and determinedly made that his reputation as a leading criminal lawyer was therein established.

---

34   *Ibid* at 281–83, App F.
35   *Ibid* at 18–21.
36   Nicholas Humphrey, *The Mind Made Flesh* (Oxford: Oxford University Press, 2002) at 235–54.

Animals had similar rights and punishments as humans did for the same crime. In all cases, their trials became full-blown legal processes, with witnesses, documentary evidence, legal aid, and some creative legal defences, both in terms of procedure and the merits. Evans tells of caterpillars who were charged in Italy in 1659 for leaving their own habitat and trespassing on fields, gardens, and orchards. The prosecutor claimed that they should stay in the forest and desist from ravaging cultivated grounds. The court ultimately invoked the biblical and superior human right to the lands, but only after it acknowledged that the caterpillars, too, had a right to life, liberty, and the pursuit of happiness.[37]

Some years later in Brazil, termites devoured the food, furniture, and the very structure of a monastery. The monks applied for interdiction and excommunication. When the termites were summoned to a hearing, their lawyers argued not only that termites had a need for sustenance, but they also praised the termites' industry, and argued that in this respect they were superior to their prosecutors. They claimed the termites had priority of possession, having lived on the land long before the monks encroached. The case ended in a compromise, and the Gray Friars were ordered to provide a suitable alternative location for the termites to live.[38]

Punishments differed as between the two courts. In the ecclesiastical cases, it was generally limited to anathema, exorcism, excommunication, or banishment, penalties which seem unlikely to have caused any insects to suffer much consternation, although perhaps only to modern thinkers looking back. Such penalties also seem to conflict with the otherwise clear church missive against attributing souls to non-human animals, but this was obviously not the only unusual thing about these trials.

In the secular domain, the punishment was of another order entirely — it was physical and often capital. Execution was sometimes preceded by whipping or maiming. In Falaise in 1386, a pig who had killed a child by tearing off the child's face and arms was sentenced to be mangled and maimed in the head and forelegs, and then hanged. The pig was first dressed in men's clothing and was executed on the public square.[39]

Sometimes guilty animals were condemned to be burned alive. Other times, judges seemed to acknowledge some degree of sentience, ordering that they need only be "slightly singed" then strangled before being thrown into the fire. Some animals were put to the rack in pursuit

---

37    Evans, above note 11 at 122–23.
38    Ibid at 123–24.
39    Ibid at 140.

of confessions. If they did not confess under torture, a death sentence could be commuted to banishment, whipping, or incarceration. Animal and human criminals were held in the same prisons, given the same treatment, and the same bill was sent to their parish for their feeding and care.[40]

Sometimes animals were acquitted. Evans recites a tale of buggery in 1750 in Vanvres. The punishment for buggery was death to both parties, usually being burned alive. However, in this case, the man was convicted, while the "she-ass" was acquitted on the ground that she was a victim of violence, having been made to participate against her own will. The parish priest and the inhabitants of the commune signed a certificate stating that they had known her for years and she had always shown herself to be virtuous and well-behaved. Evans finds that this document had a decisive influence on the court, and suggests that as a piece of exculpatory evidence, it may be regarded as unique in the annals of criminal prosecution.[41]

In addition to acquittals, there were appeals and sometimes sentences were reduced. In one case, a sow and a she-ass were sentenced to hang for a crime that Evans does not describe. On appeal, they received a new trial and the sentence was commuted to a knock on the head.[42] Some animals received a pardon. Evans cites the example of two herds of pigs whose squealing and excited behaviour caused a boy to fall and die from his injuries. The three individual pigs who knocked him over were condemned to death, and the whole herd was found guilty as accomplices, and sentenced to the same penalty. The Friar petitioned the Duke of Burgundy to a pardon, which the Duke granted, releasing the herd.[43]

In trying to understand what was really going on in these cases, a number of factors is apparent. Most notably, these trials had a strong foundation in religion. In ecclesiastical cases, courts found that their jurisdiction over animals and their particular right to excommunicate them arose directly from the biblical hierarchy, which assigned the superior position to humans. There is little doubt that, on some level, defence of that hierarchy was an important feature of animal trials, but others are apparent as well.

When it came to determining the merits of a case, courts struggled with whether the defendants were sent by God or the devil. In some cases, they found that swarms of insects and "noxious vermin" were sent at Satan's instigation, and these creatures were driven to the sea or

---

40   *Ibid* at 136–44.
41   *Ibid* at 147–51.
42   *Ibid* at 140.
43   *Ibid* at 140–145.

banished. But in others, they were seen as God's agents sent to punish humanity for its sins and promote piety, in which case exterminating the animals would be sacrilege. In these cases, courts found it more appropriate to order the guilty parties to move on after their mission was completed.

Either way, whether God or devil had sent the problem, the only proper resolution was through the church. Even in the secular courts, this was true to varying degrees. Sometimes a homicidal pig or bull was seen to be an incarnation of a demon. Aquinas himself considered beasts, birds, and creeping things to be demons in disguise.[44] Whether the church believed its own doctrine, or whether there was a more political explanation for its behaviour in perpetuating these problems and its own unique ability to redress them, is a question as old as organized religion itself, but it does seem from the records and from the widespread nature and lifespan of this phenomenon, that a broad base of people accepted these ideas.

Further, the timing of animal trials coincided with the better-known witch trials which have been the subject of abundant feminist critique.[45] Evans also gives several examples of cases in which Jews were put in the same lot with animals. He points out that Christians enlarged the Old Testament proscription against sex with animals to include a prohibition against sex with Jews themselves, noting a case in Paris where a person was convicted of sodomy for living with a Jewess and both were burned, the court finding it was precisely the same as if someone were to copulate with a dog.[46] So it is clearly not possible to

---

44    It was a prevalent belief in the Middle Ages, and taught by the Catholic church for a long time thereafter, that if a homicide was unpunished, devils could intervene and take possession of persons and places. The *aura corrumpens* could taint a dwelling such that sensitive persons could not enter without become sick or nervous. This could continue for centuries, and purchasers checked property registries not only for encumbrances by debt, but also by devils. Evans also tells of European peasants who would confine their cattle in stalls so small they could not get enough air, so that shortly after the stalls were closed for the night, the cattle would begin to fume and stamp and by the morning they were weak and exhausted. Peasants called the exorcist, who would open the windows and doors, which had the effect of not only casting out any demons, but allowing in the fresh air needed by the animals.

45    See, for example, Germaine Greer, *The Change: Women, Aging and the Menopause* (New York: Ballantine Books, 1991) at 343–62; and Andrea Dworkin, *Life and Death: Unapologetic Writings on the Continuing War Against Women* (New York: Free Press, 1997) at 20.

46    Evans, above note 11 at 153. For further analysis of the ritual exclusion of both Jews and women from moral relevancy, see Esther Cohen, *The Crossroads of Justice: Law and Culture in Late Medieval France* (Leiden: EJ Brill, 1993) at 85–94.

separate these animal trials from the deep prejudices and superstitions of their times.

More practical factors are also evident. In the case of valuable animals, like an ox or a horse, the severity of the punishment was often tempered by economical considerations. In a case in twelfth-century Burgundy, instead of capital punishment, a homicidal animal was taken to the seignor within whose jurisdiction the murder had been committed and was sold, with the profit paid to the seignor. However, if less valuable beasts, such as those belonging to Jews, committed the same wrong, they were to be hanged by the feet.[47]

Similarly, the Friar who received a pardon for the herd of pigs who abetted in murdering the boy were surely worth more to him alive than dead; the Brazilian monks who were said to be less industrious than the termites who destroyed their monastery might have been in political conflict with the authorities of the region; the man convicted of buggering the she-ass who was herself acquitted might have been out of favour with the community.

Modern notions of retribution and deterrence also beg consideration. Were the trials meant to serve as a lesson to animals not to misbehave? Were communities trying to remove the danger in their midst, particularly in the case of individual animals? This concern is apparent in modern society; when there is a news report that a person has been killed by a bear, shark, or other dangerous animal, shortly thereafter follows the story that the menacing creature has been destroyed; additionally, legislation allows for the killing of dogs who have demonstrated dangerous propensities.[48]

Was it a lesson to people? In the case of individual animals, the owner of the executed animal was punished for not better exercising control. This, too, has a modern comparator in tort law and liability attributed to the owner of an animal for harm done by that animal. In another sense as well, if the state or the church were willing to go to this kind of trouble to prosecute a pig, the community could be assured it would do the same if a person were to commit such an act.

---

47    Evans, *ibid* at 165.

48    One legal commentator has compared the prosecution of animals as practised centuries ago with the continued punishment of animals for their "crimes" against humans, citing summary and lethal proceedings against "dangerous dogs" in the United States. She suggests two primary purposes: restoration of order and achievement of revenge, and argues that these should be replaced with a renewed emphasis on due process for animals threatened with punishment for their offences. See Jen Girgen, "The Historical and Contemporary Prosecution and Punishment of Animals" (2003) 9 Animal L 97. Similar legislation exists in Canada; see Chapter 4.

Some part of the explanation for the phenomenon must also include a pre-scientific need for cognitive control of the otherwise incomprehensible happenings in the universe. Evans documents thirty-four cases of pigs prosecuted for murder, and ponders whether the thought that a baby was killed while her mother was at mass was just too arbitrary to bear, that it had to be seen as a calculated wickedness, which, however awful that was, at least had a place within the human scheme of things. In that sense, it is fair to suggest, as Evans does, that one role of the court was to tame the chaos and make sense of inexplicable events by redefining them as crimes.

Records of the time apparently reveal that while the trials were going on, there was both defence and criticism of them. The criticism, according to at least one scholar, Esther Cohen, came in part from elites who were seeking to eliminate the favourable ideas about animals held by the public. Like Aquinas, elites claimed animals should not be tried because the crime required intent, which they could not have. Cohen points out that there is some indication that in the thirteenth century, when this practice peaked, the public believed animals had reason and will.[49]

Considering all of these factors, Cohen concludes that animal trials persisted for so long because both elites and popular beliefs supported them, though for different reasons. They served important social functions of reinforcing animal-human relations, helping society believe in itself as just, and offering opportunities, such as church trials presented, for ritual purification. She sees them in this sense as a good example of how the practice of law is formed through complex interactions of multiple levels of custom and doctrine.

The sheer duration of this phenomenon defies any single explanation. In addition to all of the observations already made, it is also true that in these trials, animals were granted a kind of agency that has eluded them in courtrooms since. They were attributed an interest in living their own lives and sometimes even a right to do so, and when that right was abrogated, it was on terms similar to those applicable to humans in similar contexts. On the other hand, while animals had the right to a fair trial, they were also punished brutally for acts that were beyond their control. And whatever rights to due process they might have had in these trials did not translate more broadly. Outside the courtroom, animals were still being put to use as human resources — whether as food or clothing, as labourers or entertainers.

In their resolution of the various conflicts of daily life over the course of one thousand years, these trials were playing out the values being

---

49   Esther Cohen, "Law, Folklore and Animal Lore" (1986) 110:1 Past & Present 6.

expressed contemporaneously in the academic realms discussed in the first part of this chapter. The trials thus signify another aspect of the perpetual human ambivalence to animals, demonstrating the prolonged struggle of the former to rationalize the differences it sought to maintain with the latter, with the similarities it has been unable to deny.

## D. NEW IDEAS OF THE NINETEENTH CENTURY

By the nineteenth century, animal trials had waned and Bentham's doctrine — that the ability of animals to suffer is the basis of their entitlement to not be subjected to unnecessary suffering — had begun to take root. Humane societies emerged, and in 1835, Queen Victoria even authorized the newly formed Society for the Prevention of Cruelty to Animals to use the term "Royal," eventually becoming a patron herself.[50] Anti-cruelty legislation began to appear which purported to codify an emergent legal duty to avoid causing animals unnecessary pain and suffering. Even in the early part of the century, direct calls had begun for a different legal status for animals.

German philosopher Arthur Schopenhauer (1788–1860) was a strong critic of the idea that animals were mere things that could be seen to exist solely as means to humanity's ends and he supported the extension of legal protection to animals. He expressed revulsion at the argument that animal suffering mattered only because of how it hardened the humans who caused it and denounced a morality that allowed vivisection, hunting, coursing, bullfighting, and horse racing. He did not, however, think people had to refrain from using animals for food, satisfied that so long as the animal's death was quick, people would suffer more by not eating meat than animals would suffer by being eaten.[51]

Similarly, three other but lesser known men prefigured the debate to come. While anti-cruelty laws were fairly new, these men were already anticipating their limitations and arguing that society had to go beyond a charitable approach and recognize actual rights for animals.

In 1824, Lewis Gompertz, one of the founding members of the Royal Society for the Prevention of Cruelty to Animals, published *Moral*

---

50    Nussbaum, above note 9 at 1523.
51    Arthur Schopenhauer, "On the Basis of Morality" (1840), discussed in Norm Phelps, *The Longest Struggle: Animal Advocacy from Pythagorus to PETA* (New York: Lantern Books, 2007) at 153–54.

*Inquiries: On the Situation of Man and Brutes*, in which he argued that all creatures, whether or human or non-human, have more of a right to the use of their own bodies than does anyone else, and further that the moral duty to promote happiness applies equally to all beings.[52] Gompertz himself was a vegan, who refused to travel in horse-drawn coaches, a serious philosophical commitment at that time.

In 1892, Henry Salt's essay, *Animal Rights Considered in Relation to Social Progress*, argued a thoughtful and modern case that animals should be *liberated* from human control. Rather than receive better treatment, they should have their own legal rights just as humans do, since "the same sense of justice and compassion apply in both cases." Salt argued that the very principles that underlie our beliefs about how we should treat other human beings made it impossible to justify our treatment of animals.[53]

Several years later, in 1897, Edward Nicholson, in *The Rights of an Animal: A New Essay in Ethics*, strenuously disputed Descartes' mechanistic argument against animal consciousness, drawing on others who maintained that the ability to experience pain and pleasure entitled animals to the same natural right to life and liberty that humans have.[54]

None of these men was considered a leading thinker of his time. Gompertz was an inventor; Salt, a writer and social reformer; and Nicholson was a writer and librarian. Nor did their respective publications become widely influential in their time, although Salt's ideas were adopted decades later by Peter Singer. However, their place in history is marked for the thoughtful manner in which they approached the subject, carefully dissecting the distinctions on which others relied, asserting that animals' interests should be protected by the notion of rights at a time when women and human slaves were still fighting for or had only recently won theirs.

However, what might have ultimately been the most important development of the nineteenth century in this context came from outside law, philosophy, and ethics. It was Darwin and the theory of evolution that forever changed traditional thinking about the animal world and about humanity's place in it.[55] The works of Darwin (1809–1892),

---

52  Lewis Gompertz, *Moral Inquiries on the Situation of Man and of Brutes* (1824; repr, Lewiston, NY: Edwin Mellen Press, 1997).

53  Henry Salt, *Animals' Rights Considered in Relation to Social Progress* (New York: Macmillan, 1894).

54  Edward Byron Nicholson, *The Rights of an Animal: A New Essay in Ethics* (London: C Kegan Paul, 1879).

55  As early as 1735, Linnaeus had classified humans as primates when he created the system of biological classification of taxonomy in the first edition of his

particularly *The Origin of Species* and *The Descent of Man*, confirmed that humans are animals too, that in reality there is no such thing as a uniquely human characteristic, and that "the difference in mind between man and the higher animals, great as it is, is certainly one of degree and not of kind." He found that

> the senses and intuitions, the various emotions and faculties, such as love, memory, attention, curiosity, imitation, reason &c., of which man boasts, may be found in an incipient, or even sometimes in a well-developed condition in the lower animals.[56]

Darwin marked the beginning of a process which evolutionary science and other branches of science carried on in the ensuing decades, in which categorical distinctions between humans and all the other animals would become harder to defend.

---

*Systema Naturae.* Lamarck had developed the first cohesive theory of evolution in the early part of the nineteenth century: Stephen Jay Gould, *The Structure of Evolutionary Theory* (Cambridge, MA: Belknap Press of Harvard University Press, 2002). However, discussion about evolution and its application to humanity began in earnest with Darwin. In 1859, Darwin described the idea that new species evolve over the course of generations by means of natural selection, and that the diversity of life arose by virtue of common descent through a pattern of evolution: Charles Darwin, *On the Origin of Species by Means of Natural Selection, or the Preservation of Favoured Races in the Struggle for Life* (London: John Murray, 1859). He specifically avoided addressing human evolution at that time. It was "Darwin's bulldog," Thomas Huxley, who first made the express observation that humans and apes descend from a common ancestor, and that evolution applied as fully to humans as it did to all other life: Thomas Henry Huxley, *Evidence as to Man's Place in Nature* (London: Williams & Norgate, 1863). Later, Darwin applied the concept of evolution directly to humans in *The Descent of Man, and Selection in Relation to Sex*, 2d ed (London: Clowes and Sons, 1874).

56   Darwin, *The Descent of Man*, ibid at 126; see also Francione, *Introduction to Animal Rights*, above note 31 at 113–14.

# CURRENT IDEAS: FROM SCIENCE TO PHILOSOPHY TO LAW

It is an important and popular fact that things are not always what they seem. For instance, on the planet Earth, man had always assumed that he was more intelligent than dolphins because he had achieved so much—the wheel, New York, wars and so on—whilst all the dolphins had ever done is muck about in the water having a good time; but conversely, the dolphins had always believed that they were far more intelligent than man—for precisely the same reasons.

—Douglas Adams, *A Hitchhiker's Guide to the Galaxy*[1]

Evolution is an unusual subject with which to begin a chapter in a law text, yet its introduction, together with the knowledge subsequently provided by evolutionary biology and other scientific disciplines, has serious implications in this context. Inasmuch as it contradicts the Lockian and Cartesian assumptions on which the historical legal status of animals is based, as will be reviewed in the second part of this chapter, it is the basis of the demand for re-examination of that status, as will be discussed in the third and fourth parts.

---

1    (New York: Harmony Books, 1980) at 156.

# A. THE TWENTIETH CENTURY: THE EVOLUTION REVOLUTION

Compared to the theories preceded it, evolutionary theory takes a very different approach to the question: what is an animal? It incorporates the ideas that Darwin had presented together with all that was later learned about the structure and sophistication of animal life. The debate about the human-animal divide has itself so evolved since the emergence of the idea that humans and other primates descend from the same ancestor that it is now occupied with such subtle disputes as whether it is one or two percent by which human and chimpanzee DNA differs.[2] Whatever the genetic difference, it is trivial by comparison to the similarities; in a manner that would shock Sydney Smith, some scientists now even describe humans as the fifth great ape.[3]

Study of the great apes has had a profound impact on human identity. Well known in this regard are the researchers who came to be known as Leakey's Angels.[4] They are three women who were chosen by anthropologist Louis Leakey to go into the forest and study the great apes as participants in their own environments, rather than as specimens in captivity. He engaged American Dian Fossey to study gorillas, Canadian Biruté Galdikas to study orangutans, and Briton Jane Goodall (who ultimately became the most prolific and well known) to study chimpanzees.[5]

---

2   Roger Fouts, *Next of Kin: What Chimpanzees Have Taught Me About Who We Are* (New York: William Morrow, 1997) at 55; Jane Goodall, "Chimpanzees—Bridging the Gap" in Paola Cavalieri & Peter Singer, eds, *The Great Ape Project* (New York: St Martin's Press, 1993) at 13.

3   The reference to Sydney Smith is in Chapter 1, Section B. The great apes include chimpanzees, bonobos, gorillas, and orangutans. See "The Fifth Ape," the first of a three-part documentary series entitled *The Genius of Darwin*, written and narrated by Richard Dawkins, distributed by Channel Four Television Corporation and Richard Dawkins Foundation for Reason and Science (United Kingdom, 2008).

4   The term "Leakey's Angels" came from Biruté MF Galdikas, *Reflections of Eden: My Years with the Orangutans of Borneo* (Toronto: Little, Brown & Company, 1995).

5   A version of the story of Dian Fossey, whose strong defence of the gorillas she came to know likely led to her murder in Rwanda in 1985, was told in the 1988 Hollywood film, *Gorillas in the Mist: The Story of Dian Fossey*, directed by Michael Apted (California: Universal Studios, 1988). In Farley Mowat's biography of Fossey, he suggests she was likely killed not by gorilla poachers as some claim, but by more powerful interests who saw her as an impediment to the tourist industry and the financial exploitation of the gorillas: Farley Mowat,

Goodall has many times described what she learned over her forty years of field work in Africa. Consistent with Darwin's "different in degree, but not in kind" analysis, Goodall observed in the chimpanzees many characteristics and behaviours that they had previously been thought to lack, such as meaningful communication, sophisticated co-operation, and complex social manipulation. She has amply described gestures like kissing, embracing, holding hands, patting one another on the back, tickling, and hair pulling—gestures which she describes as not only uncannily like our own, but also used in similar contexts with similar meaning.

Goodall attributes the similar emotions and intellectual abilities in the two species to the similar structure of the brain and nervous system. She concludes

> [i]t is all a little humbling, for those cognitive abilities used to be considered unique to humans: we are not, after all, quite as different from the rest of the animal kingdom as we used to think. The line dividing "man" from "beast" has become increasingly blurred. The chimpanzees, and the other great apes, form a living bridge between "us" and "them," and this knowledge forces us to re-evaluate our relationship with the rest of the animal kingdom, particularly with the great apes.[6]

At the same time, other researchers studied dolphins, elephants, horses, dogs, crows, and numerous other species and learned things about them that had never been known and were wrongly assumed. The complete study has required a change in perspective, showing that to really understand animals, one must do so on the animals' terms rather than on ours. In other words, one does not determine whether a crow is intelligent by asking whether or not she can speak English or write poetry, but by whether she is able to process information in sophisticated and complex ways that are relevant to a crow's life circumstances.

With that perspective in mind, a vast body of literature gradually eroded the conceptual lines that had long been drawn to separate the human species from all the others. It establishes that animals live in complex social systems and that, to varying degrees, mammals, birds and even fish possess considerable intelligence, are self-conscious, invent and use tools, reason, grieve for dead companions and family members, and act altruistically. Many species have sophisticated languages,

---

*Woman in the Mists: The Story of Dian Fossey and the Mountain Gorillas of Africa* (New York: Warner Books, 1987).

6    Goodall, "Chimpanzees," above note 2 at 13–14. Goodall has authored or contributed to more than twenty books on the subject.

including dialects, which use sound, sonar or gesture to communicate complex ideas.[7]

Most significant perhaps has been the confirmation that animals feel pain in ways similar to humans. Many animals show the signs of pain that humans recognize as implying pain in one another, such as writhing, facial contortions, moaning and other vocalizations, attempts to get away from the source of pain, and fear at the prospect of its repetition. Animals produce the same biochemicals that are known to be associated with pain in human beings. They have similar physiological responses to pain, such as elevated blood pressure and dilated pupils. Further, the nervous systems humans and animals evolved are similar and serve the same purpose: a capacity to feel pain enhances a being's prospects of survival, signalling to the one experiencing it that he is in danger.[8]

---

7   Gary L Francione, *Introduction to Animal Rights: Your Child or the Dog* (Philadelphia: Temple University Press, 2000) at 113–19 [Francione, *Introduction to Animal Rights*]. Also see David Attenborough, *The Lives of Birds* (London: BBC Worldwide Ltd, 1998); Theodore Xenophon Barber, *The Human Nature of Birds: A Scientific Discovery with Startling Implications* (New York: St Martin's Press, 1993); Marc Bekoff & Jessica Pierce, *Wild Justice: The Moral Lives of Animals* (Chicago: University of Chicago Press, 2009); Gay A Bradshaw, *Elephants on the Edge: What Elephants Teach Us About Humanity* (New Haven, CT: Yale University Press, 2009); Michael Bright, *Animal Language* (Ithaca, NY: Cornell University Press, 1984); Stephen Clark, *The Nature of the Beast: Are Animals Moral?* (Oxford: Oxford University Press, 1982); Fouts, above note 2; Donald Redfield Griffin, *Animal Minds* (Chicago: University of Chicago Press, 1992) and *Animal Thinking* (Cambridge, MA: Harvard University Press, 1984); Lori Marino, "Dolphin Cognition" (2004) 14 Current Biology R910; Lori Marino, "Convergence of Complex Cognitive Abilities in Cetaceans and Primates" (2002) 59 Brain, Behaviour and Evolution 21; Jeffrey Moussaieff Masson & Susan McCarthy, *When Elephants Weep: The Emotional Lives of Animals* (New York: Dell Publishing, 1996); Joan McIntyre, ed, *Mind in the Waters: A Book to Celebrate the Consciousness of Whales and Dolphins* (New York: Scribner, 1974); James Rachels, *Created from Animals: The Moral Implications of Darwinism* (Oxford: Oxford University Press, 1990); Carolyn A Ristau, ed, *Cognitive Ethology: The Minds of Other Animals* (Hillsdale, NJ: Lawrence Erlbaum Associates, 1991); Bernard E Rollin, *Animal Rights and Human Morality*, revised ed (Buffalo: Prometheus Press, 1992); Anne E Russon & David R Begun, eds, *The Evolution of Thought: Evolutionary Origins of Great Ape Intelligence* (Cambridge: Cambridge University Press, 2004); Richard D Ryder, *Animal Revolution: Changing Attitudes towards Speciesism* (Oxford: Basil Blackwell, 1989); Frans BM de Waal, *Good Natured: The Origins of Right and Wrong in Humans and Other Animals* (Cambridge, MA: Harvard University Press, 1996).

8   Peter Singer, *Animal Liberation*, revised ed (1975; repr, New York: Avon Books, 1990) at 11.

In light of all of this information, it became inaccurate to speak of the animal world as a duality with humans on one side and all the myriad other animals together on the other. Nature is now understood to have produced a wide range of beings, each evolved over time with their own strategies for survival in their own environment and circumstances: for example, an emperor penguin cannot write a factum and a lawyer cannot incubate an egg on his feet through an Antarctic winter. And while animals differ in some ways from humans, so too do they differ from one another. In many ways, a human is more similar to a chimpanzee than a chimpanzee is to a hummingbird.

In sum, modern evolutionary, biological, behavioural, and genetic science revealed that the world consists of beings who certainly differ from one another in some ways but who are remarkably similar in others. For all the qualities that were once thought to be unique to humans, some animal will have them to some degree. It turns out that what has really been deficient these many years was not the animals, but our own ability to interpret and understand them.

As a result, Descartes' claim that all other animals are just automata devoid of the capacities that were once understood to be uniquely human, is untenable. The difference between *us* and *them* is one of degree and a line demarcating any clear separation is now difficult to draw:

> The biological reality is that all classifications are artificial. They force a certain order on to the rather chaotic mess of the natural world. Species, as we describe them, are matters of convenience rather than biological reality. The real world consists only of individuals who are more or less closely related to each other by virtue of descent from one or more common ancestors.[9]

As this knowledge moved from the scientific realm to ethics, conceptual problems began to emerge. Even Bentham had assumed that while animals were sentient, there were other qualitative distinctions that justified their instrumental use, but even these were now reduced to a matter of degree. If there were no specific characteristics to support a firm human-animal duality, and if there was in fact much more similarity than anyone had previously known, what was the justification for perpetuating the old hierarchy and the differential treatment it allowed?

---

9    Robin IM Dunbar, "What's In a Classification?," in Cavalieri & Singer, above note 2 at 110. See also Mark A Krause, *Biological Continuity and Great Ape Rights* (1996) 2 Animal L 171 at 172.

# B. EVOLUTION'S IMPLICATIONS

The implications of the new ideas about animal life began to receive broad public consideration in the 1960s, beginning in Britain. Books and popular media articles addressing the philosophical debate about animal rights generally and about particular aspects of their use in modern times, led to what philosopher Robert Garner has called a "major explosion of intellectual challenges to the moral orthodoxy"[10] regarding human treatment of animals. A group of academics at Oxford University, including animal researcher Richard Ryder, began to view the kind of exploitation to which he and others were subjecting animals as unacceptable. Ryder abandoned animal research and became a critic. He contributed to a set of articles collectively published as *Animals, Men and Morals*,[11] which was reviewed by Australian philosopher, Peter Singer, in 1973 in the *New York Review of Books*.[12]

Encouraged by the response, Singer wrote *Animal Liberation* two years later. That book brought the subject to widespread public attention and is seen as a stimulus of the modern animal rights movement. This is in part because of Singer's argument and in part because of the extensive, horrific description he provided of what the industrialized approach to animal machines had become.[13]

Like Bentham, Singer is a utilitarian who does not technically believe in "rights" as they are commonly understood. He maintains that ethically correct actions are those which lead to the greatest happiness for the greatest number, but that in doing the calculation, there is no logically defensible basis for only counting humans. Animal interests must be counted too because, in light of the post-Darwinian understanding about their fundamental similarities, there is no good reason to exclude them.

*Animal Liberation* begins with Singer's defence of Mary Wollstonecraft against Thomas Taylor's *A Vindication of the Rights of Brutes*.[14] Where Taylor had intended to demonstrate a *reductio ad absurdum* in Wollstonecraft's argument, Singer saw it as a logical conclusion. Taylor's argument had been based on "speciesism" (a term coined by Ryder but brought to

---

10   Robert Garner, *Animals, Politics and Morality*, 2d ed (Manchester: Manchester University Press, 2004) at 3.
11   Stanley Godlovitch, Roslind Godlovich, & John Harris, eds, *Animals, Men and Morals: An Inquiry into the Maltreatment of Non-humans* (New York: Taplinger, 1971).
12   Garner, above note 10 at 2–33.
13   Singer, above note 8 at 9–17 and generally.
14   See discussion in Chapter 1, Section B.

popular attention here), which, like sexism and racism, relies on morally irrelevant distinctions such as one's membership in a group as justification for differential treatment.

Relying on the biological continuum of shared characteristics and capacities in the animal world, Singer argues that the principle of equal consideration of interests applicable among humans should also include animals. In particular, he emphasizes that the most significant interest shared by animals (most particularly, but not exclusively, mammals and birds) is their sentience, or capacity to experience suffering.

Singer exemplifies the significance of sentience by way of the subject of experimentation: many people are of the view that it is unacceptable to use non-consenting human beings in scientific experiments meant to benefit other human beings even though humans are the best model of the human body, because of the pain and suffering it would cause them; however, it is acceptable to use animals. Singer maintains that when it comes to justifying the distinction, the observation that humans are more intelligent or have more developed mental capacities, whether true or not, is not morally relevant. What is morally relevant is that the animal will feel the same pain that makes it unacceptable to do the experiment on a human.[15]

When it comes to mental capacities, absolute distinctions on the basis of species are not justifiable either. All humans do not possess the same mental capacities, and further, there are some animals whose mental capacities exceed those of some humans, such as newborn babies, or even adults with severe brain damage or other serious disabilities, and this is not a justification for doing experiments on them.[16] Other than species membership, there is no single characteristic that defines all human beings to the exclusion of all animal beings. Species-im, then, is a form of discrimination as morally indefensible as any other preference for one's own kind. Singer maintains that all sentient beings should have their equivalent interests considered equally.

---

15   For Ryder's elaborated discussion of this issue, see Richard D Ryder, *Victims of Science: The Use of Animals in Research* (London: Davis-Poynter, 1975).

16   CS Lewis put it starkly and in the language of his time. He thought that it would be difficult to formulate a human right of "tormenting beasts" in terms which would not equally imply an "angelic right of tormenting man." In particular, vivisection could only be defended by showing it to be right that one species should suffer in order that another species be happier. "If we cut up beasts simply because they cannot prevent us and because we are backing our own side in the struggle for existence, it is only logical to cut up imbeciles, criminals, enemies, or capitalists for the same reasons." Clive Staples Lewis, *The Problem of Pain* (1940; repr, New York: HarperCollins, 1966) at 132–48.

On the other hand, he does not believe that sentience is always the relevant factor to consider in a given situation. He maintains that animals lack self-awareness and an interest in continuing to live, and he proposes that in some situations these distinctions can justify the continued use of animals in some ways, such as eating them, if it can be done painlessly and the animals can be replaced. In this sense, Singer has been criticized for adherence to the view that animals are essentially replaceable units with no entitlement to their own existence, and he has become a controversial figure within the very movement for animal liberation that he helped to inspire.[17] Singer does not limit these views to animals, but claims that comparative valuations can also be made in the lives of human beings, and thus the controversy regarding his work extends more deeply into the realm of bioethics.[18]

Modern animal rights theory has its essential theoretical basis in the philosophy of American philosopher, Tom Regan. Regan essentially shares Singer's view that there is no defensible basis for refusing to extend to most animals the basic moral right humans have to respectful treatment and equal consideration of their interests. Rather than regard animals as resources for human consumption, he proposes a comparable moral status to humans based on animals' own inherent value.

Regan describes animals as the subjects-of-a-life, a life which fares well or ill for them regardless of whether anybody else knows or cares about them. He rejects Singer's humane killing of animals and the general notion of using one species as a resource for another in that animals have an interest in and an entitlement to their own lives. However, while acknowledging animals' complex mental life, he finds that humans alone have a sense of the future and therefore there are circumstances where it would be acceptable to value human life more than some animal life.[19]

These philosophies, albeit relatively young and still subject to analysis and critique, raise difficult questions as they begin to respond to current knowledge, and they have shifted the debate. In the twentieth century, the public demand to generally improve the human treatment of animals grew. However, neither Singer's utilitarian approach nor Regan's rights-based approach has been implemented and there have not

17    For example, John Sorenson, *About Canada: Animal Rights* (Winnipeg: Fernwood, 2010) at 13 & 14; Michael Allen Fox & Lesley McLean, "Animals in Moral Space" in Carla Jodey Castricano, ed, *Animal Subjects: An Ethical Reader in a Posthuman World* (Waterloo: Wilfred Laurier University Press, 2008) at 145; and Francione, *Introduction to Animal Rights*, above note 7 at 135–46.

18    *Animal Liberation*, above note 8 at 17–23

19    Tom Regan, *The Case for Animal Rights* (Berkeley: University of California Press, 1983).

yet been any real substantial changes in the ways animals are used and the harms that are caused them in the process.

There are several reasons for this. First, despite evolutionary biology and the new knowledge which followed, it was never science's intent to unsettle the established human-animal hierarchy. Science itself has continued to adhere keenly to the Cartesian perspective. Many years after Darwin, in 1927 Pavlov urged that animals need only be considered in a physiological sense, and that there was no need to resort to "fantastic speculations" that they might have any subjective states.[20]

Further, even in modern times, science has not entirely displaced religion as the source of behavioural prescriptions and answers to difficult questions. Evolutionary theory contradicts material aspects of religious creationist beliefs that were deeply held for a very long time and even continue to be held in some powerful circles. It has not enjoyed a smooth course in penetrating the Western conscience.[21]

Moreover, not only science has undergone changes in the last century or two. The industrial revolution dramatically transformed Western societies. From pulling ploughs and carriages, the fundamental role of animals in the new large-scale industrialized economy also grew exponentially. While some people were debating the implications of new evidence of animal intelligence and sentience, animal use was forging ahead into ubiquity, and has become a fundamental aspect of Western economies.

In the course of all of this, individuals in society find themselves in perpetually conflicting positions. More and more people live with pets, profess to love animals, and call for better legal protection for them, while they simultaneously consume other animals and thereby (sometimes but not always unwittingly) participate in practices which would have to change or stop, if that call were answered.

Thus, the real effect of the evolution revolution has so far been confined to the realm of ideas. It has contradicted the long-term beliefs and biblical justifications that sustained the Cartesian approach to animals in philosophy and the Lockian approach to animals in law. These had relied on or assumed categorical distinctions between human beings and all of the many other species that comprise the animal kingdom, and they served as justification for differential treatment. In showing that the differences are only in degree, evolutionary theory has required philosophy to address the similarities, and philosophy in turn pressures law to do the same.

---

20    Richard D Ryder, *Animal Revolution*, above note 7 at 6.
21    Regan, above note 19 at 18–25.

On the other hand, even many years after Darwin, few people have been prepared to give up the advantages that a categorical distinction provides. Science itself has largely ignored the implications of its own findings and now proceeds on a clear contradiction: the continued use of animals in experiments rests at once on the old assumption and the new knowledge—first, that animals are sufficiently *different* from us that it is acceptable to use them as objects in experiments for our benefit, and second, that they are sufficiently *similar* to us for the results of the experiments to be meaningful. And well beyond science, animal resources are used in ever-expanding ways. Now, to the desire to use animals for sustenance or other primary factors, profit has been added and it is backed by an increasingly strong corporate interest in discouraging consumers from thinking there are any problems in the first place.

For all of these reasons, as the twentieth century closed, the search for a unique feature that would serve as the distinction necessary to perpetuate the human-animal divide persisted, even if all that was left to debate were the subtleties which Singer, Regan, and their critics have considered (animals have a mental state but is it as rich as ours?; some animals mourn their dead, but do they anticipate their own deaths coming?), and even if the resolution of those discussions has no bearing on an animal's ability to feel the pain that continues to be inflicted on them.

The twentieth-century call for legal solutions to the problems facing animals was thus answered with the same ambivalence with which it was made.

## C. THE HUMANE TREATMENT PRINCIPLE AND LEGAL WELFARISM

The surge of interest in animal welfare in the post-Bentham era did result in a new notion that animals should not be made to suffer unnecessarily. This notion was codified in the nineteenth century in anti-cruelty legislation across Canada that is considered in the next chapter. However, Locke's property notions have proved powerful and have not yielded much since their inception. As a PEI court put it in 1932 when considering the status of captive mink being raised for their fur, an animal in the class of tame animals is clearly a subject of "absolute property."[22] Thus, although laws concerning animals did change in the

---

22   *Ebers v MacEachern*, [1932] 3 DLR 415 (PEISC).

twentieth century, the legal status of animals did not and the result has been minimal in terms of meaningful improvement in their lives.

Gary Francione, American lawyer and legal scholar, explains why this is the case in his seminal text, *Animals, Property and the Law*.[23] He describes the problem as follows. The law purports to codify what he calls the *humane treatment principle*: the principle that everyone agrees that animals ought not to be subjected to unnecessary pain and suffering, and that they ought to be treated humanely, and "everyone" even includes those who directly or indirectly support animal use and exploitation.[24] However, all the while the humane treatment principle has been operational in law, animals have continued to be subjected to treatment that can only be called "barbaric" and that can not in most cases be considered to be necessary, as that word is normally understood.[25]

Francione's argument is essentially that while the humane treatment principle was well-intended and even radical in its time, as notions of property developed, it became impossible for an entity that is a chattel or a thing in law to have any meaningful recognition of its interests. There are restrictions on the use of animals, but these are not much different in practice than the restrictions law applies to uses of all property. There is a critical difference between benevolently "treating animals humanely" and attributing to animals actual "legal rights": animals do not and cannot have rights in a system that regards them as things.

McGill law professor Wendy Adams similarly explains that the essence of law is classification and everything in law depends on it. Arguably the most fundamental classification law makes is in distinguishing between persons and property. Classifying animals as property relegates them to instrumental status.[26]

---

23 Gary L Francione, *Animals, Property and the Law* (Philadelphia: Temple University Press, 1995) at 3–14. The summary provided here and following in regard to animal rights legal theory, is based largely on the Introduction set out in these pages, and is further elaborated throughout the course of the book.

24 Francione's observation is not based on empirical evidence; he reflects on his own experience and invites others to do the same; a 2010 Harris/Decima poll supports his conclusion, finding that 95 percent of Canadians agree that animal pain and suffering should be reduced as much as possible: Harris/Decima, *Humane Treatment of Animals* (3 December 2010).

25 Elsewhere he has described this as our "moral schizophrenia" concerning animals. See Francione, *Introduction to Animal Rights*, above note 7 at xix–xxi.

26 Wendy A Adams, "Human Subjects and Animal Objects: Animals as 'Other' in Law" (2009) 3:1 J Animal L & Ethics 29 at 31.

The distinction manifests in the use of the term "unnecessary," which is a central part of anti-cruelty legislation. Even to the extent that law recognizes a conflict between an animal and a human, the two parties come to court on different legal footings: one as property and the other as its owner. In order for a court to determine whether pain and suffering is necessary, it must balance the interests of the two. But it is a fundamental rule of property that property itself cannot have any rights, particularly against its owner. Legal things are not autonomous; they have no interests to be protected for their own sake. Effectively, whether something is "necessary" or not is largely predetermined by the characterization of the parties in the first place. These assumptions entrenched in law permit virtually any use of animals, however fundamental the harm that use causes them, and however trivial by comparison is the human owner's interest in causing it.

To consider the Western concept of property in its broadest sense, animal resources are objects like any other. Ownership is assigned and belongs to particular individuals who are allowed to use the resources to the exclusion of everyone else. Like any form of movable property, an animal may be the subject of absolute ownership whereby the owner is entitled to exclusive physical possession, use of the object for economic or other gain, right to contract with respect to the object, use the object as collateral for a loan, and so on. The owner can give the object away, have it taken away, or have it destroyed.

Harking back to Locke's foundational principles and the role they continue to occupy in the contemporary legal world, Francione emphasizes the importance of property in Western culture and the tendency of legal doctrine to protect and maximize its value. This normative theory, which he calls "legal welfarism," is implicit in the law and its foundations are rarely recognized or discussed.

Francione maintains that the proscription against causing unnecessary pain and suffering, while unique to animal property, does not create legal rights for animals. The limitations on animal use are interpreted against the backdrop of widespread animal use, so any difference that anti-cruelty laws might imply between animal property and other forms of property is obscured. These laws do not transcend the level of protection that facilitates the most economically efficient exploitation of the animal. In the end, legal welfarism ultimately proscribes only those uses of animals that are not efficient and that are not part of an accepted form of exploitation. A law which entrenches the assumption that it is acceptable to cause suffering in order to achieve a human end may well be more accurately characterized as protecting the interests of human owners rather than those of their animal property.[27]

Although gratuitous pain and suffering are prohibited, these are rarely found beyond the context of individual cases of egregious, aberrant behaviour in regard to a particular animal or animals. Since the determination of what is "necessary" is made by reference to the owner's own interest in her property, when it comes to institutionalized harms, it is the very industries that are engaged in the animal use that are called upon to explain why what they do is necessary. Legal welfarism is premised on the notion that law can best interpret these provisions by allowing the property owner to determine what will maximize the value of the property. It thereby puts the fox in charge of the henhouse.

Further, within the industrial context, the prohibition against "unnecessary suffering" looks only at a specific act, which occurs in the course of a broader animal use, such as the use of a bullhook to control an elephant in the circus. It does not invite an examination of the underlying assumption that elephants can be used as circus performers in the first place. The *a priori* acceptance of animal use is a structural problem inherent in the legislation that has not to date been remedied by common law principles of statutory interpretation.[28]

In the American system, property rights are constitutionally protected by the Fifth Amendment, however, these arguments are analogous in Canada where property rights are also a fundamental legal concern. The definition, allocation, and protection of property rights is the direct or indirect preoccupation of many legal fields, and provides a central premise on which others are based. Further, the language of anti-cruelty statutes is comparable between the two countries and the terminology has been interpreted in Canada similarly to the American history Francione provides.

In another way, the nature of property rights undermines the debate about how animal use should be changed or curtailed. Most harm to animals is caused on private property beyond the scrutiny of non-interested observers. Privacy legislation protects animal owners against full disclosure of what is involved in the normal practices of their use so it is difficult to have informed debate and determine whether those

---

27    *Ibid* at 34.

28    One might argue that this is not necessarily inappropriate and it should be up to legislators rather than courts to determine the broader questions of which uses of animals are permitted or whether any should be. Still, when considering whether and to what degree certain kinds of changes will substantially address a given problem, it is important to have a clear understanding of how legal limitations are built in.

practices actually have public support. At the same time, the language of the law is superficially persuasive: "unnecessary pain and suffering" is prohibited; "humane treatment" is required. Together, the reassuring language and the absence of any details to the contrary create the general sense that there is no need for public concern.

Legal welfarism has been hard to displace. Former Justice L'Heureux-Dubé has considered a similar problem in the human context, noting John Stuart Mill's observation that the law assumes that existing relationships of domination and subordination are "natural." The law, in adopting the status quo, then plays an even more insidious role, from an equality perspective, of converting into a legal relationship, a relationship of inequality which was previously a mere physical fact. Once the physical fact has reached the level of legal right, and clothed itself within the legitimacy of the law, it receives the sanction of society. Domination always seems natural to those who benefit by it. Inequality permeates institutions that people have held near and dear over centuries, so a commitment to its eradication requires that we look deep into ourselves and into the reality experienced by those that do not "by nature" dominate.[29]

Justice L'Heureux-Dubé makes these observations in reference to women's equality but they are familiar to all equality-seeking groups who question where the categorical line is drawn between inclusion and exclusion. The coherence of any legal category depends upon the validity of the processes of classifications from which the categories are derived.[30] Categories based on morally irrelevant distinctions are not sustainable.

Today all human beings are legal persons entitled to fundamental legal rights, but this has not always been the case. Throughout the course of history, reliance on "natural differences" between various empowered and disempowered groups grounded fundamental legal distinctions. In different ways, women, persons with disabilities, racialized persons, First Nations people, Jews, and others were, at one point in history, seen to be unworthy of fundamental legal rights, and

---

29   Hon. Justice Claire L'Heureux-Dubé, "New Challenges for the Legal System" in *Roads to Equality*, supp to vol 1 (Ottawa: Canadian Bar Association, Continuing Legal Education Program, Annual General Meeting, 1994) at 5–8. Christopher Stone made the same observations in the context of his argument for extending rights more generally to nature in his seminal article: Christopher D Stone, "Should Trees Have Standing? Toward Legal Rights for Natural Objects" (1972) 45 S Cal L Rev 450.

30   Adams, above note 26 at 31.

in some cases were actual chattels in whom others held proprietary right in Western societies.[31]

As seen in Chapter 1, Jewish people in medieval Europe were considered to be lower forms of life not meriting legal rights. A thirteenth-century text described Jews as "men *ferae naturae*, protected by a quasi-forest law. Like the roe and the deer, they form an order apart."[32]

Ownership of human property was the essence of American slavery; slaves were legal things with no legal status of their own: "The investiture of a chattel with civil rights or legal capacity is indeed a solecism and absurdity."[33] In the infamous *Dred Scott* case, the issue was whether an enslaved man brought to a state where slavery was prohibited could sue for his freedom. The court found he lacked standing; moreover, to permit him to proceed would deprive his owner of property without due process. The court relied on what it found to be natural differences by which slaves were "beings of an inferior order" that had "no rights which the white man was bound to respect."[34]

It was only in the twentieth century that Canadian women were found to be legal persons and holders of basic rights. In the "Persons Case" the Supreme Court considered whether the word "person" in section 24 of the *British North America Act, 1867* concerning eligibility for appointment to the Senate included women. Unanimously, the Court said no.[35] The Privy Council granted an appeal, finding that the exclusion of women was a "relic of days more barbarous than ours." It rejected the historical regard for women and outdated customs as a basis for modern statutory interpretation and adopted an approach based on the way the legal system of the day was starting to regard them, finding that "[c]ustoms are apt to develop into traditions which are stronger than law and remain unchallenged long after the reason for them has disappeared" and further:

> [T]heir lordships do not think it right to apply rigidly to Canada of today the decisions and the reasonings therefor which commended themselves, probably rightly, to those who had to apply the law in

---

31    This is not to deny that many serious problems in achieving actual equality among human beings persist; the progress referred to is of the most fundamental order, in that legal personhood of all human beings is now accepted, and with this an acknowledgement of basic rights.

32    Stone, above note 29 at 453–55.

33    *Baily v Poindexter's Ex'r*, 14 Gratt 132 at 143 (Va CA 1858).

34    *Dred Scott v Sandford*, 60 US 393 at 396, 407, and 450 (1856).

35    *Re British North America Act 1867 (UK) Section 24*, [1928] SCR 276.

different circumstances, in different centuries to countries in different stages of development.[36]

It seems obvious now that all human beings are legal persons, but that is only after the case is made, often one group at a time, that morally irrelevant distinctions do not justify differential treatment in respect of their fundamental rights. The category of legal person has had to adapt to changing knowledge and values over time. Animals are the only sentient beings who remain characterized as legal things. On the other hand, even inanimate constructs such as corporations, trusts, and estates, have legal rights and can assert their interests in law. The legal system has the flexibility required to respond to post-Darwinian knowledge about animals.

## D. EMERGENCE OF ANIMAL RIGHTS LEGAL THEORY

As legal thinking on the subject of different human groups has changed over time, legal thinking on the subject of animals is following. American civil rights lawyer, William Kunstler, states:

> It may surprise many who are familiar with my work that I have become interested in the plight of animals at a time when there seems to be more human misery and injustice than ever before. I have given considerable thought to this question, and I have resolved any doubts in favor of speaking against the exploitation of nonhuman animals . . .
>
> [I]t is unjust *to the animals themselves* to deny them their rights, irrespective of any salutary effect that it may have on relations among humans. Like us, animals are individuals with interests. Their value does not depend on their use to us any more than does the inherent value of a human being depend on that person's use to others. Justice for nonhumans requires that we recognize that all sentient beings have inherent worth that does not depend on our humanocentric and patriarchal valuation of that worth.[37]

Animal rights legal theory differs from legal welfarism in that it considers animals as individuals with their own interests that should be respected. According to Francione, the humane treatment principle should be replaced with the *principle of equal consideration* that Regan

---

36   *Re British North America Act 1867 (UK)*, [1930] 1 DLR 98 at 104–5 (PC).

37   William M Kunstler, "Foreword" in Francione, *Animals, Property and the Law*, above note 23 at x [emphasis in original].

and others proposed: where animals have similar interests to humans, they should be considered in a similar way in terms of determining the consequences of actions that will affect them, unless there is a good reason not to. The fundamental similarities between humans and other animals are those that are seen to be necessary and sufficient to attribute the status of personhood to human beings. These similarities should be thought of as though they erect rights barriers that are impervious to consequential considerations, such as how others might benefit from harming them.[38]

In many cases, the basic similarity that will be relevant is sentience. Since animals are sentient, applying the principle of equal consideration means that one basic right must be extended to them: the right not to be treated as property, or as legal things.[39] A "right" is the barrier mentioned above, which stands between its holder and everybody else. In its broadest sense, it can be understood to mean that the person who holds it has some value that must be respected, whether or not exploiting that person would be beneficial to any other person or number of people.

Invoking the term "right" in this context requires some commentary. First, in arguing that rights should be extended to animals, this is not to say these rights, like any other rights, could never be overridden, but rather that human beings have a *prima facie* duty not to cause harm to other right holders; and in order to override them, a principled approach must be articulated to provide valid moral reasons for doing so.

Second, a right to equal consideration in this sense does not mean that all the same rights apply to humans and animals. Animal rights legal theory is addressed to a being's fundamental concerns, like physical and psychological integrity, "as opposed to rights understood in more prosaic legal terms, such as contract and property rights."[40] It does not seek human rights for animals, such as the right to vote or get married.

Third, accepting this principle means that there would certainly be conflicts between human and animal right holders. This is not unusual, the interests of current right holders are often in conflict, and legal systems exist for the very purpose of attempting to negotiate them, or when that is not possible, to find a principled way to resolve them.[41]

---

38   Francione, *ibid* at 8–11, citing Regan, above note 19. See also Tom Regan, "Animal Rights and the Law" (1987) 31 Saint Louis ULJ 513.
39   Francione, *ibid* at 8–14 and generally.
40   Adams, above note 26 at 42.
41   Law can be viewed as "a mechanism for facilitating and regulating interaction between autonomous entities": *Ibid* at 45 and n 55.

Rights theory applied to animals extends the circle of those whose interests merit consideration, just as that circle has extended over time to include human groups previously excluded.

If animals are to enjoy the one right to which animal rights legal theory claims they are entitled—the right to be regarded as individuals with their own interests, and not as property—their legal status will have to be re-envisioned. The determination of the manner by which animal interests can be integrated into a human-centred legal system that accommodates animals on their own terms is a work-in-progress and the subject of considerable debate.[42] There will not be a civil war for animal rights and there is no inherent constituency able to insist upon them in the manner that disenfranchised human groups have done. The change for which animal rights legal theory calls can only be expected to take place in incremental steps, as legislation and jurisprudence evolve and transform animals from things to persons.

The twenty-first century began with one of those steps. In 2002, the Supreme Court recognized that the animal rights legal perspective is a valid one entitled to consideration in Canadian courts. Harvard College was seeking a patent for transgenic animals and the Supreme Court granted intervenor status to three organizations that sought to ensure that it specifically considered the animal rights response to whether an animal is a thing invented in a laboratory.[43] Many more steps will be taken before animals begin to enjoy any relief from the violence done to them in the name of human necessity. Some of those will be in the legal fields discussed in the coming chapters. The Supreme Court has opened the door to modern ideas.

---

42   *Ibid* at 41–51. See also Gary L Francione & Robert Garner, *The Animal Rights Debate: Abolition or Regulation?* (New York: Columbia University Press, 2010); Cass R Sunstein & Martha C Nussbaum, eds, *Animal Rights: Current Debates and New Directions* (Oxford: Oxford University Press, 2004).

43   *Harvard College v Canada (Commissioner of Patents)*, 2002 SCC 76. This case is discussed in Chapter 6.

# PART II

# LEGAL LANDSCAPE

# FEDERAL ANTI-CRUELTY LAWS

Man is the cruellest animal.

—Friedrich Nietzsche

The wide variety of human uses for animals creates legal issues in many subject areas. Federal, provincial, and municipal governments can legislate in fields including agriculture, research, hunting, fishing, trapping and other killing of wildlife, migratory birds, wildlife in captivity, import and export of animals, endangered species, companion animals in housing, licensing and other municipal concerns regarding companion animals, veterinary medicine, dangerous animals, and liability for damage done by animals. The degree of regulation varies considerably according to animal use. In the context of agriculture, extensive legislation governs the industry, both federally and provincially. By contrast, the use of animals in research, teaching, and testing has no federal oversight and within the provinces it is hardly regulated at all.

Generally applicable, and not necessarily confined to any specific subject area, are the anti-cruelty laws set out on the federal level in the *Criminal Code* (often referred to as "the Code").[1] These are "animated by the general purposes of the criminal law, which are to promote a peaceful and safe society and to prevent and punish acts which harm or threaten to harm society and which tend to undermine social values."[2]

---

1    *Criminal Code* of Canada, RSC 1985, c C-46.
2    Joanne Klineberg, "Cruelty to Animals and the *Criminal Code* of Canada" in Lesli Bisgould, ed, *An Introduction to Animals and the Law* (Toronto: Law Society

Criminal law seeks to promote treatment of animals which "reflects the values that people expect from their relations with each other, such as compassion and respect."[3] The Code "encapsulates the fundamental moral code of our society" and "sets down the minimum standard of permissible behaviour in respect of animals through a series of criminal offences."[4] These offences recognize that animals have an interest in being exposed to as little pain and suffering as possible, however they allow for animals to be subjugated and made to suffer for human ends.[5]

*Criminal Code* provisions in respect of animals have been amended several times since their inception in 1892, but their essence has changed very little. In the manner in which they seek to protect inherently conflicting interests—those of animals not to suffer, and those of people to cause such suffering—they occupy somewhat unusual territory in the criminal law, and as a result, the provisions and their interpretation are unique in several ways. In recent years, the federal government has acknowledged a need for modernization, and since 1999, there have been thirteen bills introduced in attempt to do so. To date, these have failed with the exception of amendments in respect of sentencing. In the committee debates and public discussions surrounding the various bills, the changing public perspective discussed in the previous chapter is clearly evident although it has not yet manifested in any remarkable legislative way.

This chapter is in four parts: Part A examines the development of federal anti-cruelty laws in the criminal law of Canada. Part B describes current provisions and Part C discusses issues related to their interpretation. Part D reviews the efforts to amend those provisions since 1999.

## A. DEVELOPMENT OF ANTI-CRUELTY LAWS IN THE *CRIMINAL CODE*

Canada's first federal anti-cruelty laws were enacted in 1869.[6] The essence of these provisions was adopted when the original *Criminal Code* was enacted thirteen years later, and they reflect the customs, values,

---

of Upper Canada, Continuing Legal Education, 3 October 2007) Tab 1 at 1-2 [Klineberg]. Klineberg is Counsel, Criminal Law Policy Section, federal Department of Justice.

3   *Ibid.*
4   *Ibid* at 1-1.
5   *Ibid* at 1-2.
6   *An Act Respecting Cruelty to Animals*, SC 1869, c 27, also referred to as 32–33 Vict c 27.

and knowledge of the time. From the outset, a concern for animals' well-being was set out, but a review of the historical record indicates that that concern has always been highly qualified and secondary to the interests of the people who owned and had a financial interest in them. Anti-cruelty provisions were enacted in the part of the Code addressed to property offences, Title VI, *Offences Against Rights of Property and Rights Arising out of Contracts, and Offences Connected with Trade.*[7]

The first part of Title VI had a strong emphasis on theft, of which animal theft was a significant portion. Crankshaw discussed Canada's efforts in its new legislation to address the problems that had troubled the Royal Commissioners in Britain. Despite Locke's best efforts, one persistent problem was the precise manner in which to allocate property in different kinds of animals so as to clarify the circumstances in which three categories of animals *ferae naturae* would be the subjects of larceny: those in captivity, those who had escaped from captivity and those who were captured "in the enjoyment of their natural liberty." These were codified in section 304 of the Code, entitled "Animals Capable of Being Stolen."[8]

Certain offences related to harming or threatening to harm cattle or other animals were part of a series of mischief offences, which included causing injury to buildings, landmarks, trees, and other real or personal property. Cattle was a general term which encompassed other economically valuable domesticated livestock such as horses, mules, ass, swine, sheep, goats, and any other animals of the bovine species. Harm to these animals was treated differently than the same harm or threat of harm to other animals, with a clear emphasis on the protection of the most valuable resources: attempting to injure or poison cattle, or threatening to do so, were indictable offences, while actually injuring animals other than cattle that were kept for a lawful purpose was a summary conviction offence.[9]

The cruelty to animals laws set out in sections 512 to 514 were also summary conviction offences. There were three parts to section 512 which corresponded directly to the three different goals of the legislation that were identified in Chapter 2: to protect animals' interest in not suffering, to protect people's interests in causing suffering, and to protect people from the nuisance and harm to human morality caused

---

7    James Crankshaw, *The Criminal Code of Canada* (Montreal: Whiteford & Theoret, Law Publishers, 1894) at 266–72.

8    *Ibid.* The current theft provisions in the *Criminal Code* still contain a section specifically addressed to the theft of wild living creatures in captivity and after they have escaped captivity: see s 322(5).

9    Crankshaw, above note 7 at 447–48, ss 500–2.

by certain activities involving animals. Everyone was guilty of an offence who:

(a) wantonly, cruelly or *unnecessarily* beats, binds, illtreats, abuses, overdrives or tortures any cattle, poultry, dog, domestic animal or bird; or

(b) while driving any cattle or other animal is, by *negligence* or *ill-usage* in the driving thereof, the means whereby any mischief, damage or injury is done by any such cattle or other animal; or

(c) in any manner encourages, aids or assists at the fighting or baiting of any bull, bear badger, dog, cock, or other kind of animal, whether of domestic or wild nature.[10]

Wild animals or birds kept in captivity were added to subsection (a) in 1895.[11]

Crankshaw discussed the concepts of "wanton" and "cruel" used in section 512(a) with reference to jurisprudence under its British predecessors. A wanton act was unjustifiable by the circumstances, and whether or not the harm was cruel depended not on the act itself as much as the reason for it. The mere infliction of some bodily pain was not sufficient to constitute an offence. There had to be not only some ill-usage from which the animal suffered, but also the ill-usage had to be without any necessity. The most common case in which law would apply would be where an animal was cruelly beaten or tortured for the mere purpose of causing pain or for the gratification of a malignant or vindictive temper. The mere inconvenience and discomfort attendant upon the transporting of animals from one place to another was not cruelty.

Nor was the law intended to apply when the purpose of the act was to make the animal more serviceable for the use of "man."[12] It did not prevent chastisement necessary for the training or disciplining of animals, if this was not excessive, and chastisement in good faith and for a proper purpose would not be deemed excessive. The distinction was between a justifiable motive and a malevolent spirit. Crankshaw distinguished this offence from the constraint on parents or teachers in punishing a child within moderate and reasonable limits; there were no such limits on animal chastisement, unless the excessive chastisement was also unnecessary and wantonly cruel.[13]

---

10    *Ibid* at 451, s 512 [emphasis in original].

11    *An Act further to amend the Criminal Code*, SC 1895, c 40, s 512(a).

12    Crankshaw, above note 7 at 454, citing *Lewis v Fermor* (1887), LR 18 QBD 532 [*Lewis*].

13    Crankshaw, *ibid* at 452.

The word "needless" in this context did not mean an act that might, with care, be avoided. It simply meant an act done without any useful motive, in a spirit of wanton cruelty, or for the mere pleasure of destruction. Crankshaw gave the example of an Arkansas case in which a man who had killed his neighbour's pig (the pig had been trespassing on the man's land) was convicted under a statute which made it an offence to "needlessly mutilate or kill any living creature." The court noted that he ought not to have been convicted "if he had some useful object in the killing, such as the protection of his wheat and corn."[14]

Even a lingering death did not necessarily constitute unnecessary pain and suffering. Crankshaw referred to sports that are considered to be "healthful recreations and exercise, tending to promote strength, bodily agility and courage" and noted that even the pain that comes with a lingering death is often disregarded in the customs and laws of "human and highly civilized people," citing angling and hunting as examples.[15]

As discussed more below, the general anti-cruelty prohibition contained in section 512(a) persists to date, as does the manner of its interpretation, though it has been reworded over time.[16] In 1925, a new offence was added, prohibiting abandoning an animal in distress and causing unnecessary suffering or injury by failing to provide food, water, and shelter to an animal in one's possession and control.[17] This provision, as modified, also persists to date.[18]

The offence created by section 512(b) — "while driving any cattle or other animal is, by negligence or ill-usage in the driving thereof, the means whereby any mischief, damage or injury is done by any such cattle or other animal" — is not discussed in Crankshaw's history. Its presence in the anti-cruelty section of the Code emphasizes that the notion of cruelty was rooted in the concept of using an animal badly rather than treating an animal badly. It remained in effect until the amendments of 1953–54.

Section 512(c) was an outright prohibition against the fighting or baiting animals, whether domesticated or wild. It long predated the

---

14  *Ibid* at 452–53, citing *Grise v State*, 37 Ark 456 (1881). The *Criminal Code* did not contain a general prohibition against needlessly killing any living creature; it only addressed the killing of animals in whom a person had a possessory interest, including animals who were the subject of larceny at common law, ordinarily kept in a state of confinement or kept for a lawful purpose: *ibid*, s 501.

15  Crankshaw, *ibid* at 453–54.

16  The current embodiment is s 445.1(1)(a).

17  SC 1925, c 38, s 12.

18  The current embodiment is s 446(1)(b).

Code, having arisen in response to concerns that those who would engage in these activities were of such character that they created a public nuisance or harm. For example, Section I of the *Cruelty to Animals Act 1835*[19] provided:

> And whereas divers Places in and about the Metropolis are kept and used for the Purpose of fighting or baiting of Bears or other Animals, at which Places idle and disorderly Persons commonly assemble, to the Interruption of good Order and the Danger of the public Peace; be it therefore enacted, that any Person who shall, within Five Miles of the Temple Bar, keep or use or shall act in the Management or conducting of any Premises or Place whatsoever for the Purpose of fighting or baiting of Badgers or other animals, shall, on Conviction thereof . . .[20]

Further, section III similarly adverted to the danger of "great nuisances and annoyances to the neighbourhood" caused by the impugned practices which "tend to demoralize those who frequent such places."[21]

There were two other specific anti-cruelty provisions in the original Code. In addition to the prohibition on cockfighting in section 512, section 513 made it an offence to keep a cockpit. To address the harm to the community caused by such a place, section 513 mandated that any cocks found in a cockpit would be confiscated and sold for the benefit of the municipality. That provision was modified in later years, requiring that all cocks found be confiscated and destroyed, and it persists to date.[22]

Section 514 addressed aspects of the treatment of cattle while in transit. It applied to railways and to owners and masters of vessels, where animals were travelling within a province, between provinces or to the United States, prohibiting them from confining animals for more than twenty-eight hours without a five-hour break for rest, water, and feeding, unless prevented by storm or other unavoidable cause, or necessary delay or detention. This provision has since been removed from the Code, and transportation of animals in agriculture is now regulated by relevant provincial and federal Ministries.[23]

---

19  (UK) 5&6 Will IV, c 59.

20  *Ibid*, s I.

21  *Ibid*, s III.

22  *An Act to amend the Criminal Code*, SC 1948, c 39; the current version is in s 447.

23  The permissible transit time has been considerably extended for many of these animals; ruminants may now be confined in transit without a break for more than two days: see discussion in Chapter 5.

In 1922, a fourth prohibition was added with respect to transporting an animal that was tame or sufficiently tamed so that it might serve some purpose for man's use, in a manner or position so as to cause any unnecessary suffering. A revised version of that provision persists to date.[24]

In 1930, the general anti-cruelty provision, now section 542, had two specific additions. The new section 542(e) made it an offence to wilfully and without reasonable cause or excuse, poison any cattle, poultry, dog, domestic animal, bird, or wild animal, or bird in captivity. This was the first use of the word "wilful" in anti-cruelty provisions; it would be more generally used in amendments to come. Section 542(f) prohibited trap shooting, in which birds kept captive are shot upon being released.[25] Both of these prohibitions persist to date.[26]

Other amendments were fairly minor in effect, including slight increases in penalties, while the offences remained summary conviction offences[27] until 1953–54, when the primary prohibition against cruelty was reworded to the form it has retained to present times. The various references to ill-treatment were replaced with a more general proscription against "unnecessary pain, suffering and injury" and the emphasis on cattle and other animals working in agriculture was replaced with a more general reference to harm to "an animal or bird." From that point forward, everyone commits an offence who "wilfully causes, or being the owner, wilfully permits to be caused unnecessary pain, suffering or injury to an animal or bird."[28]

This revision was the result of the changing times. Prior to the Second World War, the emphasis of the legislation had been on working animals and blood sports. As agriculture became increasingly industrialized, and with the advent of antibiotics, farmers began bringing the animals indoors where nobody could see what was happening to them. At the same time, urbanization was increasing and the interest of

---

24  A general prohibition remains against causing damages or injury to animals or birds by wilful neglect while they are in transit: s 446(1).

25  *An Act to amend the Criminal Code*, SC 1930, c 11, ss 542(e) & (f).

26  See ss 445.1(1)(c) & (d). The latter provision has rarely been interpreted. In *Prefontaine v R* (1973), 26 CRNS 367 at 377 (QCA), the Court of Appeal of Quebec stated that the purpose of the section "is certainly not to permit the shooting of pigeons under certain conditions; it is clearly intended to preclude individuals in groups from trapping small unfortunate creatures, and suddenly releasing them for purposes of being shot at."

27  *An Act to amend the Criminal Code*, SC 1935, c 56 and *An Act to amend the Criminal Code*, SC 1938, c 44.

28  *Criminal Code*, SC 1953–54, c 51, s 387. The current provision is s 445.1(1)(a).

anti-cruelty legislation shifted to the cats and dogs that more and more people were keeping as pets.[29]

Despite the addition of a "wilful" element to the general offences, these 1953–54 amendments were said to be a progressive development. When he was chief justice of the Quebec Court of Appeal, Lamer JA wrote what became the leading case interpreting the general anti-cruelty provision and the concept of "unnecessary" for modern times: "I dare to believe that we were given in 1953–4 a norm which was intended to be more sensitive to the lot which we reserve alas all too often to our animals . . . while at the same time guarding us against the danger of confusing compassion with sentimentalism." He went on at some length to assure society that the old hierarchy remained intact:

> Within the hierarchy of our planet, the animal occupies a place which, if it does not give rights to the animal, at least prompts us, being animals who claim to be rational beings, to impose on ourselves behaviour which will reflect in our relations with them those virtues we seek to promote in our relations among humans. On the other hand, the animal is inferior to man, and takes its place within a hierarchy which is the hierarchy of the animals, and above all is a part of nature with all its "racial and natural" selections. The animal is subordinate to nature and to man.[30]

Justice Lamer continued by saying that it will often be in the interests of "man" to kill, mutilate, subjugate, and tame animals "with all the painful consequences this may entail for them" and that man may kill animals if they are "too old, or too numerous, or abandoned."[31] He continued:

> This is why, in setting standards for the behaviour of men towards animals, we have taken into account our privileged position in nature and have been obliged to take into account at the outset the purpose sought. We have, moreover, wished to subject all behaviour, which would already be legalized by its purpose, to the test of the "means employed." Thus, para. (a) of s-s. (1) of s. 402[32] is not only of general application, but normalizes human behaviour from these two points of view: the purpose and the means. *While ss. 400 and 401*

---

29  Elaine L Hughes & Christiane Meyer, "Animal Welfare Law in Canada and Europe" (2000) 6 Animal L 23 at 25–26 [Hughes & Meyer].

30  *R v Ménard* (1978), 43 CCC (2d) 458 at 464 (QCA) [*Ménard*].

31  *Ibid.*

32  Section 387 was re-enacted in 1970 as s 402: RSC 1970, c C-34. It is now s 445.1(1)(a).

*of the* Criminal Code *have been enacted to condemn interference with the rights of owners of certain animals, s. 402 was enacted for the protection of animals themselves, including those, who through the interests of their owners, are protected in part by ss. 400 and 401.*[33]

He then poignantly circumscribed the effect of the new animal protection law he had just identified:

> Thus men, by the rule of s. 402(1)(a), do not renounce the right given to them by their position as supreme creatures to put animals at their service to satisfy their needs, but impose on themselves a rule of civilization by which they renounce, condemn and repress all infliction of pain, suffering or injury on animals which, while taking place in the pursuit of a legitimate purpose, is not justified by the choice of means employed. "Without necessity" does not mean that man, when a thing is susceptible of causing pain to an animal, must abstain unless it be necessary, but means that man in the pursuit of his purposes as the superior being, in the pursuit of his well-being, is obliged not to inflict on animals pain, suffering or injury which is not *inevitable* taking into account the purpose sought and the circumstances of the particular case. In effect, even if it is not necessary for man to eat meat and if he could abstain from doing so, as many in fact do, it is the privilege of man to eat it.[34]

Beyond the court's general observations noted above, it also established a principle that is sometimes overlooked in later cases, that beyond a *de minimus* argument, the amount of pain and suffering which is caused to an animal is not relevant in terms of establishing the offence:

> Certainly, the legislator did not intend, as in cases of assault among human beings, to forbid through criminalization the causing to an animal of the least physical discomfort and it is to this extent, but no more, that one may speak of quantification. With the exception of these cases, however, the amount of pain is of no importance in *itself* from the moment it is inflicted wilfully, within the meaning of s. 386(1) of the *Criminal Code*, if it was done without necessity according to s. 402(1)(a) and without legal justification, legal excuse or colour of right within the meaning of s. 386(2).[35]

---

33    *Ménard*, above note 30 at 464–65 [emphasis added].
34    *Ibid* at 465 [emphasis in original].
35    *Ibid* at 463 [emphasis in original].

Section 402 became section 446 in 1985.[36] The only amendment of any significance since 1953–54, and the most recent, was in 2008.[37] At that time, the cruelty offences themselves did not change, but they were divided into categories, set out now in sections 445.1, 446, and 447. All were changed from summary conviction to hybrid offences, and the penalties were increased.[38] Further, a provision that allowed the court to prohibit a person convicted of cruelty from owing or having custody or control of an animal for up to two years was significantly expanded, allowing a court to also prohibit a person from residing with an animal, and for any period the court considers appropriate, including a mandatory five-year minimum if there is a prior conviction.[39]

These most recent amendments constituted a significant change with respect to penalties, however, as discussed in Part D, below in this chapter, they were passed over widespread public objection. Increased penalties for crimes for which few were convicted in the first place were seen to have more meaning politically than legally.

In 2003, the majority of the Supreme Court cited bestiality and cruelty to animals as examples of crimes that do not rest on John Stuart Mill's "harm principle," the principle that "the only purpose for which power can be rightfully exercised over any member of a civilized community, against his will, is to prevent harm of others."[40] Rather, these crimes regarding animals rest on their offensiveness to deeply held social values. This was a comment made in *obiter*, but nevertheless, it bespeaks the lingering view that animals are not "others" protected by the criminal law, despite Lamer JA's specific observation in *Ménard* twenty-five years prior that the prohibition against causing unnecessary pain, suffering, and injury was enacted for the protection of animals themselves.[41]

---

36   Above note 1.

37   SC 2008, c 12, s 1.

38   For offences pursuant to ss 445.1 and 447, the maximum penalty is now five years imprisonment or eighteen months and/or a $10,000 fine: ss 445.1(2) and 447(2). For offences pursuant to s 446, it is two years imprisonment or six months and/or a $5,000 fine: s 446(2).

39   This wording is directed at closing a loophole whereby a person who continued to reside with animals even after being prohibited from having custody or control of them could claim that the animals belonged to somebody else in the household: s 447(1)(a).

40   JS Mill, *On Liberty and Considerations on Representative Government*, ed by RB McCallum (Oxford: Basil Blackwell, 1946) at 8.

41   The passage from *Ménard* is cited, above note 34. Here, the Supreme Court was responding to an argument that provisions of the *Narcotics Control Act* violated equality rights protected by s 15 of the *Charter*, and that criminal legislation

After these various amendments over the course of more than a century, anti-cruelty laws remain in a part of the Code addressed to property crimes, now Part XI, *Wilful and Forbidden Acts in Respect of Certain Property*.[42] While the language of the provisions from the outset ("in the enjoyment of their natural liberty," "escaped from captivity," "torture") to present times ("pain, suffering and injury," "distress") admits itself of a concern about animal sentience, and while significant post-evolutionary developments in science and philosophy have substantiated and expanded those concerns, the underlying premise of the legislation remains unchanged from its nineteenth-century inception.

## B. CURRENT PROVISIONS: OFFENCES

Cruelty to animals is addressed in four sections of the *Criminal Code*: 445.1, 446, 447, and 447.1, although the word "cruelty" is nowhere defined, and no form of the word is used any longer in the content of any of the actual provisions.[43] Immediately preceding these, under the heading "Cattle and Other Animals" are sections 444 and 445 which prohibit killing or injuring cattle and other animals kept for a lawful purpose. "Cattle" remains a defined term in section 2 which includes "an animal of the bovine species by whatever technical or familiar name it is known, including any horse, mule, ass, pig, sheep or goat" but the word "animal" itself is not defined in the Code. Generally, the offences are:

*Cattle and Other Animals:*
- wilfully killing, maiming, wounding, poisoning or injuring cattle: 444
- wilfully and without lawful excuse, killing, maiming, wounding, poisoning, or injuring dogs, birds, or animals that are not cattle and are kept for a lawful purpose: 445

*Cruelty to Animals:*
- wilfully causing, or, being the owner, wilfully permitting to be caused, unnecessary pain, suffering, or injury to an animal or bird: 445.1(1)(a)

---

could only be constitutionally justified by the harm principle: *R v Malmo-Levine; R v Caine*, 2003 SCC 74 at paras 106 and 117. Thanks to Professor Vaughan Black for bringing this to the author's attention.

42    *Criminal Code*, above note 1.

43    The only other place in the Code in which the word "cruelty" is used is in the obscenity provision in s 163(8). It also appears in the *Geneva Conventions Act*, RSC 1985, c G-3, Schedules III and IV as well as the *Divorce Act*, RSC 1985, c 3 (2d supp), s 8.

- as the owner or person having custody or control of a domestic animal or bird, or wild animal or bird in captivity, abandoning the animal or bird in distress, or wilfully neglecting to provide adequate food, water, shelter, and care: 446(1)(b)
- engaging in various specific acts including encouraging, aiding, or assisting at the fighting or baiting of animals or birds: 445.1(1)(b); wilfully administering a poisonous or injurious substance to a domestic or captive wild animal or bird: 445.1(1)(c); releasing a bird from captivity for the purpose of being shot: 445.1(1)(d); by wilful neglect, causing damage or injury to an animal or bird during transport: 446(1)(a); and keeping a cockpit: 447

The way in which these two sets of offences are separately outlined indicates two distinct emphases, between harm that is done to the *owner* of an animal when her animal property is damaged or destroyed (sections 444 and 445), and harm that is done to the animal *qua* animal (sections 445.1, 446, 447, and 447.1), consistent with Lamer JCA's observation in *Ménard* noted above. However, because of the specific language of the offences and the manner in which they have been interpreted, including in *Ménard* itself, the human interest has remained the prevalent concern even in the latter.

Historically there was a distinction between the offences related to harming cattle and harming other animals, but today the two prohibitions in sections 444 and 445 and the related penalties are identical. Both are now hybrid offences, subject to five years of imprisonment as an indictable offence and a fine of up to $10,000, and/or up to eighteen months imprisonment upon summary conviction.[44] These are now the same as penalties ascribed to the animal cruelty offences, with the exception of the neglect provisions in section 446, which attract a lesser penalty of imprisonment of up to two years for an indictable offence and a fine of up to $5,000, and/or six months imprisonment upon summary conviction.[45]

"Property" is defined in section 428 at the beginning of Part XI to mean "real or personal corporeal property," and the language of most of the offences does suggest a proprietary relationship with an animal, whether by reference to the animal as "domestic," "wild by nature that

---

44   Sections 444(2) and 445(2).
45   Sections 445.1(2), 446(2), and 447(2). It is also a summary conviction offence to contravene a prohibition order made pursuant to s 447.1(1)(a). Some courts have taken just these sentencing amendments to be sufficient indication of a significant increase in importance of crimes against animals, see Section C, below in this chapter.

is in captivity," or "kept for a lawful purpose," or by necessary implication in the offence. However, section 445.1(1)(a), the general and most frequently charged offence[46] of "causing unnecessary pain, suffering or injury to an animal or bird" is not qualified in the same manner and does not require that an animal be owned or kept or in a person's custody. Consistent with the finding in *Ménard* that this section was specifically enacted for the protection of animals themselves, it is unlimited in its application and should include wild, feral, stray, and other animals.

On their face, the provisions contain elements which appear to encumber the effective protection of animals. For example, section 447(3) requires that any cocks found on premises where a cockpit is located must be seized and taken before a justice who must order that they be destroyed. The use of the word "shall" prevents any consideration of what might be in the birds' own interest.[47]

Other ways are more general, for example, the *mens rea* required for most of the offences is the higher standard of wilfulness. This term typically connotes a subjective state of mind by which the Crown must prove that the accused intended the prohibited outcome, or knew that it was virtually certain to occur.[48] However, because these offences are in Part XI of the Code, the deeming provision in section 429(1) applies, which provides that if a person causes an event by doing or omitting to do an act that it is his duty to do, knowing that the act or omission will probably cause the event, and he is reckless whether the event occurs or not, he is deemed to have wilfully caused it.[49] Section 429(1) can therefore be seen to deem that wilfulness is satisfied with proof of recklessness, which requires a lesser degree of subjective awareness and is satisfied upon proof that the accused appreciated a substantial risk of the prohibited event happening. Thus, while the cruelty provisions face a higher standard of proof than many other offences, that standard should not be quite as high as in some other places where the term "wilful" is used.[50]

Two other deeming provisions bear consideration. Section 445.1(3) establishes a form of criminal negligence in respect of the general anti-cruelty offence in section 445.1(1)(a), deeming that evidence that a

---

46  Klineberg, above note 2 at 1-3.
47  The prohibition against cockfighting was introduced in the interests of human protection, as discussed above, and originally it required that seized cocks be turned over to the benefit of the municipality.
48  Klineberg, above note 2 at 1-4.
49  *Criminal Code*, above note 1, s 429(1).
50  Klineberg, above note 2 at 1-4.

person caused the pain, suffering, or injury by failing to exercise reasonable care or supervision, in the absence of evidence to the contrary, is proof that the pain, suffering, or injury was caused or permitted to be caused wilfully. Section 446(3) similarly deems that evidence that a person failed to exercise reasonable care or supervision of an animal or bird, thereby causing the damage or injury, in the absence of evidence to the contrary, is proof of wilful neglect pursuant to section 446(1)(b). As a result of these, proof that an accused failed to exercise reasonable care should satisfy the requirement for wilfulness in the first case, where the offence is related to the care or supervision of an animal, and it should satisfy the requirement for wilful neglect in the second case. Proof that a person fell substantially below the standard of care of a reasonable person should suffice, even if the person had no subjective knowledge or awareness of the respective risks.[51]

It has elsewhere been explained that the notion of "wilful neglect" is unique in the *Criminal Code* to the animal provisions, and it is an internally difficult concept since the notions of "wilfulness" and "neglect" designate mutually exclusive mental states: the former requires that an act be taken with subjective awareness that a specific consequence will occur as a result, while the latter connotes that a person fails to appreciate that very risk, even though a reasonable person would have. To some degree, the discrepancy is addressed in the manner in which section 446(3) equates evidence that a person failed to exercise reasonable care or supervision with wilful neglect, with the result that the offence is subject to the normal standard of criminal neglect.[52]

There remains a lack of certainty with respect to the interpretation of these provisions, although in some cases, courts do recognize that there is no need of proof that an accused intended to be cruel, or that she knew with virtual certainty that the act in question would cause the impugned result.[53] As seen in the next section, more problematic from the perspective of animal protection that these provisions purport to provide has been the word "unnecessary" and its reciprocal effect of permitting "necessary" suffering. The combination sets a high bar for establishing these offences.

---

51  *Ibid* at 1-4.
52  Klineberg also points out the distinction between negligence in the criminal and civil contexts. In the former, negligence does not result from a simple divergence from a reasonable standard of care, but must be a marked departure from that standard, more akin to gross negligence: *Ibid* at 1-5–1-6 and n 1.
53  *R v McHugh*, [1966] 1 CCC 170 (NSSCAD); *R v Clarke*, 2001 CanLII 12453 (NLPC); *R v Vieira*, 2006 BCPC 288; and *R v Blanchard*, 2007 CanLII 52982 (Ont SCJ).

In addition to the elements of the offence, specific defences set out in section 429(2) of the Code (legal justification or excuse and colour of rights) apply to property offences in Part XI of the Code, including crimes involving animals.

# C. ISSUES IN INTERPRETATION

Interpretation of these provisions is highly contextual and the analysis is fact-driven, so clear principles are difficult to delineate. However, themes emerge from the jurisprudence and three are discussed below: first, the provisions are rarely applied in the context of organized practices of animal exploitation, such as in industry where most animals are hurt; second, assumptions about the relative unimportance of crimes against animals seem to play a role in terms of both convictions and sentences; and third, animals are vulnerable to extreme violence and there is a need for effective legislation.

## 1)  Provisions Are Rarely Applied in the Industrial Context

Theoretically anti-cruelty laws are of general application and can apply in any context. Practically, this is not the case. The provincial animal welfare laws reviewed in the next chapter explicitly exempt most forms of institutionalized exploitation, accounting for many hundreds of millions of animals who are subjected to great pain and suffering in Canada; in the context of the *Criminal Code* where there is no specific exemption, a *de facto* exemption is either presumed or effectively written in, because of the manner in which the provisions are interpreted. An underlying assumption is sometimes evident that owners will act in their own best economic interests and not inflict more suffering than necessary on an animal and thereby diminish their property's value.[54]

---

54  This assumption was directly articulated by members of Parliament when proposed amendments to these provisions discussed in Section D, below in this chapter, were being debated. Ivan Grose, speaking to a representative of the Canada Mink Breeders Association said, "I would assume that pelts would not be first class if you were not handling the animals humanely," and Peter MacKay, who was objecting to the amendments on the basis that as a former prosecutor, he believed the existing provisions were sufficient if effectively exercised, expressed that: "farmers and furriers, and those who gain their livelihood from dealing with animals, have an obvious vested interest in treating their animals humanely": Proceedings of the Standing Committee on Justice and Human Rights (17 October 2001). Evidence of Ivan Grose at 1715, and Peter MacKay at 1640.

Exceptions are rare, and generally arise where the harm is not related directly to the actual practice, the animal resource is being wasted, and the suffering is gratuitous, such as when a herd of animals is starved.

The clearest example of the fact that the law does not normally apply against institutionalized uses of animals is the distinct absence of modern cases on point. Of the few criminal cases related to animals in the agricultural context, most predate the amendments to the Code in 1953–54 when specific reference to them was removed. Oft-cited among these older cases is *Ford v Wiley*,[55] in which the defendant in an appeal had been acquitted of having cruelly abused or tortured thirty-two oxen by "dishorning" them. The court below had considered evidence that "every tooth of the saw, as it tears through the structure" of the ox's horn, causes excruciating pain, and the inflammation following the procedure produces great and prolonged suffering. However, it found that there was no cruel intention and the defendant sincerely believed that the painful operation was for the animals' own benefit—to prevent them from seriously injuring each other and to render them more serviceable and valuable to their owners, thereby making them easier to handle, attracting a higher price, and allowing more cattle to be packed in yards and railway trucks.[56]

The acquittal was overturned on appeal. The court had clearly been affected by the graphic and horrific nature of the practice which it described at length, and the lingering effect on the animals which caused intense pain and "extreme torture"[57] by cutting through sensitive tissue, as was inevitable when the horns were cut close to the skin:

> There must be proportion between the object and the means. Mutilation of horses and bulls is necessary, and, if properly performed, undoubtedly lawful, because without it, in this country at least, the animals could not be kept at all. But to put thousands of cows and oxen to the hideous torments described in this evidence, in order to put a few pounds into the pockets of their owners, is an instance of such utter disproportion between means and object, as to render the practice as described here not only barbarous and inhuman, but I think clearly unlawful also.[58]

While the court was affected by the animals' suffering, it also went to some length to protect the notion of human necessity and the ability

---

55    (1889), 16 Cox CC 683.
56    *Ibid* at 684–85.
57    *Ibid* at 692.
58    *Ibid* at 693.

to inflict "even extreme pain" for various purposes.[59] It was not necessary in this case to sell beasts for forty shillings more, nor to pack away
a few more beasts than could otherwise be packed, nor to prevent an
occasional injury: "These things may be convenient or profitable to the
owners but they cannot with any show of reason be called necessary."
That without which an animal cannot attain full development or be fitted for its ordinary use, may be "necessary," but then only such pain as
is reasonably necessary to effect the result.[60]

A significant factor in the court's findings in this case was evidence
that the practice had been going out of favour in the last twenty years
in England and Wales and was no longer considered to be necessary
by other farmers.[61] This remains the essence of the interpretation of
necessity in this context: whether or not a practice that causes pain
and suffering is an offence can depend on how common it is. Although
dishorning was found to cause "excruciating torture," dehorning, as
it is now called, is a common practice in Canada and it can even be
encouraged with financial incentives in several provinces.[62] This might
be the most stark way in which anti-cruelty laws differ from other criminal offences: it would be absurd if other prohibited acts such as theft,
drunk driving, drug trafficking, and possession of child pornography
were removed from the purview of criminal law specifically because
many people commit them.

Sixty years later, in *R v Linder*,[63] the British Columbia Court of Appeal relied on *Ford v Wiley* for the proposition that the offence required
substantial pain, and that it was inflicted without good reason.[64] *Swan*

---

59   *Ibid* at 687–89.

60   *Ibid* at 688–89 and 693.

61   *Ibid* at 689–90. Similarly, in *Murphy v Manning* (1877), LR 2 Ex D 307, a cruelty
     charge was based on the cutting of combs on cocks, which was established as
     acutely painful by veterinary evidence that there was no portion of the comb
     without a nerve that communicated with the spinal cord. The defendant's
     acquittal was overturned on appeal, the court finding that the object of cutting
     the comb was to enable the bird to be used in fighting, which was unlawful, and
     therefore unnecessary. As in *Ford v Wiley*, the court here confirmed that acts
     may be done to animals causing them extreme pain if the cruelty is inflicted for
     some lawful purpose, such as in cutting horses. In *Lewis*, above note 12, a vet-
     erinarian was acquitted of causing cruelty in spaying sows. There was no doubt
     that he did inflict pain, and maybe torture, on the animals. However, it was the
     custom in his district to spay sows who are not kept for breeding purposes in
     order to increase their bulk and value. It was thereby beneficial to the owners of
     the animals and so to humankind.

62   See discussion in Chapter 5.

63   (1950), 10 CR 44 (BCCA).

64   Citing *Ford v Wiley*, above note 53 at 689 and 695.

v *Saunders*[65] had similarly required "unnecessary ill-usage" by which the animal "substantially suffers." In *Linder*, the issue was the normal use of a "flank strap" or "bucking strap," which was cinched around the belly of a "bucking horse" in a rodeo such that it pulled tight when the horse left the chute. The cinch was found to "at least excite and irritate the horse to cause more strenuous bucking," but not to cause substantial unnecessary pain or injury.

In a rare decision dating from 1957, the manner in which pigs were slaughtered for food was directly in issue. Pacific Meat Company in British Columbia was charged under section 446(1) (now 445.1(1)) for causing pain to the hogs that were shackled by a hind leg and swung against a metal wall with some force, then had a knife thrust into their throats, whether conscious or not. The question was not whether this caused pain, which was admitted, but whether the pain was necessary. Dismissing the charge, the court noted that hogs fulfill a purpose of providing food for human beings. Before they can be eaten, they must necessarily be killed, so the injury administered by the "sticker" to each hog is a necessity and therefore not unnecessary.[66]

The charge in *Pacific Meat Company* was unusual. Since that time, criminal law has not generally been invoked in the context of the actual practices by which animals are used and much deference is given to those in industry to know best how to handle their animal property. The interpretation of "unnecessary" in *Ford v Wiley*, largely adopted in *Ménard*, effectively excludes most such practices from judicial scrutiny. There were convictions in both of those cases, but the courts' language was carefully qualified.

In *Ménard*, the operator of an animal shelter was convicted under section 402(1)(a) (now 445.1(1)(a)) for killing animals by way of forced ingestion of carbon monoxide gas from an automobile engine connected to a small chamber. Animals were conscious for at least thirty seconds and in that time, they experienced pain, suffering, and burns from the intense heat. The court limited its findings with the lengthy general observations set out in Part A above, and also by expressing that "[o]ne cannot devote to the euthanasia of animals large sums of money without taking into account social priorities." In this case, relatively simple modifications could have been done to eliminate this suffering without much cost, but the accused had refused to adopt them even after being notified of the possibility of prosecution.[67]

---

65    (1881), 14 Cox CC 566 at 570.

66    R v *Pacific Meat Company* (1957), 27 CR 128 (BC Co Ct).

67    *Ménard*, above note 30 at 466–67.

That one need not devote large sums of money to killing unwanted animals might have been the guiding principle in a 1999 incident in New Brunswick. The matter involved a farmer who had turned to emus when his cattle operation was not successful. When emu farming failed, he tried to kill his 200 birds. Unable to shoot them, he sought the help of a local archery club, who were only able to kill a few birds, so he got further help to club the remaining birds and cut their throats. Police reportedly decided not to charge him because there was no indication of mistreatment pursuant to the *Criminal Code*. He had disposed of the animals in a way he felt was most appropriate and as far as the police officer was concerned, the animals did not suffer.[68]

In the industrial context, criminal law only seems to be invoked in cases where there is gratuitous suffering, often on the part of a large number of animals that have been starved, dehydrated, or otherwise severely neglected, and often after the humane society has attempted to intervene. An example is *R v Prince*,[69] in which a father and son were found guilty of failing to provide adequate or sufficient water, food, and care to cows, pursuant to section 446(1)(c) (now section 446(1)(b)). The father was charged in respect of one animal, and the son in respect of approximately fifty-two. The court did not describe the cows' condition but did express that it was a "frightening" and "dreadful, deplorable situation." The Ontario Society for the Prevention of Cruelty to Animals had made repeated attempts to require the men to attend to the animals and they had refused. The father's sentence was a $500 fine and twelve months probation, while the son's was five months imprisonment.[70]

## 2) Underlying Assumptions That These Are Not Serious Crimes

The second theme in the interpretation of these provisions is the operation of underlying assumptions on the part of courts and others in the justice system that hurting an animal is not a serious crime, or is not really a crime at all. There is sometimes an apparent reluctance to attach a criminal stigma by way of charges or conviction, as well as in

---

68  Gloria Galloway, "Emu Farmer Uses Club to Cull Flock After Rifle and Arrows Fail: Hard Times for N.B. Man" *National Post* (30 April 1999).

69  Transcript of Reasons for Sentence (1 November 1995) (Ont Ct Prov Div), Montgomery J, in author's file, provided by Ontario Society for the Prevention of Cruelty to Animals.

70  Similarly, see *R v Bakic*, 2004 SKPC 134 and *R v Elliott*, 2009 NSPC 5, involving approximately 100 animals and 138 animals respectively.

the sentence imposed, when the victim of the crime is an animal.[71] In a lowest common denominator approach, some courts reject criminalizing one practice by comparison to another, of which the legal merits are not in issue.

In *R v Borges*, the organizer of a Portuguese bullfight on his farm near Guelph, Ontario, was charged with having violated section 446(1)(d) of the Code (now section 445.1(b)) which prohibited, in any manner, encouraging, aiding or assisting in the fighting or baiting of animals or birds.[72] Portuguese bullfights are distinguished from Spanish bullfights in that the bull is not killed in the ring. However, the essence of the event is similarly to torment, enrage, and dominate the bull.[73]

Justice Smith began by noting that all decent people abhor cruelty to animals, which he described as "dumb creatures," noting that it is "one of our societal values that we attempt to control each other's conduct so as to prevent unnecessary cruelty and suffering to animals."[74] However, before noting Hemingway's attraction to bullfights, he observed

---

71   This observation is not premised on an assumption that more convictions or longer custodial sentences would "fix" the offenders or make them more kind to animals, which is a broader subject of debate within the realm of criminal law. It is directed more basically at the general expectation that criminal law is an important way in which a democratic society expresses and tries to protect its values.

72   *R v Borges*, transcribed reasons for judgment of Smith J (Ont Ct Prov Div) (5 February 1991), in the author's personal file, provided by the Ontario Society for the Prevention of Cruelty to Animals.

73   The videotaped evidence before the court in this case was not described at the first level, and not viewed by the court on appeal. However, in a normal Portuguese bullfight, the bull enters the arena and is chased by *cavaleiros* on horseback. The men display their horsemanship as they provoke and enrage the bull and stab several *bandarilhas* (small javelins) directly onto his back or onto a Velcro pad on his back. In the second phase, the *bandarilheiro* enters and waves a brightly coloured cape, displaying his skill as he avoids the enraged bull rushing toward him. In the third phase, a group of eight *forcados* further exhaust the bull by chasing, grabbing, and taunting him. They attack and eventually wrestle the bull to the ground. Bulls often stumble and drop to their knees from exhaustion. Former bullfighters have described practices to which the bull might be subjected prior to the event in order to drive him into a rage and deplete and weaken him to minimize the risk to the performers; these include debilitating the bull with tranquilizers and laxatives, beating the bull in the vicinity of his kidneys, rubbing petroleum jelly in his eyes to blur his vision, hanging heavy weights around his neck for days or weeks before the event, and confining him in darkness for hours before being released into the bright, noisy arena. After the event, the bull is kept to be entered in other events or is slaughtered out of the audience's view.

74   *R v Borges*, above note 72 at 125–26.

that "the criminal law is a very strong remedy and is not to be used in a general attempt, well meaning as it may be, to improve the outlook of people on the notion of how they treat animals" and later "I don't think that prosecution under the criminal law should be used to expand the societal value of being kind to animals."[75] Although he found that the bull was being antagonized, he dismissed the charge concluding, "I do not think that what happened was baiting; I do not think that what happened was necessarily cruel, although I find it personally distasteful."[76]

In expressing his own sentiments about whether or not the criminal law should improve the treatment of animals, Smith J disregarded the fact that that is what the law purported to do. In inserting a requirement to prove "cruelty," a term that did not appear in the anti-baiting section, he independently added a legal element to the offence. On appeal, Higgins J upheld the finding, accepting that even though the word "cruelty" did not appear in the provision prohibiting fighting or baiting, it had to be a form of cruelty since it was found in the "cruelty to animals" section of the Code.[77]

Justice Higgins added another element to the offence, requiring the prosecution to prove that some intentional act "generally deemed to be socially harmful or dangerous" had occurred. He was most concerned by the role of cultural differences, noting that bullfighting could not possibly be considered criminal in Spain, Portugal, and much of Latin America. As Canada was trying to be multicultural, it would not be right to require all new Canadians to throw off those parts of their former cultures which were considered by them to be sport. In this sense, he seemed to be responding to the nineteenth-century concerns of these provisions, regarding the human harms that were thought to be caused by events of this nature.

Justice Higgins further found that the trial judge was correct to have considered that animals were also subjected to stresses in rodeos and the Calgary Stampede. He wondered what difference there is between bullfighting and professional wrestling or boxing, where it is legal to batter one's opponent into insensibility, and he dismissed the appeal: "Simply because certain amusements or recreations do not suit the fancy for some of our country-men, or even to be called inhumane

---

75  *Ibid* at 126–27.
76  *Ibid* at 128 and 130.
77  *R v Borges*, transcribed reasons for judgment of Higgins J (Ont Ct Gen Div), Guelph, 1991, undated, author's personal file, provided by the Ontario Society for the Prevention of Cruelty to Animals.

by others, are we to be driven over the dividing lines to style all or even some, of such as crimes?"[78]

In R v Pedersen,[79] a man broke into a pen in which his neighbour kept thirty-one geese, ducks, and chickens as pets and he and a friend strangled, decapitated and killed all of them. He was charged with mischief, but not with any offence relating to animal cruelty. The court noted that it might be unusual that the person who kept the birds bestowed such affection on what many consider to be barnyard animals, "but to that one might respond that affection between owner and a pet is an important relationship for both, and not something to be criticized or minimized by others."[80] Still, having killed thirty-one of those animal companions, Pedersen received a one-year conditional sentence for the break and enter and mischief charge, and a custodial sentence of one day for having stolen a sign from the property.

In R v Paul,[81] the accused pled guilty to wilfully causing pain and suffering to a cat. He was asked to kill the cat, who belonged to a member of his family, and was starving. He stabbed the cat five times and then crushed the cat's skull with his boot. The court cited lengthy passages from Ménard and pointed out the necessity of animals to suffer and die as an unfortunate fact of modern society. The Crown had suggested there were more humane ways of killing the cat, but had not told the court what they were. There was no discussion as to why the animal was starving in the first place and could not have been fed. The court considered a list of factors regarding sentence, including that the accused was not subjectively cruel as he was trying to end the cat's misery, and the suffering was of relatively short duration.[82] Further, the court noted that this was only the second cruelty to animals case which he had encountered over six-and-a-half years, so general deterrence was not as important as it is in respect of other offences. Paul was sentenced to one day and was prohibited from owning animals for two years.

---

78   Differences Higgins J did not consider include the consent of both people involved in a boxing or wrestling match, and the explicit prohibition against "in any manner" encouraging, aiding, or assisting in the fighting or baiting of animals set out in the Code and unique to fights involving animals. In an older case, the term "baiting" had been found to include "harassing by the help of others," but there is no indication either court considered this: Pitts v Millar (1874), LR 9 QB 380 at 382.

79   2005 BCPC 160.

80   Ibid at para 22.

81   [1997] BCJ No 808 (Prov Ct).

82   In Ménard the court indicated that the length of time the animal suffers ought not to matter in terms of whether or not the offence had been made out; here the court did consider the length of time as a factor relevant to sentencing.

In *R v Piasentin*,[83] the offender discovered that his puppy had urinated in the basement and on his bed; he struck the puppy repeatedly to the point of unconsciousness, injuring the dog's lung, brain, and liver. The dog had to be euthanized the next day. Following a guilty plea and demonstration of genuine remorse, the court imposed a five-month conditional sentence.

The lack of legal significance of such cases is also apparent in the fact that many of them are not formally reported; references for the summaries below, as well as some of the cases mentioned above, include transcripts, reports given by humane societies, and newspaper accounts. These should be considered with a proverbial grain of salt in that in many of them there is no indication of the specific provision under which the accused was charged, nor to the totality of the issues before the court. Even bearing those limitations in mind, there are enough examples of such cases that they do seem, at least on their face, to suggest a pattern. For example:

- When an Ontario dog owner pushed his dog to the ground with such force that he broke the dog's leg and a veterinarian indicated that the force needed to cause the injury was consistent with being hit by a car, the court dismissed the charge under section 446(1)(a) of the Code (now 445.1(1)(a)) because the accused had not wilfully intended to break the dog's leg and cause the pain and suffering.[84]
- When the owners of a small zoo walked away from the animals because they were not making enough money (effectively leaving the animals to starve), the court reportedly dismissed the charge against them because they had not wilfully intended to starve the animals.[85]
- In 2010, a British Columbia couple was fined $700 each for animal cruelty after 200 animals, including horses, reptiles, llamas, exotic birds, goats, dogs, wolf-dog hybrids, cats, a boar, a lynx, and a coatimundi were found on their property in crowded, filthy conditions. The coatimundi had been living in a dog crate and had chewed his/her own paws.[86]
- In 2010, the owner of a badly neglected and starved golden retriever pled guilty to what the court reportedly called a "horrendous offence"

---

83  2008 ABPC 164.

84  Proceedings of the Standing Committee on Justice and Human Rights (5 February 2008). Evidence of Hugh Coghill, Chief Inspector, Ontario Society for the Prevention of Cruelty to Animals, speaking also on behalf of the Canadian Federation of Humane Societies [Coghill].

85  *Ibid.*

86  Wendy Stueck, "Dawson Creek Couple Receives $700 Fine for Animal Cruelty" *Globe and Mail* (18 January 2010).

of animal cruelty. The dog was emaciated, suffering from pressure sores, wearing an undersized chain choke collar, and in imminent risk of death when he was found. The sentence was a $2,000 fine and a prohibition from owning animals for ten years.[87]

- In 2009, an Alberta woman pled guilty to five animal cruelty charges after she threw five puppies in a roadside outhouse. It took rescue workers two hours to retrieve them. She was fined $500 for each puppy.[88]

- In 2007, four Alberta teens were accused of breaking into a former friend's home while the family was away, causing damage in the home, and cooking the family cat alive in the microwave. All four were sentenced to probation, a small fine, and community service after pleading guilty to a related charge of break and enter to cause mischief. Animal cruelty charges were dropped.[89]

- In 2004, a Quebec man who admitted to repeatedly running over a bear cub with his jet ski, then tying the bear's leg and holding the bear's head under water was fined for possession of a bear without a permit.[90]

- In 1997, two people were found guilty of wilfully neglecting their two dogs after the animals were found emaciated due to starvation. One died with his frozen body still chained to a doghouse. The other was euthanized after he was discovered in the couple's basement, barely able to lift his head. They were sentenced to three years probation and prohibited from owning or caring for animals for two years.[91]

- In 1993, a Quebec dog owner dragged his German Sheppard behind his car at speeds of up to eighty kilometres per hour as a punishment for running away. When the dog was unable to keep up with the car, he locked his legs but the owner hung on to the dog's collar and dragged him, ripping some of the soft pads off his feet and damaging others. Injuries on his thighs suggested the dog was also dragged on his side. After a guilty plea, he was sentenced to a $400 fine.[92]

---

87    "Ex Owner Fined for Starving Golden Retriever in Maple Ridge" *Maple Ridge Times* (24 August 2010).

88    *R v Hoath*, 2008 ABPC 287; see: "Owner of Puppies Tossed Down Outhouse Fined," *CBC News* (11 August 2009).

89    Steve Lillebuen, "Teens Get Probation in Camrose Cat-Microwaving Case" *Edmonton Journal* (17 November 2008).

90    Gary Dimmock, "Buddy Bear Free at Last: Orphaned Cub Starts a New Life After Ordeal in Gatineau River" *Ottawa Citizen* (8 July 2004) C1.

91    Pauline Tam, "Animal Lovers Jeer at Couple Given Probation After Starving Dogs" *Ottawa Citizen* (8 February 1997) C1 & C2.

92    Sean Upton, "Man Pleads Guilty to Dragging Dog with Car" *Ottawa Citizen* (2 July 1993); Citizen Staff, "Man Fined $400 for Dragging Dog" *Ottawa Citizen* (3

- In 2007, a woman in Ontario did the same thing to a dog she was looking after for the dog's owner. She dragged the dog 500 metres on a gravel road and was fined $1,000 and prohibited from owning animals for two years.[93]

By contrast, a different approach is apparent in a specific group of cases involving the shooting of trespassing dogs, which is the context in which statutory defences most often arise. The defence of colour of right and justification are invoked most frequently, though not exclusively, when a person is charged pursuant to section 445 for having killed a dog kept for a lawful purpose. Courts have said that the mere fact of trespassing is not generally a sufficient reason to kill a dog, and while a person has a right to remove an unwanted animal, she should use reasonable care or as little force as necessary.[94]

## 3) Animals are Extremely Vulnerable

The importance of effective legislation is apparent from a review of the many examples of horrific violence to vulnerable companion animals

---

July 1993).

93  Canadian Press, "$1,000 Fine for Dragging Dog" *The Province* (27 May 1997).

94  Colour of right was invoked successfully when a man shot two dogs he thought were chasing rabbits on his property in *R v Comber* (1975), 28 CCC (2d) 444 (Ont Co Ct); but it was rejected when a man shot and maimed a dog on his property who had previously killed some of his chickens: *R v Murphy*, 2010 NSPC 4. A justification defence was rejected in a number of other cases, such as where the accused shot and killed a dog on his property which was allegedly chasing and worrying his cattle, but he did not prove a reasonable apprehension that the dog was about to injure the cattle and that they could not be otherwise protected; the mere fact of trespassing was not an excuse to kill the dog: *R v Stewart*, [1937] 1 WWR 400 (Sask Pol Ct); where a man shot a dog who had left the scene after earlier worrying his sheep: *R v Etherington*, [1963] 2 CCC 230 (Ont Mag Ct); where a rancher chased two dogs off his property and then shot them, believing they were strays and wanting to protect his cattle: *R v Camber*, [1976] 5 WWR 479 (Sask Dist Ct); where the defendant strangled his neighbour's dog the day after the dog had knocked over his son; while an individual has the right to shoot a lawfully owned dog in the face of an attack on himself or his property, once the attack has stopped and there is no reasonable possibility it will resume, the right to kill no longer exists. The killing must be the only practicable way to prevent this attack, and must be done in such a manner as to spare the dog unnecessary suffering: *R v Greeley*, [2001] NJ No 207 (Prov Ct); where the defendant cattle-owner shot a dog on his property but the dog was not posing a threat to the cattle at the time, shooting was well beyond what a reasonable person would have done: *R v Klijn*, [1991] OJ No 3415 (Prov Div). Sections 444 and 445 only apply to animals kept for a lawful purpose so they would not necessarily protect a stray animal; see below note 103.

in the jurisprudence. Many cases are triggered after incidents that, however frustrating, can be expected to arise when one lives with an animal, whether the animal barks too much, escapes from the yard, urinates or defecates, or otherwise makes a mess inside. Patterns are apparent involving offenders with anger problems who find, in a nearby animal, a place to release that anger; quite a few cases involve an offender who was using drugs or alcohol. In the latter cases, courts sometimes do impose heavier sentences. Peppered within the jurisprudence are comments from some courts reflecting a strong condemnatory view of violence against animals, even for the animal's own sake.

In *R v Zeller*,[95] a person with a previous criminal record beat his pet dog to death with a shovel during an argument with his spouse. He struck the puppy on his head. The puppy went down and while his legs were shaking, the accused continued to strike his head until he was dead. He was charged with several offences, including wilfully causing unnecessary pain and suffering to an animal. He expressed remorse, which the court found was not genuine, and finding that the law does not permit the cruel and despicable death to which the puppy was subjected, sentenced him to sixty days in jail and two years probation.

In *R v Jones*,[96] a group of young people choked a dog, threw the dog across the room three times, saying "how far can a dog fly?" The dog yelped in pain upon landing and tried to hide. The dog was pulled out by the chest, dragged by the throat, and "smashed the dog around" for at least fifteen to twenty minutes. The dog was thrown over one of the youth's shoulders at least three times and was finally choked by his own leash. The accused had no prior record, he was convicted and sentenced to forty-five days with twelve months probation.

In *R v Canaday*,[97] a person attacked a cat with a broom over a prolonged period in December 2006, causing extreme pain and leaving blood, cat fur, and feces throughout the house. The cat was subsequently euthanized. The accused pled guilty and received a thirty-day sentence and six months probation.

In a case that received much notoriety in Toronto in 2001, a man ironically named Power captured a cat, set up a video camera and with two other men tortured her for six minutes. By the end, the cat had been hung from a noose, beaten, stabbed, and thrown against the wall. Her ear had been removed with pliers, her eye had been removed with dental tools and she had been disembowelled. Near the end, while the

---

95   1998 ABPC 19.

96   [1997] OJ No 1288 (Prov Div).

97   Cited in *R v Connors*, 2011 BCPC 24 at para 28.

cat still lived, Power could be seen spreading her cut skin and inhaling deeply.[98]

He was charged with wilfully causing unnecessary pain, suffering, and injury to an animal pursuant to section 446(1)(a) (now 445.1(1)(a)) and mischief. He pled guilty and at his sentencing hearing, through his lawyer, he said that he was an art student exploring the theme of cruelty to animals. He had previously filmed himself decapitate a chicken for a school project and received a good grade. He was trying to make people think about why it was acceptable to kill some animals but not others. He had not intended for the cat to suffer but the blade was not sharp enough. He requested an intermittent sentence so that he could continue to pursue these artistic studies with summer courses he would miss if incarcerated.

In reading his sentence aloud in a crowded courtroom, Ormston J indicated that the case was very high on the continuum of the worst offence, although there were worse ways this cat could have died, and that had the men intended to torture her, it would have gone on longer. The court accepted Power's explanation, finding that this was a "misguided venture conceived in furtherance of his artistic desire to challenge the conventions of a meat eating society." Further, it accepted that Power had not meant the cat to suffer; he intended to kill "it" quickly but was incompetent.[99] Power had no prior record and came from a good family. He was sentenced to ninety days intermittent as requested and a consecutive conditional eighteen month sentence for the animal cruelty offence. For mischief, he was sentenced to three years probation.[100]

The Crown appealed the sentence, seeking to require Power to serve an additional ten months in custody on the basis that the animal cruelty offence and the mischief offence attracted consecutive sentences and that both warranted incarceration. The Court of Appeal dismissed the appeal, finding that although the mischief charge had been made out, it added little to the wrong for which Power had to be pun-

---

98  Christie Blatchford, "Torture for Torture's Sake" *National Post* (14 June 2003) A1.

99  *R v Power* (2003), 176 CCC (3d) 209 at para 6 (Ont CA) [*Power*].

100  Witness account and records of the sentencing hearing, including the airing of the videotape; author's files. For further discussion of the case, see Lesli Bisgould, "Power and Irony: One Tortured Cat and Many Twisted Angles to Our Moral Schizophrenia Concerning Animals" in Jodey Castricano, ed, *Animal Subjects: An Ethical Reader in a Posthuman World* (Waterloo: Wilfred Laurier University Press, 2008) at 259.

ished, whichafter all, was the cruelty to the cat, not the interference with someone's property rights in her.[101]

  This was an ironic end to a case that raised a host of issues. The man's explanation for his actions was not consistent with the video-taped evidence, and since it was given by his lawyer, it was not subject to cross-examination.[102] It is controversial to assert that three grown men were incompetent to kill a cat when they were competent in the various mutilations described. The killing of the cat was not a legal issue in this case, only the suffering she endured first, however the events raise questions regarding inherent limitations in laws designed to protect animals who have no *prima facie* right to their own lives.[103] The Court of Appeal observed that the real wrong in this case was not to the person who might have owned this cat but to the animal her-self, lending importance to the anti-cruelty provisions. And yet, the effect was a lesser sentence than had the mischief also been penalized. On that point, the Court of Appeal might have been trying to make a point to Parliament concerning the penalty for animal cruelty. Justice Doherty noted that the trial judge had to bear in mind that six months was the maximum penalty for the animal cruelty offence at the time, adding that "[i]t may well be that the present maximum is wholly inad-equate. That is, however, a matter for Parliament."[104]

---

101  *Power*, above note 99 at paras 15 & 16.

102  The men could be heard on the videotape making comments that did not indi-cate an interest in ending the process, such as "that's good stuff, man"; author's file, above note 100. *Quaere* whether the trial judge would have responded differently had Power been purporting to artistically explore other themes like domestic violence or elder abuse in the same manner.

103  The chief inspector of the Ontario Society for the Prevention of Cruelty to Ani-mals told of a case in which a man shot and killed a stray dog for no apparent reason. Consistent with Ormston J's analysis, the man was not prosecuted be-cause no owner could be found to prove that the dog was kept for a lawful pur-pose, which would have triggered what is now s 445; in terms of anti-cruelty provisions there was, and is, no general prohibition against killing an animal: Coghill, above note 84. An unusual exception is R v *Brown* (1984), 11 CCC (3d) 191 (BCCA), where a man was convicted of killing a wandering cow pursuant to what was then s 400 of the Code (now s 444), which was not an anti-cruelty provision. He admitted he had killed and cow and butchered her for meat. The Crown could not prove the animal was anyone's property, she seemed to be a stray, and the defence argued that the reference to "cattle" did not apply to un-owned, wild cattle. The Court of Appeal of British Columbia rejected the appeal, finding that the plain meaning of the provision was that it applied to all cattle, whether wild or domestic, whether ownership is proved or not.

104  R v *Power*, above note 99 at para 16.

Maximum penalties were increased several years later in 2008. Even though none of the substantive changes to the offences that had also been sought was implemented, some post-2008 decisions indicate that some courts are ready to seize the sentencing amendments alone as recognition that things have changed significantly and animal crimes merit greater regard than they have previously received.

In *R v Munroe*,[105] the court began by noting that in increasing sentences, Parliament had given effect to widespread concerns that animal cruelty provisions in the Code had fallen drastically out of step with current social values, and the changes represented a fundamental shift in Parliament's approach to these crimes, even referring to them as a "dramatic change to the legislative landscape for those offences."[106] The court noted that such a dramatic change, whereby the overall maximum penalty had increased ten-fold, is virtually unheard of in criminal law.[107]

Munroe had subjected two dogs to what the court described as torture, using heat, electricity, and blunt force, causing hemorrhaging, a separated retina, a collapsed lung, and fourteen rib fractures to one of the dogs. Injuries to the other dog were not described. These injuries were caused over a prolonged period during which his girlfriend had been taking the dogs to the veterinarian to try to determine what was causing them. The court found that "[i]t is perfectly natural to puzzle over how a mature human being could possibly inflict injuries of this nature and extent on two companion animals."[108]

> No point is served in this case by comparing one type of offence to another to determine the appropriate range of sentence. I have, accordingly, resisted any comparison to what crimes of this nature committed against a human victim might call for by way of sentence. However, one point of distinction is significant. A person who abuses a child always runs the risk that the child will overcome his fear and report his suffering. The abuser of an animal has no such concern. So long as he commits his abuses beyond the reach of prying eyes, he need not fear that his victim will reveal his crimes. Tragically in this case, it was only in death that Abbey found her voice to identify the nature of her and Zoe's torment and the identity of their tormentor.[109]

---

105 2010 ONCJ 226.
106 *Ibid* at paras 1–3.
107 *Ibid* at paras 2 and 27 respectively.
108 *Ibid* at para 21.
109 *Ibid* at para 26.

Despite the lack of criminal record, and the Crown's submission that the sentence should be six to nine months, the court imposed a custodial sentence of twelve months and an order prohibiting Munroe from owning, having custody or control, or residing in the same premises as an animal or bird for twenty-five years.

*R v Connors*[110] is a 2011 decision in which a man pled guilty to causing unnecessary pain and suffering to a 3-month-old pitbull puppy over a fifteen-minute period. Witnesses heard smashing sounds and a dog crying in Connors's apartment. When the police arrived, the dog was on the bed apparently suffering from significant injuries. The police found dog feces on the walls, the floor, the bed sheets, in the bathroom, and in the kitchen, and the puppy's blood all over the apartment. The dog had died from internal bleeding and injuries caused by blunt force trauma, including ten broken ribs, a broken jaw and orbital bone, missing teeth, a lacerated liver, and lacerations to the tongue.

The court noted that previous cases had mostly ordered short periods of incarceration in cruelty cases, but that Parliament had concluded that the previous maximums were wholly inadequate and failed to represent the prevailing views in society as to the seriousness of these offences. The level of suffering caused was an important factor. The Crown had elected to proceed summarily, meaning the maximum penalty was eighteen months incarceration, and was seeking incarceration of three to four months and an order prohibiting Connors from owning or possessing animals for ten years. The court granted the latter order, and among other aspects of the sentence, found that six months incarceration was appropriate.

The horrific nature of these latter incidents is non-controversial, but when one considers them together with anti-cruelty jurisprudence as a whole, a question arises as to whether an act does have to be both that extreme and that extraordinary for the provisions to be effective.

Beyond the legislative provisions and their interpretation, logistical factors complicate their enforcement. Police can be involved, but often the laws are enforced when a complaint is made to a humane society. As the court in *Munroe* noted, the animal victim cannot tell someone what happened to her, so enforcement depends on there being a witness to the event, the witness being willing to complain, the humane society having sufficient resources to respond in a timely way and to sufficiently train its staff in the skills of gathering and preserving evidence, a willingness and preparedness on the part of the Crown to proceed, and the law requiring the court to give it serious attention. Humane

---

110  2011 BCPC 24.

societies have found existing legislation to be insufficient. They have expressed that crimes against animal property are minimized throughout the justice system, resulting in the withdrawal of charges, high acquittal rates, or weak sentences. In 2000, of more than 28,000 cruelty complaints received by humane societies in seven provinces, 167 were prosecuted pursuant to the *Criminal Code* and 63 resulted in convictions.[111] For many years, they and others have sought amendments to modernize the legislation and address some of these problems.

## D. ATTEMPTS TO AMEND ANTI-CRUELTY LAWS: A SAGA IN THIRTEEN PARTS

As one law professor has said, it is "quite significant that this central legislation has not been thoroughly reviewed since the advent of modern animal rights philosophies."[112] To some degree, it can be said that the federal government agreed. In 1998, it published a paper entitled *Crimes Against Animals* instituting a consultation process to gather public input regarding the changes that were needed.[113] The consultation paper began by describing the inconsistent approach people take to animals and a lack of social consensus with respect to their status. In particular,

> there is also a broad spectrum of attitudes and opinions in our society about how people should treat animals. Some people view animals as independent beings capable of pain and emotion and therefore worthy of consideration in every way that people are, while others view animals as little more than machines or products to use in any way that benefits humans, regardless of the process.[114] Falling somewhere between those two extremes is the great majority who generally feel that it is acceptable to use animals in some circumstances and

---

111 Canadian Federation of Humane Societies, *Legal Analysis re: Bill C-15B – Section 15, Cruelty to Animals* (revised October 2001), online: http://cfhs.ca/law/legal_analysis/ at 3–5.

112 Hughes & Meyer, above note 29 at 40–41.

113 Department of Justice Canada, *Crimes against Animals: A Consultation Paper* (Ottawa: Justice Canada,1998) ["Crimes against Animals"].

114 Even as the government sought to modernize existing laws, it revealed the enduring effects of the Cartesian and Lockian notions discussed in Chapter 1. Whether or not animals are capable of feeling pain and emotion or are little more than machines are questions with scientific answers and not properly categorized as matters of public opinion.

for some purposes, but that every reasonable effort should be made to reduce or eliminate unnecessary animal suffering and pain.[115]

The attitudes and opinions to which the government referred were predetermined and were not going to be measured or reviewed in the consultation. Any re-examination or debate concerning the Code's factual premise or its underlying philosophy was also circumscribed by the government, even as it was soliciting public opinion on the subject:

> It is therefore essential to note that the offence of cruelty to animals is not intended to forbid conduct that is socially acceptable or authorized by law. The current provisions do not restrict or otherwise interfere with normal and regulated activities involving animals, such as hunting, fishing and slaughter for food, and the same would be true of a reformed law. Criminal prohibitions are directed at conduct that falls outside of normally accepted behaviour.[116]

One change proposed in the consultation paper was that crimes against animals be separated from the other property offences in Part XI of the Code and moved to a general part covering various morals-based offences.[117] This was intended to acknowledge that sentient beings have significant differences from the inanimate objects otherwise addressed in Part XI, and to prevent some of the difficulties that had arisen in prosecuting these offences where the focus was on animals as mere chattels that owners may damage as they see fit. Putting animal crimes in another part would thus facilitate prosecution of gratuitous violence. However, it would not undermine the general principle that causing pain, suffering, and injury in pursuit of a lawful purpose was acceptable.

Moving these provisions to another part of the Code was not a new idea. In 1987, the Law Reform Commission of Canada had recommended that an entirely new part be created in the Code entitled "Crimes Against Animals." The Commission was anticipating that the acceptability of certain regulated uses of animals was changing, however, it left these to their respective legislative domains. What the criminal law could and should address was the growing sentiment was that it was no longer appropriate to treat crimes against animals as mere property offences:

---

115   *Ibid* at 3.
116   *Ibid* at 5.
117   *Ibid* at 7.

The new Code aims to avoid mingling cruelty to animals with property offences, to concentrate on general principle rather than on specific marginal activities and to provide for modern institutional practices like scientific experimentation. Recognizing, however, that animals are different from people, that killing animals for food, for hunting and for other purposes is socially accepted and that large-scale reform in this area cannot come overnight, the proposed Code rejects the notion of any parallel between animal crimes and crimes against the person. It does not, for instance, criminalize the killing of animals because any such message would be thoroughly diluted by all the exceptions to it, would appear hypocritical in theory and would work unfairly in practice. Instead it focuses on the central idea of unnecessary cruelty and aims, not so much to protect and preserve animal life, but rather to ensure its humane treatment.[118]

The first of thirteen bills to come after the 1998 consultation was introduced in the House of Commons in 1999.[119] Bill C-17 did move crimes against animals from Part XI of the Code to a revised Part V which would then include sexual offences and offences against public morals, disorderly conduct, and cruelty to animals.[120] Bill C-17 also introduced for the first time a definition of "animal" to mean a "vertebrate, other than a human being, and any other animal that has the capacity to feel pain."[121] Where it had previously been an offence to wilfully and without lawful excuse kill an animal kept for a lawful purpose, Bill C-17 made it an offence to kill an animal without lawful excuse; and it created two new offences of brutally or viciously killing an animal regardless of whether the animal dies immediately, and training an animal for the purpose of fighting other animals.[122] It also

---

118  *Report on Recodifying Criminal Law*, rev and enlarged ed of Report 30 (Montreal: Law Reform Commission of Canada, 1987). Discussing the Commission's proposals for revision of anti-cruelty laws, one legal commentator cited Lamer JCA's comments in *Ménard* concerning humankind's "position as supreme creatures" entitled to exploit animals, and expressed that "we may need to revamp our thinking about our role in the universe at least as profoundly as the commission has revamped the *Criminal Code*": Jeffrey Miller, "Animal Group Seeks Law Reform Comment" *The Lawyers' Weekly* (2 June 1989) at 3. The Law Reform Commission was disbanded and none of its recommendations was adopted.

119  Bill C-17, *An Act to Amend the Criminal Code (Cruelty to Animals, Disarming a Peace Officer and Other Amendments) and the Firearms Act (technical amendments)*, 2nd Sess, 36th Parl, 1999.

120  *Ibid*, s 1.

121  *Ibid*, ss 2, 181.1(8).

122  *Ibid*, ss 2, 182.1(1)(b), (c), and (f).

changed the offences from summary conviction to hybrid offences, increasing potential penalties.[123]

Just as the consultation paper had stated, the amendments introduced in Bill C-17 did not undermine the notion that a person could hurt or kill an animal for a human purpose. The general offence of wilfully causing unnecessary pain, suffering, or injury to an animal or bird did not change. As twelve other government and private members bills followed in subsequent years, amendments were made along the way, but the essence of these bills was very similar.[124]

The significance of the amendments proposed in Bill C-17 and its successors was seen to extend beyond their content. Of greater meaning was their acknowledgment of a change in public perception and expectation. While moving the offences out of the property part of the Code did not mean that animals were no longer property, it did reflect a view that there are times when it is not appropriate to think of them that way, and it is more important to consider that they are sentient beings who feel the harms inflicted on them. This conceptual change,

---

123  *Ibid*, ss 2, 181.1(3)–(7).

124  Bill C-15, *Criminal Law Amendment Act, 2001*, 1st Sess, 37th Parl, 2001. This was an extensive omnibus bill. On 26 September 2001, a motion was brought by the House Leader on behalf of the four opposition parties to divide the bill. All the elements of the lengthy bill except the animal cruelty and firearms provisions became C-15A and were passed into law within months. The animal cruelty and firearms provisions became Bill C-15B, *An Act to Amend the Criminal Code (Cruelty to Animals and Firearms) and the Firearms Act*, 1st Sess, 37th Parl, 2002. This bill passed in the House but died in the Senate when Parliament prorogued in June 2004. The next version was Bill C-10, *An Act to Amend the Criminal Code (Cruelty to Animals and Firearms) and the Firearms Act*, 2nd Sess, 37th Parl, 2002; after passing all three readings in the House of Commons and second reading in the Senate, the bill was sent to the Legal and Constitutional Affairs Committee for further study and in November 2002 the Senate ordered it to be split, with firearms provisions becoming C-10A and animal cruelty provisions becoming C-10B, *An Act to Amend the Criminal Code (Cruelty to Animals)*, 2nd Sess, 37th Parl, 2002. See also Bill C-22, *An Act to Amend the Criminal Code (Cruelty to Animals)*, 37th Parl, 3rd Sess, 2004; Bill S-24, *An Act to Amend the Criminal Code (Cruelty to Animals)*, 1st Sess, 38th Parl, 2005; Bill C-50, *An Act to Amend the Criminal Code in Respect of Cruelty to Animals*, 1st Sess, 38th Parl, 2005; Bill C-373, *An Act to Amend the Criminal Code (Cruelty to Animals)*, 2d Sess, 39th Parl, 2006; Bill S-213, *An Act to Amend the Criminal Code (Cruelty to Animals)*, 1st Sess, 39th Parl, 2007; Bill S-203, *An Act to Amend the Criminal Code (Cruelty to Animals)*, 2nd Sess, 39th Parl, 2008; Bill C-558, *An Act to Amend the Criminal Code (Cruelty to Animals)*, 2nd Sess, 39th Parl, 2008; Bill C-229, *An Act to Amend the Criminal Code (Cruelty to Animals)*, 2nd Sess, 40th Parl, 2008. For a summary of the chronology, see "Timeline: How a Bill Became a 10-year Political Football," online: http://markholland.liberal.ca/files/Timeline_How-a-bill-became-a-10-year-policital-football.

together with the elevation of the offences to hybrids with higher penalties, and the changes to the offences themselves, however limited, might have been interpreted as an acknowledgment that society wished animal interests to be recognized more seriously. For these reasons, the legislation had both extensive support from the public who wanted that recognition and opposition from organizations and industries who saw it as a threat to their practices.

Bill C-17 died on the Order Paper when Parliament dissolved. Its first reincarnation in early 2001 was C-15, then C-15B.[125] By that time, it was generating extensive public attention. Members of Parliament and their staff expressed that they had never received as much support for a legislative proposal, including the general public, the police, veterinary associations, humane societies, and a wide range of animal advocacy organizations from across the country.[126] When the bill was studied by the Standing Committee on Justice and Human Rights it was the subject of numerous deputations.

The limited nature of the amendments and the fact that they had neither the intent nor the effect of undermining traditional uses of animals was not only specifically articulated by the government but also by the Canadian Federation of Humane Societies, an umbrella organization for humane societies across the country that had actively lobbied for the amendments. It expressly indicated the organization's support for the use of animals for human purposes, including for food and research, and in hunting and trapping. Its representative at the Committee testified to personally eating a steak every Saturday night, wearing a leather belt and shoes, and to have personally approved a military research protocol in which the skin of live pigs was burned with a blowtorch.[127] Other organizations that supported the bill similarly acknowledged its limits.

---

125 *Ibid.*

126 John Sorenson, "'Some Strange Things Happening in Our Country': Opposing Proposed Changes in Anti-Cruelty Laws in Canada" (2003) 12:3 Soc & Leg Stud 377 at 378. That support persisted; see, for example, a national survey commissioned by the International Fund for Animal Welfare and the Canadian Federation of Humane Societies that determined that support was high: "85 Percent of Canadians Want Real Protection for Animals" (2006), online: http://cfhs.ca/features/cfhs_releases_poll_data_that_shows_canadians_want_effective_animal_cruelty_laws/. The support of police and some others was in part based on evidence linking human violence with violence against animals; see discussion in Chapter 1.

127 Proceedings of the Standing Committee on Justice and Human Rights (17 October 2001). Evidence of Bob Gardiner, Co-Chair, Status of Animals Committee, Canadian Federation of Humane Societies, at 1645 and 1700.

Yet the amendments were vociferously opposed, largely by corporate interest groups involved in animal exploitation. The submissions of industry representatives were similar in that they expressed their opposition to animal cruelty and abusive practices, and they supported increased penalties. However, they opposed the substantive amendments claiming, among other things, that the bill would threaten their industries and that it was an assault by "animal rights extremists" on the fundamental structures of Canadian society, which concealed a hidden agenda that would humanize animals.[128]

Ranchers and agriculture industry lobby groups were among those who protested that any increased protection of animals would subject them to what they called "nuisance prosecutions." They sought blanket exemptions for the activities undertaken in the course of their industries.[129] The Canadian Federation of Agriculture expressed that law had successfully protected animals, in particular farm animals, for the past fifty years. It was concerned that by moving the offences out of the property section, government was "raising the status of animals in society" and "as farmers [they were] concerned about [that]."[130] The Canadian Cattlemen's Association, Chicken Farmers of Canada, and the Alberta Farm Care Association opposed the amendments. The Agricultural Institute of Canada called Bill C-15B a "serious threat to responsible animal users" and claimed that moving animals from the property part of the Code would mean the loss of all legal justification for the use of animals and expose users to the "risk of nuisance prosecution"; and that the bill "threatens all people who work with animals."[131]

The Ontario Federation of Anglers and Hunters organized a letter-writing campaign and otherwise opposed the bill. The Horse Council of British Columbia warned that "extreme animal rights activists"

---

128  See, generally, Sorenson, above note 126.

129  *Ibid* at 381. In describing the efforts to amend the legislation from the perspective of the livestock industry, one legal observer wrote that throughout the years of debate, the animal cruelty bill has been generally supported by most of the Canadian public and members of Parliament, and that opposition has stemmed from animal-use industries. She described the livestock industry as one of most adversarial sectors, aggressively opposing the bill on the grounds that it would be damaging to industry practices: Christina G Skibinsky, "Changes in Store for the Livestock Industry? Canada's Recurring Proposed Animal Cruelty Amendments" (2005) 68 Sask L Rev 173.

130  Proceedings of the Standing Committee on Justice and Human Rights (17 October 2001). Evidence of Jack Wilkinson, Board Member, Canadian Federation of Agriculture, at 1610.

131  Sorenson, above note 126 at 384.

would use the new definition of "animal" to impose their agenda.[132] The Canada Mink Breeders Association expressed that the proposed changes would potentially put all animal producers at risk for currently lawful practices, of being wrongfully charged for legitimate activities.[133]

The executive vice-president of the Fur Council of Canada indicated that his intent was "to sound an alarm about the dangers of adopting certain clauses of Bill C-15B." By direct comparison to the anti-terrorism legislation that the Committee was also reviewing at the time, the anti-cruelty amendments "could be just as important, if not more important, for the security of Canadians in the long term."[134]

The medical research establishment also strongly argued against the amendments. The Canadian Council on Animal Care, the national body that purports to oversee the use of animals in research and describes itself as a quasi-regulatory body, said that while it could not promote or oppose the use of animals in science, it had a responsibility to bring its legal advisers' findings to the Committee. It indicated that experimentation on animals may involve killing, inflicting pain, depriving animals of some level of care, and administering injurious substances to them, and further, that conditions intrinsic to the experimentation can cause suffering, pain, injury, or deprivation. Therefore, it was concerned about the potential loss of defences, such as justification and colour of right, if the provisions were moved out of Part XI of the Code, particularly since animal research is not statutorily authorized in all provinces.[135] The Canadian Institutes of Health Research and the Natural Sciences and Engineering Research Council expressed that the amendments could give animal rights activists a powerful weapon which could force pharmaceutical and biotechnology companies out of Canada.[136]

There was some concern that the prohibition against "brutally and viciously" killing an animal was intended to target the annual seal hunt on Canada's east coast;[137] however, the provision was originally included in Bill C-17 after public outrage arose pursuant to an incident in the

---

132 *Ibid.*
133 Proceedings of the Standing Committee on Justice and Human Rights (17 October 2001). Evidence of Gary Hazlewood, Chair, Government Liaison Committee, Canada Mink Breeders Association, at 1535 and 1540.
134 Proceedings of the Standing Committee on Justice and Human Rights (16 October 2001). Evidence of Alan Herscovici, Executive Vice-President, Fur Council of Canada, at 1535.
135 Proceedings of the Standing Committee on Justice and Human Rights (16 October 2001). Evidence of Clément Gauthier, Executive Director, Canadian Council on Animal Care, at 1550.
136 Sorenson, above note 126 at 386.
137 The seal hunt is discussed in Chapter 8.

then minister of Justice's Edmonton riding in which two dogs were tied by their leashes to a tree then beaten to death with a baseball bat. The owner of the dogs was at risk of being evicted from his home because of barking complaints. Charges of wilfully causing the dogs unnecessary pain, suffering, or injury were stayed in the absence of any evidence that the dogs suffered, after a veterinarian testified that they likely died from one or two heavy blows to their skulls.[138]

Some members of Parliament echoed the industries' objections, claiming that the bill was the "slippery slope to legislation preventing the harvesting of wheat and cutting dandelions because wheat and dandelions are alive" or that it opened the door to "the worm police" making charges of cruelty to worms.[139]

Even if industrial practices cause much more extensive and widespread suffering than the random acts of violence directed at individual domestic animals, it was clear that Bill C-15B itself would not have criminalized them.[140] The legislation was only intended to curb gratuitous abuse that lacked any lawful purpose beneficial to human beings. Successful prosecutions would still have had to show that harm was caused wilfully and without necessity or lawful purpose.[141]

Nor did the bill establish any special prosecutorial rights for animal advocacy organizations—the responsibility of prosecuting charges remained with the Crown and the responsibility of adjudicating and sentencing them remained with judges and juries. There was no indication that the criminal justice system was administered pursuant to an animal rights agenda. While private prosecutions could be undertaken, there was no history of animal rights advocates, humane societies, or police inappropriately trying to use anti-cruelty provisions against industrial animal use. The Crown retained its authority to intervene in a

---

138  Gordon Kent, "Charges Stayed in Baseball Bat Killings of Two Dogs" *Edmonton Journal* (17 November 1998) B3; Jill Mahoney, "Judge Stays Charges for Men who Killed Dogs" *Globe and Mail* (18 November 1998) A3. For further discussion of the unreported case see, Frances Rodenburg, "Crimes Against Animals," *Animal Welfare in Focus* (Fall 1998), online: Canadian Federation of Humane Societies http://cfhs.ca/info/crimes_against_animals/.

139  *Bill C-15B*, online: Canadian Federation of Humane Societies http://cfhs.ca/law/bill_c_15b/; see a more detailed discussion in Sorenson, above note 126 at 384–92.

140  Sorenson, *ibid* at 381.

141  For a more detailed discussion of the legal issues raised by industry and how they were addressed, see documents online: Canadian Federation of Humane Societies http://cfhs.ca/law/history_of_the_amendments/ and cfhs.ca/law/legal_analysis. They are also discussed in numerous deputations to the Committees, including those cited above at notes 127, 130, 133, 134, & 135.

private prosecution and to direct a stay of proceedings, should any such inappropriate proceeding ever be commenced.[142]

The evidence that was before the Committee documented the inability of existing laws to sufficiently address even the random cases of gratuitous violence that industrial representatives said they opposed. Whether these organizations feared that their activities would be considered criminal after amendments to the anti-cruelty provisions, or whether it was a more generalized fear of the implications of entrenching a recognition that respect for animals had emerged as a strong societal value, the opposition was successful. Despite persistently strong public support and extensive media attention, Bills C-17, C-15B, and all but one of their successors failed to pass.

The closest any bill came to passing was Bill C-10B introduced in 2002, which was studied for months by the Senate's Legal and Constitutional Affairs Committee. It heard extensive public deputations, including from religious organizations that had become concerned about the potential impact of the amendments on ritual slaughter.[143] At one point, after many amendments, the bill had broad support in both the House and the Senate. However, an issue arose concerning the impact the provisions might have on Aboriginal persons, and this became a significant debate in 2003.

Some questions had been raised about whether the amendments, or amendments to the amendments, would newly include protection for wild animals and whether this would impact traditional Aboriginal practices.[144] The Senate sought to protect traditional Aboriginal rights to hunt, trap, and fish with a specific amendment, however the House of Commons found that the amendment was unnecessary and that it raised interpretation problems. The House of Commons preferred a single standard to apply across Canada.[145] The amendment was a controversy unto itself, for in seeking to protect Aboriginal practices, the implication was that they were in need of that protection, and otherwise criminally cruel. The bill moved back and for the between the

---

142  *Criminal Code*, above note 1, ss 579 & 579.1. An administrative stay is not subject to challenge except for abuse of process.

143  Proceedings of the Standing Senate Committee on Legal and Constitutional Affairs (5 February 2003). Evidence of Reuven Bulka on behalf of the Canadian Jewish Congress endorsed by the Islamic Council of Imams.

144  For example, *Debates of the Senate*, 37th Parl, 2nd Sess, vol 140 issue 60 (29 May 2003) from 1410; 37th Parl, 2nd Sess, vol 140 issue 82 (7 October 2003) from 1510; and 37th Parl, 2nd Sess, vol 140 issue 90 (28 October 2003) at 1630.

145  *House of Commons Debates*, 37th Parl, 2nd Sess, vol 138 no 113 (6 June 2003) at 1020.

House and the Senate several times and died on the Order Paper when Parliament prorogued in November 2003.

The bill that finally passed was S-203, a private member's bill that maintained the increased penalties of the earlier bills but none of their substantive amendments, so that the barriers to prosecution and conviction that had been identified by humane societies and others were not addressed. The provisions were not removed from Part XI of the Code. This bill, like its similar predecessor S-213, was received in the opposite manner of the other bills; it was widely opposed by the public, humane societies, veterinarians, and animal advocacy organizations on the basis that it failed to address the much needed comprehensive changes that had been embodied in previous bills, and it was supported by the Ontario Federation of Anglers and Hunters, the Canadian Professional Rodeo Association, the Atlantic Centre for Comparative Biomedical Research, the National Coalition of Animal-based Sectors, and other animal-using organizations.[146] It was fast-tracked and enacted on 17 April 2008, six months after introduction. Government members acknowledged the bill's weaknesses but wanted to address the subject once and for all. Two subsequent attempts to introduce the substantive changes did not succeed, but yet another private member's bill was introduced in June 2011.[147]

146 A petition with more than 111,000 signatures was tabled in the House of Commons in 2007 opposing the bill: "Criminal Code Amendments," online: Canadian Federation of Humane Societies http://cfhs.ca/law/history_of_the_amendments; see also Proceedings of the Standing Senate Committee on Legal and Constitutional Affairs (4 December 2006) and Proceedings of the Standing Committee on Justice and Human Rights (31 January 2008 and 5 February 2008).
147 Bill C-232, *An Act to Amend the Criminal Code (Cruelty to Animals)*, 1st Sess, 41st Parl, 2011.

# PROVINCIAL ANIMAL WELFARE LEGISLATION

The question is not Can they *reason*? Nor, Can they *talk*? but, Can they *suffer*?

— Jeremy Bentham

In much of Canada, there are agencies officially authorized to protect animals and prevent cruelty. Some provinces have limited legislation which establishes humane societies or societies for the prevention of cruelty to animals (SPCAs) and delineates their authority in respect of animals who are abandoned or in distress, and in respect of offences related to animal welfare. Others have broader legislation addressing these matters and also touching on a variety of other health, safety, and welfare issues. Some jurisdictions have hardly any such legislation, and Quebec has none whatsoever. This chapter provides an overview of those agencies and that legislation. The legislation is discussed more specifically as relevant in the chapters below.

## A. ANIMAL WELFARE AGENCIES

Animal welfare agencies such as humane societies and SPCAs (terms used interchangeably below) are among the oldest social institutions in the country. In Canada, as in Britain, they emerged in the nineteenth century to protect disempowered people and animals alike. The Toronto Humane Society was established in 1887 to protect animals and children from cruel treatment, the family domain being a matter of relatively private concern at the time.[1] For its first two decades, the main function of the Nova Scotia SPCA, incorporated in 1877, was providing marriage counselling and legal aid for estranged couples and "harassed spouses." In 1906, provincial social services assumed the care of children, however after the Halifax explosion in 1917, the SPCA assisted hundreds of injured and orphaned children, and as late as 1932 it was investigating and reporting incidents of cruelty to children.[2] Similarly, the Winnipeg Humane Society was initially the Society for the Prevention of Cruelty to Women, Children, and Animals. It retained that broad focus from 1894 until 1911.[3]

The link connecting support for vulnerable persons and animals was broken by the development of government departments or government funded social agencies for the former, while animals were left to the continued authority of the humane societies. These latter organizations, while often created by legislation and acting pursuant to statutory powers, are not government agencies. They generally receive some government funding, but they depend largely on public donations, fundraising initiatives, and volunteer contributions to pursue their work.

Humane societies occupy an awkward position in the realm of animal protection. They are expected to provide the solution to human-animal problems but their power is constrained by their limited funding and statutory authority. Moreover, the lack of societal agreement as to what the core of these problems really is inclines to inhibit their effectiveness. Throughout their lengthy histories, humane societies have struggled internally with conflicting views about what the protection of animals and the prevention of cruelty mean, and whether they should be proactive agencies focused on reforming or eradicating the sources of animal suffering, or more reactive agencies limited to "clean(ing) up after them."[4]

This has been the case even from the outset. In the 1920s, the Victoria branch of the British Columbia SPCA fought over opposition to vivisection and those who sought to abolish it were forced out.[5] The

---

1   John Kelso, *Early History of the Humane and Children's Aid Movement in Ontario* (Toronto: William Briggs, 1911); Charlotte Montgomery, *Blood Relations: Animals, Humans, and Politics* (Toronto: Between the Lines, 2000) at 45.

2   *History of the Nova Scotia SPCA*, online: www.spcans.ca/about/history.html.

3   *History of the Winnipeg Humane Society*, online: www.winnipeghumanesociety. ca/history-of-the-winnipeg-humane-society.

4   Montgomery, above note 1 at 47–54.

5   *Ibid* at 44.

tumultuous history of the Toronto Humane Society is replete with such disputes. For several years in the 1980s, it was widely respected for its efforts to directly address the use of animals in research, agriculture, fur, and other areas, however, directors who supported this work were eventually voted off the board, staff who undertook it were terminated, and the organization has focused on more traditional work related to companion animals since that time.[6]

Even that work can be controversial. Like many humane societies, the Toronto Humane Society has had to determine how to handle the constant stream of unwanted animals left in its care. It has adopted a "no-kill" policy, refusing to kill healthy animals for lack of a home, while others, including the Ontario SPCA (OSPCA), do not adhere to that principle. Long-standing conflict between the Toronto Humane Society and the OSPCA culminated in the latter laying criminal cruelty charges against staff and board members of the former in 2009 related to the condition in which the animals in its shelter were living.[7] The incident and the extensive media coverage it generated raised much public debate about which agency was most to blame for its approach; one was seen to be too willing to kill unwanted animals, while the other was not willing enough.[8] There was hardly any discussion about why so many animals are bred and then abandoned, creating the problem in the first place.

At the other end of the spectrum, a more insidious aspect of the conflicts within humane societies includes the control sometimes taken by those who would undermine efforts to curb practices that

---

6    *Ibid* at 57–70.

7    This story was covered by print, radio, and television media across the country; Kate Hammer, "Toronto Humane Society Officials Arrested, Face Animal-Cruelty Charges" *Globe and Mail* (26 November 2009). Charges were later dropped but there was protracted litigation including an application commenced by the OSPCA pursuant to the *Charities Accounting Act*, RSO 1990, c C.10 and the *Corporations Act*, RSO 1990, c C.38; it was given temporary control of the Toronto Humane Society premises and authority over the fate of the animals there, see, for example, *OSPCA v Toronto Humane Society*, 2010 ONSC 608 and 2010 ONSC 1953. These decisions contain useful discussion about the authorities of these agencies.

8    Six months after Toronto Humane Society representatives were charged with cruelty, it emerged that the OSPCA was in the process of killing 350 animals after an outbreak of ringworm, a treatable illness, in its shelter. Ninety-nine animals were reportedly killed before extensive public criticism led to new plans to treat and find homes for the rest. Daniel Dale, "OSPCA to Euthanize 350 Animals at York Region Shelter" *Toronto Star* (11 May 2010); "Analysis: Tables Have Turned in Dispute Between Animal Charities" *Toronto Star* (13 May 2010); and "What Went Wrong at the OSPCA" *Toronto Star* (16 May 2010).

harm animals. In 1998, legal proceedings were taken against the Grey-Bruce Humane Society (GBHS) in Ontario. The OSPCA, of which GBHS was an affiliate,[9] had adopted policies aimed at discouraging harmful practices, including hunting, hunting with dogs, and trapping. The president of the GBHS was a hunter who hunted with dogs and operated a dog trial compound (in which dogs are trained to run down foxes, coyotes, and other animals confined in electrified enclosures) while the vice-president was a trapper. Dog trial compounds were going to be prohibited by impending provincial wildlife legislation and the OSPCA had expressed an intention to strictly monitor grandparented compounds because of a concern about the suffering they engendered.

Two members of the GBHS commenced an application against the GBHS pursuant to the *Charities Accounting Act*,[10] alleging that executive officers who engaged in activities which violate OSPCA policies were in a conflict of interest and could not comply with their fiduciary and other duties to the corporation. The officers claimed that it was open to the corporation to choose not to act on wildlife issues and limit its focus to domestic animals.[11] The OSPCA did not take a position in the litigation, and the court implied that the applicants were the real problem, wondering what it would take for them "to find joy in working with the humane society,"[12] and the application was dismissed.

---

9  The *OSPCA Act*, below note 27, required that in order for a society to profess to function with the object of animal welfare or the prevention of cruelty to animals, it had to be incorporated and become affiliated with the OSPCA: ss 3 and 10. Affiliates were required to comply with OSPCA bylaws and policies, and evidence was produced that GBHS had done so: *Weinberg*, below note 10.

10  *Charities Accounting Act*, above note 7. *Weinberg v Grey-Bruce Humane Society*, file no 3274/98 (Ont Ct Gen Div) [*Weinberg*].

11  This begged the question to the extent that even domestic animals were affected by the impugned practices; hunting with dogs and dog trial compounds directly include dogs, and domestic animals are caught as non-target species in traps. There were also concerns about how GBHS was protecting domestic animals at the time; it had no animal shelter and there were reports of agents allegedly refusing to take any action in circumstances in which animals seemed to be clearly suffering: Montgomery, above note 1 at 50.

In a local newspaper, the president's daughter defended her father and the thrill of hunting with reliance on the biblical passage in which God gave humanity dominion over animals, asking "What do they think animals were put on this good green earth for?" *Ibid* at 54.

12  The applicants had initiated another proceeding against GBHS. It had received a substantial bequest for an animal shelter but it had no shelter, nor any plans to build one. The applicants sought to require GBHS to build and maintain a shelter pursuant to the bequest: *Weinberg v Grey-Bruce Humane Society*, Ont Ct Gen Div, file no 181/96, discussed in Montgomery, above note 1 at 47–54.

Other humane societies have been rebuked for aligning themselves more closely to those who exploit animals than the animals themselves, such as the Alberta SPCA that has been criticized for being too close to the agriculture industry and defensive of the Calgary Stampede.[13]

Beyond these conflicts, in a general way, animal welfare agencies are usually most occupied with traditional matters of taking in lost or abandoned animals, encouraging people to spay and neuter their pets, and investigating cruelty cases. As noted, sometimes they pass policy statements condemning the harm inherent in practices such as factory farming, circuses, rodeos, hunting and trapping, and exotic pets; however, their actual activities are usually focused on specific cases "against bunnies as prizes at Easter or horse-drawn wagon rides in downtown traffic—rather than at the routine treatment of animals in normal daily life."[14]

The Canadian Federation of Humane Societies is an independent umbrella organization for humane societies across the country. It has no statutory authority, but it is recognized within official circles in Canada, taking moderate positions on the use of animals in various fields and working collaboratively with "key stakeholders" in animal use industries.[15] It is invited to represent the interests of animals when the federal government brings welfare and user groups together to discuss issues such as transport of animals and genetic engineering. It has participated as the only non-industry representative in the development of voluntary national codes of conduct for the agriculture industry. It is the only non-industry member of the Canadian Council on Animal Care, which purports to oversee the use of animals in research. These activities can be seen to bring a perspective to these initiatives that would otherwise be lacking, or to validate and thereby quell any criticism of the harmful practices that follow.

A journalist who studied animal welfare agencies in the context of the broader world of animal advocacy within Canada concluded that the essence of animal welfare work of this nature is not so much

---

13   Montgomery, *ibid* at 55.

14   *Ibid* at 42–43. There are some advocacy organizations with the name "humane society" that are non-profit or charitable organizations entirely separate from government or any statutory authority, such as the Vancouver Humane Society and the Nova Scotia Humane Society (distinct from the British Columbia SPCA and the Nova Scotia SPCA respectively). These organizations can sometimes be more proactive in terms of their positions and activities in effort to curb practices that harm animals.

15   Canadian Federation of Humane Societies, "Who We Are," online: www.cfhs. ca/info/who_we_are/.

the protection of animals as human society. It seeks to "protect some humans from other humans with bad attitudes, as evidenced by their treatment of animals," and further:

> It is about channelling human feelings of compassion for animals in safe and useful ways and about how to keep society humming along without the twinges of conscience or the opposition that the blatant human abuse of animals might generate. In short, animal welfare advocates generally want the status quo, with better manners. With a few exceptions, whenever animal welfare organizations get carried beyond the status quo towards calls for serious change in the human treatment of animals simply for the sake of the animals, the members pushing in that direction end up being labelled as extremists and are either pushed out or sidelined.[16]

At its essence:

> [B]y treating those who call for greater change as extremists and by providing a non-challenging animal organization for business or government to consult or support, the animal welfare movement acts as a kind of foil. Intentionally or not, it seems more commonly to head off calls for reform than to pave the way for real improvement in animals' lives, although welfare advocates might argue that they are softening up social attitudes and making small strides so that some day animals will be better and more respectfully treated. This is like the paradox of the best of food banks or wage subsidy programs. They offer immediate relief to limited numbers and take the edge off demands for a change in welfare rates or employer practices that might mean lasting help for many more.[17]

These animal welfare agencies, pursuant to the legislative authority delegated to them, the financial limitations within their budgets, and the broader political and ideological complexities noted, operate under a weighty public expectation that they are generally responsible for the welfare of animals across Canada.

---

16   Montgomery, above note 1 at 78–79. Montgomery was referring not only to humane societies but also to advocacy organizations pursuing animal welfare, as opposed to animal rights.

17   *Ibid* at 43.

# B. PROVINCIAL AND TERRITORIAL LEGISLATION

The first anti-cruelty legislation in Canada was enacted in Nova Scotia in 1822.[18] Since that time, every province and territory but Quebec has enacted some form of animal welfare legislation. The level of regulation varies. The legislation is generally administered under the auspices of the jurisdiction's Ministry of Agriculture or Natural Resources, whose focus and expertise is generally in consumptive animal activities, although there are exceptions, such as in Ontario where it is the Ministry of Community Safety and Correctional Services:

- Alberta: *Animal Protection Act*[19]
- British Columbia: *Prevention of Cruelty to Animals Act*[20]
- Manitoba: *The Animal Care Act*[21]
- New Brunswick: *Society for the Prevention of Cruelty to Animals Act*[22]
- Newfoundland and Labrador: *Animal Health and Protection Act*[23]
- Northwest Territories: *Dog Act*[24]
- Nova Scotia: *Animal Protection Act*[25]
- Nunavut: *Dog Act*[26]
- Ontario: Ontario *Society for the Prevention of Cruelty to Animals Act*[27]
- Prince Edward Island: *Companion Animal Protection Act*[28]

---

18   Elaine L Hughes & Christiane Meyer, "Animal Welfare Law in Canada and Europe" (2000) 6 Animal L 23 at 26 [Hughes & Meyer].

19   RSA 2000, c A-41.

20   RSBC 1996, c 372 [BC *Prevention Act*].

21   CCSM, c A84 [Manitoba *Animal Care Act*].

22   RSNB 1973, c S-12 [NB *SPCA Act*].

23   SNL 2010, c A-9.1. This legislation received assent on 24 June 2010 but as of July 2011 it had not been proclaimed. It is more elaborate than the fairly typical legislation it replaces: *Animal Protection Act*, RSNL 1990, c A-10. The new extended legislation addresses traditional animal protection as well as animal health which appears to relate generally to commercial animal exploitation (extensive regulation-making powers are established, but no regulations are yet in force), "nuisance animals," and "heritage animals."

24   RSNWT 1988, c D-7.

25   SNS 2008, c 33.

26   RSNWT (Nu) 1988, c D-7.

27   RSO 1990, c O.36 [*OSPCA Act*].

28   RSPEI 1988, c C-14.1. PEI also has a separate *Animal Health and Protection Act*, RSPEI 1988, c A-11.1, which addresses animals defined as "livestock" and applies to industrial contexts including agriculture and research.

- Quebec: *An Act Respecting Societies for the Prevention of Cruelty to Animals*[29]
- Saskatchewan: *Animal Protection Act, 1999*[30]
- Yukon: *Animal Protection Act*[31]

Some acts are fairly succinct and similar, establishing the SPCA and its authorities, including those in British Columbia, Nova Scotia, Ontario, and Yukon. These jurisdictions generally have separate legislation addressing aspects of animal health and welfare in the context of agriculture and some other commercial practices. Some, like those of Manitoba, Newfoundland and Labrador, and Prince Edward Island, are broader schemes that encompass those other practices, to varying degree, although Prince Edward Island's is specific to companion animals. Others fall somewhere between: New Brunswick includes retail sales of animals and kennels and other matters such as issues related to animal "nuisances"; Alberta has a very succinct Act, but regulations include some livestock and transportation issues; Saskatchewan includes "service animals" and protection of certain animals against dogs. Some legislation applies to wildlife in captivity; in Nunavut and Northwest Territories it is limited to dogs.

In terms of the core "humane society functions" they create, these acts operate in a similar manner, beginning by establishing the humane society or SPCA and its powers. They then designate officers, such as SPCA agents, or where there is no humane society, provincial animal protection officers or police officers to exercise authority under the legislation. Inspection, investigation, and enforcement powers generally arise in relation to an animal's "distress" or in some cases, to positive duties of care. The acts create offences and penalties related to causing distress, unnecessary suffering, and a variety of specific offences that vary by province. Three aspects of the legislation common to most jurisdictions are reviewed below: abandonment and distress; investigative, inspection, and enforcement powers; and offences and penalties. Quebec, Northwest Territories, and Nunavut are separately addressed.

The societal ambivalence in respect of animals that has been previously discussed is manifest in this aspect of the law. The legislation vacillates as to whether animals are respected individuals whose inter-

---

29   RSQ c S-32 [Quebec *SPCA Act*]. This legislation allows for the creation of local or regional SPCAs but does not give them any authority, nor does it establish any provisions with respect to the care or treatment of animals in the province.

30   SS 1999, c A-21.1.

31   RSY 2002, c 6 as amended by SY 2008, c 13.

ests merit meaningful protection. In some cases, it borrows family law terminology, allowing agents to "take custody" of an animal; in others, animals are "seized," can be the subjects of a lien, and ownership interests in them are transferred like in other legal things. Animals can be "euthanized" or they can be "destroyed." Several jurisdictions have considerably raised penalties in recent years, implying a strong concern for the welfare of the animals covered; by contrast, agencies who rescue suffering animals can sell or "otherwise dispose of" those whose care has not been paid for. Some provisions are about animals but not their welfare, they are aimed at protecting people from animal nuisances or at safeguarding the service being provided by animals to persons with disabilities or the police. Sometimes provisions are broadly interpreted in favour of animal interests, while in others human interests and business purposes prevail.

These laws tend to reflect their historical roots and adopt the same sort of "utilitarian calculus"[32] that federal legislation does, focusing on pets and denying protection to the overwhelming majority of animals by exempting the activities by which their suffering is caused; suffering that is prohibited when caused to individual animals in random occurrences is explicitly permitted when it is predictably caused to large numbers of animals in prescribed settings.

It is the concept of "cruelty" at the heart of the legislation which, in large measure, perpetuates the distinction. Although generally not defined or interpreted, one court pointedly found the usual meaning of the word to reflect a "disposition to inflict suffering; delight in or indifference to another's pain; mercilessness; hard-heartedness," which implies an intention.[33] Legally, this is inaccurate because *mens rea* should not have to be proved in these provincial offences as in the criminal context; however, the malevolent state of mind which the word "cruelty" connotes does tend to permeate the legislation and its interpretation. The preoccupation of the law to date has not been the harm itself, but the reason it is caused.

Traditionally, protecting animals from "cruelty" has therefore meant something very specific and fundamentally different from protecting them from suffering. In this sense, a subtle but cardinal purpose of animal welfare legislation can be seen to be protecting people's interests in these animals. People tend to have an interest in protecting their companions from harm, which is of a different order than their interest in the welfare of animals they will eat or use in other impersonal

---

32    Hughes & Meyer, above note 18 at 38–40.
33    *R v Vaillancourt*, 2003 NSPC 59 at para 18 [*Vaillancourt*].

ways; [34] people also have an interest in being able to subordinate even the former to financial or other personal priorities they might have. If new legal approaches are to develop in accordance with new ideas about respect for animals, these constraints should be understood.

## 1)  Animals, Abandonment, and Distress

Unlike the federal anti-cruelty provisions, which do not define the word "animal," most provinces do define the term fairly broadly. For example, in Alberta, it "does not include a human being";[35] in Manitoba, it is a "non-human living being with a developed nervous system" and the legislation further distinguishes between "companion animals" and "commercial animals."[36] British Columbia does not define animal, but excludes wildlife that is not in captivity.[37]

While some of the legislation specifically prohibits causing animals unnecessary pain, suffering, or injury, similar to the *Criminal Code*,[38] it commonly operates around a determination of whether an animal is "abandoned" or "in distress." Abandoned animals are generally those who have been left for a specified period without food, water, or shelter, or who have been left a certain period of time after they were expected to be retrieved from a veterinarian or boarding facility, or who are found on premises in respect of which a tenancy agreement has been terminated.[39]

Distress can include a range of elements which are qualified to varying degree, but generally refers to a state in which an animal is: deprived of adequate shelter, ventilation, space, food, water, veterinary care, or reasonable protection from injurious heat or cold; injured, sick, in pain, or suffering; abused or subjected to undue hardship, privation, or neglect.[40] In addition to prohibiting distress, some statutes establish

---

34  Abandoned companion animals can be seen to fall in the broad category of animals that people generally care about, even if that may not be the case for the specific individuals who meet the definition.

35  Alberta *Animal Protection Act*, above note 19, s 1(1)(a).

36  Manitoba *Animal Care Act*, above note 21, s 1(1).

37  BC *Prevention Act*, above note 20, s 2.

38  RSC 1985, c C-46.

39  For example: Alberta *Animal Protection Act*, above note 19, s 4(1); Manitoba *Animal Care Act*, above note 21, s 1(1).

40  For example, Alberta *Animal Protection Act*, ibid, s 1(2); and BC *Prevention Act*, above note 20, s 1(2). The standard can be quite high, see Manitoba *Animal Care Act*, ibid, s 6(1), which requires "acute" pain and prohibits exposing an animal "unduly" to cold or heat, or subjecting an animal to conditions that will "significantly impair" health or well-being.

positive animal care duties. These can be seen as more directly preventative in that they do not necessarily require an animal to suffer before they can be enforced.[41]

Cases have held that allowing an animal to be, or to continue to be, in distress is a strict liability offence.[42] In *R v Muhlbach*, the court emphasized that while *mens rea* does not need to be proved, the *actus reus* has to be proved beyond a reasonable doubt given the quasi-criminal nature of the proceeding, and the accused is entitled to raise a due diligence defence;[43] an appeal of an acquittal on a charge of permitting an animal to be in distress was dismissed in that case. However, in *R v Benoit*, where the accused's due diligence defence relied in part on the lack of published or objective standards with respect to what constitutes distress or neglect, the court rejected the argument, finding that it would be impractical to require standards for all the animals that are protected by the legislation.[44]

All of this legislation protects the ability to cause distress to animals in the course of "generally accepted practices," which are explicitly excluded from its purview. Alberta's provision is typical, indicating that there is no offence if the distress results from an activity carried on in accordance with the regulations, or with reasonable and generally accepted practices of animal care, management, husbandry, hunting, fishing, trapping, pest control, or slaughter.[45] Where a distress charge was laid in Alberta after two peace officers and a veterinarian observed numerous animals in poor condition(s), including a steer with a grossly enlarged scrotum, a cow with a limp that was missing part of her hoof

---

41  For example, Alberta *Animal Protection Act, ibid*, s 2.1; and *OSPCA Act*, above note 27, s 11.1. In Manitoba, similar duties must be satisfied, but only so as not to "significantly" impair the animal's health or well-being: Manitoba *Animal Care Act, ibid*, s 2(1).

42  *R v Loerzel*, 2007 SKCA 107 at para 13; *R v Lupton*, 2005 NSPC 11 at para 30; *R v Bailey*, 2009 NSPC 3 at para 63; and *R v MacIsaac*, 2008 NSPC 81 at paras 16 & 17. See also *R v Gerk*, 2001 ABQB 87 [*Gerk*], where nineteen bison were obviously undernourished and in distress, according to the observation of an SPCA agent and a veterinarian. The offender argued that so long he provided some food and water, a conviction could not stand. The court rejected the argument, finding that a lack in either quantity or quality of sustenance could sustain a conviction; paras 8 and 13.

43  2011 ABQB 9 at para 11.

44  2010 NSSC 97 at paras 34–36. Evidence that puppies were infected with roundworms and parasites, that their bellies were so distended and distorted that they could barely move, that they were very thin and lacked muscle mass, was sufficient to demonstrate their distress.

45  Alberta *Animal Protection Act*, above note 19, s 2(2); see also BC *Prevention Act*, above note 20, s 24.02.

wall, empty water bowls, stagnant standing water containing manure, external parasites on some animals, an emaciated and dehydrated "downer" cow lying on the ground,[46] and dead calves and cattle on the land, the accused was acquitted on the basis that the animals were being cared for pursuant to reasonable and generally accepted practices of animal care.[47]

The exclusions can be quite extensive. In Manitoba, the legislation establishes owners' duties in respect of animals, prohibits causing or permitting distress, as well as inflicting acute suffering, serious injury or harm, or extreme anxiety or distress that significantly impairs health or well-being. Yet none of these already qualified prohibitions applies where the harm is caused by a treatment, process, or condition that occurs in the course of an "accepted activity."[48] Thirteen accepted activities are set out in the Act (agriculture, exhibitions and fairs, zoological displays, slaughter, medical care, discipline and training, protection of people or property, sporting events, fishing and hunting, trapping, research and teaching, pest control, predator control, and euthanasia) and the regulations add circuses and kennelling, breeding, and retail sale of companion animals.[49]

In New Brunswick, the term "distress" is not used. Instead, this Act creates a positive duty to provide food, water, shelter, and care in accordance with the regulations, and makes it an offence for failing to do so.[50] However there is no offence if a person treats an animal in a manner consistent with codes of conduct specified by schedule, or with generally accepted practices or procedures.[51] The regulation regarding "pet establishments" including shelter, retail stores, and kennels, exempts training operations, research and educational facilities, premises that board or sell livestock, zoos, circuses, and other premises.[52] Similarly in Newfoundland and Labrador, the prohibition against distress does

---

46    "Downer" is a term used to describe an animal, usually a cow, who is so debilitated by illness or injury that she cannot get up.

47    *Muhlbach*, above note 43.

48    Manitoba *Animal Care Act*, above note 21, ss 2, 3, and 6.

49    *Ibid*, s 4 and *Animal Care Regulation*, Man Reg 126/98, s 1.2. Manitoba regulations incorporate by reference and specify as acceptable the industry-prepared recommended codes of practice and other standards or codes of practice it adopts by way of lengthy schedules, see s 2 and Schedules A and B. Other provinces do as well; see for example New Brunswick: *General Regulation*, NB Reg 2000-4, Schedule A.

50    NB *SPCA Act*, above note 22, s 18.

51    NB Reg 2000-4, s 4(2).

52    *Pet Establishment Regulation*, NB Reg 2010-74, s 3. It also regulates horse and pony hauling contests: *Horse and Pony Hauling Contests Regulation*, NB Reg 85-182.

not apply in respect of prescribed animals, conditions, and treatments that occur in the course of an accepted activity.[53] Specific prohibitions against docking horses' tails and cropping dogs' ears are also inapplicable when they occur in the course of an accepted activity.[54]

In Prince Edward Island, the legislation is confined to companion animals, including establishments where they are boarded, trained, sold, and displayed. The Act prohibits wilfully causing a companion animal unnecessary pain, suffering, or injury and causing and permitting an animal to be in distress; however, neither of these prohibitions applies where the pain, suffering, injury, or distress occurs in the course of accepted activity, which includes research and teaching involving animals, euthanasia, and any activity designated by the regulations.[55]

In Ontario, before the *Ontario Society for the Prevention of Cruelty to Animals Act* was amended in 2009, it did not contain the exemptions that other provinces had. However, the amendments brought extensive exclusions and broad authority for regulations prescribing activities, classes of animals, circumstances, conditions, persons, and classes of persons that are exempt from otherwise mandatory standards of care.[56] Similarly, prohibitions against causing or permitting an animal to be in distress do not apply in respect of activities permitted under provincial wildlife legislation, nor to activities carried on in accordance with generally accepted practices, to prescribed classes of animals living in prescribed circumstances or conditions, nor to prescribed activities.[57] Regulations further exclude persons who are hunting from the distress prohibition.[58] Animals in research are also excluded from the ambit of the SPCA pursuant to the province's *Animals for Research Act*.[59]

In the previous chapter, it was noted that the industrial practices by which animals are harmed are generally excluded from the purview of the criminal law (not explicitly, as in provincial legislation, but effectively, by way of interpretation of the offences) and that, in the industrial context, it is generally only where the animal resource is being wasted and the suffering is gratuitous that any offences are seen to arise. The same applies in the provincial realm. The practices themselves are statutorily protected in the manner described above, however, many cases do arise where animals, generally in an agricultural context, are

---

53  NL *Animal Health and Protection Act*, above note 23, s 18.
54  *Ibid*, ss 25 & 26.
55  PEI *Companion Protection Act*, above note 28, ss 1(2)–(4) and 3.
56  *OSPCA Act*, above note 27, ss 11.1 and 22(1), and *Standards of Care*, O Reg 60/09.
57  *OSPCA Act*, *ibid*, s 11.2.
58  *Exemptions*, O Reg 62/09, s 1.
59  RSO 1990, c A.22, s 18(9).

found to be in distress as a result of extreme neglect unrelated to any human purpose, such as being starved or dehydrated.[60]

## 2) Investigative, Inspection, and Enforcement Powers

The authority of humane society agents generally includes the enforcement of the provincial legislation as well as other laws in force in the province pertaining to the welfare of animals or the prevention of cruelty, including criminal laws. In respect of such laws, agents can generally exercise police officer powers; conversely, police officers often have enforcement authorities under the animal welfare legislation, together with or in the absence of an operating humane society.[61]

Typically under the provincial animal welfare legislation, where agents have reasonable and probable grounds for believing an animal is abandoned or in distress, they can enter a place other than a private dwelling house, with or without a warrant, for purposes of investigation.[62] A warrant is generally required to enter private dwelling places.

Additionally, agents often generally have inspection powers and can enter places other than dwelling houses even in the absence of suspicion of a violation, to determine whether standards of care are being met, or other aspects of compliance with the legislation. These can be important preventative powers, however they can also be unclear, particularly where they include premises where animals are kept for commercial purposes, but where a finding of distress or laying of charges in respect of duties or standards of care is precluded by the legislation.[63]

If an animal is found to be abandoned or in distress, the agent or officer is authorized to take further steps, including, in some provinces, ordering the owner to take specific steps to relieve the distress, or if the owner cannot be found or is unwilling or fails to comply with an order,

---

60   There was severe neglect, abuse, emaciation, disease, rot, filth, and stench among the corpses and living horses in *R v Carter*, 2006 ABPC 341. See also *R v Sudweeks*, 2003 BCSC 1960 [*Sudweeks*]; *Marshall v British Columbia Society for the Prevention of Cruelty to Animals*, 2007 BCSC 1750 [*Marshall*]; and *Gerk*, above note 42.

61   For example, *OSPCA Act*, above note 27, s 11.

62   The provisions vary. For example, in Alberta, no warrant is necessary if an animal is believed to be in distress and obtaining a warrant is not practical in the circumstances: Alberta *Animal Protection Act*, above note 19, ss 3 & 4; similarly, in Ontario, no warrant is necessary if an animal is believed to be in "immediate distress": *OSPCA Act*, ibid, s 12(6). BC provides the same authority, only for a higher standard called "critical distress": BC *Prevention Act*, above note 20, s 14.

63   For example: NS *Animal Protection Act*, above note 25, ss 21 and 28; *OSPCA Act*, ibid, ss 11.1 and 11.4.

or where there is no provision for making such orders, taking custody of the animal and arranging for care as required.[64] In some cases, a court order is required to remove animals. There is generally authority for euthanizing animals found to be in a state where prolonging their life would result in undue suffering, sometimes referred to as "critical distress."[65]

Some courts, including the British Columbia Court of Appeal, have found it appropriate to give the authority to take custody of animals broad, purposive interpretation on the basis that one of the purposes of the legislation is to allow the humane society to take steps to prevent suffering.[66] Courts have sought to balance fairness to animals and to their owners; for example, where the Ontario SPCA seized a group of eighteen animals, the Court of Appeal for Ontario confirmed that a veterinarian need not examine every individual to substantiate the SCPA's concern regarding the well-being of the group.[67]

Warrantless searches and other aspects of the humane society's authority to enter the premises or the manner in which it exercised that authority have often been challenged as unreasonable under section 8 of the *Canadian Charter of Rights and Freedoms*,[68] but these challenges have been generally unsuccessful across the country.[69]

---

64   For example: BC *Prevention Act*, above note 20, ss 10.1 and 11; Manitoba *Animal Care Act*, above note 21, ss 9, 10, and 10.5; and *OSPCA Act*, ibid, ss 13 & 14.

65   For example, Alberta *Animal Protection Act*, above note 19, s 3(3); BC *Prevention Act*, ibid, s 12; and NB *SPCA Act*, above note 22, s 17.

66   *Ulmer v British Columbia Society for the Prevention of Cruelty to Animals*, 2010 BCCA 519 at para 37, leave to appeal to SCC refused, [2011] SCCA No 33. A further purpose identified in *Ulmer* was to allow owners to retrieve their animals only if they are able to satisfy the society that they will be taken care of; however, not all provinces allow the agency that discretion. In most cases, where there is no charge pending, animals must be released to their owners if their outstanding expenses are paid. Ontario has also applied a liberal, purposive interpretation in the interest of relieving the suffering of animals as expeditiously as possible: *R v Baker*, 2004 CanLII 569 at paras 10 & 11 (Ont SCJ), aff'd (2004), 73 OR (3d) 132 (CA) [*Baker*].

67   *Bevan v Ontario Society for the Prevention of Cruelty to Animals*, 2007 ONCA 119 at paras 19 & 20.

68   *Canadian Charter of Rights and Freedoms*, Part I of the *Constitution Act, 1982*, being Schedule B to the *Canada Act 1982* (UK) 1982, c 11 [*Charter*].

69   No violation was found in *Baker*, above note 66; *R v Ringler*, 2004 ONCJ 104; *McAnerin v British Columbia Society for the Prevention of Cruelty to Animals*, 2004 BCSC 1430; *Sudweeks*, above note 60; or *Friesen v Saskatchewan Society for the Prevention of Cruelty to Animals*, 2008 CarswellSask 438 (QB). In *Gerk*, above note 42, a s 8 *Charter* argument was rejected on appeal for not having been raised at first instance. But see *R v Bingley*, 2010 NSPC 72; part of the evidence was excluded in *R v Nickason*, 2004 BCPC 316.

Where a humane society takes custody of an animal in the absence of his owner, it is required to give the owner several days to retrieve him. Return of the animal to the owner is typically contingent on the owner paying the society's costs for the animal's care, and if she does not or cannot, her request for return of the animal can be refused. In this regard, business purposes carry as much weight as benevolent ones and the potential results for animals themselves can fall anywhere on a spectrum of being adopted to a loving home, being sold for use in experiments or other purposes, or being killed. The humane society's possessory and proprietary interests in the animals are generally pre-scribed and provisions specifically address the transfer of ownership interests in the animal, sometimes expressly indicating that the animal becomes the "property" of the humane society.[70]

If accounts are satisfied, humane societies do not generally retain any residual authority to maintain custody of the animal solely based on welfare concerns. In some provinces, they can apply to court for an order granting them custody of the animal pending the outcome of charges against the owner, regardless of whether costs are outstand-ing.[71] In *British Columbia Society for the Prevention of Cruelty to Animals v Montroy*, a couple charged with causing distress to their dog wanted him returned to their care before trial, and the court refused.[72] It took specific notice of the legislature's use of the word "custody" rather than "possession," the latter being a right attendant upon ownership. The court found that the use of "custody" directed it to consider the matter more in the context of child custody, where the applicable test is not a balance of convenience, but "best interests." It found that it was in the dog's bests interests to remain in SPCA custody where he was thriving, while granting the owners "access" to visit him in the interim.[73]

---

70   For example, BC *Prevention Act*, above note 20, s 19.1, and Alberta *Animal Pro-tection Act*, above note 19, s 7.

71   For example, in Ontario, if there are grounds for believing an animal might be harmed if returned, a court can authorize the SPCA to keep an animal it has removed, if the owner or custodian has been charged with violating a law pertaining to the welfare or prevention of cruelty to animals in connection with the same fact situation that gave rise to the removal: *OSPCA Act*, above note 27, s 14(1.1). See also Alberta *Animal Protection Act*, *ibid*, s 13, and BC *Preven-tion Act*, *ibid*, s 25. By way of exception, New Brunswick seems to empower the SPCA to satisfy itself that an animal it has seized will be properly cared for before it releases the animal to an owner: NB *SPCA Act*, above note 22, s 16(5).

72   1997 CanLII 3288 (BCSC).

73   *Ibid* at paras 33–40. The dog had been discovered in a plastic bag in a dumpster with only his head protruding. A veterinary examination revealed that he had chronic medical problems resulting from a long period of neglect. The accused

Similarly, in *Brown v British Columbia Society for the Prevention of Cruelty to Animals*, where the SPCA had seized several horses found to be in distress, the owner claimed they were chattels and that if they were not returned, her business as a horse breeder would suffer.[74] The court found that any prejudice to owners has to be weighed against prejudice to the health and well-being of animals if they were returned. If found further that the mandate of the act is such that protection of animals in and from distress will generally, if not always, outweigh whatever prejudice might accrue to an owner as a result of being temporarily deprived of their use.[75]

By contrast, property interests have prevailed in other cases, such as when a court ordered the return of three horses to a breeder, although they were emaciated and sick, because the humane society had failed to properly communicate with the owner.[76] Similarly, the SPCA seized at least thirty cats and dogs in distress from a breeder where they were living in filthy and unsafe conditions, amidst a vast amount of feces, urine, rotting food, broken glass, and garbage, in intense heat and inadequate ventilation. The court ordered the cats returned because "other than the deplorable conditions in which the cats lived" there was no evidence of health concerns, and the owner had been denied natural justice and procedural fairness.[77]

---

claimed they had no idea how he came to be in the dumpster but the court was cautious; the fact that the trial was a long way off was troublesome, but not more important than Jasper's best interests.

74  1999 CanLII 5502 (BCSC).

75  *Ibid* at paras 21–29. The SPCA seized nine horses, who were in such poor body condition due to inadequate nutrition that two of them died shortly thereafter. The SPCA arranged veterinary and other care for the surviving horses. The owner of the horses brought an action against the SPCA, claiming that once the SPCA returns the animals to good condition, they are no longer in distress and must be returned to their owner. The court rejected the argument, finding that it must be satisfied that if animals are returned, they will remain in good condition. It might have been inclined to return the horses with conditions regarding their care and protection, except that this was the second incident in less than two years. The principle that the court had to be satisfied that the animals will remain in good condition if returned was followed in *Marshall*, above note 60.

76  *Van Dongen v Society for the Prevention of Cruelty to Animals*, 2005 BCSC 548.

77  *Haughton v British Columbia Society for the Prevention of Cruelty to Animals*, 2009 BCSC 1773 at paras 93–97 [*Haughton*]. Haughton was charged both provincially and federally with cruelty to animals, and one of her bail conditions prevented her from having dogs and cats in her care. However, she renovated her facility and bail review granted her return of the animals. The SPCA sought to have its costs of more than $46,000 paid before the animals were released; the court reduced these to just over $34,000: *Haughton v British Columbia Society for the Prevention of Cruelty to Animals*, 2010 BCSC 406.

The costs associated with humane society involvement are a significant aspect of these legislative schemes. In some cases, owners can be ordered to pay the costs directly, or to reimburse the humane society for costs it incurs in the process. As noted, if the owner does not appear, or does not or cannot pay the costs, the society is authorized to sell or dispose of the animal as it sees fit.[78] The cases are somewhat inconsistent as to determining the costs to which a humane society is entitled. Where the Ontario SPCA removed eighty-seven birds and animals in distress from premises that were not maintained or clean, where they had insufficient food, water, and care and had to provide for them until legal proceedings were resolved, the court refused to enforce any boarding costs, reducing the SPCA's claim for almost $170,000 to just over $5,000.[79] By contrast, where the SPCA seized dozens of sled dogs who were in distress, several of whom had to be euthanized, the court upheld an order of almost $120,000 for the costs it incurred for their care and treatment.[80]

Some of the acts create administrative tribunals to which an owner can appeal some of the orders made by the humane society, such as the Animal Cruelty Appeal Board in Nova Scotia,[81] or the Animal Care Review Board in Ontario;[82] in other cases or contexts, provision is established for applications to court.

## 3) Offences and Penalties

To assist in enforcement, several provinces have provisions protecting peace officers and others acting in good faith from legal action.[83] In

---

78   While they can occupy a significant portion of the legislation, costs provisions do not necessarily have the effect this might imply. The veterinary and other costs of caring for an animal or group of animals can be extensive. Where it is apparent those costs might not be recoverable from the owner, there can be a disincentive on financially constrained SPCAs to act; as noted above, the statutory authority given to these agencies is accompanied by limited funding. The authority to sell animals whose care has not been paid for also puts the SPCA in a conflicted position, where it is expected to protect animals but also potentially to sell them, in order to recoup their own expenses, to be used in practices where they might be badly hurt.

79   *Ontario Society for the Prevention of Cruelty to Animals v Straub*, 2009 CanLII 25138 (Ont SCJ).

80   *Beynon v Ontario Society for the Prevention of Cruelty to Animals*, 2004 CanLII 24563 (Ont SCJ). See also *Haughton*, above note 77.

81   NS *Animal Protection Act*, above note 25, s 31.

82   *OSPCA Act*, above note 27, s 16.

83   For example: BC *Prevention Act*, above note 20, s 25.1; Manitoba *Animal Care Act*, above note 21, s 38; PEI *Companion Protection Act*, above note 28, s 17; and

Alberta, that immunity extends to a person who reports an in animal distress.[84] By contrast, Yukon's legislation was recently amended to prohibit making a frivolous or vexatious complaint regarding an animal in distress and as a further disincentive to reporting, the expenses incurred by the government of Yukon or the RCMP are recoverable as against the individual. Animal protection officers are specifically authorized to refuse to investigate complaints they find to be frivolous or vexatious, or if they are satisfied there is insufficient evidence to warrant further action.[85]

The legislation typically establishes a provincial offence related to causing or permitting an animal to be "in distress," and sometimes for causing an animal unnecessary pain, suffering, or injury, or for failing to meet established standards of care. At least one case has specifically considered whether provincial legislation is *intra vires*, in light of the anti-cruelty provisions in the *Criminal Code*, finding in the affirmative; while both statutes deal with the same subject matter, there is no conflict between the two and therefore no issue of paramountcy.[86]

The various acts also include their own specific additional offences, a common one being a prohibition against animal fighting.[87] There are also some distinct requirements that appear in particular provinces' legislation. For example, Ontario requires veterinarians who have reasonable grounds to believe an animal has been or is being abused or neglected to report it to the OSPCA.[88] Yukon requires a person who strikes and injures an animal while operating a vehicle to stop and use reasonable diligence to notify the owner or an animal protection officer and take other reasonable and appropriate action so the animal may receive proper care if injured or be properly disposed of if killed.[89]

Penalties vary. The lowest penalty is in Prince Edward Island, which has no imprisonment and a maximum fine of $5,000.[90] In Yukon,

---

Saskatchewan *Animal Protection Act, 1999*, above note 30, s 17.

84   Alberta *Animal Protection Act*, above note 19, s 14.

85   Yukon *Animal Protection Act*, above note 31, s 2.3.

86   *Vaillancourt*, above note 33. It is not uncommon for charges to be laid under both the *Criminal Code* and the provincial animal welfare act, and the *vires* of the legislation does not become an issue, for example *R v Lohse*, 2010 BCCA 395; *Haughton*, above note 77, and *R v Perrault*, 2007 NSPC 14.

87   For example, New Brunswick *General Regulation*, NB Reg 2000-4, s 6; in Ontario, the prohibition extends to keeping equipment used for fighting: *OSPCA Act*, above note 27, ss 11.2(3) & (4).

88   *OSPCA Act*, ibid, s 11.3; a similar duty has recently been added to BC, *Prevention Act*, above note 20, s. 22.1.

89   Yukon *Animal Protection Act*, above note 31, s 10.3.

90   PEI *Companion Protection Act*, above note 28, s 15.

the penalty was recently increased from a $500 fine to a fine of up to $10,000 and twenty-four months imprisonment, or both; further, each day the offence continues is considered to be a separate offence.[91] In British Columbia, an individual, or a corporation and its representatives, can be fined up to $75,000, imprisoned for up to two years, or both.[92] Other provinces fall in between.

In addition to fines and imprisonment, penalty provisions commonly allow courts to prohibit a person from owning, or having custody or control of an animal for whatever amount of time the court finds appropriate.[93] In *R v Chan*, the court made it clear that its jurisdiction extends to restraining an offender from having custody of any animal, not just the specific animal involved in the charge at issue.[94] A literal interpretation of the statute that would suggest otherwise would result in an absurd consequence: the purpose of the legislation is to protect animals generally, so it makes no sense that the legislature would require an animal to be abused before that protection could be invoked.

---

91   Yukon *Animal Protection Act*, above note 31, s 12.

92   BC *Prevention Act*, above note 20, s 24.1. The amendments followed recommendations of a task force appointed after public outcry when a sled-dog company brutally slaughtered 100 of its sled dogs when business was down a year after the Vancouver Olympics: see Introduction. The amendments do not prevent an owner from killing 100 healthy animals for any reason whatsoever, be it a matter of finance, preference, or convenience. A new provision, s 23.2(2), addresses the method of killing animals. It prohibits causing distress while killing an animal, however this prohibition is subject to the exemptions for causing distress in the course of reasonable and generally accepted practices in s 24.02.

93   For example, Alberta *Animal Protection Act*, above note 19, ss 12(2) & (3). In PEI, the provision is explicitly limited to companion animals; it also authorizes a court to order that ownership of all companion animals owned by the defendant vests in the humane society: PEI *Companion Protection Act*, above note 28, ss 16(1)(a) & (b).

94   1999 ABPC 68 at paras 19–31 [*Chan*]. The offender had locked his cat in the trunk of his car for a number of days and it was minus four degrees Celsius when the cat was discovered dehydrated, stressed, and starving. The court found the offender's attitude toward animals to pose a real and present threat to the well-being of animals that might fall under his control, and he was prohibited from having custody of any animal for two years. But see *R v McConkey*, 2008 ABPC 37 [*McConkey*], where a couple pled guilty to causing distress to four very badly neglected dogs, at least one of whom had to be euthanized. While the court found that the behaviour would normally disentitle them from owning animals, it did not require them to give up their other dog and three cats, expressing reluctance to inflict on those animals the stress of being removed from their long-time home, possibly to a "death sentence" if they could not be relocated.

The fine and prohibition aspects of the penalty provisions are frequently applied, while custodial sentences have, to date, been exceedingly rare. Considering that charges often ensue only after the offender has been given one or more opportunities to remedy the animal's suffering, sentences have generally been insubstantial from the perspective of denunciation, deterrence, and rehabilitation.[95]

## 4)  Quebec, Northwest Territories, Nunavut

Quebec is the only jurisdiction in Canada that does not have any animal welfare legislation whatsoever. It has legislation which authorizes the creation of societies for the prevention of cruelty to animals, which allows for the creation of local or regional SPCAs, but it does not give them any powers.[96] A case arose in 2006 after one such humane society found two lost dogs and placed them in an adoptive home. When their owner later appeared, the humane society refused to divulge the contact information for the family to whom the dogs had been adopted. The owner argued that the humane society had failed to provide a reasonable opportunity for her to retrieve them, and the issue went to litigation.[97] The court found this to be an unprecedented case and resorted

---

95    For example, in *Chan, ibid*, the cat owner was fined $1,500 and prohibited from owning an animal for two years. In *McConkey, ibid*, the couple had ignored an SPCA warning to remedy the distress; they were each fined $750 and prohibited from owning animals for five years, except for their four pets. In *R v Ryan*, 2004 BCSC 1168, many dogs were found in pain, injured, and neglected, with matting, fleas, lice, teeth problems, difficulty walking, dirty housing, and disease; the offender had been given several opportunities to remedy the problem and the court called it an "egregious offence"; a $2,000 fine was upheld on appeal, together with a ten-year prohibition order. In *Sudweeks*, above note 60, the offender left forty horses and seven dogs without sufficient food or water when he left the country for several weeks. The animals were found to be starving and suffering, in urgent need of food, water, and veterinary care; at least one horse had died and another had to be euthanized; some horses were infested with lice and worms and their feet revealed longstanding lack of care; the sentence was a $4,000 fine and a lifetime prohibition order. In *R v Glodkiewicz*, 2006 ABPC 185, a couple left their dog in the car when it was twenty-seven degrees outside; when firefighters rescued him, it was 124 degrees in the car; the dog recovered from hyperthermia; the court found the couple was genuinely remorseful and fined them each $200.

96    Quebec *SPCA Act*, above note 29.

97    *Perreault c Société pour la prévention contre la cruauté envers les animaux (SPCA) de l'Ouest du Québec inc*, 2006 QCCQ 6770.

to the *Civil Code*'s general property law provisions addressing lost or forgotten moveable goods to resolve the dispute.[98]

Northwest Territories and Nunavut are not far ahead of Quebec in that their animal welfare legislation is limited to a few provisions in their respective *Dog Acts*.[99] For many years, these were identical statutes comprised of several sections, predominately addressing nuisance and safety issues caused by dogs, with very limited provisions prohibiting owners from leaving dogs unfed or without water sufficiently long enough to amount to cruelty or to cause the dog to become a nuisance, and prohibiting a person from punishing or abusing a dog in a manner to an extent that is cruel or unnecessary and providing for circumstances, whether welfare or nuisance related, in which dogs can be seized, sold, and otherwise disposed of.[100] The interests of dogs remained a low priority when modest amendments to each act came into effect in 2011. In the Northwest Territories, amendments include the addition of a duty of care, a requirement to prevent undue suffering when destroying a dog, and a slight expansion of the definition of "distress," while excluding distress that is caused in the court of an accepted activity.[101]

## 5) Exceeding the Limitations within Animal Welfare Legislation

The discussion above highlights some of the limitations within animal welfare legislation. A 2011 dissenting decision of the Alberta Court of Appeal offers a contextual analysis of that legislation which is more consistent with current knowledge and concern about animals. It identifies both the pressing need for legal progress in this area and the theoretical basis for it; and while such progress is being implemented, it provides interim support for a significantly broader interpretation of existing legislation that has animal protection as its aim.

In *Reece v Edmonton (City)*,[102] two animal advocacy organizations and a resident of Edmonton applied for a declaration that the City of Edmonton was in breach of Alberta's *Animal Protection Act*. The city owns the Valley Zoo and the subject of the allegations was Lucy, a lone elephant who lives there. The Act prohibits causing or permitting animals to be in distress similarly to other provinces. Alberta is also one

---

98  *Ibid* at paras 30 and 55. *Civil Code of Québec*, RSQ c C-1991, ss 939–46.

99  NWT *Dog Act*, above note 24, and Nunavut *Dog Act*, above note 26.

100  *Ibid*, ss 4 & 5 of each act.

101  *Ibid*, ss 4–6.

102  2011 ABCA 238 [*Reece*].

of the jurisdictions that create affirmative animal care duties;[103] and the regulations require that a person who owns or controls a licensed zoo must comply with certain standards.[104] The applicants alleged that in failing to meet several of those standards, the city was violating the Act, and they sought declaratory relief to that effect.[105]

Like its equivalents in other provinces, the *Animal Protection Act* grants peace officers the powers of investigation, inspection, and enforcement discussed above, and it authorizes the approval of humane societies, such as the Edmonton Humane Society (EHS), which are independent agencies charged with administering the Act. The EHS had failed or refused to take any enforcement action on Lucy's behalf.[106]

The city successfully brought a motion to dismiss the application as an abuse of process. The dismissal was upheld by the majority of the Court of Appeal, invoking a broad interpretation of that doctrine. While acknowledging the long-standing principle that declaratory relief can be granted to a private litigant respecting a public wrong, the majority expressed that this was only appropriate where the applicant also suffered some private wrong. While also acknowledging that a long

---

103  Above note 19, ss 2 & 2.1 respectively.

104  *Animal Protection Regulations*, Alta Reg 203/2005, s 2(3): "A person who owns or controls a zoo for which a zoo permit is issued under the *Wildlife Act* must comply with the Government of Alberta Standards for Zoos in Alberta, prepared by the Alberta Zoo Standards Committee of Alberta Sustainable Resource Development and Alberta Agriculture, Food and Rural Development, September 30, 2005."

105  The case is discussed further in Chapter 8. Extensive expert evidence filed by the applicants described numerous problems associated with requiring an elephant to live alone, in a cold climate where she is confined indoors much of the year, and in the particular conditions to which Lucy is subjected. In her dissenting judgment, Fraser CJA found that the evidence revealed a disturbing image of the magnitude, gravity, and persistence of Lucy's ongoing health problems and the severity of the suffering she continues to endure from the conditions in which she has been confined. Noting that it would be naive to assume that problems do not arise from the mere fact of keeping elephants in captivity, the evidence nevertheless exposed who is responsible for Lucy's living conditions and suffering, and showed that her health problems and her social isolation have been caused or aggravated by her living conditions at the Valley Zoo: *Reece*, above note 102 at paras 103 and 107, and n 69.

106  The majority's reasons briefly mention that one of the applicants had written to the EHS objecting to the conditions in which Lucy was being kept, that EHS investigated and replied that it had concluded "by the information provided" that it would not be in Lucy's best interest to be transported: *ibid* at para 4. (The applicants had identified an elephant sanctuary in California which was willing and able to accept Lucy.) Further information regarding efforts to encourage EHS to take enforcement action, as well as other aspects of the case are discussed online: www.savelucy.ca.

line of cases had relaxed the test for standing in public law matters, it found that there are still limits, such as where an applicant is seeking a declaration in respect of the breach of a penal statute.[107] Its analysis could have the effect of preventing anyone other than the specific authorities established under the Act from acting on the laws contained therein. It also reinforces the narrow reading of animal protection laws that has long beset them.

However, the thorough and strenuous dissent of the chief justice could be the most important development for animals in Canadian jurisprudence to date. Chief Justice Fraser of the Court of Appeal would have granted the appeal, on the basis that it raises serious issues about how society treats sentient animals and about fundamental democratic principles and the rule of law, including the right of people to ensure the government itself is not above the law. That alone—the simple act of connecting fundamental democratic principles to laws affecting the treatment of animals—gives animal interests a legitimacy that they have generally been denied. The decision goes much further still.

The chief justice observed that the old common law view that animals are property to be used—and sometimes abused—as humans see fit, was tempered long ago by legislative reform and the evolution of the law, as manifest in both the *Animal Protection Act* and the province's wildlife legislation.[108] She emphasized that animal protection laws were enacted to protect animals' interests, and not those of their owners.[109] While this legislation does not grant animals the full range of rights advanced by some, it does give them some rights, limited though they may be.[110]

Viewed through the animal welfare lens, the chief justice found that the appeal raised important issues fundamental to the effective protection of animals in the province, namely, under what circumstances can

---

107  See *ibid*, paras 21–36. In passing, the majority also cited, at para 27, *Cassells v University of Victoria*, 2010 BCSC 1213, in which the applicant sought to restrain the respondent from killing rabbits on its campus. The application was dismissed in part because the court found the applicant was essentially seeking a declaration that the respondent was in breach of animal welfare statutes and that she did not have the standing to do so (citing paras 3 and 82–83 of *Cassells*, *ibid*).

108  *Wildlife Act*, RSA 2000, c W-10. This legislation also has equivalents in other provinces: see Chapter 8.

109  *Reece*, above note 102, paras 2–3 and 91.

110  In so doing, Fraser CJA notes the loaded nature of the very term "rights" and uses it to mean the limited basket of rights, entitlements, benefits, and protections conferred for the benefit of animals under the province's law. These include the right to be free from pain and suffering, and to be provided with adequate food, shelter, space, and care: *ibid* at para 43 and n 10.

citizens or advocacy groups be granted public interest standing to seek a declaratory judgment that the government itself has failed to comply with animal welfare laws? And, under what circumstances, if any, and to whom, is a civil declaratory judgment an available remedy where the alleged unlawful government acts may also be the subject of prosecution under a regulatory animal welfare statute? Who, if anyone, is entitled to access the courts, and under what circumstances, to protect animals to the extent that the legislature has defined?[111]

The chief justice carefully reviewed (a) the historical and legal context of animal protection laws, (b) the changing legal paradigm, in which the animal welfare model replaced an exploitive one, (c) the flaws in the animal welfare model, and (d) proposals for reform.[112] She observed that the evolution of the law in this area is part of the relevant context, and that there is an ongoing debate about the sufficiency of the animal welfare model.[113] Without expressing any personal views in the debate, the incontrovertible fact of its very existence is the point.

In regards to legal paradigms, she observed that the animal welfare model currently in place replaces an exploitative one. The fact that criminal law prohibits deliberate cruelty is so ingrained in society that it is considered a rule of civilization. Yet, how society treats animals goes far beyond simply prohibiting the most egregious forms of abuse. This is the point of provincial animal welfare legislation, which in Alberta, includes not only prohibitions in respect of distress, but also affirmative animal care duties. The animal welfare model continues to be the norm in Canada, and it still involves attempting to balance animal pain against human need or pleasure. However, Fraser CJA expressed that while these fundamental questions are for the legislature to answer, there might be circumstances in which the law's current way of balancing competing values should be recalibrated, have other values included in the balance, or perhaps adopt an entirely different model that places greater emphasis on animal rights.[114]

She went on to observe that while the animal welfare model codified by legislation constituted a significant step forward, it has attracted considerable criticism in recent years for a variety of reasons which touch on issues within the jurisdiction of the judiciary. The issues identified by the chief justice include those that have been discussed

---

111 *Ibid* at paras 47 and 53.
112 *Ibid* at paras 51–71.
113 For a discussion concerning the difference between the animal rights model as compared to the animal welfare model illustrated by the "humane treatment principle," see Chapter 2.
114 *Reece*, above note 102 at paras 54–58.

throughout this book. First, laws are substantively inadequate to properly protect the interests of animals, in that they are laden with many delimiting qualifications such as "unreasonable" and "undue."[115] Chief Justice Fraser cites one scholar's observation that the idea that animal suffering should be minimized is "really only the beginning of the debate about how animals should be treated in modern society."[116] Second, the utilitarian balancing test at the heart of animal welfare always gives undue weight to human needs, no matter what the purpose. Third, laws that do exist are inadequately enforced for several reasons, ranging from insufficient funding to failing to take the rights of animals seriously. Fourth, efforts by citizens or advocacy groups to protect animal interests are often silenced by denying legal standing to both them and the animals they seek to protect.[117]

Reviewing a variety of proposals for reform, including the right to legal personhood, the chief justice concluded that while there were substantial differences among the proposals, they all agreed on one critical point: if animals are to be protected in any meaningful way, they or their advocates must be accorded some form of legal standing at law.[118]

The chief justice acknowledged the importance of understanding the nature and extent of the deficiencies of the animal welfare model because they underscore why courts should interpret the animal protection laws that we do have in a generous manner. She summarized these as including:

> inadequate consideration of animals' interests in law-making; priority for human interests always; restrictive judicial interpretation of protective legislation; common law precepts that treat animals as property and deny them or their advocates legal standing; limitations on what constitutes legitimate legal argument; restrictions on what is accepted as evidence; and anemic enforcement of animal protection legislation.[119]

On the basis of these observations, the chief justice identified four important consequences of the province's animal welfare legislation.[120]

---

115  *Ibid* at para 60.

116  Citing Peter Sankoff & Steven White, eds, *Animal Law in Australasia: A New Dialogue* (Annandale, NSW: Federation Press, 2009) at 9. Sankoff is a Canadian professor of law.

117  *Reece*, above note 102 at paras 59–64.

118  *Ibid* at paras 65–70.

119  *Ibid* at para 71.

120  *Ibid* at paras 88–91.

First, it reflects public policy and the need and importance of protecting animals, a highly vulnerable group who have no capacity to consent to what we do to them. Second, while animal rights are not at the end of the spectrum advocated by some, the provincial legislature has nevertheless made the policy choice of according animals the protection of certain rights. Third, since those rights are limited, courts should not diminish the full import of animal protection laws by creating unnecessary barriers to those seeking compliance; they should take a generous approach to the grant of public interest standing for those seeking to enforce the restrictive rights that do exist. Fourth, such legislation is "not simply for show, to assuage our collective conscience, promising much but delivering little."[121] The "overarching purpose is to protect animals—not their owners."[122]

From this, the chief justice concluded that the provincial legislature had clearly accepted that a civilized society should show reasonable regard for vulnerable animals, and therefore there should be some effective means of vindication if such laws exist, asking rhetorically: "Is there no one who can intervene under any circumstances no matter how egregious to protect vulnerable animals from mistreatment by government?"[123] Noting that Lucy could not start her own legal action, Fraser CJA added that it arguably remains an open question whether the common law has now evolved to the point where, depending on the circumstances, an animal might be able to sue through a litigation representatives to protect herself.[124]

With all of these novel matters at issue, the chief justice was of the view that the application for declaratory relief should not have been summarily dismissed. Her considered analysis gives animal interests the serious recognition that has eluded them in much Canadian jurisprudence. It describes animals over whom humans exercise dominion and control as a "highly vulnerable group."[125] It establishes that while the animal welfare paradigm was a first step toward checking animal exploitation, it is nevertheless inherently flawed and insufficient. It endorses the notion of animal rights. It calls for real legal progress through both judicial and legislative means. While written in dissent, its premises are sound and its reasoning is compelling. It could be the source of important legal developments to come.

---

121  *Ibid* at para 91.
122  *Ibid*.
123  *Ibid* at para 162.
124  *Ibid* at para 179 and n 143. Efforts to bring legal action on behalf of animals have been proposed and undertaken in other jurisdictions, see Closing Thoughts.
125  *Ibid* at para 88; see also para 72.

# PART III

# SPECIFIC USES OF ANIMAL THINGS

# COMPANIONS

Animals have these advantages over man: They have no theologians
to instruct them, their funerals cost them nothing, and no one starts
lawsuits over their wills.

—Voltaire

Voltaire was right about the theologians. As for the funerals and the
wills, things have changed since the eighteenth century. Animals might
not be troubled with making arrangements of their own, but their human companions certainly are. Millions of cats and dogs, together with
a wide variety of other animals, live in Canadian homes now, and a
multi-billion dollar industry has grown around breeding, feeding,
dressing, grooming, training, boarding, walking, and otherwise caring
for them, both in life and in death.[1] Modern household pets have been
singled out for special treatment as the beloved animals. Our attachment to them can be so strong that it has begun to manifest in a variety
of new legal problems that are explored in this chapter.

Still, there is a distinct tension between the love for these animals and all the strings attached to it. Domestic pets occupy a unique
conceptual space where they are expected to not really be like animals at all. They are not overtly treated like Cartesian machines in

---

1    In 2007, there were approximately 7.9 million cats and 5.9 million dogs in
     Canadian homes; see discussion in John Sorenson, *About Canada: Animal Rights*
     (Winnipeg: Fernwood, 2010) at 105–6.

the way commercially-used animals are, but in many ways they have been, and continue to be, manipulated to accord with human preferences. Over thousands of years of domestication, their biological and physical makeup has been modified. They have been selectively bred to diminish their size (the word "pet" is a diminutive of "petite"); to favour juvenile traits, such as large eyes and floppy ears, which make them appear more dependent than their wild progenitors; and to make them more submissive.[2]

In modern times, they are subjected to a variety of surgical procedures, whether to make them less animal-like, such as cutting dogs' vocal cords or removing cats' claws, or to make them conform with popular trends and status symbols, such as the removal of unseemly tails or cropping ears to make them stand up again. They are often expected to behave more like machines than animals—machines that walk, stop, and sit according to a person's commands, and do not bark or jump. Harsh methods of training and control are sometimes used. Pets can be perpetually confined in the backyard or in indoor cages so as not to cause a mess while they are alone; they can be abandoned at the humane society or just abandoned. They are beloved companions, but we hold fast to our place as their masters.

In this context, as in others, law struggles with the ambivalence. Pets are now the subjects of custody disputes, housing conflicts, and estates problems. The industry that breeds them is awash in public criticism and law is called upon to respond. When these animals cause harm to others, both damages and liability concerns raise atypical legal issues. When these animals are hurt themselves, meaningful compensatory damages are sought. But what are meaningful compensatory damages in this context? Who is being compensated, and for what?

Lawyers and courts wrestle in this realm with the thematic questions: What is an animal? Is it a thing or a being? What is its value—can it be replaced like a commercial good, or is it unique? The answers to date have conflated these ideas. Some courts openly begrudge wasting resources on conflicts related to animals. Others apply traditional property law principles, while lamenting that law has not yet developed a framework within which to give more serious regard to the animals that are so important in people's lives. Either way, even as pets receive more legal attention than other animals, it has largely been on the same basis: it is the person's interest to be protected, whether instrumental or emotional. Even here, animals matter because and to the extent that they matter to *us*.

---

2   Erika Ritter, *The Dog by the Cradle, the Serpent Beneath: Some Paradoxes of Human-Animal Relationships* (Toronto: Key Porter, 2009) at 239–40.

However, in some cases, the pressure to shift law's emphasis and incorporate new notions of respect for animals is apparent. Some courts are making way for incremental changes which promote their status, whether by rejecting the anachronistic classification of animals as commercial goods or by importing notions of "custody" and "best interests" from family law to animal problems, thereby acknowledging that the person's interests are not the law's only concern. The status of a pet begins to change from an owned thing to a being towards whom people have duties.

As new areas of law emerge or as the beloved animals enter the fact situations of traditional areas, there are opportunities to move away from the animal-as-thing approach. It is therefore important that when a legal problem is conceptualized, the implications are carefully considered from the outset: Do they reinforce old ideas that the value of an animal is for his owner to decide, or do they foster recognition that the animal matters for his own sake?

Of the non-exhaustive range of legal problems around companion animals, three categories are discussed below. The first part considers the industry that breeds them; the second part discusses legal issues that arise when people and their pets cause harm to one another; and the third part reviews issues related to animals in the family that arise in housing, family, and estates law. Various aspects of the use of lost, unwanted, or abandoned pets as research subjects are discussed in Chapter 7.

# A. COMMERCIALLY PRODUCED COMPANIONS

## 1) Breeding Operations

Overall, the industry that produces these animals treats them as commodities, in accordance with established legal and industrial norms. It both creates and responds to fluctuating demands for particular types of animals that represent status or power. Purebred dogs are selectively bred to meet market demand for size, temperament, security, and convenience. While there are some reputable small-scale breeders, most dogs sold in Canadian pet stores are from facilities that have come to be known as "puppy mills."[3] Their practices are aimed at producing the

---

3    Puppy mill dogs are also advertised in local newspapers, and sold at flea markets and in other circumstances.

greatest volume of product at the lowest possible cost, and as a result animals are often bred in conditions of neglect and deprivation.

Prior to the early 1990s, most commercially bred dogs were imported from the United States. Extensive media attention on the American industry and advocacy in Canada led to conditions being attached to the import of dogs. Agriculture Canada began, and the Canadian Food Inspection Agency continues, to require handwritten veterinary certification that pet dogs entering the country unaccompanied by their owner are at least eight weeks old, free from clinical evidence of disease, vaccinated, and can be transported without undue suffering.[4] Many shipments of dogs from American puppy mills could not meet these standards and that aspect of the trade was curbed.[5]

However, the failure to establish concurrent provisions with respect to unregulated breeding in Canada has shifted the production internally. The practice is now widespread in Canada, with many hundreds of such operations across the country. Puppy mills are often makeshift facilities that operate in and around people's homes and farms. They can have dozens or many hundreds of animals at any one time. The puppies are sold directly to the public or to pet shops, sometimes by way of a broker. Puppy mills increasingly register their dogs through online registration bodies that are not recognized in Canada; in any event, even established kennel clubs purport to certify only the breed and not the circumstances into which the puppy was born.

In these operations, animals often live in cramped conditions, either in small cages or stalls, where they are stressed and subject to fights and injuries, or on short tethers, often with minimal room to move and minimal shelter. Lack of sanitation is common; in some facilities, cages are stacked atop one another where excrement and food remains drop on animals below. Food is minimal in quantity and quality and veterinary care is rare. Female dogs are almost always pregnant, usually having two litters every year. By age six to eight, they are too worn out to produce any more and they are abandoned or killed.[6]

---

4    Import Reference Document AHPD-DSAE-IE-2002-3-4, s 2(4) pursuant to the Health of Animal Regulations, CRC, c 296, ss 10–12. The certification must be prepared less than seventy-two hours before the dog is imported: s 2(4)d. There are also provisions regarding the importation of cats, but these only address rabies vaccinations for animals over three months old: s 1. There are some "kitty mills," but cats are readily available as pets and are not generally bred in the same intensive operations that dogs are, with the exception of certain uncommon breeds.
5    Animal advocacy organizations are seeing some indication that border enforcement is waning and an increase in American puppies is beginning again.
6    See Sorenson, above note 1 at 106–8; Karen Gormley & Jim Berry, "Animal Welfare Position Papers, Puppy Mills, and You" (2009) 50:11 Can Vet J 1166; and

Repeated selective breeding of related purebred dogs has created genetic health problems endemic to the breed, including hip dysplasia, cancer, epilepsy, and serious respiratory and skin problems. Other physical and psychological illnesses arise from the conditions in which they live. Many have difficulty adjusting to life with people due to lack of handling and socialization, so in addition to often being sick, they can be fearful or aggressive.

Puppy mills can be found across the country, but many are in Quebec, the only province with no specific animal welfare legislation. Even outside Quebec, few provincial animal welfare acts directly address the issues that breeding operations present. Some provinces regulate retail stores and the conditions in which the animals live in pet shops, but these laws do not affect the industry that produced them. Some provinces regulate kennels but they also tend to adopt industrial standards and because those standards are so low, prosecutions are rare and convictions rarer still.

For example, in *R v Chapman*,[7] the operators of a licensed dog kennel were charged for failing to provide adequate medical care pursuant to New Brunswick's animal welfare legislation.[8] There were 350 dogs on the property with various illnesses including anal prolapse, distemper, and respiratory disease. One dog had such severe periodontal disease that his teeth and the flesh around his mouth were rotting. Another had to be euthanized. The court dismissed the charge, finding that the accused had the right to operate a kennel and that they had met all obligations under the Act and the Code of Practice for kennel operations.

Considering the extent of commercial dog breeding and its well-known brutality, it is the subject of few reported cases. Of those, some are judicial review proceedings brought by owners seeking the return of their animals,[9] and fewer are offence-related. Where charges do arise it is generally pursuant to provincial animal welfare legislation; charges pursuant to the anti-cruelty provisions in the *Criminal Code* are even less frequent.[10] Many of the facilities are on private property in

---

Charlotte Montgomery, *Blood Relations: Animals, Humans and Politics* (Toronto: Between the Lines, 2000) at 228.

7   2009 NBPC 28.

8   *Society for the Prevention of Cruelty to Animals Act*, RSNB 1973, c S-12.

9   For example: *Chatwin v Society for the Prevention of Cruelty to Animals*, 2008 BCSC 796; *Camping v British Columbia SPCA*, 2006 BCSC 1640; and *Pieper v Kokoska and British Columbia Society for the Prevention of Cruelty to Animals*, 2004 BCSC 1547.

10  *Criminal Code* of Canada, RSC 1985, c C-46, ss 445.1–47.1.

remote rural areas. These are rarely registered in any formal way, so humane societies, where they exist in these areas, generally have no authority to inspect without grounds. Even where such agencies exist, whether they have inspection powers or receive specific complaints, there are logistical disincentives to enforcement. Seizing suffering animals from a large breeding operation means having to pay significant costs associated with the medical care, food, and lodgings they require, which is a challenge where budgets are limited and shelters are full, or where there is no shelter in the first place.

Nor has commercial breeding been a priority of the relevant government authorities. Trying to find a way to require the government to enforce existing laws was the issue in *Teja's Animal Refuge v Quebec (AG)*.[11] A non-profit organization involved in rescuing animals in Ontario (TAR) commenced litigation in Quebec regarding a large commercial dog breeding facility there. TAR had received complaints about the conditions and treatment of animals, documented what it regarded to be violations of the *Animal Health and Protection Act*[12] over many months, and brought these to the attention of the Ministry of Agriculture, Fisheries and Food. The documented problems included a lack of ventilation, insufficient heating, chronic overcrowding, unhealthy conditions, lack of veterinary care, and physical abuse of the animals.

The Ministry took few steps to enforce the Act, so the organization sought a declaration that the minister was in breach of his animal protection duties for failing to enforce the relevant provisions and for refusing to exercise his discretion under the Act. It asked the court's direction to establish a norm for the appropriate level of animal protection required under the Act. The organization's standing was in issue, but it was ultimately not addressed since the Court of Appeal dismissed the proceeding on the basis that it did not present a justiciable issue: the court was unwilling to delimit the appropriate level of animal health protection as determined by the minister.

Cases where there are convictions give a sense of the gravity of the problem.[13] In *R v Bailey*,[14] the SPCA found puppies living in dirty cardboard boxes and cages full of urine and feces; some had distended bel-

---

11   2009 QCCA 2310.

12   *Animal Health and Protection Act*, RSQ c P-42. This legislation generally governs animals in agriculture although it includes language regarding the safety and welfare of animals generally, and it established minimal requirements regarding food, care, and living conditions of animals kept for sale or breeding.

13   In addition to the cases discussed, see *R v Hiebert*, 2003 CanLII 47922 (Man Prov Ct).

14   2009 NSPC 3.

lies, protruding ribs and anuses; some were crying and could not walk; and they were in need of food and water. The accused claimed they were not breeders but brokers, who had sold 28,000–30,000 animals over thirteen years, or approximately 200 animals per month. They were convicted of *Criminal Code* offences related to obstructing peace officers, and of causing or permitting animals to be in distress pursuant to Nova Scotia's *Animal Cruelty Prevention Act*.[15]

In *R v Materi*,[16] the accused had eighty-seven dogs who were very thin, had distended abdomens, feces matted in their fur, food mixed with feces and urine, no shade, and contaminated water. Some had painful yeast infections in their ears or untreated injuries and open wounds, evidence of fighting caused by the stress of crowding. The court found that the puppy mill, a term it specifically invoked, did not meet minimal standards and the accused were convicted on two counts of animal cruelty under the *Criminal Code* and one count of causing or permitting animals to be in distress under British Columbia's *Prevention of Cruelty to Animals Act*.[17] The circumstances were "sufficiently egregious" that a jail sentence was called for, but since the offender was not a danger to the community, he received a six-month conditional sentence and was prohibited from owning animals for life, although he could continue to reside with his wife's two pets.[18]

Both the *Criminal Code* and provincial animal welfare acts allow for such prohibition orders to be made upon conviction. Provincial acts tend to authorize a court to prohibit a person from owning or having custody of an animal for whatever period it considers appropriate. The *Criminal Code* includes an additional element allowing courts to prohibit a person from "residing with" animals, which closes a loophole whereby a person could otherwise claim his spouse is the owner and custodian of the animals.[19] Courts could potentially prohibit a breeder from ever owning animals again, and have done so on occasion (as in *Materi*). However, where the fact that breeding is the person's business might evoke enhanced concern about her inability or unwillingness to properly care for animals, the practical result tends to err more in her favour, as courts are reluctant to prevent a person from pursuing her livelihood.

In *Haughton v British Columbia Society for the Prevention of Cruelty to Animals*,[20] the SPCA seized twenty-six dogs and six cats in distress

---

15    SNS 1996, c 22, now the *Animal Protection Act*, SNS 2008, c 33.
16    Excerpt from Oral Reasons for Judgment, 2005 BCPC 85.
17    RSBC 1996, c 372.
18    *R v Materi*, Excerpt from Reasons for Sentence, 2005 BCPC 86.
19    *Criminal Code*, above note 10, s 447.1.
20    2009 BCSC 1773.

from a breeder who was a long-time member of the Canadian Kennel Club. The dogs had various illnesses and injuries: one had a swollen knee and was limping; one had visible pressure sores on his hind legs and walked with extreme difficulty; one was so thin the ribs and hips were easily discernible. Enclosures had no food or water, or very dirty water; some were full of broken glass, wire, chewed up garbage, and feces. The cats were in filthy quarters full of mould-covered feces and urine, with no food or water. The breeder denied the animals were in distress and claimed that they were seized in violation of her rights of natural justice and procedural fairness. The court found the animals were in distress, but agreed that the breeder's rights had been violated, and that the SPCA's refusal to return the animals to her affected her livelihood and her reputation, not only as a breeder, but as sheep and cattle rancher. On judicial review, the matter was remitted back to the SPCA to review changes made to the premises and decide whether some or all of the dogs ought to be returned.

In *R v MacIsaac*,[21] two Nova Scotian women plead guilty to causing distress after numerous animals were seized from their property. They were prohibited from owning or having custody of animals for twenty years, with the exception of five dogs who could be kept until their deaths but not replaced, and authority was given to the SPCA to enter the residence to ensure compliance with the order. Two factors seem to have played a role in the breadth of the sentence; first, it was a joint submission by the Crown and the offenders, and second, it was not a commercial breeder but a non-profit animal rescue facility from which the offenders did not gain any income.

## 2) Actions by Purchasers of Sick Puppies

At the other end of the commercial transaction are individuals who purchase the sick animals who are the products of this trade. In some cases, people who have no other apparent recourse invoke consumer protection laws to recover the damages incurred in treating the animals. Claiming that an animal is a defective consumer good reinforces the very categorization that allows such practices to flourish in the first place, and although there are cases where it seems to resolve the immediate problem, it ultimately undermines itself as an argument. The language of such cases tends to obscure the individual animal whose suffering is the point and emphasizes that the only relevant loss is that experienced by her owner.

---

21   2008 NSPC 81.

In *Pezzente v McClain*,[22] a woman spent more than $10,000 on veterinary bills after the Samoyed she bought from a breeder had many health problems. She sued for breach of warranty. The defendant argued that the money she spent far exceeded the commercial value of the dog, that one does not spend $10,000 to fix a $350 stereo and if one does, the costs of the decision should not have to be borne by the vendor. The British Columbia Provincial Court agreed and found that if the plaintiff had purchased a stereo, the most she could recover in damages is the $350 she paid for the defective product. It ordered the breeder to refund the $350 or replace the dog.

In so doing, the court relied on *Gandy v Robinson*,[23] an earlier decision of the New Brunswick Court of Queen's Bench. A man bought a dog from a breeder, spent $1,400 replacing the dog's hip after hip dysplasia was diagnosed, then sued the breeder for damages, claiming the dog was "defective." The court cited the 10,000-year-old "contract" between man and dog by which dogs agree to perform certain tasks for people, like provide companionship and security, and people agree to provide dogs with food, water, shelter, companionship, and care. The claim was dismissed on the basis that the veterinary fees the plaintiff chose to incur were paid as consideration under that metaphoric contract in return for the dog's performance of his tasks.

By contrast, in *Montier v Hall*,[24] the Alberta Court of Queen's Bench upheld an award of compensation for veterinary expenses for a couple who bought a sheepdog who had recurrent bladder infections and lameness due to fractured bones, later diagnosed as osteoporosis. She was euthanized. The purchase agreement warranted the puppy against serious hereditary defects or illness, but limited the damages to replacement with another puppy. The couple argued that this limitation effectively precluded any remedy for breach of the health guarantee, violating the province's fair trade laws. The court agreed, finding that even though the $840 veterinary bills exceeded the cost of the animal, these were reasonable steps to see if the "defective puppy" could be "corrected."

In an unusual turn of the tables, in *Watson v Hayward*,[25] a breeder refused to return a miniature dachshund she claimed was being im-

---

22    2005 BCPC 352 at para 16. Similarly, see *Armstrong v Ayoub*, 2002 CanLII 9423 (Qc CQ). By contrast, see *Ferguson v Birchmount Boarding Kennels Ltd*, discussed below note 38.

23    [1990] NBJ No 565.

24    2002 ABQB 70. *Quaere* whether this approach to damages would be upheld if the damages at issue were more significant.

25    2002 BCPC 259.

properly cared for by the man who had bought her. The purchaser (Watson) left the dog (Sophie) with the breeder (Hayward) for one week while he was out of town. Hayward found Sophie to be badly neglected. Her toenails were so long they were growing under her feet and interfered with her walking. She was grossly obese: her head was so fat she could not turn it, her breathing was laboured and she could not stand for any length of time. She had a serious ear infection.

Hayward claimed it was a condition of Sophie's sale that Watson would take proper care of her, provide a good home, and return her to Hayward in the event the conditions could not be met. Watson denied agreeing to any such conditions and claimed that as Sophie's legal owner, he had a fundamental right to determine what was in her best interests, and he was *prima facie* entitled to possession while the contract issues were litigated. The court cited previous jurisprudence in which pet adoption agreements had been found to limit the rights of a new owner in order to protect the animal's interests. It found that in a case of this sort, the balance of convenience was not the sole consideration, noting the SPCA's authority to retain custody of an animal when it was in the animal's best interests. The court found it appropriate to do the same in this context, and left Sophie with Hayward pending resolution of the litigation, allowing Watson twice-weekly access.

## 3)  Pre-emptive Legal Initiatives

With the failure of animal welfare laws to protect animals in commercial breeding, and the conceptual and practical limitations inherent in consumer protection laws, pre-emptive initiatives are seen as an alternative. Humane societies encourage people to adopt and save an existing animal from death rather than perpetuate an exploitive industry and breed more animals, some of whom will, in turn, end up in those shelters.

The City of Richmond, British Columbia codified that perspective when it passed a bylaw prohibiting the sale of all puppies and dogs from retail pet stores within its jurisdiction.[26] Three pet stores sought to quash the bylaw, claiming it was unreasonable, discriminatory, and passed in bad faith. The Supreme Court of British Columbia found that the municipality did not have to prove the bylaw was effective, just that there was a rational connection between the bylaw and its objective.

---

26   It relied on its authority under the province's municipal legislation, the *Community Charter*, to regulate in relation to business, including the power to prohibit and impose requirements respecting persons, property, things and activities: SBC 2003, c 26, ss 8(3) and (6)–(8), and 12(1).

In this case, the municipal purposes, being to reduce the number of unwanted and abandoned dogs and to improve the conditions of dogs sold as pets in Richmond, were valid, other allegations were rejected, and the bylaw was upheld.[27]

The Richmond bylaw is a disincentive to commercial breeding, particularly if other jurisdictions follow suit. Similar municipal authorities exist in other provinces.[28] These authorities can play additional roles in protecting animals. Municipalities can establish standards for keeping animals and prohibitions on keeping certain species.[29] Strictly enforced bylaws requiring cats and dogs to be licensed and establishing significant fines for breach of the bylaw have been successful in reducing the number of animals ending up in shelters, because they cause people to reflect seriously on their desire to get an animal in the first place, and because they provide the means for lost animals to be returned.[30]

## B. CIVIL CONSEQUENCES WHEN PEOPLE AND ANIMALS HARM EACH OTHER

### 1) Harm to a Companion Animal

Traditionally animals are chattels and when they are damaged, their owners are compensated according to their market value, as seen above. However, increasingly, courts are recognizing that there is more to the relationship a person has with her dog than to the relationship she has with her stereo and it is not sufficient to reimburse the purchase price so she can buy a new one. Courts now grant damages for the emotional distress caused to a person when her companion is harmed, even if that companion is not human.

---

27   *International Bio Research v Richmond (City)*, 2011 BCSC 471.

28   For example, s 7(h) of Alberta's *Municipal Government Act*, RSA 2000 c M-26, permits a council to pass bylaws for municipal purposes respecting wild and domestic animals and activities in relation to them; ss 10(2) and 11(3) (clause 9) of Ontario's *Municipal Act, 2001*, SO 2001, c 25, authorize municipalities to pass bylaws respecting animals.

29   Municipal efforts to prohibit the keeping of exotic animals are reviewed in Chapter 8.

30   One of the most successful municipalities in this regard is Calgary, see online: The City of Calgary www.calgary.ca/portal/server.pt/gateway/PTARGS_0_0_784_203_0_43/http%3B/content.calgary.ca/CCA/City+Hall/Business+Units/Animal+and+Bylaw+Services/Animal+Services/Licensing+your+pets/Licensing+Your+Pets.htm.

It is specifically the damages to the person that law has so far compensated; there is not yet a notion of general damages to compensate the animal's suffering directly. In reinforcing that an animal's value is determined by his owner, this development might not be much progress at all. On the other hand, it can perhaps be said that the formal legal admission that a dog is not just a replaceable thing does begin to erode the fixed property status that has been such a scourge. As the notion develops further, it can become a step toward recognition of animals' inherent value. As seen below, the complementary idea that the environment has compensable intrinsic value is developing and this could lead to similar arguments on behalf of animals.

Legal disputes tend to most often arise when animals receive negligent care from a veterinarian, while being groomed or boarded, while being transported in the cargo hold of an airplane, or when attacked by another animal. The cost of litigation compared to the potential damages that have traditionally been available has limited the number of cases that arise. Of those that do, many are resolved out of court or are unreported, although this can be expected to change with their increasing frequency.

Damages are increasingly available for mental distress inflicted on a person when her companion is harmed. Such awards tend to be minimal; however, as the principle comes into more common usage, those damages will likely increase in accordance with traditional jurisprudence on the subject, which considers the degree and nature of the mental distress suffered by the plaintiff to be the ultimate issue, so long as it was foreseeable and is reasonably proportionate to the events which caused it.[31]

Early cases often relied on breach of contract principles, including distress. In *Surette v Kingsley (cob Paws for Thought)*, a cat was injured during grooming and the plaintiff was awarded $250 for the anxiety she suffered as a result; she relied on both negligence and breach of contract, and the decision is unclear as to which was the basis for the award.[32] In *Weinberg v Connors*, the plaintiff operated an animal adoption service and in order to protect the animals he placed, he included a term requiring adoptees to keep him advised of the cat's whereabouts

---

31 Kate Kempton, "When Animals are Harmed: Remedies and Damages" in Lesli Bisgould, ed, *An Introduction to Animals and the Law* (Toronto: Law Society of Upper Canada, 3 October 2007) Tab 3 [Bisgould]. The paper also discusses the American context where there are many more such cases, and where success in the claim varies considerably by state.

32 [2000] NBJ No 532 (Sm Cl Ct).

for one year.[33] When the defendant failed to do so, he was found to have breached the contract and to have thereby caused the plaintiff anxiety, for which the plaintiff was awarded $1,000, even in the absence of any harm to the cat.

In *Newell v Canadian Pacific Airlines*, one dog died and another was injured after inhaling carbon monoxide on a plane.[34] There was a contractual duty to transport the animals safely, and the emotional distress of their owners was found to be a reasonably foreseeable consequence of the breach, resulting in a $500 damages award.[35]

An Ontario case that more significantly recognizes damages for emotional distress in this context is *Somerville v Malloy*, where the plaintiff's Chihuahua died after he and the dog were attacked by the defendant's pit bull terrier.[36] The court awarded $20,000 for general damages. While it did not break down the respective amounts, it appears from the court's description that the bulk of the plaintiff's suffering was attributable to the loss of his dog. His own injuries were fairly minor and the loss of his dog was described in some detail: "The experience of having his beloved pet ripped from his arms and torn to near death before his eyes has had a devastating and lasting effect on him."[37] The court specifically found it appropriate to award damages for emotional trauma and mental shock.[38]

That decision was cited with approval in *Ferguson v Birchmount Boarding Kennels Ltd* where Ontario's Divisional Court upheld an award of $1,400 for mental distress after the plaintiff's dog escaped from the kennel where he was boarded during the plaintiff's vacation.[39] The kennel was found liable in both tort and contract for having failed to take reasonable steps to ensure that its fences were secure. The plaintiff gave evidence of her emotional distress, including suffering from insomnia and nightmares as a result of the loss of her companion. The court specifically found that mental distress was a proper head of damages.

---

33   (1994), 21 OR (3d) 62 (Gen Div).

34   (1976), 14 OR (2d) 752 (Co Ct).

35   Animals can be injured during transport by the way in which they are handled or stored, or as a result of the heat, cold, or bad air quality where they are held. Sometimes they are lost like luggage. Animals on planes raise unique issues in terms of liability because of the *Canada Transportation Act*, SC 1996, c 10. See Kempton, above note 31 at 3-8–3-10.

36   [1999] OJ No 4208 (SCJ).

37   *Ibid* at para 8.

38   *Ibid* at paras 15–17.

39   (2006), 79 OR (3d) 681 (SCJ).

Most noteworthy was its rejection of the categorization of a companion animal as just another consumer product as "incorrect in law."[40]

A development of significant potential is the notion of compensable "intrinsic value" that has been endorsed by the Supreme Court in the environmental context. In a decision known as *Canfor*,[41] the defendant was found negligent in causing a forest fire. The Crown, as plaintiff, sought compensation for lost trees: both the market value for trees that could be harvested, and the environmental value of those that could not. The Supreme Court rejected the latter claim on the facts of the case in the absence of evidence as to how such damages might be quantified, however, it endorsed the concept. The environmental value of the trees, or their intrinsic or inherent worth, was seen to be separate from and beyond market value, recognizing that trees, ecosystems, and other parts of the environment are important in and of themselves. Although quantification might be difficult, the Court found that it is compensable and some valuation is possible.[42]

This decision reflects the broader notion of environmental rights that has emerged over the last several decades as a more general respect for nature has been making its way into legal discourse. In his seminal 1972 essay, "Should Trees Have Standing?", American legal scholar Christopher Stone took a novel step in addressing the relationship between granting rights to an "other" (in that context, trees and other things in nature) and the parallel moral understanding of the other as "one of us." He cites Darwin for the proposition that moral development has been a continual extension in the objects of humanity's social instincts and sympathies.[43] Professor Stone's titular question was considered laughable to some at the time. Several decades later, the Supreme Court recognized that environmental protection had emerged as a "fundamental value in Canadian society."[44]

As notions of an environmental intrinsic value take hold, the intrinsic value of animal life should necessarily follow, whether because animals are a part of the environment or because of even more valued qualities, such as sentience, which they are now known to possess.[45] This approach has more theoretical appeal than the instrumental arguments it would replace. It would release those otherwise caught in a

---

40   *Ibid* at paras 20 and 25.
41   *British Columbia v Canadian Forest Products Ltd*, 2004 SCC 38.
42   *Ibid* at paras 132–47.
43   Christopher D Stone, "Should Trees Have Standing? Toward Legal Rights for Natural Objects" (1972) 45 S Cal L Rev 450.
44   *114957 Canada Ltee v Hudson (Town)*, 2001 SCC 40 at para 1, L'Heureux-Dubé J.
45   See discussion in Chapter 2.

catch-22 from having to reinforce old principles which undermine the very claim asserted. It could also be a principled basis from which to begin to recognize harm caused to non-companion animals, including animals in the wild.

## 2) Harm by a Companion Animal

Harm done by a companion animal has at least two legal implications: first, the liability of the person responsible for the animal, and second, the liability attributed to the animal directly.

### a) Liability of a Person for Harm Caused by an Animal

The common law classifies animals in two general categories: animals *ferae naturae* that are inherently dangerous, and animals *mansuetae naturae* that are not. Common law has long held that an owner is strictly liable for damage done by dangerous animals, without any proof of negligence. However, the owner or keeper of an ordinarily harmless animal, such as a dog, would not be held to strict liability unless she was aware of the animal's dangerous disposition. This awareness is called *scienter*, and it is a matter to be proved by a plaintiff seeking damages. The requisite knowledge must relate to the particular propensity that caused the damage.[46]

To establish *scienter*, a plaintiff must first prove that the defendant was the animal's owner or keeper;[47] second, that the animal had manifested a propensity to cause the type of harm occasioned; and third, that the defendant knew of that propensity.[48] *Scienter* is the premise of the adage that "every dog is entitled to one bite." However, some cases have found that it is not necessary for the animal to have actually done the type of harm in question on a previous occasion, it is sufficient if, to the defendant's knowledge, the animal had manifested a trait to do that kind of harm.[49] Where *scienter* does not apply, an action for harm done by a domesticated animal might also be based on nuisance, negligence,

---

46  *Janota-Bzowska v Lewis*, [1997] BCJ No 2053 (CA) [*Janota-Bzowska*]; *Raisbeck v Desabrais*, [1971] 1 WWR 678 (Alta CA); and *Richard v Hoban* (1970), 2 NBR (2d) 493 (QB). See also discussion in Douglas Christie, "Dog Bites and Tiger Scratches — Liability for Animals that Cause Harm" in Bisgould, above note 31, Tab 4 at 4-1-4-6.

47  See *McLean v Thompson*, 2009 BCPC 415 at paras 37–40 [*McLean*], confirming that a person can be liable if she has assumed responsibility or accepted the charge or duty in respect of the animal, whether she is the "owner" or the "keeper."

48  *Janota-Bzowska*, above note 46 at para 20.

49  *Xu v Chen*, 2008 CarswellBC 1693 (BC Prov Ct).

or trespass.[50] Defences could include provocation, trespass, or voluntary assumption of risk.

Classification of a particular animal species is a question of law for the court to decide based on judicial notice or expert evidence.[51] Wolf-dog hybrids[52] and coyote-dog hybrids[53] have been determined to be in the dangerous category. However, in regards to dogs in particular, the common law assumption that domesticated animals are not inherently dangerous, and are therefore in the category of harmless animals, has been modified over the years by statute.

Provincial and territorial statutes now apply to the harms that might be caused by domesticated animals, particularly dogs. These are either specific dog or animal liability acts or bylaw-making authorities in respect to animals given to municipalities. This legislation abolishes *scienter* as it applies to the behaviour of dogs (or other animals where they are included),[54] and a dog is "effectively reclassified by statute as a wild animal."[55] This removes the "free bite" other domesticated animals retain and makes owners strictly liable, even in the absence of any indication of dangerous propensities on the part of their dogs.

Animal liability legislation generally does several things. It establishes liability on the part of a person for damages caused by her dog; it authorizes designated authorities to make orders to control animals who have proven to be a threat to the safety of the community, including possible destruction orders;[56] and it can exclude specific breeds that are perceived to be categorically dangerous.

## b) Liability of the Animal for Harm Caused

In addition to addressing civil liability, animal liability legislation creates regulatory violations and provincial offences, with a variety of penalties. At one end of the spectrum, fines can be imposed for lesser infractions such as allowing dogs to "run at large."[57] Penalties along

---

50 Liability insurance such as home owners' insurance, pet insurance, or automobile insurance might respond to such claims, depending on the circumstances, see Christie, above note 46 at 4-31–4-32.

51 *McQuaker v Goddard*, [1940] 1 KB 687 at 700–1.

52 *McLean*, above note 47.

53 *Temple v Elvery*, [1926] 3 WWR 652 (Sask Dist Ct).

54 In most jurisdictions, there is explicit statutory language abolishing *scienter*; in others, it is effectively abolished by the standards established by the legislation.

55 Christie, above note 46 at 4-2.

56 Depending on the province, this can be a municipality and the municipal authority it designates, or a court directly.

57 Similar consequences can also be triggered if a dog disturbs the neighbourhood, for example, Nova Scotia's *Municipal Government Act*, SNS 1998, c 18, ss 175–79;

the spectrum of offences can also include incarceration.[58] At the more serious end of the spectrum, regardless of whether or not any person is convicted of an offence, all of these statutes allow that dogs determined to be dangerous can be seized and destroyed, with or without a court order, possibly immediately at the scene of an incident. The authorities established under these acts can be quite emphatic and the standards quite low, sometimes allowing animals to be killed if they have worried or injured livestock[59] or even if they are merely "at large."[60]

It is rare for jurisdictions to directly factor in the dog's perspective and allow for consideration of unusual circumstances that might have justified the incident or address the likelihood of future incidents, although Prince Edward Island[61] and Ontario[62] do.[63] Saskatchewan includes provocation as an element of two of the four alternative criteria for determining whether a dog is dangerous.[64] In Manitoba, while proof of provocation does not affect the dog's fate, courts can consider contributory negligence in assessing damages in a civil action.[65]

Overwhelmingly, all of the legislation focuses heavily on the conduct of the dog and does not sufficiently address the owner's behaviour and the role he might have played, either in the specific circumstances of an incident, or in affecting the dog's demeanor more generally. Human behaviour might be modified through law or education, whereas focusing on the dog's actions not only affects the individual dog in a potentially lethal way, it also leaves the person free to get a new dog and recreate the problem. Some have argued that a negligence-based approach with emphasis on the person's role is more reasonable from the perspective of both human and dog safety.[66]

---

and New Brunswick's *Provincial Dog Regulation*, NB Reg 84-85.

58   For example, Manitoba's *Animal Liability Act*, CCSM c A95, s 9; and Ontario's *Dog Owners' Liability Act*, RSO 1990, c D.16, s 18.

59   For example, in Manitoba, any person can request a destruction order for a dog, wild boar or other prescribed animal that has worried, injured, or killed livestock within the last six months: *ibid*, s 7(1).

60   For example, see Newfoundland and Labrador's *Dog Act*, RSNL 1990, c D-26, s 4.

61   *Dog Act*, RSPEI 1988, c D-13, s 16(7)

62   *Dog Owners' Liability Act*, above note 58, s 4(6).

63   Some municipal bylaws also include consideration of provocation; for example, City of Winnipeg's *Pound By-Law*, 2443/79, s 20.1(4).

64   *Municipalities Act*, SS 2005, c M-36.1, s 375(1)(a) and (c).

65   *Animal Liability Act*, above note 58, s 2(1); see also *Dog Owners' Liability Act*, above note 58, s 2(4).

66   See Jacquelyn Shaw, *Canada's Dangerous Dog Laws* (East Lansing, MI: Animal Legal & Historical Center, 2009) online: Animal Legal & Historical Center www.animallaw.info/nonus/articles/ddcadangerousdogs.htm, and Lynn A

Some courts have overturned "dangerous dog" findings, showing appreciation for the significance of the order and even considering the problem as though the dog was the accused. In *Bolen v Regina (City)*,[67] a husky named Diego was walking unleashed past a home outside of which a cat was leashed and a "cacophonous fracas" ensued.[68] Diego was designated dangerous pursuant to a Regina bylaw but the designation was overturned on appeal. The court observed that Diego was "sentenced without hope of parole" to wear a muzzle whenever he was off his owner's property and this was a "life sentence" which seemed "cruel and unusual." In particular, because the punishment accorded the dog left no discretion to the court, a judge should "show some flexibility or restraint in deciding whether a dog is mischievous or playful as compared to vicious or menacing when he worries a cat."[69]

In *R v Houdek*,[70] a Labrador cross named Maxine was designated a dangerous dog after she jumped over the fence and got into a fight with the neighbours' dogs. Nobody was hurt, but because there had been a series of aggressive acts on Maxine's part, an order under the municipal bylaw imposed numerous conditions related to her future control. The Court of Queen's Bench for Saskatchewan granted an appeal, finding it necessary to bear in mind that dogs bark and snarl for many reasons, and the assessment must be in the context of a dog acting in the normal way of canines. When it might lead to a dog being declared dangerous, "the quality of mercy should not be restrained." The court abrogated the finding and substituted "a verdict of not guilty."[71]

There is also authority for overturning an order directing that a dog be killed. In *R v Solomon*,[72] the Ontario Court of Justice held that such a decision could be set aside on any of the following four grounds: if it is unreasonable; if it can not be supported by the evidence; if there was an error of law; or if it involves or results in a miscarriage of justice.[73] The court applied criminal law sentencing principles, noting that the test is whether the sentence is fit from an analytical point of view. While an appeal court should be hesitant to interfere with the discretion of the trial judge, it is appropriate to do so if the wrong principles were

---

Epstein, "There Are No Bad Dogs, Only Bad Owners: Replacing Strict Liability with a Negligence Standard in Dog Bite Cases" (2006) 13 Animal L 129.

67   2004 SKQB 263.

68   As described when considered in *R v Houdek*, below note 70 at para 19.

69   *Bolen v Regina (City)*, above note 67 at paras 6, 7, and 9.

70   2008 SKQB 434.

71   *Ibid* at paras 24 & 25.

72   2005 ONCJ 353.

73   *Ibid* at para 7.

applied, if correct principles were applied incorrectly, if evidence was ignored or exaggerated in its application, or if improper evidence was applied.[74]

In British Columbia, the limits of appellate review have been the subject of dispute. Municipal animal control officers have the authority to take certain steps with respect to "dangerous dogs," including applying to the provincial court for an order that the dog be destroyed. There is disagreement within the jurisprudence as to whether courts have the authority to review the determination that the dog is dangerous or only whether the animal control officer reasonably believed it. In *Capital Regional District v Kuo*,[75] the British Columbia Court of Appeal acknowledged the uncertainty, but declined to resolve it where the issue had become moot and lacked the necessary adversarial context.

Unlike the United States where "death penalty" cases are sometimes aggressively and publicly fought, they have received little attention in Canada to date. They are nevertheless inherently controversial, in that animals pay the ultimate price when their behaviour is often the result of circumstances brought about by the people around them, including where people failed to exercise reasonable precautions to prevent the harm, where dogs are poorly socialized in the breeding conditions discussed above, or where they are treated with neglect, aggression, or violence.

This becomes a particular concern in the context of breed-specific controls. In 2005, Ontario implemented a "pit bull ban" by way of amendments to its *Dog Owners' Liability Act*.[76] It was not the first such ban in the country, as Winnipeg has prohibited the keeping or harbouring of any pit-bulls since 1990 by way of municipal bylaw.[77] However, Ontario's legislation has unprecedented implications for dogs in the province. The Act prohibits the keeping of a list of species of animals considered to be pit bulls, and explicitly shifts the onus to persons accused of having a pit bull to disprove it. It places various restrictions on the ownership and transfer of pit bulls and imposes strict and sweeping controls on grandparented "restricted pit bulls" which apply to all but those who are using pit bulls in research, the use of which is explicitly protected.

Most dramatically, the Act establishes a mandatory order requiring a pit bull to be killed in a variety of circumstances, including those in which the dog himself has caused no harm. A court must order a pit

---

74  *Ibid* at para 13.
75  2008 BCCA 478.
76  Above note 58, s 1(1), definition of "pit bull."
77  City of Winnipeg, *Pound By-Law*, above note 63, s 20.2.

bull to be killed if he is found to have bitten or attacked a person or domesticated animal, if he "poses a menace" to the safety of persons or domestic animals, or even if his owner is found to have contravened laws relating to pit bulls or a related court order.[78] Mitigating circumstances that courts may take into account in making orders regarding other dogs are explicitly eliminated from consideration in the case of pit bulls.[79]

This legislation has been the subject of much public debate. Critics claim that breed-specific bans detract from addressing the real source of the problem. They put the emphasis on the dog rather than on the person's treatment of the dog, or management of the conditions in which the dog is put, and these can have dramatic consequences for individual dogs. Further, critics claim that emphasizing pit bulls as particularly dangerous as compared to other dogs is inaccurate and unsafe.[80]

Some of these issues were raised when the legislation was constitutionally challenged in *Cochrane v Ontario (AG)*.[81] Of particular concern in that case was the definition of a pit bull which included "a dog that has an appearance and physical characteristics that are substantially similar" to those of specific breeds included in the definition.[82] Cochrane argued that because imprisonment could arise from conviction under the Act, the definition of "pit bull" was constitutionally overbroad and vague contrary to section 7 of the *Charter*;[83] that a provision which allows a document from a veterinarian stating that a dog is a pit bull within the meaning of the Act to stand as proof that the dog is a pit bull violates the presumption of innocence and the right to a fair trial, thereby offending section 11(d) of the *Charter*; and that the

---

78   Above note 58, ss 4(8) & (9).

79   *Ibid*, s 4(6).

80   A study in the *Canadian Veterinary Journal* found that between 1990 and 2007, there were twenty-eight identified fatalities from dog bites. Predominant factors were owned, known dogs; residential location; children's unsupervised access to an area with dogs; and rural/remote areas. In Canada, a higher proportion of sled dogs and possibly mixed-breed dogs, as well as multiple dogs, caused fatalities, than in the United States. See Malathi Raghavan, "Fatal Dog Attacks in Canada, 1997–2007" (2008) 49:6 Can Vet J 557. See also *Cochrane v Ontario (AG)*, 2007 CanLII 9231 (Ont SCJ).

81   *Ibid*.

82   The others are a pit bull terrier, Staffordshire bull terrier, American Staffordshire terrier, and American pit bull terrier, s 1(1).

83   *Canadian Charter of Rights and Freedoms*, Part I of the *Constitution Act, 1982*, being Schedule B to the *Canada Act, 1982* (UK) 1982, c 11 [*Charter*].

designation of a particular breed of dogs is *ultra vires* the provincial government.[84]

After a lengthy analysis, the Superior Court of Justice rejected the argument that the legislation was *ultra vires*. However, it found that while the definition of "pit bull" was not overbroad, it was vague and violated section 7. Further, inasmuch as the definition improperly relieved the Crown of the burden of proof by creating a mandatory presumption in its favour, it violated the presumption of innocence and section 11(d). Neither provision was justified by section 1 of the *Charter*. However, on appeal, the Court of Appeal overturned the findings of *Charter* violations and upheld the legislation.[85]

The controversy regarding Ontario's breed-specific prohibition continues. A private member's bill introduced in May 2010 would repeal the provisions.[86] For now, the provisions are in force and enforced. In *R v Huggins*,[87] a pit bull named Ginger and a shepherd/collie mix named Buddy had a fight in a local dog park. Ginger inflicted serious wounds on Buddy and bit his owner. While Ginger's owner was acquitted of a charge under the *Dog Owners' Liability Act* for having failed to exercise reasonable precautions, Ginger was ordered to be killed. On appeal, the summary conviction appeal judge overturned the order on the basis that the language of the legislation was ambiguous and could lead to an absurd result; for example, if a pit bull bit a burglar breaking into his home, the pit bull would have to be killed.[88] However, on further appeal, the Court of Appeal found the language to be clear and unambiguous about what is to happen "when a pit bull contravenes" the provisions and the order to kill Ginger was reinstated.[89]

---

84  In this case, the issue was the constraints imposed on a grandparented dog named Chess and the mandatory killing provisions were not in issue. However, while ss 7 and 11(d) of the *Charter* are being considered, it is interesting to imagine the case that might be argued from the perspective of a dog, facing death because of the action of her caregiver, who wishes to assert a right to be presumed innocent and a right to life, liberty, and security of the person. One can also imagine why a dog in this situation would benefit from legal representation of her own interests, inasmuch as they could conflict with those of her caregiver when blame for the incident is being determined.

85  *Cochrane v Ontario (AG)*, 2008 ONCA 718, leave to appeal to SCC refused, [2009] SCCA No 105.

86  Bill 60, *Public Safety Related to Dogs Statute Law Amendment Act, 2010*, 2d Sess, 39th Leg, Ontario, 2010.

87  2010 ONCA 746.

88  *Ibid* at paras 8 & 9.

89  *Ibid* at paras 29 & 30.

## C. FAMILY MATTERS: HOUSING, FAMILY, AND ESTATES LAW

### 1) Animals in the Home: Issues in Rental Units and Condominiums

In 1989, a sixteen-year-old cat named Fluffy was residing in a Toronto apartment with disabled tenants who relied on pension benefits. Their lease contained a clause prohibiting pets on the premises. The couple was aware of the clause when they signed the lease, but this was the only apartment they could afford. Fluffy was partially blind, her claws had been removed, and she was spayed. She had not been the subject of any complaints. However, a worker saw her in the unit and advised the landlord, who sought to terminate the tenancy. The tenants lost a lengthy, well-publicized court battle because they knew of the provision when they signed the lease and the landlord enforced the provision against all animals on the premises.[90]

The negative publicity generated by the "Fluffy the Cat" case led to amendments in Ontario's residential tenancy legislation and now "no pets" clauses in residential leases are void pursuant to section 14 of the *Residential Tenancies Act*.[91] There must be grounds in order to evict a tenant who keeps a pet, such as undue damage to the unit or substantial interference with others' reasonable enjoyment of the premises.[92]

For undue damage to terminate a tenancy, the damage caused must be beyond that caused by normal living. For example, in *File No SOL-08628*, the Ontario Rental Housing Tribunal dismissed a landlord's application to evict where he alleged there were excessive dog feces accumulating in the back yard and a strong cat odour. The Tribunal stressed that uncleanliness might equate to damages, but only in extreme circumstances.[93]

Similarly, for an animal's presence to substantially interfere with reasonable enjoyment, the bar is high and the landlord must establish requirements set out in section 76, which was specifically established for applications concerning pets. The Tribunal may not make an order

---

90   *Cassandra Towers v Ryll*, [1989] OJ No 1233 (Dist Ct).
91   *Residential Tenancies Act, 2006*, SO 2006, c 17.
92   *Ibid*, ss 62 and 64.
93   *File No SOL-08628*, [1999] ORHTD No 22 at para 7. But see *File No SOL-49554*, [2004] ORHTD No 46, where a landlord's application to terminate a tenancy was granted upon evidence that the tenants left their dog unattended for long periods, the dog barked a lot, and used the balcony to defecate and urinate.

terminating the tenancy based on the presence, control, or behaviour of an animal unless it is satisfies of one of three criteria:

- The past behaviour of an animal of that species has substantially interfered with the reasonable enjoyment of the complex, and the specific animal at issue caused or contributed to the substantial interference;
- the presence of an animal of that species has caused the landlord or another tenant to suffer a serious allergic reaction and the specific animal at issue caused or contributed to the allergic reaction; or
- the presence of an animal of that species or breed is inherently dangerous to the safety of the landlord or other tenant.[94]

A leading Ontario case addressing termination for substantial interference on the basis of having a pet is *Kay v Parkway Forest Developments*,[95] where the Divisional Court held that the issue is a question of fact to be determined on the basis of the nature of the conduct complained of; duration, extent, and seriousness of the complaint; the nature of the premises; the nature of the complaints; and the reasonable expectations and feelings of other tenants.

In a case before the Landlord and Tenant Board in 2010, a landlord sought unsuccessfully to evict a tenant who had three dogs—two of whom were pit bulls—along with other animals. The dogs had been grandparented under the *Dog Owners' Liability Act* discussed above. They had never been aggressive, and were found to be peaceable, quiet, and well-behaved. One of the landlords had a phobia of them, but it was unrelated to anything these particular dogs had done. Even if pit bulls were inherently dangerous within the meaning of the legislation, they would have had to do something to contribute to the landlord's fears to be the subject of an eviction order.[96]

A new provision in the history of residential tenancy legislation in Ontario requires the Board to review the circumstances and consider whether it should exercise discretion to grant relief from eviction, even if an animal has caused undue damage or substantially interfered with reasonable enjoyment.[97]

Other provinces do not render void "no pets" clauses. British Columbia does the opposite; its legislation specifically allows for terms or conditions in tenancy agreements prohibiting pets or restricting the size, kind, or number of pets a tenant may keep, and governing a

---

94   *Residential Tenancies Act, 2006*, above note 91, s 76.
95   (1982), 35 OR (2d) 329 (Div Ct).
96   *File No TSL-29326*, 2010 LNONLTB 38.
97   *Residential Tenancies Act, 2006*, above note 91, s 83(2).

tenant's obligations in respect of pets.[98] It also establishes "pet damage deposits" and inspection rights in respect of new pets.[99] Manitoba has fairly detailed pet damage deposit provisions, including specific authority to order a pet removed if a deposit is not paid, and to terminate a tenancy where no deposit is paid and the pet is not removed; the legislation also allows the landlord to give the tenant rules about pets.[100] Northwest Territories creates "pet security deposits" with authority to terminate a tenancy where the obligation to pay it has been breached; it also creates inspection powers when a tenant acquires a pet.[101] Other provinces do not have specific provisions with respect to pets, but the general provisions addressing impairment of safety, interference with reasonable use and enjoyment, and damage to the premises could apply to pets, in the manner discussed above in respect of Ontario.

While a blind old cat inspired substantial legislative change in the residential tenancies context, this did not protect a blind old dog living in a rental unit within a condominium. In *Metropolitan Toronto Condominium Corp No 949 v Irvine*,[102] a sixteen-year-old deaf, blind poodle named Mickey was living with a couple in a condominium apartment. The tenancy agreement included a "no pets" clause and the condominium's declaration prohibited pets in the building. The "no pets" clause was unenforceable pursuant to the *Landlord and Tenant Act*,[103] which was in Part IV of the Act, and section 80 provided that Part IV of the Act took precedence over any other Act or agreement to the contrary. The court held that section 108 prohibited an order "based on the provisions of an agreement." However, the condominium corporation sought its remedy on the basis of the declaration legislatively authorized under the *Condominium Act*.[104] The declaration was registered on the creation of a condominium corporation and could prohibit pets. Pursuant to its provisions, a lessee was also subject to the duties imposed by the declaration. Mickey was ordered to go.[105]

---

98  *Residential Tenancy Act*, SBC 2002, c 78, s 18.

99  *Ibid*, ss 18 and 23, respectively.

100  *Residential Tenancies Act*, CCSM c R119, ss 29.1, 29.2, and 95(3)–(5).

101  *Residential Tenancies Act*, RSNWT 1988, c R-5, ss 14.1, 14.2, and 15.

102  (1992), 24 RPR (2d) 140 (Ont Ct Gen Div), aff'd (1994), 42 RPR (2d) 319 (Ont CA).

103  RSO 1990, c L.7, s 108 (since replaced by the *Residential Tenancies Act, 2006*, above note 91).

104  RSO 1990, c C.26, since replaced by *Condominium Act, 1998*, SO 1998, c 19.

105  While this decision was upheld by the Court of Appeal, the case might be made that a declaration is an agreement; for example, a mortgagee, if any, must consent to the terms of the declaration. There is other Court of Appeal jurisprudence which strongly implies that a declaration is not a unilateral document but an agreement with owners of the units which cannot be unilaterally altered; see

Mickey generated as much media attention as Fluffy did; callers to radio shows offered to adopt him, many decried the apparent harshness of evicting a deaf, blind poodle near the end of his life. However, the publicity did not lead to legislative amendments in the condominium context, and there has been much litigation regarding pets in condominiums, particularly in Ontario and British Columbia, but also in other jurisdictions.

The difference lies in the different settings. Condominiums are seen as a unique kind of living arrangement where unit owners, who are entitled to the benefits of property ownership, have at the same time chosen to make their home in a specific kind of community setting. As a result, courts have taken a deferential approach to the community's choices, allowing the community to decide their own living arrangements and enforcing their expectations. To date, courts have not seen fit to subordinate the rights and expectations of condominium unit owners to those of tenants. However, even within the framework of the governing condominium legislation, issues arise regarding the validity of the condominium's administration and there is room for interpretation.

One Ontario court resolved a case similar to Mickey's in a different manner. In *215 Glenridge Ave Ltd Partnership v Waddington*,[106] a tenant with two cats in a condominium unit signed an agreement that included an unenforceable pet prohibition, and the condominium prohibited pets, both in its declaration and its rules. The court dismissed the landlord's application under the *Condominium Act, 1998* for an order removing the cats, finding that the no-pets rule contravened section 58(1) of the Act which allows prohibitions of pets only if they compromise safety, security, or the welfare of unit owners, or if they unreasonably interfere with the use and enjoyment of common elements.

This case has been criticized in that the court appears not to have considered that the prohibition was also contained in the condominium's declaration,[107] however, the condominium owner did not appeal the decision. When the condominium corporation later instituted new proceed-

---

*Re Carleton Condominium Corporation No 279 and Rochon* (1987), 59 OR (2d) 545 (CA).

106  (2005), 75 OR (3d) 46 (SCJ).

107  Audrey M Loeb, *Condominium Law and Administration*, 2d ed, loose-leaf (Toronto: Thomson Canada Limited, 1989–, 2006 supplement), vol 3 at 3–30.5. Loeb and James have also supported the finding that a condominium's rules cannot contain an outright prohibition on pets, and a prohibition should properly be in the declaration.

ings for the same relief, they were dismissed as an abuse of process and the dismissal was unanimously upheld by the Court of Appeal.[108]

When it comes to resolving a pet issue in a condominium, the matter will therefore largely depend on whether the requirement sought to be enforced is contained in the condominium's declaration, bylaws, or rules. The declaration is sometimes called the building's constitution. It is registered when the corporation is created and it generally takes a large majority of owners to agree to amend it. Bylaws are rules that are not as entrenched, and they are often subject to reasonableness and other limitations which expose them to challenges to which the declaration is not subject.

Where declarations prohibit keeping pets, or limit the number of pets that can be kept in a unit, or their size, they are generally enforced, even where owners claim a lack of knowledge of the prohibition or that they were assured by a realtor or others that pets were permitted.[109] The underlying notion is that owners of a condominium unit are entitled to rely on the declaration and if a particular unit owner has been misinformed, he can take appropriate legal action against the source of misinformation to recover his losses. The value of the human-animal relationship has not yet been tested in this context to determine whether recoverable costs could include moving to a location where pets are permitted, or whether such costs would be considered unreasonable, and the person would be expected to remove the dog.

Exceptions to the general enforceability of provisions in the declaration have arisen, such as where a cat had resided in a unit for more than ten years, with the knowledge of representatives of the condominium corporation, and where enforcement of the prohibition had only recently been stepped up;[110] where an 85-year-old deaf woman relied on her dog to enable her to function, even though the condominium corporation had refused, after being asked to amend the declaration to permit the woman to have her dog;[111] and where unit owners swore that they were not aware of the prohibition, and had not received a copy of

---

108  *Niagara North Condominium Corp No 125 v Waddington*, 2007 ONCA 184.
109  For example: *Peel Condominium Corp No 449 v Hogg* (1997), 8 RPR (3d) 145 (Ont Ct Gen Div); *Peel Condominium Corp No 338 v Young*, 1996 CarswellOnt 1232, additional reasons at 1996 CarswellOnt 1522 (Ont Ct Gen Div); *York Condominium Corp No 585 v Gilbert*, 1990 CarswellOnt 2929 (Ont Dist Ct); *Peel Condominium Corp No 78 v Harthen* (1978), 20 OR (2d) 225 (Co Ct).
110  *Metropolitan Toronto Condominium Corp No 949 v Staib*, 2005 CarswellOnt 6959 (CA), leave to appeal to SCC refused, 2006 CarswellOnt 2060 (SCC).
111  *Waterloo North Condominium Corp No 198 v Donner* (1997), 36 OR (3d) 243 (Gen Div).

the proposed declaration when they signed the agreement of purchase and sale, the court exercised its broad discretion in regard to ordering performance of a duty, and ordered they could keep their dogs but not replace them or add any more.[112]

While the language varies by province, bylaws and rules are generally subject to "reasonableness" requirements and have been challenged with varying degrees of success. In *Halifax County Condominium Corp No 21 v Savage*,[113] keeping pets was described as a right incidental to ownership and a bylaw that prohibited all pets was beyond the powers of the corporation. By contrast, in *Condominium Plan No 8810455 v Spectral Capital Corp*,[114] a "no pets" bylaw was reasonable and enforceable against an owner whose real estate agent had told her pets were allowed, and who had not looked at the bylaws herself though she had been given a copy.

In *York Condominium Corp No 382 v Dvorchik*,[115] the condominium's rules prohibited pets over twenty-five pounds. The unit owners had a wheaten terrier who had been the "runt of the litter," however, she gained weight, and when she reached thirty-two pounds, the condominium corporation sought to have her removed. Its application was initially unsuccessful as the rule was found to be unreasonable given the lack of evidence that dogs over the weight limit were any more of a threat to safety, security, or welfare of other owners than smaller dogs. However, the Court of Appeal allowed an appeal, finding that a court should not substitute its own opinion about the propriety of a rule enacted by a board unless it was clearly unreasonable or contrary to the legislative scheme. This case has been said to have shifted the onus, at least in Ontario, where previously it had been up to the corporation to defend the reasonableness of a challenged rule and now the individual unit owner must prove the rule is unreasonable.[116] Still, there is more room for courts to exercise their discretion to allow pets to stay in apparent contravention when it is a rule or bylaw being challenged, rather than a provision in the declaration.[117]

---

112  *York Condominium Corp No 228 v McDougall* (19 July 1978) (Ont Co Ct), cited in Loeb, above note 107 at 3-25–3-26.
113  1983 CarswellNS 263 (TD).
114  (1990), 14 RPR (2d) 305 (Alta QB).
115  (1992), 24 RPR (2d) 19 (Ont Ct Gen Div), rev'd (1997), 12 RPR (3d) 148 (CA).
116  Loeb, above note 107 at 4-46–4-47.
117  For example, *Metropolitan Toronto Condominium Corp No 601 v Hadbavny* (2001), 48 RPR (3d) 159 (Ont SCJ); note the case refers to "by-laws" but it was a rule at issue.

Human rights issues arise with respect to animals on whom persons with disabilities rely. It is generally the case that where there is reliable medical evidence confirming both the disability and the dependence on the animal, a prohibition against keeping the animal is not enforceable, either in a rental unit or in a condominium. A leading case in this area is *Niagara North Condominium Corp No 46 v Chassie*.[118] However, in declining to follow that case, the British Columbia Human Rights Tribunal found that there was no evidence that British Columbia had reached the same consensus that Ontario had about the value of pets. It dismissed the complaint of a tenant in social housing who had two small dogs. He had fibromyalgia, depression, and hearing loss, and claimed the dogs helped him with feelings of social isolation. The Tribunal found a lack of sufficient evidence linking the disabilities with the accommodation requested.[119]

Human rights law has also allowed a person to have a pet outside the disability context. In *Campbell v Yukon Housing Corp*, the Board held that precluding low-income tenants in subsidized housing from having pets while market rent tenants could have them was based on the assumption that members of the class would not meet their obligations, and this was systemic discrimination.[120]

## 2) Family Law: Disputes over Custody of the Animal

Animals are also beginning to appear more commonly in family law cases and they create an unusual problem because of the competing concepts of property and companionship that they engage. As the caselaw develops, some courts seem to be more comfortable importing notions of custody and best interests into consideration than others, but none has made these a clear priority to date.[121]

---

118  (1999), 173 DLR (4th) 524 (Ont Ct Gen Div). Some provinces' human rights legislation specifically addresses what it refers to as "service animals"; in others, the claim would rely on the general prohibition against discrimination on the basis of disability with respect to accommodations. This subject has the potential to engage competing interests between members of protected groups inasmuch as some people have disabilities which require them to live in an animal-free environment, see *Sakellariou v Strata Plan VR 4136*, 2009 BCHRT 289.

119  *Strumecki v Capital Regional Housing Corp*, 2005 BCHRT 386. Similarly, in the condominium context, see *Niagara North Condominium Corp No 125 v Kinslow*, 2007 CarswellOnt 7444 (SCJ).

120  (2005), 56 CHRR D/151 (Y Bd Adj).

121  For a full discussion of the legal issues that arise in the Ontario context, see Sandra J Meyrick, "Dog Files: Pets, Animals and the Family Law Act" in Bisgould, above note 31 at Tab 5, 5B-1.

In the early case of *Rogers v Rogers*,[122] the Ontario District Court began by observing that it is beyond question that a pet is a personal chattel and subject of absolute property. It considered how the chattel was ordinarily used and enjoyed by the respective spouses as a family asset. It also found that the welfare and best interests of the animal are a factor to consider, noting that a dog has feelings and must be treated humanely with all due care and attention to the dog's needs. However, these were not the primary considerations as in child custody disputes. The court compared the matter to disputes regarding any "work of art, antique piece of furniture or heirloom that spouses wish to keep, preserve and enjoy . . . ."[123] On the other hand, unlike works of art, the spouse to whom custody was not granted, was granted alternating weekend possession.

Similarly, in *Ridgeway-Firman v Firman*,[124] the court granted the wife's motion for interim relief including the return of two dogs on the basis that the child was entitled to have the comfort of the two dogs. In *Gauvin v Schaeffer*,[125] a couple separated and the husband claimed that a dog they had purchased during the marriage was his sole property. The court found that the generic separation agreement clause dealing with division of personal property applied to the dog and ordered that the dog "be distributed equally" between the former spouses.[126] In *Judge v Judge*,[127] the wife took the children and the cats when the parties separated. She commenced a new relationship with a partner who was allergic to cats. Rather than give the cats to her former husband, she gave them up. The husband had pleaded poverty to limit his child support obligations, so the wife claimed he did not have the economic means to care for the cats. The court rejected the husband's claim for possession, finding that the wife was not acting spitefully, that she had a greater proprietary right to the cats and her actions were governed by what she thought was their best interests.[128]

In *Gardiner-Simpson v Cross*,[129] a former couple came to court after shared ownership of their dog was unsuccessful. The court was sympathetic to their predicament, noting that the love that humans can develop for their pets is no trivial matter, "and the loss of a pet can be

---

122 [1980] OJ No 2229 (Dist Ct).
123 *Ibid* at paras 18 and 26–29.
124 [1999] OJ No 1477 (Gen Div).
125 2003 SKQB 78.
126 *Ibid* at paras 12 & 13.
127 [1998] OJ No 1792 (Gen Div).
128 *Ibid* at para 14.
129 2008 NSSM 78.

as heartbreaking as the loss of any loved one."[130] Emotions notwith-
standing, the court noted that the law continues to regard animals as
personal property and that are no special laws for pets as there are for
children. Laws that prohibit cruelty to animals do not dictate that an
animal should be raised by the person who loves the animal more or
would provide a better home environment. As such, "slightly distasteful as it may be," the issue had to be decided on the basis of who had
the better property claim.[131]

In *Warnica v Gering*,[132] a man sought access to a dog that a couple
had bought during their relationship. The court found that pure property law principles were insufficient to resolve the dispute. A pet does
not lend itself to physical division and few would want to sell the animal
with the proceeds to be divided equally. A pet could be shared, however,
the court did not think it appropriate to be "in the business of making custody orders for pets, disguised or otherwise."[133] The court observed that while pets are of great importance to human beings, they are
not children and the dispute should not occupy more of the court's or
the parties' resources than it merited.[134] It ordered that the dog remain
with the woman. The Court of Appeal for Ontario dismissed the appeal,
unanimously agreeing that the case was a waste of the court's time.[135]

The Saskatchewan Court of Queen's Bench was more scathing in
its criticism of the resources wasted in an animal custody dispute. In
*Ireland v Ireland*,[136] a separated couple had been able to agree on all
issues relating to family property except for the family dog. The court
saw the dispute as an "unacceptable waste of these parties' financial
resources, the time and abilities of their very experienced and capable
legal counsel and most importantly the public resource of this Court."[137]
Stating that a dog is a dog, it dismissed any notion that principles that a
court might apply to child custody disputes should be applicable to the
disposition of a pet. It refused to establish any principles at all in adjudicating on the issue, for fear that doing so may invite further applications, and resolved the matter on pure property principles, ordering
that the dog would be the exclusive property of the wife, who had to
pay half of the dog's purchase price to the husband.

---

130  *Ibid* at para 3.
131  *Ibid* at para 5.
132  [2004] OJ No 5396 (SCJ).
133  *Ibid* at paras 18–19.
134  *Ibid* at paras 19–20.
135  *Warnica v Gering*, [2005] OJ No 3655 at paras 5 & 6 (CA).
136  2010 SKQB 454.
137  *Ibid* at para 9.

The resentment some courts have expressed about resolving disputes over animals stands in stark contradiction to the accepted use of resources for resolving disputes over all sorts of inanimate property. Under the pressure of increasing demand, courts will have to develop a principled approach to animal disputes that better reflects modern sentiment. The language that some courts have already begun to import will enable them to do it.

## 3)  Estates Law: Caring for Animals after Death

When American hotelier Leona Helmsley died in 2007, there was much ado about the $12 million trust fund established in her will for her dog, Trouble. In litigation initiated by disgruntled relatives, the trust was undone and most of the money was awarded to two grandsons who had been disinherited on the basis that their grandmother was not of sound mind when she created the trust agreement. Two million dollars remained in trust for Trouble, who was taken in by the general manager of a Helmsley hotel.[138]

When author Dorothy Parker was found dead in her Manhattan apartment in 1967, her little dog C'est Tout was found whimpering beside her. Parker had left the bulk of her estate to a charity. She had made no provision for C'est Tout, who was taken to the local pound and never heard of again.[139]

Increasingly, people are interested in providing for animals after their deaths, whether allocating a portion of their estate to organizations that help animals generally, or for the benefit of specific animals. The former is uncomplicated enough in terms of established legal principles, while the latter has distinct complications. In the United States, the law is more developed,[140] while in Canada, there is a lack of legislation dealing with pets in the context of estate planning, particularly making clear provision for the creation of trusts.[141]

The law distinguishes between making provisions for many animals, which is seen as a community benefit and therefore charitable,

---

138  Barry Seltzer & Gerry W Beyer, *Fat Cats & Lucky Dogs: How to Leave (Some of) Your Estate to Your Pet* (Delray Beach, FL: Prism, 2010) at vii–ix [Seltzer & Beyer].

139  *Ibid* at xv.

140  See Gary W Beyer, "Pet Animals: What Happens When Their Humans Die?" (1999–2000) 40 Santa Clara L Rev 617, and online: www.animallaw.info/articles/arus40sanclr617.htm.

141  Laura M Tyrrell, "Estate Planning for Pets" in Bisgould, above note 31, Tab 5 at 5A1. The discussion in this section is a summary of the issues discussed more fully in that paper at 5A-7–5A-10.

and providing for a specific individual, which is neither.[142] Here again, the conflict between property and non-property interests in animals is manifest. Because a pet is property, she cannot be a direct beneficiary of an estate. The essence of property is that it has no rights and in particular, no right to own property. Therefore, if a person leaves a portion of her estate directly to an animal, the gift will not be upheld. On the other hand, animal property can itself be bequeathed, and the person to whom an animal is bequeathed becomes the owner of the animal with all attendant rights, including the right to sell, give away, or kill the animal. If a person dies intestate, the pet passes to the next of kin like other property in accordance with provincial law.[143]

While a person to whom an animal is bequeathed may choose to kill him, a provision in a will directing a trustee to do so might not be upheld. In a notorious New Brunswick case, *Re Wishart Estate*,[144] the deceased directed that his four horses, Barney, Bill, Jack, and King, be shot by the Royal Canadian Mounted Police after his death. When the will was challenged, the lawyer who had prepared it testified that Wishart loved the horses and the purpose of the direction was to ensure they would not be abused when he was not there to care for them.

The court cited literary passages concerning the high regard in which horses have always been held. It noted strong public objection across the country to killing these horses, that many qualified persons had offered to care for them, and that the New Brunswick SPCA had offered to ensure they were properly placed and cared for.[145] The court finally held that it could not decide on the basis of sentiment or public opinion, but legal principles. To destroy healthy animals "for no useful purpose" would benefit nobody and be a waste of resources and estate assets, therefore, the horses became the property of the residuary beneficiaries of the estate. Practically, however, the length of the decision, the issues covered by the court, and the specific orders it made with respect to the welfare of the horses all suggest that the court's concern exceeded the traditional legal principles by which it felt itself constrained.

Creating a trust for a pet raises a variety of issues that have not been directly addressed in Canadian law. An Ontario estates lawyer has posited that a trust for a pet would likely be characterized as a non-

---

142  *Granfield Estate v Jackson* (1999), 27 ETR (2d) 50 (BCSC).

143  Tyrell, above note 141 at 5A-2.

144  1992 CanLII 2679 (NBQB).

145  In anticipation of the next chapter in this book, it bears noting that the court further observed that had the subject animals been pigs, they would not have drawn the same opposition.

charitable purpose trust.[146] At common law, a non-charitable purpose trust is unenforceable and invalid because there is no ascertainable beneficiary who can enforce it and because it violates the rules against perpetuities[147] and indefinite duration.[148] American courts have found pet trusts to be invalid on the basis the trust is intended to last for the duration of the pet's life. While that life is, in most cases, unlikely to exceed twenty-one years, the courts have found that the life to be measured for purposes of determining the perpetuity period must be a human life.[149] However, Canadian legislation modifies these rules in the context of non-charitable purpose trusts. In Ontario, for example, a trust for a specific non-charitable purpose is valid if it takes effect within twenty-one years of the testator's death and it is possible that a pet trust could be upheld pursuant to this provision.[150]

A nineteenth-century British case, which appears to remain good law,[151] upheld a trust created for pets, finding it to be an exception against the general rule against non-charitable purpose trusts. In *Re Dean*,[152] the deceased directed his trustee to pay £750 annually to look after his horses and hounds, for the animals' lifetimes but not longer than fifty years. Because the trust was for specific animals, and not for the benefit of animals generally, it was non-charitable. Because it had no human beneficiaries, but directed a trustee to apply money for a specific purpose, it was a purpose trust. While the trust had no beneficiary with capacity to enforce it, the court found it was valid.

Because of the manner in which pet trusts have been found to be invalid in the United States, many states have passed specific legislation allowing for them to be created.[153] Until there is clarity in Canada, experts have posited that a trust might be created naming an appointed caregiver as the beneficiary,[154] or that a pet can be bequeathed to a caregiver with

---

146  Tyrell, above note 141.
147  The rule against perpetuities provides that an interest in a will must best within twenty-one years of the testator's death, or within twenty-one years of a life in being at the time the interest is created.
148  The rule against indefinite duration provides that an interest is not valid if it lasts beyond the perpetuity period.
149  Christine Cave, "Trusts: Monkeying Around With Our Pets' Futures: Why Oklahoma Should Adopt a Pet-Trust Statute" (2002) 55 Okla L Rev 627.
150  *Perpetuities Act*, RSO 1990, c P.9, s 16.
151  Tyrell, above note 141 at 5A-8–5A-9.
152  (1889), 41 Ch D 552; cited in Tyrell, *ibid* at 5A-8.
153  Tyrell, *ibid* at 5A-9.
154  *Ibid* at 5A-10. The theory is that the trust would be valid because of the caregiver's ability to enforce it. The rule against perpetuity could be addressed by making the trust valid for the length of the caregiver's life plus twenty-one

a specific gift.[155] As in other areas, law will have to evolve to respond to growing pressures. Taking the best interests of the animals themselves into account seems a natural extension of established principles. If an animal were a legal person, the establishment of a trust on her behalf would fit even more neatly within those established principles.

---

years, ending earlier if the animal died within that time. The testator would bequeath the animal to a trustee, in trust, under instruction to deliver the animal to the caregiver, and specify a gift to be set aside for the caregiver's benefit. Payments could be payable on terms, such as allowing for period inspection to ensure the caregiver was taking proper care of the animal.

155  See also Seltzer & Beyer, above note 138.

# CHAPTER 6

# FOOD

Laws, like sausages, cease to inspire respect in proportion as we know how they are made.

—John Godfrey Saxe, American poet, *The Daily Cleveland Herald*, 1869

In *R v Dudley and Stephens*,[1] the necessity defence was rejected in the case of two sailors charged with murder after they killed and ate their companion while shipwrecked at sea; as far as the common law was concerned, no matter how dire the circumstances, it could never be legally necessary to kill another human being to sustain oneself. The subject of this chapter is the law in respect to the beings we do permit ourselves to eat. Agriculture falls under both federal and provincial jurisdiction and there is extensive legislation at both levels, in addition to industry-created recommended codes of practice. In order to understand how the laws governing this vast industry are interpreted and applied, one must have a sense of the context. In this chapter, Part A provides a brief overview of the modern industry; Part B is an overview of animal life in that industry; and Part C reviews the legislative scheme.

---

1   [1881–85] All ER 61 (QB), as discussed in the Introduction.

# A. OVERVIEW OF THE MODERN AGRICULTURE INDUSTRY

Since the Second World War, consumption of animals and animal products has become big business. In Canada, we now kill at least 700 million animals for food every year.[2] In the United States, the number is greater than 9 billion animals and globally, the meat, dairy, and egg industry kills 56 billion animals every year.[3]

Like any transformative sociological and economic development, the dramatic increase in animal consumption is attributable to a number of factors; however, the most unequivocal are the industrialization of agriculture and its partnership with the research industry. Early in the twentieth century, animal slaughter was already a highly mechanized process.[4] After the Second World War, breeding and raising animals became increasingly efficient, allowing animals to be produced on a scale that had never been seen before. "Farmers" became "producers" and Old MacDonald's farm ceased to resemble children's drawings.[5]

The availability of antibiotics allowed for the intensive confinement of animals. This brought the animals indoors, out of public view. Major corporations with no connection to agriculture, such as bus compan-

---

2   The exact number is unknown. Agriculture and Agri-Food Canada collects slaughterhouse statistics in respect of some species raised and killed on land, but not fish and other sea creatures. The 700 million number is based on 2008 statistics for hogs, cattle, calves, sheep, and lamb slaughtered in both federally and provincially inspected facilities, and poultry, including chickens, turkeys, ducks, and geese: Canadian Food Inspection Agency, compiled by Agriculture and Agri-Food Canada, online: www4.agr.gc.ca/AAFC-AAC/display-afficher. do?id=1177676316971&lang=eng.

3   See 2007 statistics collected by Food and Agriculture Organization of the United Nations' Global Livestock Production and Health Atlas, online: http://kids.fao.org/glipha (enter theme: Livestock population).

4   Upton Sinclair's 1906 novel, *The Jungle* (New York: Bantam Books, 1981), alerted readers to the brutal conditions for both workers and animals in the turn-of-the-century Chicago stockyards. Their methods inspired Henry Ford in his conception of the assembly line production of cars. The novel is thought to have been a factor which led to the United States' first meat inspection legislation, and the development of the Bureau of Chemistry, which became the Food and Drug Administration.

5   Thousands of pigs can be kept in a single building; at least 15,000 pigs living in one building in Alberta were killed in a fire: "Massive Blaze at Cluny Hutterite Colony" *ctvcalgary.ca* (1 August 2009), online: http://calgary.ctv.ca/servlet/an/ local/CTVNews/20090801/CGY_pig_fire_090801/NFL. Egg producers keep an average of anywhere from approximately 11,000 layers (Alberta) to 50,000 (Newfoundland and Labrador), and the number is growing: Egg Farmers of Canada, *2010 Annual Report* (Ottawa: Egg Farmers of Canada, 2011) at 25.

ies, life insurance companies, and oil companies, became the owners or part owners of farming operations, thereby gaining tax concessions and diversifying their profits. Living animals began to be regarded as machines that convert low-priced fodder into flesh. Growth hormones made them grow bigger and faster and continuing innovations have sought an ever more efficient conversion ratio.[6] Across North America, small producers have had to adopt modern methods, establish a niche, or go out of business. There continue to be family farms in Canada, but they are much like the belugas of the St. Lawrence River, polluted by the effluent of mega-corporations and headed for an unpleasant death.[7]

Globally, the industrialization of agriculture has had catastrophic[8]

---

6   Research now also includes the growing field of biotechnology. For example, biotechnology manipulates the DNA of animals like the Enviropig engineered at the University of Guelph, Ontario, so as to produce waste with less phosphorous, and AquaAdvantage Salmon, developed in Newfoundland and Prince Edward Island, engineered to grow bigger and faster.

7   To note an exception, as people begin to learn about and respond to the harms of industrialized agriculture, a small but apparently growing movement seeks to return to more local and sustainable organic farming. As subsidies and tax incentives continue to favour large, factory operations, the long-term fate of the new wave of family farms remains precarious.

8   Approximately 1.5 billion cows populate the earth, occupying nearly one quarter of the planet's landmass. The population is destroying natural habitat and interrupting ecosystems on six continents. Herding is a primary factor in the destruction of the world's remaining tropical rain forests. Millions of acres of ancient forest in Central and South America are felled and cleared to make room for pastureland to graze cows for richer nations. Herding is responsible for much of the spreading desertification in sub-Saharan Africa and western rangelands in the United States and Australia. Runoff from feedlots is a major source of pollution and a serious threat to water safety. Cows are a major source of global warming, emitting methane gas, which prevents heat from escaping the Earth's atmosphere. The list goes on.

See Jonathan Safran Foer, *Eating Animals* (New York: Little, Brown and Co, 2009); Jeffrey Moussaieff Masson, *The Face on Your Plate: The Truth About Food* (New York: WW Norton & Company, 2009); Food and Agriculture Organization of the United Nations, *Livestock's Long Shadow: Environmental Issues and Options* by Henning Steinfeld (Rome: Food and Agriculture Organization of the United Nations, 2006); Erik Marcus, *Meat Market: Animals, Ethics, and Money* (Minneapolis: Brio Press, 2005); Stuart Laidlaw, *Secret Ingredients: The Brave New World of Industrial Farming* (Toronto: McClelland & Stewart, 2004); Eric Schlosser, *Fast Food Nation: The Dark Side of the All-American Meal* (New York: Houghton Mifflin, 2001); Howard F Lyman with Glen Merzer, *Mad Cowboy: Plain Truth from the Cattle Rancher Who Won't Eat Meat* (New York: Touchstone, 1998) [Lyman & Merzer]; Jeremy Rifkin, *Beyond Beef: The Rise and Fall of the Cattle Culture* (New York: Penguin Books, 1992); Orville Schell, *Modern Meat: Antibiotics, Hormones, and the Pharmaceutical Farm* (New York: Vintage Books, 1985); Mark Gold, *Assault and Battery: What Factory Farming Means for Humans*

results for the environment and for human health and security.[9] Intermittent crises bring aspects of these practices to light in Canada. In 2000, E. coli from manure that had been spread on a farm entered a nearby well and contaminated the water supply of Walkerton, Ontario, killing seven people and making 2,300 sick.[10] Bovine spongiform encephalopathy (BSE), or mad cow disease, caused by feeding vegetarian cows the parts of other cows, emerged in Alberta in 2003 and several more times in subsequent years. The disease sickened several Canadians and killed dozens of cows; thousands more cows were preemptively killed to prevent its spread.[11] In 2004, the Canadian Food Inspection Agency (CFIA) ordered 19 million birds to be killed to control the avian influenza found in British Columbia.[12]

When these crises arise, beyond the human health issues, the central matter of public concern becomes the financial losses of the industry

---

and Animals (London: Pluto, 1983); and Jim Mason & Peter Singer, Animal Factories (New York: Crown Publishers,1980).

9   In developing countries, millions of people are pushed off their ancestral lands to make room for the conversion of farmland from local, subsistence grain production to commercial animal feed. Half of the world's grain harvest is fed to animals while more than one billion people live with chronic hunger and malnutrition. In the industrialized world, people die from diseases that are partially or directly caused by eating too much grain-fed animal flesh and other animal products. The human food and water supply are contaminated by antibiotics and growth hormones, which are consumed when people eat drugged animals or use the water into which the farm's effluent has entered. Antibiotic resistant superbugs arise from the indiscriminate overuse of low-dose drugs in farmed animals. The list goes on.

   See references, ibid, and Vandana Shiva, Stolen Harvest: The Hijacking of the Global Food Supply (Cambridge, MA: South End Press, 2000) and Biopiracy: the Plunder of Nature and Knowledge (Boston: South End Press, 1997).

10   Honourable Dennis R O'Connor, Report of the Walkerton Inquiry: The Events of May 2000 and Related Issues (Toronto: Ontario Ministry of the Attorney General, 2002) at 2–6.

11   Variant Creutzfeld-Jakob Disease, Current Data, National Creutzfeldt-Jakob Disease Surveillance Unit, University of Edinburgh (March 2011), online: www.cjd.ed.ac.uk/vcjdworld.htm. Bovine spongiform encephalopathy is the disease in animals; Creutzfeldt-Jakob disease is the disease in humans. Specific numbers are difficult to confirm and thought to be underestimated because of the disease's long incubation period.

12   See Karen Davis, "The Avian Flu Crisis in Canada: Ethics of Farmed-Animal Disease Control" (Keynote presentation at Two Days of Thinking About Animals in Canada, Brock University, St Catharines, Ontario, 25 February 2005), online: www.upc-online.org/slaughter/22805karenflu.htm; and Vancouver Humane Society, "A Gentle and Easy Death? An Examination of Animal Welfare Issues during the 2004 Avian Influenza Outbreak in British Columbia" (January 2005), online: www.vancouverhumanesociety.bc.ca/downloads/reports/AvianFlu.pdf.

itself. More than $1 billion in aid was paid to cattle ranchers and other animal producers as a result of BSE[13] and the litigation that arose was concerned with a range of issues, all economic.[14] Very little debate took place concerning the practices which caused these crises in the first place, or about whether they should be changed. Nor was there much discussion about the suffering that a disease like BSE causes to cows, or of the certain violence in the mass slaughter of millions of confined birds.

Democratic debate about the degree to which a society supports particular activities requires a regular stream of accurate information, but it is difficult to obtain information from Canadian authorities about farming practices under the *Access to Information Act*.[15] When Canada's Information Commissioner released its Report Card in April 2010, it gave the CFIA a "D" for not meeting its obligations under the Act,[16] and the Canadian Association of Journalists awarded the CFIA its Code of Silence Award in 2008 for "its dizzying efforts to stop the public from learning details of fatal failures in food safety."[17]

---

13    "Mad Cow in Canada: The Science and the Story" *CBS News Online* (24 August 2006), online: www.cbc.ca/news/background/madcow/.

14    *Hunt Farms Ltd v Canada (Minister of Agriculture)*, [1994] 2 FC 625 (CA): appeal of a decision refusing an interlocutory injunction concerning the alleged "wrongful slaughter" of animals in reaction to the mad cow threat; *Kohl v Canada (Department of Agriculture)*, [1995] FCJ No 1076 (CA): application for judicial review of the decision of the minister of agriculture ordering the destruction of the applicant's bulls to aid in eliminating the threat of the disease spreading; *Sauer v Canada (AG)*, 2007 ONCA 454: defendants' unsuccessful effort to strike parts of a class action started by an Ontario cattle farmer on behalf of 100,000 commercial cattle farmers in seven provinces, alleging negligence and negligent regulation; certification of the class was addressed in *Sauer v Canada (Agriculture)*, 2008 CanLII 43774 (Ont SCJ). Similarly, see *Bernèche c Canada (PG)*, 2007 QCCS 2945. BSE was also a factor in a family law case, affecting the valuation of a ranch: *Swaren v Swaren*, 2007 ABQB 193 at para 77; and in an income tax case, where the profitability of a farming operation was found to have been adversely affected by BSE: *Gunn v Canada*, 2006 FCA 281 at para 12.

15    RSC 1985, c A-1.

16    Office of the Information Commissioner of Canada, *Out of Time: Special Report to Parliament 2008–2009 Systemic Issues Affecting Access to Information in Canada* (Ottawa: Office of the Information Commissioner of Canada, April 2010) at 81–84.

17    Canadian Association of Journalists, "Canadian Food Inspection Agency Wins CAJ Secrecy Award" (23 May 2009), online: www.newswire.ca/en/releases/archive/May2009/24/c7044.html. See also World Society for the Protection of Animals, "Curb the Cruelty: Canada's Farm Animal Transport System in Need of Repair" (2010), online: www.wspa.ca/ati/CurbtheCrueltyReport.pdf at 6 [WSPA Report]. The WSPA describes its efforts to obtain copies of CFIA reports used to assess compliance with animal transport regulations under the *Health of Animals Act*. It took almost a year to receive any of the requested files and some of the reports it finally received were incomplete or illegible, while others appeared to be missing.

In the United States, the problem of ensuring there is sufficient information in the public realm to sustain an informed discussion is magnified. Food disparaging laws, of which Oprah Winfrey learned first hand,[18] prohibit the criticism of agricultural products.[19] Recent bills in four states proposed making it illegal to record images or sounds of a farming operation, even from off the property, without the owner's consent.[20] Whether these prefigure Canadian initiatives to come remains to be seen, but some indications are already apparent, such as the passage in every province of right-to-farm legislation which, like its American equivalents, protects farming operations from nuisance actions arising from "normal" or "acceptable" farming practices.[21]

---

18  In 1998, Oprah Winfrey and her guest, former cattle rancher Howard Lyman, were sued by a feedlot operator after Lyman appeared on the show discussing beef production in relation to the mad-cow scare. Oprah famously declared that she had eaten her last burger. The feedlot operator sued, claiming a loss of more than $12 million, alleging that Lyman and Winfrey's statements were not based on reliable facts. A jury eventually rejected the claim. However, Oprah did not speak publicly on the issue thereafter and she has declined to make videotapes of the original interview available to inquiring journalists. She and Lyman were able to access legal representation that would likely be beyond the means of other critics. See Sheldon Rampton & John Stauber, *Mad Cow USA: Could the Nightmare Happen Here?* (Monroe, ME: Common Courage Press, 1997) at 192 [Rampton & Stauber]; and Lyman & Merzer, above note 8 at 15.

19  This type of law exists in at least thirteen states. They vary, but typically allow a food manufacturer or processor to sue anyone who makes a disparaging comment about their products. Many of these laws establish a lower standard of proof, and in some states, the onus is shifted entirely to the defendant. Many allow for punitive damages and legal fees for plaintiffs alone, regardless of the outcome. For a list of and links to these statutes see online: Coalition for Free Speech: Food Speech cspinet.org/foodspeak/laws/existlaw.htm. For a history of these laws, see Rampton & Stauber, *ibid* at 17–24 and 137–45.

20  The bills failed, narrowly in some cases: Florida: SB 1246; Iowa: HF 431 and HF 589; Minnesota: HF 1369 and SF 118; and New York: S 5172-2011. For discussion and links to further information, see Simon Fodden, "U.S. Farm Bills: Don't Look, Don't Tell" Slaw (7 July 2011), online: www.slaw.ca/2011/07/07/u-s-farm-bills-dont-look-dont-tell.

21  Alberta: *Agricultural Operation Practices Act*, RSA 2000, c A-7, Part 1; British Columbia: *Farm Practices Protection (Right to Farm) Act*, RSBC 1996, c 131; Manitoba: *Farm Practices Protection Act*, CCSM c F45; New Brunswick: *Agricultural Operations Practices Act*, SNB 1999, c A-5.3; Newfoundland and Labrador: *Farm Practices Protection Act*, SNL 2001, c F-4.1; Nova Scotia: *Farm Practices Act*, SNS 2000, c 3; Ontario: *Farming and Food Production Protection Act, 1988*, SO 1998, c 1; Prince Edward Island: *Farm Practices Act*, RSPEI 1988, c F-4.1; Quebec: *An Act Respecting the Preservation of Agricultural Land and Agricultural Activities*, RSQ c P-41.1; and Saskatchewan: *Agricultural Operations Act*, SS 1995, c A-12.1

# B. OVERVIEW OF ANIMAL LIFE IN INDUSTRIAL AGRICULTURE

Lack of progress in ameliorating our treatment of nonhumans is attributable to several causes, many of which may be traced to people's ignorance about the animal abuse that they themselves indirectly support. The ultimate consumer of the veal, pork, chicken and eggs simply has no more conception of what went on before these neatly packaged farm products arrived at the retail level than the purchasers of Civil War clothing had of the conditions under which enslaved black hands planted and picked the cotton from which its threads were made.[22]

Every year, between 2 and 3 million animals arrive at Canadian slaughterhouses already dead.[23] The intensive confinement in which most animals are now reared is more than they can take. Their natural behaviours are inhibited and they live much, if not all, of their lives crowded and stressed, often sick, injured, and in pain. Pre-emptive mutilations without anaesthetic are the norm. Animals who hurt each other are a liability, and it is more economically efficient to remove part of the animal than the source of her stress. Manipulations of the animals' physiognomy in response to consumer preferences for certain kinds of meat produce deformed creatures who cannot support their own weight. Many animals only go outside to be loaded on the trucks that take them to market and slaughter. Transport itself is traumatic. From the animals' perspective, every aspect of the process raises issues to which law fails to respond. Regular practices in respect of the three animals Canadians most like to eat are summarized below.[24]

22    William M Kunstler, "Introduction" in Gary Francione, *Animals, Property and the Law* (Philadelphia: Temple University Press, 1995) at x.

23    WSPA Report, above note 17 at 11.

24    There are numerous resources discussing animals in intensive farming in the United States; for example, see above note 7. For Canada, see John Sorenson, *Animal Rights* (Black Point, NS: Fernwood, 2010) at 37–58; Charlotte Montgomery, *Blood Relations: Animals, Humans and Politics* (Toronto: Between the Lines, 2000) at 128–91 [Montgomery]; WSPA Report, *ibid*; Twyla Francois, *Broken Wings: The Breakdown of Animal Protection in the Transportation and Slaughter of Meat Poultry in Canada* (Vancouver, BC: Canadians for the Ethical Treatment of Food Animals, 2010), online: www.cetfa.com/documents/Broken%20Wings. pdf; Canadian Coalition for Farm Animals, "Gestation Stalls and the Welfare of Sows in Canada: A Summary of the Scientific Literature" (2006), online: www. vancouverhumanesociety.bc.ca/downloads/reports/SOW-GESTATION.pdf; "Battery Cages and the Welfare of Hens in Canada: A Summary of the Scientific

## 1)  Pigs

Breeding pigs live most of their lives pregnant, in crowded and noisy buildings, in individual metal "sow stalls" that are so small they cannot turn around or move forward or backward. Waste is left to collect beneath them so they are always inhaling the fumes of their own urine and feces. Babies are nursed through the bars of "farrowing crates" so as not to be crushed in the small space. After approximately two-and-a-half years, breeding productivity diminishes, and when sows are then sent to slaughter, many have pneumonia and other respiratory illnesses.

Piglets are moved to group pens. Extreme crowding causes frustration and aggression and the animals bite each other, so, without anaesthetic, they are castrated, their teeth are clipped, and their tails are cut off. The tusks of breeding boars are sometimes cut prior to transport when animals are mixed. The tusks contain nerves, and "tusk trimming"—also known as "boar bashing"—can expose the pulp that contains these nerves.

Having been confined most of their lives, pigs have leg, joint, and cardiovascular problems, making it difficult for them to climb the transport ramp when being loaded on to trucks. Federal regulations discussed below allow pigs to remain on the truck, in heat or cold, without food, water, or rest, for up to thirty-six hours. It is a federal offence to use an electric prod on a pig's face or genitals, however truck drivers have difficulty seeing what they are hitting through port holes in the sides of trailers, and pigs are routinely shocked in these sensitive areas. In addition to causing severe pain, electric prods increase the rate of "metabolic downers," animals who are too sick or weak to stand on their own, and "blood splash," heavy bruising and broken blood vessels that create dark patches in the pork people later eat.

## 2)  Cows

Modern dairy cows are expected to produce a high yield of milk. The resulting huge udder distorts their walking to such an extent that they often become lame. They commonly have mastitis, which causes swelling in the affected glands; treatment requires drawing off accumulated pus from the infected canal and the injection of antibiotics into their teats. To produce milk, cows must be in a constant cycle of pregnancy

---

Literature" (2005), online: www.vancouverhumanesociety.bc.ca/downloads/ reports/BatteryReport.pdf. See also *Bacon, the Film*, DVD, directed by Hugo Latulippe (Montreal: National Film Board of Canada, 2002); *A Cow at My Table*, VHS, directed by Jennifer Abbott (Vancouver: Flying Eye Productions, 1998).

and delivery. Mother and calf are separated within hours or days of birth. Males move into veal production and some females move into dairy herd replacement. The rest are slaughtered, the mother is artificially inseminated, and the process begins again.

Being kept crowded indoors much of the time is another source of foot damage and lameness. Dairy cows are the most common "downers," or non-ambulatory animals who are injured or diseased and unable to stand as a result of injuries such as dislocated hips, spinal injuries, hind quarter paralysis, broken bones, torn tendons and ligaments, neck and head injuries, prolapsed uteruses, milk fever, and swollen abscesses. Federal regulations allow cows, sheep, goats, and other ruminants to be in transit for more than two days without food, water, or rest. They go to slaughter by age six or seven, although out of confinement they live into their twenties.

Veal calves are separated from their mothers before they can walk and transported to a facility where they are commonly raised in individual stalls or huts, or sometimes in pens. In stalls, they are sometimes restrained by tethers that allow them to stand up and lie down, but in order to prevent tangling and choking, the tethers are not long enough to allow the animals to turn around in their stalls or move. In group pens, because calves were removed prematurely from their mothers, they tend to suck on each other's ears, tails, navels, or scrotums and this can lead to injury. Milk-fed veal, which provides the lightest colour meat, comes from calves slaughtered generally at about five months of age before their flesh gets too tough.

Both dairy and beef producers seeking to maximize output engage in such practices as "embryo transfer," which can result in cows giving birth to calves that are too large for the birth canal and cause extreme pain and injury during birth. Caesareans are common, and since a breeding cow will have several in her lifetime, these can lead to chronic abdominal pain. Cows bred for beef consumption also undergo preventative mutilations to prevent the harms done by overcrowded, frustrated animals. Most of these animals have their horns removed. The most common method of dehorning has been the use of a saw or other sharp device to cut them off, a procedure that was referred to as "excruciating torture" in a British case more than 100 years ago.[25] A newer method prevents horn growth by heat cauterization with a hot iron and chemical cauterization with caustic paste. Many males are castrated without anaesthetic by methods including a knife, crushing the spermatic cords, or cutting off the blood supply to the testicles and scrotum with a tight rubber ring.

---

25   *Ford v Wiley* (1889), 23 QB 203.

At the slaughterhouse, animals are stressed, scared, and exhausted. Many suffer bruising and internal injuries during loading and transport from blows or falls. They are moved along by way of beatings, kicks, shouting, and electric prods. They slip and fall on busy, noisy, slippery slaughterhouse floors. The regulations discussed below require animals to be stunned into unconsciousness before being bled to death, however stunning pens are also noisy and busy. If the bolt is placed incorrectly or the animal jerks her head, the stun is not effective. Either way, she is shackled by a hind leg to a conveyor and moved to the bleeding area where her throat is cut. Her heart must be beating to pump out the blood.

## 3)  Chickens

Most Canadian eggs are produced by hens in "battery cages." Laying hens are selected for high egg production and not high meat yield, so male chicks are not worth rearing. They are tossed into containers to be gassed, or drowned, or to suffocate or be crushed under the weight of chicks thrown on top of them, but commonly, they are chopped up in a high speed macerator.

At approximately eighteen weeks, female birds are put in battery cages, stacked up to eight tiers high, for the rest of their lives. In nature, hens are active, walking, running, pecking, foraging, dust-bathing, and nest-building. In intensive confinement, they stand or crouch on bare sloping wire, often suffering damage to their feet and claws. They cannot stretch their wings. The frustration of intensive confinement causes feather-pecking, vent pecking, and cannibalism, therefore their nerve-rich beaks are amputated with a hot blade or laser, often causing chronic pain. By one or two years of age, a normal hen would have produced dozens of eggs, but a battery hen has produced hundreds. She is considered "spent" and slaughtered.

Chickens destined to be eaten are slaughtered at five to seven weeks old. The extremely fast growth rate is a factor in the high levels of leg problems and chronic pain from skeletal problems that "broilers" experience. The toes of male broiler breeders are cut off or microwaved to the skin of their feet ("de-toeing"). Scissors are used to cut off their combs ("dubbing") and to remove the snood of turkeys ("de-snooding"). Often broilers have fractured legs as their limbs are not strong enough to carry their bodies. The demand for white meat and drumsticks has led to selection for unnaturally large chests and thighs. This, together with growth promoters, causes these birds to be twice as heavy at several weeks of age as full grown chickens normally are. Many develop ulcerated feet and hock burns. Toward the end of their lives, some broilers are so crippled they cannot walk.

Broilers are bred for "greediness" so that they fatten as quickly as possible. Those used for breeding, however, are kept on minimal rations that leave them hungry and pecking at empty water troughs, eating feces and litter. Drinking large quantities of water to assuage their appetites produces wet droppings and soggy litter so water supply is also sometimes restricted. The pronounced head shaking sometimes seen in breeders is thought to be caused by the stress of constant hunger and unnaturally frequent breeding.

When birds are reared together in such great numbers, proper inspection of individuals is impossible. Impacted eggs, prolapses, and disorders of the kidney and liver commonly affect battery hens. Many spent hens have malignant tumours. They are constantly exposed to high ammonia levels from their excretions and they regularly inhale toxic fumes, dust, and feathers. Dead hens can be left to decompose in cages with live hens for prolonged periods. Many dead and dying broilers also go unnoticed and decompose on the shed floor. Many die from starvation, dehydration, heat stress, or heart attacks.

Most birds are offloaded from trucks to highly mechanized and automated assembly lines where their legs are put in metal shackles and they are moved, upside down, along a conveyer belt. Their heads are dragged though a water bath charged with a low voltage electric current. When stunning is ineffective, the birds just receive painful shocks; however, when it is effective, it can cause broken bones. If the electric current is reduced so fewer bones are broken, birds might have their necks cut or miss the stunner altogether. The machine carries on to an automated knife which slits their throats but birds that are too large or small can get cut in the eyes, head, or breast. Death is supposed to occur through blood loss. Whether or not their throats are properly cut, they move on to be immersed in a scalding tank, full of boiling water, to loosen their feathers. The system is imperfect and many are still alive at the time.

## 4)  Spin-offs and Niches of the Industry

In the agricultural context, there are many related practices, each with its own nuances and legal implications. Wildlife and exotic animals are also raised for food in increasingly confined operations. *Foie gras* is made from the diseased liver of a duck or goose that has been confined and fattened by methods including force feeding. Sharks are thrown back to the sea to drown after their fins are cut off to make the shark fin soup found in Canadian restaurants. In Western provinces, pregnant horses are confined so that their urine can be collected. Estrogen is extracted from the urine and used in the manufacture of Premarin, a hormone replacement drug prescribed to women undergoing menopause; the foals are unwanted and often slaughtered.[26] Horse slaughter itself is controversial and Canada's industry is among the largest in the world.[27] Most horses slaughtered are race or workhorses no longer fit for their former burdens, or unwanted pets. The business in Canada grew dramatically after the United States prohibited slaughtering horses for food in 2007. Canada exports horse meat to Europe and Asia. Approximately 93,000 horses were killed in Canada in 2009.[28]

Agricultural uses of animals have spawned their own form of entertainment, including horse riding, horse-racing, rodeo, and Canada's notorious Calgary Stampede. The Stampede events involve dominating, scaring, stressing, hurting, and sometimes killing animals.[29] In 2010, two horses died of heart attacks, one horse's back was broken from bucking too hard, one died of health problems forty minutes after a chuckwagon race, and two others were killed after suffering injuries.[30]

---

26   The name derives from its source: pregnant mare urine. The drug was introduced in 1942 and the industry thrived for decades in Ontario until objections to catheterized mares living in horrible conditions led to licensing regulations, which eventually ended the practice in the province. It persists today in Manitoba, Saskatchewan, and Alberta. The horses are perpetually pregnant and confined in indoor stalls with bags attached to them to collect the urine. There have been many allegations concerning the poor conditions in which these horses live, including being kept dehydrated so as to increase concentration levels of estrogen. Garth S Jowett & Victoria O'Donnell, *Propaganda and Persuasion*, 4th ed (Thousand Oaks, CA: Sage Publications, 2006) at 342 and Montgomery, above note 24 at 151–53.

27   Melissa Fung, "No Country for Horses" on *CBC The National* (first aired 10 June 2008), online: www.cbc.ca/thenational/indepthanalysis/story/2009/10/01/national-horses-061008.html.

28   Barry Shlachter, "U.S. Horse Slaughter Ban a Boon to Canada, Mexico" *Ottawa Citizen* (5 July 2011); Gloria Galloway, "Protesters Call for End to Canada's Horse Slaughter" *Globe and Mail* (4 October 2010); "CBC Probe Raises Questions about Horse Slaughtering" *CBC News* (11 June 2008), online: www.cbc.ca/news/canada/story/2008/06/10/horses-slaughter.html; and Humane Society International Canada, "Horse Slaughter," online: www.hsicanada.ca/horses/horse_slaughter/.

29   Vancouver Humane Society, "The Calgary Stampede" (2011), online: www.vancouverhumanesociety.bc.ca/campaigns/the-calgary-stampede.

30   "Horse Dies During Chuckwagon Race at Calgary Stampede" *The Canadian Press* (9 July 2011), online: www.thestar.com/sports/article/1022466--horse-dies-during-chuckwagon-race-at-calgary-stampede.

If there has ever been an anti-cruelty conviction arising from a Stampede event, it is difficult to find.

# C. OVERVIEW OF THE LAW

There is voluminous regulation of this industry. However, the purpose of legislation is the key to its interpretation so, in this context, one must begin by distinguishing between laws meant to protect animals and laws meant to protect the products to be made of them. Minor aspects of the latter might have an incidental benefit to animals themselves. For example, every jurisdiction has regulatory requirements regarding adequate lighting, safe equipment, secure ramps, and so on. An animal does have an interest in walking on secure ramps. However, the impact of such regulation on animals is trivial in the context of the profound multi-faceted suffering which is an inherent part of modern agriculture.

While agricultural laws are replete with references to animals, consideration of the living creature is almost nowhere to be found. Even in the limited places where legislation purports to require humane treatment or to prohibit undue or avoidable suffering, such adjectives presuppose that some amount of suffering is due and acceptable.[31] With increasingly mechanized operations hurriedly processing 700 million animals every year, the notion of humane practices becomes absurd. These animals are brought into existence for the purpose of being killed. Some amount of beating, mutilation, intensive confinement, stress, sickness, injury, fatigue, pain, fear, and suffering is both predicted and permitted. The premature death of many animals is expected. In this context, even regulations that seem to address their welfare cannot reasonably be expected to be broadly interpreted in their favour.

Most aspects of the daily existence of these animals are not regulated in the first place. Governments have opted to defer much of their authority to standards created by the industry itself. These standards and codes of practice are referenced in some of the relevant legislation, usually more often as a defence to a charge than a positive duty. However, often they are nothing more than voluntary recommendations. In any event, if the standard is to do what everybody else in a competitive industry is doing, there is no incentive to consider the non-economic interests of the animals, which require capital outlays and reduce profits. Ironically, it is the fact that so many producers engage in these pernicious

---

31   For further discussion of the constraints within these terms, see Chapter 3.

activities that protects their legal status as "generally accepted" where such acts could otherwise attract criminal censure. The governance of this industry facilitates the infliction of the most profound privation and suffering on hundreds of millions of animals every year.

## 1)  Relevant Federal Legislation

Federal legislation applies when animals or animal products move between provinces or out of the country. Four federal statutes are engaged in respect of the treatment of animals raised for food: the *Health of Animals Act*,[32] the *Meat Inspection Act*,[33] the *Agriculture and Agri-Food Administrative Monetary Penalties Act*,[34] and the *Criminal Code* of Canada.[35]

The enforcement agency for the *Health of Animals Act* and the *Meat Inspection Act* is the Canadian Food Inspection Agency (CFIA), but it can also include police officers and designated provincial authorities. *Criminal Code* offences relating to cruelty to animals are generally enforced by agents of provincial humane societies or police.

The federal framework has been summarized as follows:

> Canada does have regulations on the transport of animals to slaughter and on what happens in the abattoirs themselves. But relentless budget cuts and a government distaste for regulation have led to limited enforcement of the rules on the treatment of live animals. Efforts to deal with recognized weaknesses in slaughterhouse or transport systems have depended upon the enthusiasm of overworked civil servants willing to buck a trend. The federal mandate appears to be a hands-off, after-the-fact sort of surveillance instead of on-site monitoring. The agriculture industry has not been the subject of shrewd government scrutiny. Instead, it has become a collection of clients for whom the rules are tailored and from whom fees are collected. For animals, that has proved a deadly attitude. The emphasis has been on cost-saving and partnership.[36]

### a)  *Health of Animals Act*
The purpose of this legislation specifically includes animal protection; its full title is "An Act respecting diseases and toxic substances that may affect animals or that may be transmitted by animals to persons,

---

32   SC 1990, c 21.
33   RSC 1985, c 25.
34   SC 1995, c 40.
35   RSC 1985, c C-46.
36   Montgomery, above note 24 at 133.

and respecting the protection of animals."[37] Most of the provisions are aimed at preventing disease or toxicity in animals that might be passed to consumers or spread among animals with financial implications for the industry. Some of these, such as the many sections dealing with cleaning, disinfecting, and maintaining a sanitary condition, might have an incidental beneficial effect on animals. However, to the extent that such regulations aim to protect consumers, they do not address other ailments in animals or the variety of physical and mental stresses that are not perceived to affect consumers.

This is not for lack of authority. The Act establishes broad regulation-making powers for the purpose of protecting human and animal health through the control or elimination of diseases and toxic substances and generally for carrying out the purposes of the Act. In particular, pursuant to subsection 64(1)(i), regulations may be passed for the humane treatment of animals and generally:

(i)    governing the care, handling and disposition of animals;
(ii)   governing the manner in which animals are transported within, into or out of Canada; and
(iii)  providing for the treatment or disposal of animals that are not cared for, handled or transported in a humane manner.

Nevertheless, most of the welfare-related provisions in the legislation are concerned with import, export, and transport. It gives no consideration to what happens to animals during the course of their daily lives; in fact, a sick animal who is required to be killed under the Act may actually be reserved by the minister to be used in experimentation: section 13(2)(a).

Transportation is an insufficient concern but not an unimportant one. The ongoing reduction of slaughter facilities, industry concentration in fewer locations, the size of the country and the extent of the trade in live animals with the United States and other countries, make long distance transportation a common event.[38] The *Health of Animals Act* already allows animals to be transported for long periods of time without food, water, or rest, but that time starts at zero when animals cross the national border and become subject to the importing country's legislation. Canada puts no limit on the total length of the journey

37   Above note 32.
38   Spent hens are typically transported up to 800 kilometres and sometimes up to 2,400 kilometres to slaughter. In 2008, more than 9.4 million pigs and 1.5 million cows were exported to the United States and Mexico. Canada also exports cows to Columbia and pigs to countries including Russia, South Korea, Venezuela, and Vietnam for breeding purposes: WSPA Report, above note 17 at 4–7.

and the food, water, and rest intervals are among the longest in the world.[39]

The export of an animal from Canada by vessel or aircraft generally requires, among other things, certification by veterinary inspector that there has been compliance with all the prescribed requirements respecting the health, protection, and transportation of the animal.[40]

Offences are generally punishable on summary conviction and carry a maximum fine of $50,000, six months imprisonment or both (sections 65 and 66). The limitation period is two years after the minister became aware of the subject-matter of the proceedings (section 68). The vast majority of reported cases are not with respect to offences, but compensation to producers pursuant to sections 51 and 52,[41] for animals ordered destroyed.

### b)  Health of Animals Regulations

Of the eleven regulations pursuant to the *Health of Animals Act,* the main one of interest is the *Health of Animals Regulations.*[42] It addresses export, import, and transportation. Most of the importation provisions (Parts II through VII) concern measures to control the spread of diseases specific to the various species, including conditions of import for each species. Most of the exportation regulations (Part VIII) concern communicable diseases and human health. Only Part XII considers animal welfare at any length.[43] It applies to the transportation of animals entering or leaving Canada, or within Canada, whether on railway cars, motor vehicles, aircraft, or vessels. Section 137 broadly provides that every animal is subject to inspection at all times; however, as seen below, this provision is largely theoretical.

---

39   *Ibid* at 5.
40   *Health of Animals Act*, above note 32, s 19(1)(b). The minister may exempt animals and shipments from this provision by regulation.
41   For example, *Kreshewski v Canada (Minister of Agriculture)*, 2006 FC 1506.
42   CRC, c 296.
43   The only other sections of this regulation that touch on animal welfare include a prohibition on exporting animals from Canada to any country other than the United States without the consent of an inspector, if they have not been at the place of embarkation for at least twelve hours: s 71(1). This does not apply to animals exported from an airport: s 71(2). Thus, an animal in transit can be denied a rest period with an inspector's consent, if the destination is the United States or if the animal is sent by air. Section 79.19(8) requires operators of hatcheries to ensure that any chick or unhatched embryo that is killed in a hatchery is killed "in a humane manner."

*i)  Ill and Injured Animals*

Section 138(2) prohibits loading or transporting an animal:

   (a)  that by reason of infirmity, illness, injury, fatigue or any other cause cannot be transported without undue suffering during the expected journey;

   (b)  that has not been fed and watered within five hours before being loaded, if the expected duration of the animal's confinement is longer than 24 hours from the time of loading; or

   (c)  if it is probable that the animal will give birth during the journey.

Section 138(2.1) specifies that for the purpose of paragraph (2)(a), a non-ambulatory animal is an animal that cannot be transported without undue suffering during the expected journey. Further, subsection 138(4) purports to prohibit a railway company or motor carrier from continuing to transport an animal that is injured, or becomes ill or otherwise unfit for transport during a journey, except to the nearest suitable place at which they can receive proper care and attention.

*ii)  Loading and Unloading*

Section 139 prohibits (1) beating an animal being loaded or unloaded, or (2) loading or unloading an animal, "in a way likely to cause injury or undue suffering." It also addresses ramps, gangways, chutes, boxes, or any other apparatus which must be used and maintained so as not to cause injury or undue suffering, and secure footholds with slopes that are not excessive, unless the animals are loaded in containers.

Places where animals are loaded and unloaded for food, water, and rest are required to protect them from "extremes of weather" (section 145). Subsection 148(5) requires the pen in which animals are unloaded to have sufficient space for all animals to lie down at the same time, properly designed racks and troughs, well-drained and clean floors that provide safe footing, an adequate amount of bedding, and protection from inclement weather.

*iii)  Transportation Conditions*

Overcrowding is prohibited but broadly defined in section 140 to mean crowding "to such an extent as to be likely to cause injury or undue suffering." Sections 141 to 142 address the segregation of animals, the requirement that animals be able to stand in a natural position without coming into contact with a deck or roof, and drainage or absorption of urine.

Section 143 establishes a series of conditions related to the vehicle of transportation. Rather than positively protect animals from insecure fittings, undue exposure to the weather, and inadequate ventilation, the provision prohibits transporting an animal "if injury or undue suffering is likely to be caused" in these ways. Section 144 requires that animal containers must be adequately constructed and maintained so that: (a) animals may be fed and watered without being removed; (b) animals may be readily inspected; and (c) so as to prevent the escape of liquid or solid waste. Ventilation for air and sea carriers is addressed in sections 146 and 147. The regulations anticipate that animals will die, be killed, and be seriously injured while in transit, and they establish reporting and record-keeping requirements for carriers in sections 150 and 151.

Sections 152 to 159 address sea carriers transporting livestock. No veterinary inspector is generally required to be on board. Animals must be securely tied: if bovine, by the head or neck to a securing rail with a halter or a rope; if equine, by ropes in such a manner as to prevent the animal from biting other animals or striking the head on the deck above; if sheep, goats, or pigs, in pens or enclosed containers. Adequate lighting is required. Animals are not supposed to be kept near the engine or boiler room casing unless the casing is covered by adequate insulation. Vessels must keep a suitable humane killing device in good working order on board, along with an adequate quantity of ammunition and a sufficient quantity of suitable veterinary drugs. Injured animals must be destroyed by the humane killing device unless they can be kept alive without undue suffering.

### iv) Food, Water, and Rest

Section 138(2) provides that animals are supposed to be given food and water within five hours before being loaded, if the expected duration of confinement is longer than twenty-four hours from the time of loading. This does not apply to chicks, if the expected duration of confinement is less than seventy-two hours from the time of hatching.

Pursuant to section 148, equines, "swine," and other monogastric animals may be confined in a carrier, regardless of heat, cold, or other conditions, for up to thirty-six hours. Cattle, sheep, goats, or other ruminants may be confined for up to forty-eight hours; however, ruminants can be confined for even longer, up to fifty-two hours, if their final destination is within Canada, and they may be fed and given water and rest at that destination. Chicks of any species may be confined without food or water for up to seventy-two hours from the time of hatching.

If animals are unloaded for food, water, and rest during the journey, they are supposed to be rested for at least five hours before reloading, and be given suitable food and potable ice-free water, and fresh bedding is supposed to be placed in the carrier. No rest stops are required if the carrier is suitably equipped to feed, give water, and allow rest for the animals and they are fed and given water and rest at specified intervals. Section 149 provides for special food and hours of feeding for calves too young to be fed exclusively on hay and grain.

### c) Interpreting and Enforcing the *Health of Animals Act*

In several cases, the Federal Court of Appeal has found a violation of section 138(2) of the *Health of Animals Regulations,* which prohibits transporting an animal who cannot be transported without undue suffering.

In *Canada (AG) v Porcherie des Cèdres Inc*,[44] a pig was found lying on his side, panting and shivering, unable to flee despite being afraid of the veterinarian examining him. He had an open fracture of one leg, with necrosis of the skin, muscle, and bone tissue, which had lasted at least ten days. The producer told the veterinarian it was a little scratch and that the diseased foot just had to be cut off. The Review Tribunal[45] dismissed a charge, finding that "undue" suffering in section 138(2) meant "excessive" suffering, of which there was no evidence since the pig had sustained the injury before being transported. The Federal Court of Appeal rejected this interpretation as an error of law. In the context of the legislation, the term meant "undeserved," "unwarranted," "unjustified," or "unmerited" suffering.[46] It concluded that "the transportation of an injured, and therefore suffering, animal *could only* cause unjustifiable or inappropriate suffering to that animal."[47] The illness and considerable injury sustained by the pig before the time of loading meant that he could not be loaded and transported without undue suffering on the journey.

In *Canadian Food Inspection Agency v Samson*,[48] a pig was injured prior to being transported from Ontario to Quebec. The pig was in so much pain that he later had to be euthanized. The Review Tribunal found that "undue suffering" was a subjective determination and although there was little doubt that the animal was injured and likely very uncomfortable while being loaded and transported, the injury had preceded those events. Because there was no evidence that the condi-

---

44    2005 FCA 59 [*Porcherie des Cèdres Inc*].

45    The Agriculture/Agri-Food Review Tribunal ("Review Tribunal") hears appeals of fines issued under the *Agriculture and Agri-Food Administrative Monetary Penalties Act*, above note 34, which arise out of violations of the *Health of Animals Act* and other legislation. It is discussed further below.

46    *Porcherie des Cèdres Inc*, above note 44 at para 26.

47    *Ibid* at para 27 [emphasis added].

48    2005 FCA 235 [*Samson*].

tion was worse after shipping than before, there was no undue suffering. However, the Federal Court of Appeal, relying on *Porcherie des Cèdres*, again found that section 138(2) does not require that an existing condition be aggravated during transport to apply.

> What the provision contemplates is that no animal be transported where having regard to its condition, undue suffering will be caused by the projected transport. Put another way, wounded animals should not be subjected to greater pain by being transported. So understood, any further suffering resulting from the transport is undue. This reading is in harmony with the enabling legislation which has as an objective the promotion of the humane treatment of animals.[49]

*Samson* was in turn relied on in *Fermes G Godbout & Fils Inc v Canada (Canadian Food Inspection Agency)*,[50] where the Federal Court of Appeal dismissed applications for judicial review by farmers found to have violated section 138(2). The farmers argued that any suffering caused to an animal destined for human consumption was economically justifiable. The court rejected the argument, finding that one of the important objectives of the *Health of Animals Act* is to prevent the mistreatment of animals, and therefore economic considerations cannot in and of themselves warrant the infliction of undue or unwarranted suffering. Subsection 138(4) showed Parliament's intent by obliging a carrier to stop the transport of an animal that becomes injured, sick or otherwise unfit for transport during the trip. Transport must end at the nearest place where the animal can receive proper care and attention.

These cases suggest that under scrutiny, some practices will not be legally tolerated. However, such scrutiny is rare.[51] Most farm animals are transported multiple times, often over long distances across provincial and national borders in apparent violation of the regulations before they are finally killed. Many animals are in conditions as bad as or worse than those that were ultimately rejected by the court. Very few cases before the Review Tribunal concern animal welfare issues, and of those that do, fines are low, amounting to the cost of doing business.[52]

Cows, pigs, horses, sheep, chickens, and other animals regularly arrive at Canadian livestock markets and slaughterhouses sick, emaciated, weak, crippled, severely wounded, and injured. Catching, trans-

---

49   *Ibid* at para 12.
50   2006 FCA 408 at paras 10 & 11.
51   WSPA Report, above note 17 at 33. The CFIA prosecution bulletins indicated one animal welfare conviction under the *Health of Animals Act* between January 2008 and March 2010.
52   *Ibid* at 33. In 2006, fines ranged from $500 to $2,000.

port, and slaughter cause severe trauma, particularly to birds. Lack of exercise and constant egg-laying in the case of battery hens, cause them to lose calcium, and their bones become so brittle that they can snap when catchers pull them from their cages. Chickens are thrown into crates or drawer-like containers to be loaded on to trucks, often packed in so tightly there is no space between them. Some are crushed. Some are drenched by heavy rain. Some freeze to death in long hours in sub-zero temperatures, or, if they do not die, parts of their nearly featherless bodies are frozen to the truck and then amputated when the birds are later pulled out. In hot weather, they suffer or die from heat stress or suffocation. Spent hens in particular travel long distances to slaughter since only a few plants specialize in killing them.

Severely compromised and downed animals of all species are transported in contravention of regulations and they are often left to suffer for long periods of time.[53] It is not uncommon for animals to have been standing or lying in their own waste, in overcrowded conditions, in extreme heat, cold, rain, or snow, without adequate protection, ventilation, or bedding, for many hours.[54] Even after long journeys, animals often have to wait hours more on the truck, lined up behind other trucks, awaiting their turn at busy facilities. The millions of animals who succumb before they can be slaughtered in the facility are referred to as "DOA" (dead on arrival).

The regulations rest on an assumption that an inspector or a veterinarian is readily available, however, this is not the case. Enforcement resources are increasingly limited, government regulation is seen more as a corporate nuisance than a citizen's right in the current climate, and regard for animals is a low priority among Canadian governments.[55] CFIA employs approximately 980 meat inspectors (including 291 veterinarians) and 329 terrestrial animal health inspectors (including 195 veterinarians) in Canada. There are 772 federally registered slaughter, processing, and rendering plants, and these can be extensive operations. CFIA animal health inspectors are also responsible for the animals transported to more than 430 provincially registered slaughterhouses

---

53  CFIA inspection reports reveal incidents such as a downed cow in Alberta who had been on the road for at least eight hours, and was dragged off the truck and left on a pile of dead animals for more than two days. Two employees saw her struggling to get up and vocalizing in apparent distress, but it was more than fifty-eight hours before she was euthanized. In another incident in Nova Scotia, a sow with hind-leg paralysis was left in a stockyard for three days before she was euthanized: *Ibid* at 22.

54  *Ibid* at 4.

55  Montgomery, above note 24 at 153–66.

across the country and at border crossings, and they are supposed to conduct random inspections along the highway.[56]

These inspectors have multiple responsibilities in the broad field of food inspection, and animal welfare is not necessarily their priority or area of expertise. Most inspectors review a small number of animals and trucks arriving at each facility. Among other things, this means that the decision about whether or not a suffering animal should be euthanized is left to the company that owns her, that created the conditions in which she was hurt in the first place, and that stands to lose profit if she does not make it to slaughter. En route, all discretion is in the hands of the drivers. There are no mandatory training requirements for either animal handlers or truck drivers.

The fact that CFIA is severely under-resourced is part of the explanation for its weak and inconsistent reporting and enforcement. CFIA policy is that if more than one percent of broiler chickens or more than four percent of spent hens arrive dead, it warrants further inspection, but would not necessarily be reported as non-compliant.[57] This might be a reasonable incurred loss in the transportation of other fragile products, yet one might have different expectations in the case of livestock. However, in many CFIA reports where animal welfare problems are noted, the enforcement action specified is a verbal warning or education provided through a pamphlet. Sometimes loads are marked as compliant even where problems are noted, and even where violations of the regulations are apparent.[58] Inspectors also face resentment, hostility, or intimidation, and veterinarians have quit because of the stress.[59]

### d)  *Meat Inspection Act*

The full title of the *Meat Inspection Act* is "An Act respecting the import and export of and interprovincial trade in meat products, the registration of establishments, the inspection of animals and meat products in registered establishments and the standards for those establishments and for animals slaughtered and meat products prepared in those establishments." The Act provides that no meat may be exported out of Canada or conveyed from one province to another unless it was pre-

---

56   *Health of Animals Regulations*, above note 42, s 137; WSPA Report, above note 17 at 23–27.

57   WSPA Report, *ibid* at 11.

58   *Ibid* at 28–33. The report cites a number of examples from across the country where injured, crippled, and dead pigs were noted, but do not indicate any violation or enforcement action.

59   *Ibid.*

pared or stored in a registered establishment, and it authorizes regulations governing their operation.

Summary conviction and indictable offences are created in section 21; penalties include fines of up to $50,000 and six months imprisonment or both for the former, and fines of us to $250,000 and two years imprisonment or both for the latter. Regulations may provide for inspection, prescribe the equipment and facilities to be used, the procedures to be followed, and the standards to be maintained to ensure the humane treatment and slaughter of animals (section 20(f)). Despite this responsibility and the broad authority given to support it, the regulations are thin and the term "humane" is undefined.

### e) *Meat Inspection Regulations*

Lengthy and detailed provisions contained in section 28 of the *Meat Inspection Regulations*[60] address the design, construction, and maintenance of the physical establishment; these are clearly directed toward the safety of the meat for human consumption and not the welfare of the animal, although section 28(3)(c)(ii) requires registered establishments to have facilities for conveying injured or disabled animals in a humane manner. Floors, ramps, gangways, and chutes must be constructed and maintained in a manner that provides secure footing for the animals and prevents injury during movement.

Part III of the regulation, entitled "Examination, Inspection, Humane Treatment and Slaughter, Packaging and Labelling" establishes the rules for handling and slaughtering of food animals in registered establishments. Considering that these rules govern the deaths of many millions of animals every year, they are not extensive; most of them address human safety and post-mortem issues. They are replete with vague, undefined qualifications like "humane," "undue," and "avoidable" which, among other things, create disincentives and challenges to enforcement.

Section 61.1 requires that calves be condemned if the operator or a veterinarian has reasonable grounds to believe that the calf was not transported in accordance with the provisions of the Code of Practice for Veal Calves.[61] Section 62 (1) is the general provision related to animal welfare; it provides that no animal shall be handled in a manner that subjects the animal to avoidable distress or pain. Subsection (2) is more specific, prohibiting the application of goads or electric prods to the animal's anal, genital, or facial region.

---

60   SOR/90-288.
61   Codes of practice are discussed in the next part.

Different species are to be kept apart, as are diseased or injured animals and animals that are a potential danger to other food animals (section 63). Holding pens for animals awaiting slaughter are to be "adequately" ventilated and not "overcrowded" (section 64). Animals awaiting slaughter are supposed to be provided with access to potable water but not food unless they are held for twenty-four hours (section 65).

Every animal in a registered establishment is supposed to be inspected and approved for slaughter by an official veterinarian or inspector within twenty-four hours prior to slaughter (section 67). Operators are required to comply with any instructions from an official veterinarian that a food animal must be condemned or must be held and segregated from all other food animals for rest, treatment, or slaughter (section 68).

Section 79 addresses slaughter and provides that every animal that is slaughtered must, before being bled, either (a) be rendered unconscious or be killed in a manner that ensures that the animal does not regain consciousness before death; or (b) in the case of a bird or a domesticated rabbit, by rapid decapitation. The methods approved in subsection (a) for rendering an animal unconscious are: (i) a blow to the head by means of a penetrating or non-penetrating mechanical device; (ii) exposure to a gas or a gas mixture; or (iii) the application of an electrical current.

Animals to be ritually slaughtered in accordance with religious law do not have to be rendered unconscious before slaughter. They are supposed to be restrained and slaughtered by means of a cut resulting in a rapid, simultaneous, and complete severance of the jugular veins and carotid arteries in a manner that causes them to lose consciousness immediately (section 77). The equipment used for restraining, slaughtering, or rendering unconscious; the condition of the equipment or instrument; and the operator's competence and physical ability to use the equipment or instrument, should not subject the animal to avoidable distress or pain (section 80).

### f) *Agriculture and Agri-Food Administrative Monetary Penalties Act*

The *Agriculture and Agri-Food Administrative Monetary Penalties Act* establishes a system of administrative monetary penalties (AMPs) for the enforcement of several Acts, including the *Health of Animals Act* and the *Meat Inspection Act*. It reinforces the low values of these animals by allowing an administrative process of monetary payments to take the place of more serious forms of accountability for violations in respect of their most important interests. Section 17 specifically provides that a violation under the Act is not an offence under the *Criminal Code*.

While defences of due diligence or honest and reasonable mistake of fact are not available, common law defences of justification and excuse are (sections 17 and 18). The standard of proof is the civil standard of balance of probabilities (section 19). Continuous violations are treated as separate violations in respect of each day in which they are continued (section 21). The violations themselves are created in the Regulations.

### g)  *Agriculture and Agri-Food Administrative Monetary Penalties Regulations*

The contravention of a provision of the *Health of Animals Act* or Regulations, or the refusal or neglect to perform any specified duty imposed by *Health of Animals Act* that is set out by way of Schedule is a violation that may be addressed by way of AMP pursuant to section 2 of the *Agriculture and Agri-Food Administrative Monetary Penalties Regulations*.[62]

The penalty for a violation committed by an individual other than in the course of business, and not to obtain a financial benefit, is $500 if it is minor, $800 if it is serious, and $1,300 if it is very serious (section 5(1)). Violations committed in the course of business or in order to obtain a financial benefit have higher penalties of $1,300, $6,000, and $10,000 respectively (section 5(3)). The "total gravity value" of serious and very serious violations is based on consideration of three factors: (i) prior violations (up to the past five years), (ii) the degree of intention or negligence, and (iii) the harm done or that could be done (including monetary losses to any person): section 6.

Schedule 1 to the regulation classifies the violations as minor, serious, or very serious. Violations for most of the provisions of the *Health of Animals Regulations* discussed above are "serious." Some are considered "very serious," such as beating an animal being loaded or unloaded contrary to section 139(1). Some are considered "minor," such as transporting animals that cannot stand in their natural position contrary to section 142(a).

In *Doyon v Canada (AG)*,[63] the Federal Court of Appeal was critical of the entire framework from the perspective of those charged with violations, finding that the Act has "imported the most punitive elements of penal law while taking care to exclude useful defences and reduce the prosecutor's burden of proof." Like the cases discussed above, *Doyon* also involved the transport of a suffering pig. However here, the court took a more traditional approach. Its circular articulations of the proper way to interpret section 138(2) of the *Health of Animals Regulations* dem-

---

62   SOR 2000-187.
63   2009 FCA 152.

onstrate the inherent problems with legislation that permits a person to cause an animal to suffer and purports to regulate the nature and degree of that suffering.

The court confirmed that section 138(2) is not limited to cases where an animal's condition is worsened as a result of transport [64] and it does not permit the transportation of a healthy animal in conditions that would cause undue suffering. [65] On the other hand, it expressed that not all suffering that exists before transportation will necessarily lead to a violation;[66] nor does the fact that an animal is compromised and suffering necessarily mean that she cannot be transported, especially if she remains ambulatory; there is no absolute prohibition against transporting an emaciated hog to the slaughterhouse.[67] After observing that due diligence had been removed as a defence, the court went on for several paragraphs to consider what was essentially a due diligence defence and determined that it was "not in [the producer's] interest to incur a $2000 penalty for a hog worth $100,"[68] and granted the producer's application for judicial review.

### h)  *Criminal Code*

The *Criminal Code* includes several offences in relation to cruelty to animals in sections 444 to 447.1.[69] "Cattle" is a defined term in section 2 which includes "an animal of the bovine species by whatever technical or familiar name it is known, including any horse, mule, ass, pig, sheep or goat." Generally, the sections potentially relevant to animals used in agriculture create the following offences:

*Cattle and Other Animals:*
- wilfully killing, maiming, wounding, poisoning, or injuring cattle: 444

---

64  *Ibid* at para 33.
65  *Ibid* at para 47.
66  *Ibid* at para 46.
67  *Ibid* at para 47.
68  *Ibid* at para 56. The court noted that the applicant was a pork producer with twenty-nine years of experience; that of his own accord he had taken a course on the transportation and euthanasia of compromised hogs; that he had no prior record when the proceeding was instituted; that he had seen the hog in question over a long period; and that he had ensured the hog would be transported in isolation.
69  These are generally sections 446 and 447. There are also several offences designed to protect an owner's interest in preserving her animal property; for example, see sections 444 and 445. For a more thorough discussion of these provisions see Chapter 3.

- wilfully and without lawful excuse, killing, maiming, wounding, poisoning, or injuring dogs, birds, or animals that are not cattle and are kept for a lawful purpose: 445

*Cruelty to Animals:*
- wilfully causing, or, being the owner, wilfully permitting to be caused, unnecessary pain, suffering, or injury to an animal or bird: 445.1(1)(a)
- as the owner or person having custody or control of a domestic animal or bird, or wild animal or bird in captivity, abandoning the animal or bird in distress or wilfully neglecting to provide adequate food, water, shelter, and care: 446(1)(b)
- wilfully administering a poisonous or injurious substance to a domestic or captive wild animal or bird: 445.1(1)(c)
- by wilful neglect, causing damage or injury to an animal or bird during transport: 446(1)(a); and keeping a cockpit: 447

Practically, many, if not all, of the practices by which animals are turned into food could be considered to be violations of these sections of the *Criminal Code*.[70] However, as discussed more thoroughly in Chapter 3, the interpretation of "unnecessary" which courts have applied to date does not question the validity of the use to which an animal is put. The *status quo* is assumed to be acceptable and the "unnecessary" qualification is applied only in the context of particular practices which occur in the course of the activity. While from this one might conclude that some of the particularly problematic practices described above would thereby be rendered unlawful, the interpretation which courts have given the term is circular.

In *R v Pacific Meat Company*,[71] the company was charged under this section for causing pain to hogs that it shackled by their hind leg, swung against a metal wall with some force, and then thrust a knife into their throats whether they were unconscious or not. The question in the case was not whether this caused the animals pain, which was admitted,

---

70    Among other things, they cause pain, suffering, or injury to animals for an ultimate purpose which is not "necessary" in any true sense of the word. Relying on animals for food may be done for reasons of custom, convenience, or preference, but it cannot be considered necessary in most parts of Canada today. See John Robbins, *Diet for a New America: How Your Food Choices Affect Your Health, Happiness and the Future of Life on Earth* (Walpole, NH: Stillpoint Publishing, 1987); Neal D Barnard, *Food for Life: How the New Four Food Groups Can Save Your Life* (New York: Harmony/Random House, 1993); and T Colin Campbell with Thomas M Campbell II, *The China Study: Startling Implications for Diet, Weight Loss and Long-Term Health* (Dallas: BenBella Books, 2005).

71    [1957] BCJ No 98 (Co Ct).

but whether that pain was necessary. The court dismissed the charge, assuming without considering the basis on which killing animals for food is itself permissible. The practices used to cause the animal to die were then deemed necessary and automatically protected.

> Hogs fulfil a purpose of providing food for human beings. Before the hogs can be eaten by mankind they must of necessity be killed, so that the fatal injury that is administered to each hog by the "sticker" is a necessity and therefore not "unnecessary."
>
> . . .
>
> [I]f someone who was not employed in a slaughter house was to shackle a hog as described in this case, and if such a person hoisted the animal as herein described, just to hear it squeal or for any other sadistic reason, and if evidence was adduced that the hog in fact suffered pain in the process, than I would hold that such pain and suffering was "unnecessary" and that such a person would be guilty. But I am dealing with a case involving two human individuals whose regular employment involves the necessity of slaughtering hogs to provide food for mankind.[72]

Similarly, in *R v Ménard*, Lamer J, speaking for the Court of Appeal for Quebec, expressed that whether necessary or not, eating meat is the privilege of humanity:

> "Without necessity" does not mean that man, when a thing is susceptible of causing pain to an animal, must abstain unless it be necessary, but means that man in the pursuit of his purposes as a superior being, in the pursuit of his well-being, is obliged not to inflict on animals pain, suffering or injury which is not inevitable taking into account the purpose sought and the circumstances of the particular case. In effect, even if it not be necessary for man to eat meat and if he could abstain from doing so, as many in fact do, it is the privilege of man to eat it.[73]

The *Criminal Code* might condemn some of the most egregious and wasteful abuses of animals used in food production, such as when owners let entire herds starve to death, but activities which are institutionally abusive, standard practice, and commonly done, have not attracted the courts' censure to date.

---

72   *Ibid* at paras 8 and 14. This is an old case, but the specific practices of animal production and slaughter are not commonly subject to criminal charges.

73   *R v. Ménard* (1978), 43 CCC (2d) 458 at 465 (Que CA) [emphasis in original].

## 2) Relevant Provincial Legislation

> [A]t just the federally regulated slaughterhouses between two and three million animals arrive dead or dying or so ill they must be destroyed—year after year after year. That figure does not include the number of injured animals that arrive and, if they are still considered fit for human consumption, are sent directly to slaughter.
>
> Provincially inspected slaughterhouses, where meat is produced for domestic consumption, are considered to be generally less demanding.[74]

Provincial legislation generally applies to animals or animal products that remain within the province. It is up to each province to determine whether or not to permit meat that has not been slaughtered and prepared at a registered slaughterhouse to be sold to local retailers or consumers. The legislation takes a deferential approach to industry, and harms caused by its practices are protected in three general ways ways: they are insulated against nuisance claims; they are excluded from compliance with animal welfare legislation; and the welfare of animals is not seriously required in other legislation governing the industry.

First, as noted above, many provinces have enacted legislation that protects farm operations against nuisance claims, as long as the operation is in compliance with the regulations, local land-use bylaws, and what are usually called "normal farm practices."[75] Most statutes, such as Ontario's, set out a general definition for normal farm practice as one that:

(a) is conducted in a manner consistent with proper and acceptable customs and standards as established and followed by similar agricultural operations under similar circumstances, or

(b) makes use of innovative technology in a manner consistent with proper advanced farm management practices.[76]

Terms like "proper and acceptable" are not defined. Instead, normal farm practices are generally understood to be the things which colleagues or competitors in similarly situated operations do. There is no requirement that they be the safest, least painful, or most environmentally sound practices available. The industry is given license to choose its practices and should it so choose, to collectively adopt "slipshod

---

74    Montgomery, above note 24 at 153.
75    Above note 21.
76    *Farming and Food Production Protection Act*, above note 21, s 1(1).

methods in order to save money."[77] As more farms convert to intensive operations, intensive practices become the norm, regardless of other considerations. In this manner, at least within the realm of nuisance and related actions, this legislation protects the practices by which animals are harmed.[78]

Second, the animal welfare legislation discussed in Chapter 4 generally establishes certain basic requirements regarding the care of animals in one's possession and authorizes agents to take certain actions based on their knowledge or suspicion that an animal is in distress. However, it excludes animals raised in accordance with generally accepted practices or codes of practice, or it excludes animals in food production specifically. For example:

11.1 (1) Every person who owns or has custody or care of an animal shall comply with the prescribed standards of care with respect to every animal that the person owns or has custody or care of.

(2) Subsection (1) does not apply in respect of,

(a) an activity carried on in accordance with reasonable and generally accepted practices of agricultural animal care, management or husbandry;

. . .

11.2 (1) No person shall cause an animal to be in distress.

(2) No owner or custodian of an animal shall permit the animal to be in distress.

. . .

(6) Subsections (1) and (2) do not apply in respect of,

. . .

(c) an activity carried on in accordance with reasonable and generally accepted practices of agricultural animal care, management or husbandry . . . .[79]

---

77   JJ Kalmakoff, "The Right to Farm: A Survey of Farm Practice Protection Legislation in Canada" (1999) 62 Sask L Rev 225 at 243.

78   The legislation can be quite extensive in scope; for example in British Columbia, it includes practices used in respect of a wide variety of exotic animals by way of the *Specialty Farm Operations Regulation*, BC Reg 53/99.

79   *Ontario Society for the Prevention of Cruelty to Animals Act*, RSO 1990, c O.36, ss 11.1–11.2. See also Alberta: *Animal Protection Act*, RSA 2000, c A-41, s 2(2); British Columbia: *Prevention of Cruelty to Animals Act*, RSBC 1996, c 372, s 24(2); Manitoba: *Animal Care Act*, CCSM c A84, s 2(2); New Brunswick: *Society for the Prevention of Cruelty to Animals Act*, RSNB 1973, c S-12 and *General Regulation*, NB Reg 2000-4, s 4(2); Newfoundland and Labrador: *Animal Health and Protection Act*, SNL 2010, c A-9.1, s 18(3); Nova Scotia: *Animal Cruelty Prevention Act*, SNS 1996, c 22, s 11(4); Quebec: *Animal Health Protection Act*, RSQ c P-42, s 55.9.15; PEI: *Animal*

Compliance with industry-created standards provides an automatic exclusion or a defence for practices which might otherwise be unlawful in light of the harm they cause, condoning whatever practice that the industry itself has adopted.

Newfoundland and Labrador does not establish exemptions in this manner; rather, its animal welfare legislation includes a provision that gives the very animal welfare laws it establishes the lowest priority of all other legislation pertaining to animals:

> 21.  Nothing in this Act shall be construed as affecting a right, power, duty or prohibition relating to animals conferred or imposed under another Act and where a conflict exists between this Act and that other Act, that other Act prevails.[80]

Even to the extent that general animal welfare legislation does apply to farming operations, it has other limitations. Humane society agents are either not entitled to access private property without sufficient grounds, which are unlikely to come to their attention without access to the property; or, where agents are entitled to inspect such facilities, their ultimate powers are constrained by the fact that generally accepted practices are beyond their purview. Nor is it the function of humane societies, whose authority is normally based on specific instances of animal distress, to fundamentally modify industrial practices and eliminate the kind of institutionalized suffering that is the norm in a large industry.

On the occasions when charges are laid under animal welfare legislation in the agricultural context, it is not in the context of normal practices but only where large numbers of animals are subjected to gratuitous neglect and suffering.[81] In this regard, one of the biggest cases in Canadian history arose in Manitoba in 2010. The RCMP and provincial agriculture officials raided a feeder barn and found hundreds of dead pigs and more than 2,200 others living knee-deep in filth and sewage with no food, water, or light. Many pigs had died from manure gas poisoning from poor ventilation in the crowded building. Hundreds of others had fallen through a broken slatted floor and drowned in sewage. A few days after the raid, the building burned to the ground

---

*Health and Protection Act*, RSPEI 1988, c A-11.1, s 8(2); Saskatchewan: *Animal Protection Act*, 1999, SS 1999, c A-21.1, s 2(3); Yukon: *Animal Protection Act*, RSY 2002, c 6, s 3(3). Northwest Territories and Nunavut do not have equivalent legislation.

80  *Animal Protection Act*, RSNL 1990, c A-10, s 21.

81  See for example: *R v Loerzel*, 2007 SKCA 107; *R v Baker*, 2004 CanLII 33290 (Ont CA); and *Bevan v Ontario Society for the Prevention of Cruelty to Animals*, 2007 ONCA 119. Also see discussion in Chapter 4.

in a massive fire. Twenty-three charges were laid under the *Animal Care Act*[82] and the producer eventually pled guilty to several of them. His sentence included a $60,000 fine and a lifetime prohibition against owning or possessing animals; identical charges against his wife were stayed, reportedly on the undertaking that she would be prohibited from owning or possessing pigs for five years.[83]

Third, the many provincial acts which regulate different aspects of agriculture do not seriously address the interests of the animals themselves, even where they are specifically authorized to do so. To varying degrees, they address aspects of the animals' lives: they regulate ramps and lighting and equipment, in a manner similar to federal legislation. They also regulate transport and slaughter, but with fewer limitations than in federal legislation. For example, some provinces expressly allow crippled, injured, or dead animals to be transported.[84]

Provincial agricultural laws do not generally address the routine issues that affect animals in their daily lives. They allow harmful practices including branding animals, and in some cases, financially encourage dehorning animals. Inspections by provincial authorities tend to be on an *ad hoc* basis; inspectors do not generally conduct regular inspections of farming operations themselves, nor are there always inspectors at the slaughter site. Ritual slaughter is most commonly done at provincial facilities and provincial legislation makes an exception for it in the same manner that federal legislation does. The summaries below identify relevant provincial legislation to assist the reader's further investigation.

### a)   Alberta

The *Agricultural Pests Act;*[85] the *Animal Health Act;*[86] the *Animal Protection Act;*[87] the *Dairy Industry Act;*[88] the *Livestock Identification and Commerce*

---

82   CCSM c A84.

83   Dean Pritchard, "Pig Farmer Guilty of 'Disastrous' Cruelty," *QMI Agency* (3 June 2011), online: cnews.canoe.ca/CNEWS/Crime/2011/06/03/18232196.html. See also, online: www.cetfa.com/index.php?option=com_content&view=article&id= 408%3Amartin-grenier-lifetime-ban-on-owning-livestock&catid=1%3Alatest& Itemid=107. The Manitoba Pork Council's response was to call for self-regulation, see Ron Friesen, "Port Council Asks for Self-Regulation after Animal Cruelty Case" *Manitoba Co-operator* (9 June 2011), online: www.agcanada.com/Article. aspx?ID=37545.

84   See Saskatchewan's *Livestock Inspection and Transportation Regulations, 1978,* Sask Reg 242/78: crippled, injured, or dead animals may be transported if they are separated from the others and unloaded at the nearest stockyard, s 21.

85   RSA 2000, c A-8.

86   SA 2007, c A-40.2.

87   RSA 2000, c A-41.

88   RSA 2000, c D-2.

*Act*;[89] the *Livestock Industry Diversification Act*[90] (licences domestic cervid[91] production farms, which keep wildlife in captivity for purposes of reproduction or sale as breeding stock or meat); the *Livestock and Livestock Products Act*;[92] the *Meat Inspection Act* (governs inspection and slaughter);[93] and the *Stray Animals Act*[94] (establishes liability and provides for the captures, impoundment, and destruction of trespassing livestock, and establishes the right to kill dogs that are pursuing, worrying, or destroying livestock).

## b)  British Columbia

The *Agri-Food Choice and Quality Act*;[95] the *Agricultural Produce Grading Act*;[96] the *Animal Disease Control Act*;[97] the *Prevention of Cruelty to Animals Act*;[98] the *Food Safety Act*[99] including the *Meat Inspection Regulation*[100] (applies to slaughter establishments that are not registered under the federal *Meat Inspection Act*, and to the slaughter of animals by the owner for personal use); the *Game Farm Act*[101] (addresses game farms for fallow deer, bison and reindeer); the *Livestock Act*[102] (addresses the capture of animals at large and authorizes killing a dog found running at large or attacking or viciously pursuing livestock); the *Livestock Identification Act*;[103] the *Livestock Lien Act*;[104] and the *Milk Industry Act*.[105]

## c)  Manitoba

The *Animal Care Act*,[106] (including the *Animal Care Regulation*[107] which incorporate by schedule all recommended codes of practice and other

---

89  SA 2006, c L-16.2.
90  RSA 2000, c L-17.
91  Of the deer family.
92  RSA 2000, c L-18.
93  RSA 2000, c M-9.
94  RSA 2000, c S-20.
95  SBC 2000, c 20.
96  RSBC 1996, c 11.
97  RSBC 1996, c 14.
98  RSBC 1996, c 372.
99  SBC 2002, c 28.
100  BC Reg 349/2004.
101  RSBC 1996, c 168.
102  RSBC 1996, c 270.
103  RSBC 1996, c 271.
104  RSBC 1996, c 272.
105  RSBC 1996, c 289.
106  Above note 82.
107  Man Reg 126/98.

standards or codes of practice); the *Animal Diseases Act*;[108] the *Dairy Act*[109] (will be repealed when the *Food Safety and Related Amendments Act*[110] comes into force); the *Livestock and Livestock Products Act*;[111] the *Livestock Industry Diversification Act*[112] (regulates game production farms); and the *Public Health Act*[113] (including the *Food and Food Handling Establishments Regulation*[114] which addresses slaughterhouses and meat processing plants).

### d) New Brunswick

The *Natural Products Act*;[115] the *Diseases of Animals Act*[116] (including the *General Regulation*[117] addressing the inspection of animals in slaughterhouses and livestock yards); the *Public Health Act*[118] (including the *Abattoir Regulation*);[119] the *Society for the Prevention of Cruelty to Animals Act*; the *Poultry Health Protection Act*;[120] and the *Sheep Protection Act*[121] (which deals with compensating owners of sheep when their sheep are killed by dogs and authorizes killing a dog found injuring sheep).

### e) Newfoundland and Labrador

The *Animal Protection Act*[122] (this is the province's current animal welfare law, however, both it and the *Livestock Health Act*[123] are repealed by the *Animal Health and Protection Act*,[124] a comprehensive Act which has received royal assent but not yet been proclaimed. The new Act addresses animal health, animal protection, nuisance animals, heritage animals, and licensing, distinguishing between companion animals and livestock. The Animal Protection provisions in Part II of the Act do not apply where they conflict with parts I or III.); the *Food and Drug*

---

108 CCSM c A85.
109 CCSM c D10.
110 SM 2009, c 8, s 39.
111 CCSM c L170.
112 CCSM c L175.
113 CCSM c P210.
114 Man Reg 339/88 R.
115 SNB 1999, c N-1.2.
116 SNB 1974, c D-11.1.
117 NB Reg 83-105.
118 SNB 1998, c P-22.4.
119 NB Reg 2009-140.
120 RSNB 1973, c P-12.
121 RSNB 1973, c S-7.
122 RSNL 1990 c A-10.
123 RSNL 1990 c L-22.
124 SNI 2010, c A-9.1.

Act;[125] the *Meat Inspection Act* (addresses slaughter);[126] and the *Poultry and Poultry Products Act.*[127]

## f) Northwest Territories

The *Herd and Fencing Act*[128] addresses some issues of cruelty to horses, cattle, sheep, swine, and goats.

## g) Nova Scotia

The *Agriculture and Marketing Act*[129] (permits the killing of dogs found on the premises of fur farms); the *Animal Health and Protection Act;*[130] the *Animal Protection Act;*[131] the *Baby Chick Protection Act;*[132] the *Dairy Industry Act;*[133] the *Meat Inspection Act*[134] (addresses slaughter, but does not regulate slaughter at increasingly popular farmgate operations, where people buy the meat directly from the farmer); and the *Sheep Protection Act*[135] (establishes a method of compensation for the owner of a sheep that is killed or injured by a dog).

## h) Nunavut

The *Herd and Fencing Act*[136] addresses some issues of cruelty to horses, cattle, sheep, swine, and goats.

## i) Ontario

The *Animal Health Act, 2009;*[137] the *Food Safety and Quality Act, 2001*[138] (creates a licensing scheme for food related activities, including slaughter; under the *Disposal of Deadstock* regulation,[139] "fallen animals" are supposed to be promptly killed, without being moved before being killed, in a humane manner; the *Meat* regulation[140] addresses slaughter);

---

125 RSNL 1990 c F-21.
126 RSNL 1990 c M-2.
127 RSNL 1990, c P-18.
128 RSNWT 1988, c H-2.
129 RSNS 1989, c 6.
130 RSNS 1989, c 15.
131 SNS 2008, c 33.
132 RSNS 1989, c 29.
133 SNS 2000, c 24.
134 SNS 1996, c 6.
135 RSNS 1989, c 424.
136 RSNWT (Nu) 1988, c H-2.
137 SO 2009, c 31.
138 SO 2001, c 20.
139 O Reg 105/09.
140 O Reg 31/05.

the *Livestock Community Sales Act*;[141] the *Livestock and Livestock Products Act*;[142] the *Livestock, Poultry and Honey Bee Protection Act*[143] (compensates animal owners for the loss or depreciation in value of a protected animal, and establishes circumstances under which one has the right to kill a dog); the *Milk Act*;[144] and the *Ontario Society for the Prevention of Cruelty to Animals Act*.[145]

## j)   Prince Edward Island

The *Animal Health and Protection Act*[146] (the *Animal Protection Regulations*[147] incorporate by reference several Recommended Codes of Practice); the *Dairy Industry Act*;[148] the *Farm Practices Act*;[149] and the *Public Health Act*[150] (establishes a licensing scheme for commercial slaughterhouses; the *Slaughter House Regulations*[151] set out requirements concerning the operation of licensed slaughterhouses, but do not apply to farmers who slaughter animals on their own property for their own use).

---

141  RSO 1990, c L.22; this legislation will be repealed by proclamation of the Lieutenant Governor, SO 2009, c 31, ss 73 and 75(1).

142  RSO 1990, c L.20.

143  RSO 1990, c L.24. This Act will be repealed upon proclamation of the Protection of *Livestock and Poultry from Dogs Act*, pursuant to the *Open for Business Act, 2010*, SO 2010, c 16, Sched 1, ss 4(1) and 10(2). The new Act is largely similar, and it incorporates municipal liability where a dog kills or injures livestock or poultry, and authorizes municipalities to pass bylaws establishing similar liability when the livestock or poultry is killed by a wild animal.

144  RSO 1990, c M.12. There is no caselaw addressing the welfare of animals under this legislation, however, existing jurisprudence does reinforce the status of animal as units of production. In *R v Schmidt*, 2010 ONCJ 9, a dairy farmer was acquitted of a number of offences related to selling raw unpasteurized milk. In his defence, he explained that he was not selling the milk to the public, but that he was running a "lease-a-cow" program where he retained ownership and was the lessee of his thirty cows to people who wanted unpasteurized milk. The decision is under appeal at the time of writing.

145  RSO 1990, c O.36.

146  RSPEI 1988, c A-11.1.

147  PEI Reg EC71/90.

148  RSPEI 1988, c D-1.

149  RSPEI 1988, c F-4.1.

150  RSPEI 1988, c P-30.

151  PEI Reg EC478/62.

### k)  Quebec

The *Animal Health Protection Act*;[152] the *Farm Producers Act*;[153] and the *Food Products Act*[154] (including the *Regulation Respecting Food*[155] which minimally address the welfare of animals in transport and slaughter-houses; fish are referred to here as "live freshwater products").

### l)   Saskatchewan

The *Agricultural Operations Act*;[156] the *Animal Identification Act*;[157] (the *Brand Regulations*[158] provide for the size and style of brands to be applied to an animal by hot or cold device, but no requirement for anaesthetic or pain relief); the *Animal Products Act*[159] (addresses the production, manufacture, sale, purchase, transport, and inspection of animals and animal products without a license; regulations address keeping animals, stockyards, and transport); the *Animal Protection Act, 1999*;[160] the *Diseases of Animals Act*;[161] and the *Horned Cattle Purchases Act*[162] (financially encourages the dehorning of cattle by way of a method of lesser payment for cattle with horns).

### m)  Yukon

The *Animal Protection Act*[163] is the territory's animal welfare legislation. Similar to its provincial equivalents, the prohibition against causing an animal to be or to continue to be in distress does not apply if the distress results from an activity carried on in accordance with reasonable and generally accepted practices of animal management, husbandry, or slaughter if these practices are carried out in a humane manner.

## 3)  Recommended Codes of Practice

The most notable aspect of the production of animals for food is that most details of their daily lives are not prescribed by legislation but

---

152  RSQ, c P-42.
153  RSQ, c P-28.
154  RSQ, c P-29.
155  RRQ, c. P-29, r 1.
156  SS 1995, c A-12.1.
157  RSS 1978 (Supp), c A-20.1.
158  RRS, c A-20.1, Reg 1.
159  RSS 1978 (Supp), c A-20.2.
160  SS 1999, c A-21.1.
161  RSS 1978, c D-30.
162  RSS 1978, c H-6.
163  RSY 2002, c 6.

by voluntary codes of practice established by the industry itself. Recommended codes of practice are developed and reviewed under the auspices of the National Farm Animal Care Coalition (NFACC). Its twenty-six members are largely representatives of producer or "commodity" groups, but also include animal scientists, federal and provincial governments, truckers, and one animal welfare organization, the Canadian Federation of Humane Societies. NFACC is funded by the federal government through Agriculture and Agri-Food Canada.[164]

The following codes have been developed to date: Cattle—Beef (1991); Cattle—Dairy (2009); Cattle—Veal (1998); Bison (2001); Deer (1996); Goats (2004); Horses (1998); Mink (1988); Pigs (1993); Pigs, Addendum—Early-Weaned Pigs (2003); Poultry—Chicken, Turkeys, and Breeders from Hatchery to Processing Plant (2003); Poultry—Layers (2003); Ranched Fox (1989); Sheep (1995); and Transportation (2001). The review process is supposed to be every five years, but as the dates indicate, they are reviewed far less often. Codes are available on NFACC's website.[165]

The codes of practice are guidelines for the care and handling of farm animals. They contain recommendations for housing and management, transportation, processing, and other husbandry practices that are considered acceptable within the industry. The codes use both permissive and mandatory language. Even where the language is mandatory, in the absence of a corresponding statutory duty, there is no obligation to comply; however, even where the codes are referenced in legislation, they cannot be seen to offer meaningful animal protection. They endorse intensive agriculture, including some of the most harmful of the prevailing intensive production practices. They endorse the lengthy transportation times set out in federal regulations. Their content is often undermined with the same qualifications seen in legislation: they discourage causing "unnecessary" suffering and "avoidable" distress, thereby approving the suffering and distress that industry actors consider appropriate.

The code for pigs approves the gestation and farrowing crates for breeding and nursing pigs discussed above, in which animals are so thoroughly confined they can stand up and lie down but not move beyond that, even to turn around (section 2.3.6.1). Attendants are advised to avoid pulling pigs' ears and to avoid pulling their legs in directions in which they do not naturally move (section 2.3.6.1.3.1). Tooth trim-

---

164   National Farm Animal Care Council, *Annual Report* (2005–2006), online: www. nfacc.ca/pdfs/nfacc/Annual Report 2006.pdf.

165   National Farm Animal Care Council, online: www.nfacc.ca/codes-of-practice.

ming, tail trimming, castration, and tusk trimming are explicitly approved (sections 2.3.6.1.3.2 and 2.3.6.1.3.6).

For dairy cattle, tie stalls and other housing systems may be with or without outdoor access (section 2.3.2.1.1). Cattle need not have more space than that which allows them to stand up, lie down, and adopt normal resting postures (section 2.3.2.1.1.2). Aversive behaviours such as hitting, shouting, aggressive tail twisting, electric prods, and kicking should be avoided, but this is a recommendation and not a requirement (section 2.3.2.3.2). It is similarly recommended but not required to aim for prevalence of less than ten percent obvious or severe lameness, less than ten percent sole ulcers, and less than fifteen percent digital dermatitis (section 2.3.2.3.5). It is recommended that only trained people load, unload, and transport cows (section 2.3.2.5.1.3).

The code for veal calves endorses the confinement of calves in veal crates (section 2.3.3.1.2). It indicates that transportation personnel are responsible for the welfare of calves and should be properly instructed. The infliction of physical injury to calves is discouraged (section 2.3.3.1.8).

Intensive indoor confinement of beef cattle is approved, and the code recommends only that animals should be able to stand up and lie down, and that any tethering devices should not interfere with their ability to do so (section 2.3.1.1) Hot iron branding is said to be necessary in some circumstances (section 2.3.1.11). It is recommended that downers should not be dragged, that vehicles should not be parked in direct sunlight, and that the use of electric prods, canvas slappers, and similar devices should be minimized (section 2.3.1.15).

Battery operations for chickens and turkeys are approved. Morphological alterations to beaks, toes, combs, and snoods should be avoided, except where necessary. High speed maceration is described as a practical and humane method of "euthanasia." Carbon monoxide gas and electrocution are not recommended for reasons of human safety (section 2.3.4.1). The code allows forced moulting (section 2.3.4.4), a process in which hens are deprived of food and water for one or two weeks until they lose one quarter to one third of their body weight. This shuts down the reproductive system and causes birds to lose their feathers and begin another lay of eggs, accelerating the normal resting phase. It is not uncommon for hens to die from the trauma.

The use of codes and generally accepted practices allows an industry which has broad effects on all animals, both human and nonhuman, to regulate many important aspects of its own behaviour in accordance with its own priorities. Codifying the *status quo* offers no incentive to producers to exceed it. Codes are used not only as a defence to any charge that might be laid, but more broadly to deflect growing criticism of intensive handling systems. In perpetuating this state of affairs, corporations have normalized a state of disgrace, and both federal and provincial governments have abdicated their responsibilities.

# CHAPTER 7

# RESEARCH TOOLS

You do not settle whether an experiment is justified or not by merely showing that it is of some use. The distinction is not between useful and useless experiments, but between barbarous and civilized behaviour. Vivisection is a social evil because if it advances human knowledge, it does so at the expense of human character.

—George Bernard Shaw[1]

It is in the realm of research that the implications of animals' legal status as property are brought into greatest relief. In medical, scientific, and commercial experiments using live animals, sometimes referred to as *in vivo* research or "vivisection," hurting animals is an intrinsic part of the activity; in this realm, it is *prima facie* acceptable to knowingly cause pain, suffering, injury, disability, disease, fear, and stress and to require animals to live in unnatural, uncomfortable, and lonely conditions.

Research is the most challenging subject for some people who have ethical concerns about the treatment of animals and it is sometimes seen as an unfortunate necessity: how can anyone support leaving any stone unturned when it comes to seeking the cure to human diseases that so deeply affect us and our loved ones? Yet when scrutinized, the subject raises the most difficult problems in respect of justifying the instrumental use of animals.

---

1    Preface to *The Doctor's Dilemma* (1911; repr, New York: Penguin Books, 1957).

Part A is an introduction to the issues surrounding the use of animals in experimentation. Part B describes the peer-review system of oversight administered by the Canadian Council on Animal Care. Part C reviews the relevant legislative schemes. Part D considers particular implications of biotechnology and intellectual property.

# A. ISSUES IN THE USE OF ANIMALS IN EXPERIMENTATION

Animals are used in research conducted in and by universities, hospitals, federal and provincial government departments, and pharmaceutical, biotechnological, and other commercial operations. They are used for a wide variety of purposes (which include but are not limited to the pursuit of ways to prolong human lives), all of which are generally categorized under three headings: teaching, testing, and research.

In teaching, students from primary grades through university are required to watch demonstrations or actually participate in vivisection (of living) or dissection (of dead) individual animals. In testing, animals are used in drug and toxicology studies for medical, pharmaceutical, or other commercial purposes. Some animals have chemicals applied to their eyes or skin in order to test new cosmetics or personal care, household cleaning, and industrial products. Sometimes animals are force-fed toxic substances to see what level causes reactions like convulsions, paralysis, tremors, bleeding from bodily cavities, or death; they can be put in chambers where they are forced to inhale heavy concentrations of substances like hair spray, disinfectants, and industrial chemicals. They are used widely for pharmaceutical tests and even for military purposes, like testing chemical and nerve gas.

Animals are used in both pure and applied research. Commercial agricultural research aims to create turkeys with more white meat or juicier thighs, chickens who fatten faster or have no feathers, and dairy cows who give more milk. In medical research, they are used to develop and test surgical procedures and devices. They can be given diseases, burned, maimed, electrocuted, shaken, paralyzed, blinded, and deprived of food, water, and companionship. They can be forcibly addicted to substances, sometimes by being restrained for hours a day and subjected to electric shocks or food deprivation to encourage them to self-administer drugs or alcohol. They can be used in psychological studies related to learned helplessness, maternal deprivation, social isolation, stress, and depression.

Although humans would be the best models for studies related to human disease and matters affecting the human body, ethical concerns preclude the use of unconsenting humans in experiments.[2] The use of consenting humans in research is prohibited for the kinds of things that are done to animals, and, where it is permitted, it is subject to controls and extensive ethical debate.[3] It is therefore inaccurate to say that we will not leave any stone unturned in the quest to cure human diseases. However important such cures are, some things are even more precious: an individual's right to her own life, liberty, and bodily integrity takes priority over the knowledge that might be gained if she were used instrumentally for the benefit of others.

When we then turn to animals to be surrogate models for the human body, we create a logical contradiction: research is done on animals on the basis that they are *like us* (and therefore the results of experiments done on them will be meaningful to us), but it is justified on the basis that they are *not like us* (and therefore it presents no ethical barriers). That contradiction is a premise of the practice and it is the basis of much of the objection to it.[4] However, the contradiction is obscured in

---

2    This statement is subject to qualification. First, children and some adults lack the capacity to give informed consent and they can be involved in experimental studies; however, substitute consent must be given on behalf of such persons by someone concerned for their interests. It is also true that apart from well-known atrocities committed in the Second World War, marginalized and otherwise disempowered human beings have been used in many experiments, in many places in the world, without their consent and sometimes even without their knowledge. However, such acts are generally deplored and those who engage in them strenuously seek to protect them from public awareness. See: Andrew Goliszek, *In the Name of Science: A History of Secret Programs, Medical Research and Human Experimentation* (New York: St Martin's Press, 2003).

3    Canadian Institutes for Health Research, Natural Sciences and Engineering Research Council of Canada and Social Sciences and Humanities Research Council of Canada, *Tri-Council Policy Statement: Ethical Conduct for Research Involving Humans*, 2d ed (December 2010), online: www.pre.ethics.gc.ca/pdf/ eng/tcps2/TCPS_2_FINAL_Web.pdf.

4    Animal rights philosophy poses the question: what are the morally relevant differences that justify subjecting sentient animals to treatment for the benefit of humans which is unacceptable for humans themselves? Otherwise put: if the very factors which are the basis for rejecting the use of humans in experiments (such as loss of liberty or loss of life, and the pain and fear they will suffer) will be experienced by those who are being used instead, how is the differential treatment justified? These questions are explored in Gary L Francione, *Animals, Property and the Law* (Philadelphia: Temple University Press, 1995) at 165–84 [Francione, *Law*]; William Paton, *Man and Mouse*, 2d ed (New York: Oxford University Press, 1993); Bernard E Rollin, *The Unheeded Cry: Animal Consciousness, Animal Pain and Science* (Oxford: Oxford University Press, 1990); Gill Langley, ed, *Animal Experimentation: The Consensus Changes* (New York: Chapman & Hall, 1989); Carl Cohen, "The Case for the Use of Animals in Biomedical Research" (1986) 315 New England Journal of Medicine 865; and Richard

the public realm. The research industry emphasizes the serious human problems that it promises to solve, thereby perpetuating the notion that vivisection is an unfortunate necessity and making any claims about being mean to mice seems silly by comparison; it also assures the public of the humane care it provides to animals living in laboratories and it portrays its critics as emotional and soft, or violent and dangerous, or both.[5] In this manner, widespread public scrutiny of the practice is discouraged and deflected.

To categorize the use of animals in experimentation as an unfortunate necessity is not just a factual assertion, but a moral one. The practice is often framed as a choice between killing an animal or allowing a human being to die. This is a simplistic reduction of the research process itself, in which it is rarely, if ever, a single experiment that brings a conclusive result, but rather knowledge accumulated on the basis of an aggregate of accrued information. It is also misleading from an ethical perspective because a choice so posed has already been made. The very act of considering whether taking one life will save another reduces the status of the first to a mere instrument. That is why one does not speak of the necessity of using a human being in an experiment or of taking a human organ without consent; the use of the term "unfortunate necessity" presupposes a categorically different moral status.[6] The term invites still more scrutiny in the commercial domain.

---

D. Ryder, *Victims of Science*, 2d revised ed (London: National Anti-Vivisection Society, 1983). For more general analysis which includes examination of the use of animals among other issues in science, see Bernard E Rollin, *Science and Ethics* (New York: Cambridge University Press, 2006).

5   In Ontario, where a government inspector is required to inspect registered research facilities, requests under the *Freedom of Information and Protection of Privacy Act*, RSO 1990, c F.31, to obtain copies of inspection reports have been denied on the grounds that disclosure of the information is a serious threat to the safety or health of an individual or could endanger the security of a building. The government has not provided any clear explanation as to what the alleged threat is or how the release of laboratory inspection reports could seriously threaten the safety of people who work at a research facility. Rather it invokes unsubstantiated allegations about extremists in the animal rights movement who use acts of violence to promote their cause. In some such requests, the Canadian Council on Animal Care has intervened to argue against the release of information. See Charlotte Montgomery, *Blood Relations: Animals, Humans and Politics* (Toronto: Between the Lines, 2000) at 117–19 and 127 [Montgomery]. Also see note 68, below in this chapter.

6   For further discussion, see Francione, *Law*, above note 4 at 165–233. The legislative regime governing animals in research in the United States, which Francione discusses, is significantly different than Canada where there is hardly any legislation at all; however, his general observations and analysis apply in

The word "humane," when used in the context of experimentation, does not adhere to any dictionary meaning, nor to the manner in which it is commonly understood to be characterized by tenderness and sympathy. Juxtaposed against a setting in which severe harm is caused to members of one group (animals) in order to avoid harm being caused to another group (humans), "humane" acquires an inimical meaning: any requirement to mitigate the harm need only be considered if it will not in any way interfere with the experiment, and the nature of the experiment itself is limited only by the researcher's imagination. As to whether the public would agree that the actual acts undertaken are humane, that is a matter for public debate. Yet meaningful debate requires that all parties to it be informed of the relevant factual basis, such as the specific things that are done to animals and the purpose for which they are done, and such debate is hindered by a lack of information in the public realm.

There is currently no legal duty on researchers themselves or any agency on their behalf to make such information publicly available. When it is sought by way of freedom of information requests, disclosure is opposed and has so far been largely rejected.[7] Research protocols that outline the number and species of animals to be used in a particular experiment, the procedures to which they will be subjected, and the level of invasiveness associated with the procedure are confidential. Only general details of the overall picture are shared with the public. It is generally only where research is published, after the fact, that information enters the public realm and may be found and interpreted by those who understand scientific journals. Even then, when a report of a scientific discovery is made, the details of what the animals experienced in the course of the study are not the point of the report.[8]

---

the Canadian context. See also Gary L Francione, *Introduction to Animal Rights: Your Child or the Dog?* (Philadelphia: Temple University Press: 2000) at 31–49 [Francione, *Introduction to Animal Rights*]; and Angus Taylor, *Animals & Ethics: An Overview of the Philosophical Debate*, 3d ed (Peterborough, ON: Broadview Press, 2009) at 119–45.

7   See note 5, above in this chapter.

8   A recent exception was a study in mouse pain conducted at McGill University: DJ Langford *et al*, "Coding of Facial Expressions of Pain in the Laboratory Mouse" (June 2010) 7:6 Nature Methods 447. The aim was to develop a system for coding the severity of pain through assessing various facial grimaces made by unanesthetized mice in response to painful stimuli of varied intensity. Techniques for producing pain included actions on their tails (hot-water immersion, radiant heat, application of a binder clip), injection of irritants into the feet, and induction of bladder inflammation with a chemical that causes painful cystitis in humans. Another was intraperitoneal injection of acetic acid, which caused the mice to

Confidentiality is an important aspect of the perpetuation of this practice; it is easier to accept when one is amorphously curing a dreaded disease than when people are informed of the specific procedures to which animals are subjected under that guise. With scientists seen to be the "miracle workers of a secular age,"[9] deference is given to the industry to determine what is necessary and humane and to decide for itself what is acceptable practice. In regards to its use of animals, the industry is subject to hardly any legislative control or public scrutiny. Decisions about what can be done to animals are left to a private, interested, and unchallenged group.[10]

Medical, pharmaceutical, biotechnological, and other kinds of research constitute a competitive, multi-billion dollar industry. Procedures, processes, and the products that derive from it can earn substantial profits and be the subject of valuable patent protection. Capital flows into the manufacture of cages and numerous other supplies needed to house, feed, and experiment on animals. Research subjects are bred and sold by large corporations with their own patent-protected strains of animals who are selectively bred and sometimes genetically altered to meet researchers' needs[11]: animals are bred to have certain sorts of seizures, be susceptible to particular cancers, to have muscular dystrophy or diabetes, no immune response, or be anemic.

When it comes to cats and dogs, however, many animals used in Canadian laboratories are former pets who are acquired from pounds (sometimes called shelters) for a nominal fee. Animals are also procured from farms and auction markets, commercial livestock operations, from other studies, institutions, or animal users, or from the wild,[12] including many primates.[13] It is unknown exactly how many animals

---

develop abdominal constriction and writhing. The researchers concluded that a "mouse grimace scale" could be constructed from five facial grimaces characteristic of animals feeling "moderate" and "severe" pain. Because causing pain and observing the animals' reaction to it were the actual object of the study, those details are discussed openly in the report. The study has been the subject of some controversy, see online: http://principalinvestigators.org/mcgill-study-compliant. However, the authors of the study indicated that all animal experiments were approved by the McGill University (Downtown) animal care and use committee.

9　Montgomery, above note 5 at 78.

10　*Ibid* at 101.

11　See, for example, Charles River International Laboratories, Inc., online: www. criver.com.

12　Canadian Council on Animal Care, *Guidelines on Procurement of Animals Used in Science* (Ottawa: Canadian Council on Animal Care, 2007), online: www.ccac. ca/Documents/Standards/Guidelines/Procurement.pdf.

13　For a discussion about the hundreds of cynomolgus monkeys captured by the Canadian government in the Philippines in 1983 to be used in a breeding pro-

are used in experiments in Canada every year. The Canadian Council on Animal Care collects statistics from the facilities which participate in its program[14] and in 2009, those facilities reported using 3,375,027 amphibians, cats, cephalopods, chinchillas, dogs, domestic birds, farm animals, fish, fur animals, gerbils, guinea pigs, hamsters, marine mammals, mice, non-human primates, rabbits, rats, reptiles, and wild species from Canada and elsewhere.[15] It appears as though researchers in Canada do not currently use great apes, although such use in not prohibited in Canada as it is in some other countries.[16]

Apart from ethical questions about how to justify the use of animals in research when their use is premised on their similarities to humans, there is considerable skepticism of the soundness of the practice from a scientific perspective.[17] Published reports are qualified by

---

gram to repeat quality tests of polio vaccine, see Montgomery, above note 5 at 108–9 . At least 100 monkeys died in the process of capture and transport. The conditions in which the survivors were required to live in federal government laboratories were the subject of long-term criticism.

14  As discussed in the Section B(1), below in this chapter.

15  Canadian Council on Animal Care, *2009 CCAC Survey of Animal Use* (Ottawa, 2010), Table 1, online: www.ccac.ca/en_/publications/audf/stats-aud/data-2009. [*2009 CCAC Survey*]. For a variety of reasons, this number is thought to be significantly lower than the total number of animals used throughout Canada as there are many facilities CCAC does not inspect; the animals killed to be used in dissection are not counted; and many uncounted animals are killed in an effort to create certain strains of transgenic animals; see Montgomery, above note 5 at 100–1.

16  New Zealand was the first country to prohibit the use of great apes in invasive research in 2000 and since that time others have prohibited or limited their use, including Australia, Austria, Belgium, Japan, Holland, Sweden, and the United Kingdom: Andrew Westoll, *The Chimps of Fauna Sanctuary: A Canadian Story of Resilience and Recovery* (Toronto: HarperCollins, 2011) at 220–22. (This book tells the story of a private sanctuary near Montreal, which gives a home to a wide variety of animals in need, including chimpanzees who had been used in many years of experiments in American research laboratories.) The United States and Gabon might be the only two countries left that do experiments on chimpanzees: Brian Vastag, "Chimpanzee Research an Endangered Species as Experts Debate Usefulness, Ethics" *Washington Post* (13 August 2011).

17  For example, Arthur Birmingham LaFrance, "Animal Experimentation: Lessons from Human Experimentation" (2007) 14 Animal L 29; Christopher Anderegg *et al*, *A Critical Look at Animal Experimentation*, 6th ed (Cleveland: Medical Research Modernization Committee, 2002); C Ray Greek & Jean Swingle Greek, *Specious Science: How Genetics and Evolution Reveal Why Medical Research on Animals Harms Humans* (New York: Continuum, 2002); Francione, *Introduction to Animal Rights*, above note 6 at 31–49; Alix Fano, *Lethal Laws: Animal Testing, Human Health and Environmental Policy*, 2d ed (New York: St Martin's Press, 1997); Neal D Barnard & Stephen R Kaufman, "Animal Research is Wasteful

the concern about extrapolation of results from one species to another, particularly where the results were reached in a highly controlled and artificial context. Many examples exist of products that were found to be safe when tested on animals but had harmful effects when used on humans.[18] There is a "striking paucity" of quantitative data confirming the value of the animal model for human health.[19] There is also criticism concerning the duplication of experiments, outdated methods, and the triviality of purpose in some cases.[20] Alternatives to the use of animals are increasingly available, however their development lacks the funding that traditional methods receive and there is no legal obligation to pursue them.[21]

## B. PEER REVIEW AND THE CANADIAN COUNCIL ON ANIMAL CARE

In the 1960s, ethical concerns about the use of animals in research were getting public attention, in large part because of the theft of pets that were ending up in North American laboratories.[22] The Medical Research Council requested that the National Research Council introduce a committee to investigate the care and use of experimental animals in Canada. Rather than establish legislative control and oversight of the practice,

---

and Misleading" (February 1997) 276:2 Scientific American 80; Robert Sharpe, *Science on Trial: Human Cost of Animal Experiments* (Sheffield, UK: Awareness, 1994); Pietro Croce, *Vivisection or Science: A Choice to Make* (Massagno, Switzerland: CIVIS, 1991); Andrew N Rowan, *Of Mice, Models and Men: A Critical Evaluation of Animal Research* (Albany: State University of New York Press, 1984). Also see discussion in Kathy Hessler, "Perspectives philosophiques sur la recherche animale" in Mártine Lachance, ed, *L'animal dans la spirale des besoins de l'humain* (Cowansville PQ: Yvon Blais, 2010) at 267; and in John Sorenson, *Animal Rights* (Black Point, NS: Fernwood, 2010) at 138–42 [Sorenson].

18   *Ibid.*

19   Sorenson, *ibid.*

20   As discussed in authorities cited in note 16, above in this chapter. See also: Anne Innis Dagg, "Blame and Shame? How Can We Reduce Unproductive Animal Experimentation?" in Jodey Castricano, ed, *Animal Subjects: An Ethical Reader in a Posthuman World* (Waterloo, ON: Wilfred Laurier University Press, 2008) at 271–84.

21   For example, see Johns Hopkins Center for Alternatives to Animal Testing, online: http://caat.jhsph.edu/.

22   Francione, *Law*, above note 4 at 190–200; see also Judith Reitman, *Stolen for Profit: How the Medical Establishment Is Funding a National Pet-Theft Conspiracy* (New York: Pharos Books, 1992).

the committee recommended a voluntary control program exercised by scientists in each institution, subject to peer review.

## 1) Canadian Council on Animal Care

The Canadian Council on Animal Care (CCAC) was subsequently established in 1968, and in 1982 it was incorporated as a non-profit corporation, entirely independent of government.[23] The CCAC describes itself as a quasi-regulatory body.[24] It is funded primarily with public monies provided by the Canadian Institutes of Health Research (CIHR) and the Natural Sciences and Engineering Research Council of Canada (NSERC), although it has also adopted a cost recovery program in recent years where institutions that wish to be assessed must pay a fee for that assessment.[25] The CCAC's stated purpose is to act in the interests of the people of Canada to ensure that the use of animals, where necessary, for research, teaching, and testing employs optimal care according to acceptable scientific standards, and to promote an increased level of knowledge, awareness, and sensitivity to relevant ethical principles.[26]

The twenty-two permanent members of the CCAC are not representative of the people of Canada generally, but of organizations and agencies directly interested in participating in or promoting the business of animal research. They include federal government departments with scientific interests; representatives of academic facilities of medicine, dentistry, and psychology and universities generally; associations representing scientists and specialists in animals used in laboratories; federal agencies that give research grants; charities that give research grants to study human disease; and zoologists. The Canadian Federation of Humane Societies (CFHS) is a limited term member.[27]

CCAC accepts the use of animals in research as necessary. It requires the institutions that participate in its program to confirm that they have considered alternatives to the use of animals, but it creates no obligation or meaningful incentive to develop such alternatives in

---

23  Beyond the more precise references in the footnotes below, the information in this section is discussed more thoroughly in Montgomery, above note 5 at 96–127.

24  Canadian Council on Animal Care, *The Canadian Council on Animal Care*, online: www.ccac.ca/en_/about.

25  Canadian Council on Animal Care, *Cost Recovery Services and Fees*, online: www.ccac.ca/en_/assessment/cost.

26  Canadian Council on Animal Care, *Mandate and Purpose*, online: www.ccac.ca/en_/about/mandate.

27  Canadian Council on Animal Care, *Member Organizations*, online: www.ccac.ca/en_/about/structure/members.

the first place. It has no record of criticizing the use of animals in research nor in calling for eradication of the practice; its record is of defending the practice and advocating on behalf of the interests of the research industry.[28]

## 2) System of Oversight

The CCAC's system of oversight includes an assessment program and a requirement for participating facilities to establish animal care committees.[29] Government departments are required to participate in the CCAC program, as are institutions that rely on public funding. However, if a pharmaceutical or biotechnology company, or other private institution does not wish to participate, it does not have to. As universities increasingly work in partnership with private corporations to collaborate on research, the need for government funding and CCAC oversight is diminished.

Assessments of institutional animal care and use programs are based on CCAC documents. It has produced a two-volume Guide to the Care and Use of Experimental Animals.[30] It also establishes guidelines that address various issues in the use and care of animals in science such as endpoints, euthanasia, laboratory animal facilities, and pro-

---

28   See several examples set out in Montgomery, above note 5 at 115–17. In an unusual move for an organization that describes itself as a quasi-regulatory body, CCAC raised concerns regarding proposed amendments to improve Canada's criminal anti-cruelty legislation. The organization's executive director told the federal Standing Committee on Justice and Human Rights that the use of animals for research deserved its special attention. The CCAC was concerned about the lack of definition of "unnecessary pain," "kills an animal brutally," "reasonable care," and "suitable and adequate food and water" contained in the proposed amendments. Further, since research on animals can cause them pain, suffering, injury, and deprivation, the CCAC was troubled that proposed amendments might potentially have removed the defences on which animal researchers would rely in doing their work: Proceedings of the Standing Committee on Justice and Human Rights (16 October 2001), evidence of Clément Gauthier, Executive Director, Canadian Council on Animal Care at 1550. See further discussion in Chapter 3.

29   For a description of the system of oversight in the United States, see Francione, Law, above note 4 at 185–233. While that system operates pursuant to federal legislation, it is similarly designed to the CCAC system in some ways and the limitations to enforcement give a sense of the comparable limitations in the Canadian context.

30   Canadian Council on Animal Care, CCAC Guide to Care and Use of Experimental Animals, 2d ed (Ottawa: Canadian Council on Animal Care, 1993) vol 1, online: www.ccac.ca/Documents/Standards/Guidelines/Experimental_Animals_Vol1. pdf. Volume 2 is under revision and not available online.

curement of animals.[31] These guidelines are the industry's own expression of the things it deems acceptable to do.

The assessment program has panels of peer groups visit participating facilities every three years, with significant notice and planning. The panel consists of a CCAC assessment director, a veterinarian, one or two scientists from different facilities, and a community representative selected from a list of people nominated by the Canadian Federation of Humane Societies, usually from the geographical area of the institution.

Members of the assessment panel get a list of the laboratory research projects, with a brief description and data about the numbers of animals used, the species, and what is being done to them. Panel members can ask for more information, including copies of the research protocols submitted to the institution or granting agency for approval. Panel members look at how the facility handles research proposals as well as particular projects. They meet *in camera* with institute officials and members of the institution's animal care committee to express any concerns. Assessment of the facility does not generally include observation of animals who are in the midst of an experiment, but can include a tour of the facilities where animals awaiting their turn are held.

After the assessment, the panel sends a written report to the laboratory, which has several months to reply to any concerns. The CCAC then rates the institution as in compliance with its standards, in conditional compliance, on probation, or in non-compliance. CCAC has no meaningful authority to penalize institutions it finds to be in non-compliance. In theory, CIHR or NSERC can freeze or cut funding to an institution found to be in non-compliance, however this penalty has never been implemented in the history of the CCAC, even though some laboratories have been found to be in non-compliance.[32]

Institutions assessed by CCAC must have their own animal care committees. There is no specific composition prescribed; the CCAC notes that membership will vary, but should include: scientists and/or teachers experienced in animal use; an institutional member who does not use animals; experienced veterinarian(s); a technical staff representative; a student representative where students are present; a coordinator; and others as needed. The only suggested outside presence is one or more community representative(s), usually appointed by senior administrators at the university. Animal care committees are supposed to educate, assess, and ensure compliance with CCAC guidelines, as

---

31  Canadian Council on Animal Care, *Development of Peer-Based Guidelines*, online: www.ccac.ca/en_/standards/guidelines/development.

32  Montgomery, above note 5 at 97. Also see discussion regarding an investigative report on CBC's *Disclosure* in Sorenson, above note 17 at 137.

well as review protocols, and ensure that alternatives to the use of animals have been sought; however, there is no duty on an animal care committee itself to make any effort to develop such alternatives, nor is there any specific indication as to the extent of the effort a researcher must make to seek alternatives, nor as to whether anything beyond her own assurance is sufficient to satisfy the animal care committee.

Like the CCAC, animal care committees are composed almost entirely of people who share the interests of the institution and who share the view that it is acceptable to use animals in this way. Those who want their own protocols to be approved or who want to work harmoniously with colleagues have a disincentive to criticize or reject another's proposal. For the community member, who is there at the invitation of the institution, the process can be intimidating. Even when a community member expresses contrary views, this does not necessarily change the end result.[33]

## 3) Information Provided to the Public

All information related to individual institutional animal care and use programs, including institutional animal use data and assessment information, is entirely confidential, including pre-assessment documentation, information obtained during the assessment process, assessment reports, and all post-assessment documentation. CCAC takes the view that confidentiality is necessary to foster frank and open discussions. It denies that confidential in this sense means "secret" and describes it rather as "restricted to those authorized to have access."[34] In addition to a confidentiality promise, which panel members must sign for the CCAC, the institutions being inspected can require panel members to sign their own extensive confidentiality agreements. Institutions may choose to release information about CCAC findings, but, in the few instances that they do, it is generally to announce their receipt of a Good Animal Practice certificate.

---

33   Montgomery, *ibid* at 101–5. Montgomery discusses an incident in which the former president of the Canadian Federation of Humane Societies voted against renewing an experiment at a Toronto hospital when she served on its animal care committee. The experiment involved immobilizing cats with metal bars inserted into their backs. Rather than refuse to renew the research because of a single dissenting vote, the other members of the committee decided it would henceforth require two negative votes to veto a project.

34   Canadian Council on Animal Care, *Confidentiality of Assessment Information*, online: www.ccac.ca/Documents/Standards/Policies/Confidentiality_of_assessment_information.pdf.

The CCAC publishes some data that it gathers from the facilities in assessments, including the total number of animals used in Canada in those facilities, the species used, the general purpose of the use,[35] and the category of invasiveness of the experiments. It does not provide any description of what is done to animals in the course of these uses. It does not reveal which laboratories are subject to its assessment, nor does it report on any violations of its standards.

Categories of invasiveness are used by researchers to describe what they anticipate to be the level of invasiveness or severity of their proposed research.[36] Categories A and B involve little or no pain or distress. Category C entails minor stress or pain of short duration. Category D addresses moderate to severe distress or discomfort, such as prolonged physical restraint, radiation sickness, exposure to noxious substances with no escape, or the stress of maternal deprivation. Category E is for experiments which cause severe pain, at, near, or above the pain tolerance threshold of unanesthetized conscious animals, including such things as exposure to painful levels of drugs or chemicals.

In 2009, the institutions that provided information to the CCAC reported using 822,981 animals in Category D experiments and 145,632 animals in Category E experiments.[37]

In Category D, 2,358 of the animals used were dogs. Of these dogs, 1,161 were "purpose-bred" while 1,197 were "random source," the category that includes lost and abandoned pets received from pounds as well as excess dogs sold by pet breeders. Cats were 1,016 of the animals used in Category D experiments, and of these, 171 were purpose-bred while 845 were random source.[38] CCAC does not reveal which prov-

---

35  The purpose of animal use, or "PAU," is indicated in a series of general categories: PAU 0 includes breeding colony/stock (animals held in breeding colonies that have not been assigned to a particular research, teaching, or testing protocol); PAU 1 includes studies of a fundamental nature in sciences relating to essential structure or function (such as biology, psychology, biochemistry, pharmacology, physiology, and so on); PAU 2 includes studies for medical purposes, including veterinary medicine, that relate to human or animal disease or disorders; PAU 3 includes studies for regulatory testing of products for the protection of humans, animals, or the environment; PAU 4 includes studies for the development of products or appliances for human or veterinary medicine; and PAU 5 includes education and training of individuals in post-secondary institutions or facilities. No further description is provided: *2009 CCAC Survey*, above note 15, "Definitions" (last page).

36  Canadian Council on Animal Care, *Categories of Invasiveness in Animal Experiments* (1991), online: http://ccac.ca/Documents/Standards/Policies/Categories_of_invasiveness.pdf.

37  *2009 CCAC Survey*, above note 15, Table II.

38  *Ibid.*

inces use random source animals or what is done to the animals — it only publishes the total number of animals reported in that category across the country.

# C. LEGISLATIVE OVERVIEW

## 1)  Federal Legislation

There is no federal legislation specifically governing the use of animals in research. While many, if not all, of the things done to animals in laboratories would be offences under the *Criminal Code* if done to human beings,[39] these provisions are not applied to animals. Nor have *Criminal Code* anti-cruelty provisions[40] been applied in the context of animals in research, with one exception. In 1985, a psychologist and the chief veterinarian of the University of Western Ontario faced prosecution as a result of a cholesterol study in which a baboon (called B-43 by the university, and "Debbie" by the public, when it became aware of her) was fully restrained in a plexiglass chair, motionless and alone in a windowless room for four months.[41] A private prosecution for cruelty to animals led to a trial that lasted several days; charges were withdrawn after the university agreed to terms regarding Debbie's retirement and its future use of baboons.[42] The experiment was supported by the Medical Research Council and the Ontario Heart and Stroke Foundation, and the protocol was approved by the CCAC.[43]

Federal laws can apply to certain aspects of the practice, such as the procurement of animals. The *Health of Animals Act*[44] and *Health*

---

39   RSC 1985, c C-46. Some of the most obvious offences would include: administering poison or other destructive or noxious thing (s 245); setting a trap, device, or other thing likely to cause death or bodily harm (s 247); assault (s 265); assault with a weapon (s 267); aggravated assault (s 268); torture (s 269.1); kidnapping (s 279); forcible confinement (s 279(2)); and trafficking in persons (s 279.01). Thanks to Professor Vaughan Black for raising this point.

40   *Ibid*, ss 445–47.1.

41   Montgomery, above note 5 at 62–63. One news report described Debbie as having sores on her bottom, hair loss, a limp body, and trembling at the approach of a human visitor: Lynne Thomas, "The Plight of B43" *Globe and Mail* (10 November 1984).

42   Personal file in the author's possession. The private prosecutor has been unable to confirm Debbie's fate.

43   Tim Beardsley, "Canada Baboon Cruelty Trial" *Nature* (7 February 1985) at 421.

44   SC 1990, c 21.

*of Animals Regulations*[45] create import and export requirements addressing certain aspects of testing, inspection, permit issuing, and quarantine; and they establish certain requirements with respect to transportation. Permits might be required to acquire and transport fish and marine mammals, pursuant to the *Fisheries Act*.[46] The *Wild Animal and Plant Protection and Regulation of International and Interprovincial Trade Act*[47] (Canada's enabling legislation for CITES, the *Convention on the International Trade in Endangered Species of Wild Fauna and Flora*[48]) establishes import and export requirements for animals on the CITES list. New substances, including certain living organisms such as genetically engineered livestock, are subject to the *New Substances Notification Regulations (Organisms)*[49] pursuant to the *Canadian Environmental Protection Act, 1999*.[50]

Other federal law can be implicated indirectly in this realm. For example, in early 2011, Air Canada was subject to criticism for shipping forty-eight monkeys from China to Canada to be used in research.[51] It claimed to be bound by a 1998 decision of the Canadian Transportation Agency (CTA).[52] In that case, Air Canada had refused to carry a shipment of monkeys destined for research from Barbados to Canada, on the basis of industry practice to prohibit the carriage of goods which may constitute a nuisance or the transportation of which might be considered offensive by passengers. The Primate Research Center and Wildlife Reserve of Barbados filed a complaint pursuant to the *Canada Transportation Act*,[53] claiming that the refusal to carry the monkeys was unfair, abusive, and discriminatory. The CTA agreed, finding that the opinion of certain individuals that such carriage is offensive on hu-

---

45   CRC, c 296.
46   RSC 1985, c F-14.
47   SC 1992, c 52.
48   Can TS 1975 No 32.
49   SOR/2005-248.
50   SC 1999, c 33.
51   Nicole Saute, "Flying Monkeys Raise Eyebrows" *Toronto Star* (25 January 2011) A2. Research monkeys are usually transported in cramped crates in the plane's cargo hold. Air Canada is one of a small number of airlines that continues to transport primates for research; by contrast, British Airways has a policy of not carrying any live animals that are for use in any laboratory or for experimentation or exploitation.
52   Decision No 10-A-1998 (19 January 1998), (Canadian Transport Agency), online: www.otc-cta.gc.ca/eng/ruling/10-a-1998.
53   SC 1996, c 10; in particular, ss 18, 110, 111, and 122 of the *Air Transportation Regulations*, SOR/88-58.

mane and moral grounds was not sufficient to constitute an annoyance under the legislation.[54]

## 2) Provincial Legislation

Ontario is the only jurisdiction that has enacted a statute specifically addressing the use of animals in research. Other jurisdictions either have no legislation addressing the use of animals in research, or the relevant provisions are contained in the province's animal welfare legislation, in which research is protected by way of exemption for generally accepted practices or activities. In some provinces, compliance with CCAC standards is required, however there is not always a clear way of verifying compliance. Similar to the federal context, provincial wildlife legislation might create certain requirements in respect of the procurement of certain animals for research.

### a)   Overview of Ontario's *Animals for Research Act*

Ontario's *Animals for Research Act*[55] creates a system based on the registration of research facilities and the issuance of licences for facilities that supply animals. The Act establishes pounds and a requirement that pound animals are deemed to be available for research if they are not claimed by their owners within the redemption period defined therein.[56] Parliamentary debates from 1969[57] indicate that there were two primary motivations for creating such a system. The first was to ensure that medical and scientific facilities were supplied with animals for experimentation (including former pets — seen by some to be more suitable for research, and more affordable). The second stated purpose

---

54   The CTA relied on the fact that there was no evidence that the passengers on that particular plane even knew that monkeys destined for medical research were there, and therefore they could not be so annoyed in any event. The ironic conclusion reinforces the role of secrecy in protecting potentially offensive activities from criticism.
     In 2007, Air Canada stopped shipping beagles, the most popular purpose-bred dogs used in experiments, after passenger complaints about dogs yelping from the cargo hold, circumstances that came within the limits of the CTA's ruling.
55   RSO 1990, c A.22.
56   Pounds created under this legislation are distinct from humane societies created under the auspices of the *Ontario Society for the Prevention of Cruelty to Animals Act*, RSO 1990, c O.36 which do not have the same obligation to turn over the dogs and cats in their possession to research.
57   Ontario, Legislative Assembly, *Hansard*, Nos 242 & 243 (11 December 1969) at 9511–541.

was to prevent unnecessary cruelty to animals by ensuring that facilities are licensed and inspected.[58]

The definitions in section 1(1) establish a broad scope for activities done pursuant to the legislation. "Animal" is a live, non-human vertebrate; "research" is the use of animals in connection with studies, investigation, and teaching in any field of knowledge, including the use of animals for the performance of tests, the diagnosis of disease and the production and testing of preparation intended for use in the diagnosis, prevention, and treatment of any disease or condition; "research facilities" are premises on which animals are used in research and include premises used for the collecting, assembling, or maintaining of animals in connection with a research facility; and "supply facilities" are premises other than a research facility used for the breeding and rearing of animals under a contract between the supply operator and the operator of a research facility.

All research facilities that use animals must be registered, and are required to submit such reports respecting animals used in the research facility for research to the director (designated by the Minister of Agriculture, Food and Rural Affairs) as may be prescribed by the regulations (sections 4 and 15). Supply facilities must be licensed pursuant to section 2. Licences and registrations for both supply and research facilities may be revoked where facilities, materials, and equipment are not property maintained; where the operator has not complied with provisions of the Act or regulations, or any other Act relating to the cruelty, maltreatment, or neglect of animals (sections 2 and 4).

The Act authorizes the appointment of a chief inspector who is a veterinarian and other inspectors who can enter premises where animals are used or intended to be used in research, as well as any pound. In practice, enforcement has not been a significant government priority.

---

58  *Ibid.* Some argued that the legislation would protect stray animals from theft by animal dealers; that it would ensure that only unwanted animals who would otherwise be destroyed would be used in experiments; that it would protect the welfare of animals beyond the safeguards in the *Criminal Code*; that medical schools must have the things they need to teach those who will care for the sick; that animals need to be stressed so that scientists can learn how to minimize the same stress in people; that the legislation would dispel the public's worry about cruel experiments; and that there are not enough purpose-bred animals for research, so medical facilities have no other choice than to use pound animals. Others objected to the legislation on the basis that the majority of animals in pounds are wanted, lost pets; that animals bred for domestic purposes and companionship should not be used in this way and it is a betrayal of the public trust to do so; and that no animals should be considered to be used as experimental resources in the first place.

For many years, there has only been one inspector for all of Ontario, a province in which there are seventy-nine registered research facilities, some of which have multiple sites, such at the Universities of Toronto and Guelph. In total, there are at least 120 research sites across the province.[59]

Two provisions in the legislation address animal pain and both of these are qualified by the word "unnecessary." Section 16(1) requires an animal used in an experiment that is likely to result in pain to be anaesthetized so as to prevent him from suffering from unnecessary pain. Section 16(2) requires the use of analgesics adequate to prevent an animal from suffering unnecessary pain during his recovery from any experiment. These provisions directly exclude animals used in pain experiments, or in experiments where monitoring pain is part of the study, or where interfering with the natural process by way of anaesthetic or analgesic might otherwise hamper the results. More generally, where hurting animals is the object of the activity, such provisions are ineffective in protecting animal interests in any meaningful way.

Section 17 requires registered research facilities to establish an animal care committee, with a similar role to those established by the CCAC. One member must be a veterinarian, but there is no requirement for a community or arm's-length member. If an animal care committee has reason to believe that an offence has been or will be committed under section 16, it is required to order that any connected research be stopped, and that any animals in severe pain or illness as a result of the research be humanely destroyed. In this regard, section 17(4) refers to "the committee" and does not clearly empower individuals whose concerns are not shared by the rest of the institutional members.

Ontario's animal welfare legislation, the *Ontario Society for the Prevention of Cruelty to Animals Act*, is expressly excluded from applying in respect of animals in the possession of the operator of a registered research facility or of a licensed operator of a supply facility (section 18(9)).

The *Research Facilities and Supply Facilities* regulations[60] provide minimum standards for the housing and care of animals in research, and the *Transportation* regulations[61] prescribe conditions for transporting animals used or intended for use by a research facility. The *Pounds* regulations[62] provide minimum standards for the housing and care of animals in pounds and establish record-keeping requirements.

---

59   Author's records based on conversations with Ministry representatives including Ontario's inspector.

60   RRO 1990, Reg 24.

61   RRO 1990, Reg 25.

62   RRO 1990, Reg 23.

They also address the killing of unwanted animals, called "euthanasia," which can be done by methods including shooting and electrocution for dogs, as well as a variety of other methods (sections 21 and 22).

An effort to amend the legislation in 1987 to give municipalities the choice of whether or not to provide pound animals to research did not receive a third reading.[63] In 1988, when international awareness grew regarding the use of animals in cosmetic and product testing, Bill 190[64] was introduced which would have amended the Act to prohibit the use animals in non-medical experimentation involving the Draize irritancy eye test, the LD50 acute toxicity test, and similar tests.[65] This Bill did not pass a third reading either.[66]

---

63   Bill 21, *An Act to amend the Animals for Research Act*, 1st Sess, 33d Leg, Ontario, 1985. Supporters of the bill echoed concerns raised when the Act was introduced, and were concerned that three days was not sufficient time to allow a person to find a lost pet. Objections were that disallowing researchers to use animals from pounds would badly cripple medical research; that animal care committees ensure animals are being treated humanely; that if people were better pet owners, pounds would not be overrun with animals.

64   Bill 190, *An Act to amend the Animals for Research Act*, 1st Sess, 34th Leg, Ontario, 1988.

65   The Draize test is an acute toxicity test generally used for testing cosmetics. It involves applying a test substance to the eye or skin of a restrained, conscious animal and leaving it for a set amount of time before rinsing it out and recording its effects. The animals are observed for up to fourteen days for signs of erythema and edema in the skin test, and redness, swelling, discharge, ulceration, hemorrhaging, cloudiness, or blindness in the eye. The most common subjects are albino rabbits because their eyes do not tear and therefore do not wash away the substance; however, dogs are also used. Apart from the suffering they cause, the test is criticized as unscientific because of the differences between rabbit and human eyes. The LD50 (short for Lethal Dose) is the dose of a toxin, radiation, or pathogen required to kill half the members of a tested group after a specified test duration. It is used as a general indicator of a substance's acute toxicity. The LD50 is subject to criticism for the painful deaths and other effects it has on test animals and for its unreliability, imprecision, and variability as it relates to humans.

66   The tests were said to be unnecessary in that alternatives were available; that many products on the market had already been tested on animals and did not require further testing; that the tests can be misleading; that there was broad public support to abolish such tests; that they are not used for medical research; and that other jurisdictions in Europe and the United States had abolished these tests, or were considering doing so. Opposition to the bill claimed that animal tests are necessary, that tests are administered safely, and the current Act sufficiently ensured the care and safety of animals through inspections: see Ontario, Legislative Assembly, *Hansard*, No 118 (8 December 1988) 6590.

## b)  Pound Seizure in Ontario

The *Animals for Research Act* creates Canada's only remaining pound seizure laws, which operate in the following manner. Section 14(1) authorizes the use of animals in research who have been acquired from any of three sources: registered research facilities, pounds, and licensed supply facilities.[67] In regards to pounds, section 20(1) establishes a redemption period of three days during which a pound is not permitted to destroy an animal in its possession, allowing a brief opportunity for lost pets to be found. Municipalities may fix a longer redemption period by bylaw (section 20(2)). During the redemption period, pound operators are supposed to take all reasonable steps to find the owner of the dog or cat (section 19(4)).

Subsection 20(6) prohibits a pound from euthanizing a dog or cat after the redemption period, and provides the pound operator with three options: return to the original owner, sell or donate to a new owner, or sell to a research facility. Subsection 20(7) establishes four circumstances in which dogs and cats may be destroyed: if the animal's owner has so requested in writing; if an inspector or veterinarian has ordered the dog or cat be destroyed pursuant to subsection 20(11); if the operator has satisfied all requests from research facilities; or, during the redemption period, the dog or cat is ill or injured and incapable of living without suffering and all requests from research facilities have been satisfied.

Subsection 20(11) provides that an inspector or veterinarian can order a dog or cat to be destroyed (1) during the redemption period, if the dog or cat is ill or injured and incapable of living without suffering, or (2) where the dog or cat has not been redeemed, and is not suitable for use in research by reason of ill health, injury, malnutrition, excessive age, or other infirmity.

The combined effect of these provisions is that even if a pound operator believes that it is more humane for a particular animal to be euthanized than sold for research, the pound operator may not make that choice. Similarly, an inspector or veterinarian may order a dog or cat to be destroyed after the redemption period, even if the animal is not ill or injured, but such an order may only be given where the inspector or veterinarian determines that the animal is unsuitable for use in research. This prevents an inspector or veterinarian from choosing euthanasia as a humane alternative for any dog or cat that is suitable

---

67   However, a person who wishes to use an animal that is not of a type that may be readily purchased or otherwise acquired under s 14 by reason of its species or strain, or by reason of any specific disease condition or condition desired of the animal, is exempt from s 14: *General* regulation, RRO 1990, Reg 22, s 10.

for research. If there is demand from research facilities, dogs and cats suitable for research cannot be euthanized.

Therefore, while it is not quite accurate to say that pounds in Ontario are required to give up cats and dogs for research, their ability to euthanize those animals is restricted unless research facility requests have been met and the cumulative effect of these restrictions pressures pounds to cooperate. Pounds do sell cats and dogs to research,[68] although some pounds make arrangements with animal protection organizations to rescue unwanted animals and avoid the conflict.[69]

These provisions raise questions about the nature of pounds, the incompatible roles they are expected to fulfill, and the lack of public awareness[70] in this regard. It is fair to assume that the public expects

---

68  Pound seizure is not often publicly discussed, but in 2001, a thirteen-year-old golden retriever named Royal wandered off his property in Dundalk, Ontario. Someone found him some distance away and turned him over to the local dog pound. He was wearing a collar embroidered with his name with two dog tags, he was tattooed, his nails were clipped, and he was a little overweight. Despite the indications that he was a wanted dog, the pound sold him to a conditioning facility of the University of Guelph to be used in research. Finding him to be too old, the facility killed him. The pound sold Royal before the redemption period expired and the university accepted him without any confirmation in that regard. All the while, the family who lost him had been calling all appropriate authorities, placing newspapers ads, and doing everything they could to find him. The operators of the pound were charged pursuant to s 20 of the Act for failing to notify the OSPCA after it impounded a dog with an identification tag and for selling the dog before the expiry of the redemption period. They pled guilty, were convicted and fined in 2002. There was no penalty against the University of Guelph. See *Ontario (Agriculture, Food and Rural Affairs) (Re)*, Order PO-2103, 2003 CanLII 53854 (ON IPC) "Background" [Order PO-2103]; and *Action Alert*, Animal Alliance of Canada (2 November 2001), online: http://archive.groovy.net/citizens/animal1.htm.

69  For example, Animal Alliance of Canada, a non-profit advocacy organization, operates a rescue network called Project Jessie. Volunteers drive to cooperative pounds around the province to pick up dogs and cats who are vulnerable to being sold for research and place them in new homes, online: www.projectjessie.ca.

70  The incident described in note 68, above in this chapter, generated much critical publicity and concern about the use of pound animals in research. To collect information regarding the practices of the particular pound, as well as more general information regarding the acquisition, use, and disposal of pound-source dogs, access to pound inspection records, information on which City of Toronto pounds send animals to research facilities, and records of the number of animals requisitioned to be sent to research facilities, were requested from the Ministry of Agriculture and Food by a non-profit animal protection organization. The records were refused and appeals to the Information and Privacy Commissioner were largely dismissed on the basis that the Ministry did not control the records: Order PO-2103, above note 68 and *Ontario (Agriculture and Food)*

pounds to be places that safeguard lost animals or where someone looking for a pet can adopt one. However, the fact that pounds are established and regulated under the *Animals for Research Act*, the particular provisions discussed above, and the nominal maximum fees ($6 for a dog and $2 for a cat) which pounds can charge a research facility, suggest that the purpose of pounds is to be a supplier of animals for the research industry.[71]

### c) Other Provincial Jurisdictions

Animal welfare legislation in Alberta, Manitoba, New Brunswick, Nova Scotia, PEI, and Saskatchewan specifically mention research, and most of them make reference to some or all of the CCAC standards. This can be either by way of a positive duty to comply, or by way of a defence created for persons who are in compliance with the standards. Other provinces do not specifically address the subject.

Provincial animal welfare legislation generally prohibits causing distress in animals, or in some cases establishes positive animal care duties.[72] The acts generally empower agents authorized thereunder to inspect or investigate places where animals are held, or where animals are thought to be in distress, and this can include research facilities. However, no offences generally arise when that distress is caused or those duties are not met in the course of generally accepted practices. In this manner, animal welfare legislation protects the rights of industrial actors, including researchers, to hurt animals.

The statutes in these provinces do not encourage pound seizure of cats and dogs from pounds in the way that Ontario does, however, they do not discourage it. Generally, if a humane society cannot locate an animal's owner within the prescribed time, or if the owner does not or cannot pay the expenses incurred on the animal's behalf, the humane society can give away or sell the animal and the animal

---

(*Re*), Order PO-2365, 2005 CanLII 56482 (ON IPC); or that the release of such records would endanger the security of research facilities: *Ontario (Agriculture, Food and Rural Affairs) (Re)*, Order PO-2197, 2003 CanLII 53947 (ON IPC). These claims were strenuously disputed by the requester.

71  *General* regulation, above note 67, s 5(1). Section 4(1) of this regulation requires the operator of every research facility to submit an annual report to the director stating the total number of every species of animal used for research in the facility that year, the total number of dogs and of cats acquired from the different sources (including pounds), and the total number of dogs and of cats that in any experiment or surgical procedure did not recover from anaesthesia.

72  See discussion in Chapter 4.

becomes the property of the person to whom she is sold.[73] It is open to municipalities outside of Ontario to pass bylaws prohibiting the sale of impounded animals in their care to research.

In Alberta, the prohibition against causing or permitting an animal to be in distress contained in section 2 of the *Animal Protection Act*[74] does not apply if the distress results from an activity carried on in accordance with the regulations. The *Animal Protection Regulations*[75] define "research activities" in section 2(2) to include the use of animals in scientific investigation; scientific training or teaching other than as part of a school or in a school building; and testing of products including medical devices and biological, chemical, and pharmacological products. Section 2(1) of the regulations provides that "a person who owns or has custody, care or control of an animal for research activities must comply with the following Canadian Council on Animal Care documents," and it lists all twenty-two CCAC standards.

In Saskatchewan's *Animal Protection Act, 1999*,[76] an animal is not considered to be in distress if the animal is handled in a manner consistent with a standard or code of conduct, criteria, and practice that is prescribed as acceptable (section2(3)(a)). Acceptable codes and practices are set out in Part II of the Appendix to the *Animal Protection Regulations, 2000*[77] and they include the CCAC Guide to the Care and Use of Experimental Animals, as supplemented by policies and guidelines published and revised from time to time.

Under Manitoba's *Animal Care Act*,[78] the prohibition against causing suffering, harm, injury, or anxiety to an animal does not apply where it is caused by a treatment, process, or condition of an "accepted activity" (section 3(2)), nor is an animal considered to be in distress as a result of any treatment, process, or condition that occurs in the course of an accepted activity (section 6(2)). Research and teaching involving animals is an accepted activity pursuant to section 4(1). Accepted activities must be carried out in a manner consistent with a standard or code of conduct, criteria, or procedure specified as acceptable in the regulations, and consistent with generally accepted practice or procedures for such activity and that does not cause needless suffering (section

---

73    For example, see Alberta's *Animal Protection Act*, RSA 2000, c A-41, s 7(1) and Saskatchewan's *Animal Protection Act , 1999*, SS 1999, c A-21.1, s 10(1).

74    *Ibid.*

75    Alta Reg 203/2005.

76    Above note 73.

77    RRS, c A-21.1, Reg 1.

78    CCSM, c A84.

4(2)). Section 4(4) of the *Animal Care Regulation*[79] provides that animals raised for the purposes of, or used in, research and teaching activities, must be kept in accordance with the CCAC's Guide to the Care and Use of Experimental Animals policies and guidelines. Section 4(5) requires that research involving animals be reviewed and approved by an animal care committee structured according to the criteria set out in the same CCAC documents.

The New Brunswick *Society for the Prevention of Cruelty to Animals Act*[80] does not contain any provisions directly relating to animals in research and experimentation. Section 18 creates an affirmative duty to provide food, water, shelter, and care to an animal, and an offence for failing to comply. However, pursuant to section 4(2) of the *General Regulation*,[81] no one can be convicted of an offence under section 18(2) of the Act for treating an animal in a manner consistent with a standard or code of conduct, practice, or procedure set out in the Regulations, which includes the CCAC's *Guide to the Care and Use of Experimental Animals* by the CCAC.[82] Further, section 19(1) of the Act requires a person who destroys or assists in the destruction of an animal to do so in a humane manner in accordance with the regulations, which also includes acting in accordance with the CCAC Guide.

Nova Scotia's *Animal Protection Act*[83] defines "research activities" as the use of animals in scientific investigation, scientific teaching or training, or the testing of products including medical devices and biological, chemical, and pharmacological products, that are subject to prescribed standards and guidelines with respect to the care of animals in those activities (section 2(1)(k)). The Act does not apply to mandatory testing procedures undertaken by a research laboratory that are required by Health Canada, the World Health Organization, or any other organization prescribed in the regulations (section 3(3)). The legislation explicitly gives authority to the Nova Scotia Society for the Prevention of Cruelty to inspect premises in which animals are kept for research activities, as well as for breeding and sale (section 28). Where an inspector believes that an offence is being committed in respect of research animals, the inspector must consult or be accompanied by a representative of the animal care committee — or consult with the CCAC — if the facility is part of the CCAC assessment program (section 28(2)). The Act permits the passage of regulations prescribing

---

79   Man Reg 126/98.
80   RSNB 1973, c S-12.
81   NB Reg 2000-4.
82   *Ibid*, s 4(2) and Schedule A.
83   SNS 2008, c 33.

standards of care and standards of design, construction, and maintenance with respect to animals kept for sale, breeding, and research; the regulations must be consistent with CCAC guidelines and no action may be taken against a person who complies with those guidelines (sections 40(1)(a), (3), and (4)).

In Prince Edward Island, the *Animal Health and Protection Act*[84] exempts distress that results from an accepted activity, or an activity carried on in accordance with generally accepted practices (section 8). The Act also allows for regulations to be made respecting the use of animals for the purpose of medical or scientific research (section 16(e)). The *Animal Protection Regulations*[85] provide in section 5 that with respect to the use of animals for the purposes of medical or scientific research, the standards of care are those contained in the CCAC's Guide to the Care and Use of Experimental Animals.

### d) Another Aspect of Provincial Legislation: A Student's Right to Refuse

All provinces have human rights legislation which protects an individual against discrimination on the basis of a variety of enumerated grounds, including religious beliefs or creed.[86] A student who does not wish to engage in dissection or vivisection for course credit should be able to rely on that right so as not to be required to participate in practices which violate his beliefs. The duty to accommodate in human rights law[87] should include the duty to provide an alternative, and many such alternatives are readily available.[88]

No Canadian case has yet addressed the question of whether a deeply held spiritual, ethical, or philosophical belief in the sanctity of animal life constitutes a "creed" pursuant to human rights legislation. However, several Canadian complaints have been resolved on

---

84   RSPEI 1988, c A-11.1.

85   PEI Reg EC71/90.

86   For example, Alberta: *Alberta Human Rights Act*, RSA 2000, c 25.5, s 4; Nova Scotia: *Human Rights Act*, RSNS 1989, c 214, s 5; and Ontario: *Human Rights Code*, RSO 1990, c H.19, s 1.

87   The duty to accommodate is discussed in *British Columbia (Superintendent of Motor Vehicles) v British Columbia (Council of Human Rights)*, [1999] 3 SCR 868; and *British Columbia (Public Service Employee Service Relations Commission) v British Columbia Government and Service Employees' Union*, [1999] 3 SCR 3.

88   See Johns Hopkins Center for Alternatives to Animal Testing, above note 21. See also online: www.dissectionalternatives.org; and www.teachkind.org/dissectalt.asp.

that basis without the need for legal adjudication.[89] A recent British case lends support to the argument. A professional gardener lost his job when his employer learned that he was a hunt saboteur,[90] and an employment tribunal ruled that his animal rights beliefs in the sanctity of life were a philosophical belief akin to religion under the relevant employment law.[91] In the United States, the right of a student to object to vivisection or dissection in the classroom is protected by a variety of doctrines under federal and state law.[92]

# D. BIOTECHNOLOGY AND ANIMALS AS INTELLECTUAL PROPERTY

Genetic engineering, or biotechnology, creates new forms of life by re-combining genes from widely different sources and transferring genes between very different organisms. Its rapid and largely unregulated progress has profound implications for all aspects of human life and for life itself.[93] Animals are an integral part of every stage of development, including research, development, and application of biotechnological

---

89   Complaints to both high schools and colleges have been resolved by way of assertion of the student's human rights by correspondence and negotiation, culminating in the student being provided with an alternative activity that did not require using an animal.

90   This term is used to describe people who intentionally interrupt hunting, usually by making noise or otherwise scaring away the animals being pursued by hunters. It is practised in the United Kingdom and sometimes in the United States.

91   *Hashman v Milton Park (Dorset) Limited t/a Orchard Park* (31 January 2011), Case Number 3105555/2009 (Employment Tribunals), online: www.bindmans.com/fileadmin/bindmans/user/Departments/Employment/Hashman_judgment.pdf.

92   Gary L Francione & Anna E Charlton, *Vivisection and Dissection in the Class-room: A Guide to Conscientious Objection* (Jenkintown, PA: The American Anti-Vivisection Society, 1992).

93   The implications are biological, philosophical, social, environmental, geopolitical, and economic, and include matters related to health and food security on local and global scales. See, for example, Bill McGibbon, *The End of Nature* (New York: Random House, 2006) at 66 and 128–83; David Suzuki, *From Naked Ape to Superspecies: Humanity and the Global Eco Crisis*, revised ed (Vancouver: Greystone, 2004); Jeremy Rifkin, *The Biotech Century: Harnessing the Gene and Remaking the World* (New York: Tarcher/Putnam, 1998); Vandana Shiva, *Biopiracy: The Plunder of Nature and Knowledge* (Boston: South End Press, 1997); and Ted Howard & Jeremy Rifkin, *Who Should Play God? The Artificial Creation of Life and What it Means for the Future of the Human Race* (New York: Delacorte Press, 1977).

innovations. In various aspects of biotechnology, animals themselves or their body parts are the ultimate product. Like research generally, some genetic technologies are considered to be life saving, while others have purely commercial application.

Transgenic animals are used in biological studies of regulatory gene elements and in medical research as models of human disease. Research in genetic engineering has created mice prone to such things as malignant tumours, sickle-cell anemia, cystic fibrosis, and other diseases.[94] Transgenic animals are used in toxicology as responsive test animals. In agriculture and aquaculture, their genome is manipulated so that they will grow faster or yield more meat. They are considered valuable for developing drugs, producing vaccines, and for more directly commercial purposes, including production of pharmaceuticals. "Pharming" in animals refers to the insertion of particular genes into animals in order to produce human pharmaceuticals such as proteins in their milk, blood, urine, or tissues.[95] In this manner, they are transformed into little, individual protein factories, whereas in "xenotransplantation" (species-to-species transplantation), animals become individual organ factories.

One of the particular concerns about biotechnology is the lack of public awareness of the extent and content of the practice and its potential risks.[96] Xenotransplantation provides a good example of that problem in the Canadian context. In 1998, twelve genetically altered pigs

---

94  Montgomery, above note 5 at 88.

95  Nexia Biotechnologies in Quebec developed a mammary cell lactation system at McGill University, which has the commercial capacity to produce building blocks for pharmaceuticals and industrial bioproducts in transgenic animals. It cloned African dwarf goats who had received a spider silk gene, so that their progeny would secrete spider silk protein in their milk. The protein is extracted for a variety of potential medical, military, and industrial applications, including the production of bio-steel, a light, biodegradable fabric thought by some to be strong enough to stop bullets and shield spacecrafts from meteorites. Some of the goats were sold to the United States Defense Department: *Nexia Biotechnologies* (Montreal: McGill University, Office of Technology Transfer, 2002), online: www.mcgill.ca/files/ott/nexia.pdf.

96  One of the first books to discuss the problems appearing in cloned animals was Bernard E Rollin, *The Frankenstein Syndrome: Ethical and Social Issues in the Genetic Engineering of Animals* (New York: Cambridge University Press, 1995). For example, when the United State Department of Agriculture inserted human growth hormone genes into pigs and sheep, the animals had life-shortening pathological changes, including kidney and liver problems, and a wide variety of diseases and symptoms like lethargy, lameness, uncoordinated gait, and abnormal skull growth which led to bulging eyes and defective vision, thickened skin, being prone to gastric ulcers, severe synovitis, degenerative joint disease,

were imported to Canada from Britain. Since a significant problem with transplants is rejection, the pigs were engineered with human genes so as to make their organs more human-like and less likely to be rejected when ultimately transplanted into humans.[97] The pigs were owned by Imutran, a British pharmaceutical company that was a subsidiary of Novartis Pharmaceuticals. About the same time, Novartis provided a $1.5 million endowment to establish Canada's first university research chair in xenotransplantation at the University of Western Ontario.[98] In 1999, researchers at the University of Guelph Ontario were breeding humanized pigs and the organs of these transgenic pigs were later transplanted into baboons at the University of Western Ontario, as a first step toward human clinical trials.

The development of humanized pigs raises many questions relevant to the public interest.[99] However, the pigs were imported without the involvement of Health Canada. Government attention and public awareness began after much of this had happened. In February 1999, the Canada Gazette published an "Intent to Develop a Regulatory Framework for Xenografts — Notice to Interested Parties" with public comments due later that year.[100] In July 1999, Health Canada released its "Proposed Canadian Standard for Xenotransplantation" for public comment. In July 2000, the Canadian Public Health Association was commissioned by Health Canada to carry out a fourteen-month public consultation on the subject. The *National Post* reported in August 2000 that UK biopharmaceutical company PPL Therapeutics was negotiating with Canadian centres to see Canada become the centre of its xenotransplant program.[101]

---

heart disease, nephritis, pneumonia, problems in sexual behaviour, infertility, tendencies toward diabetes, and a compromised immune system (at 188).

97  Primates had been considered as a source of organs as they might have offered fewer rejection problems; however, ethical concerns arose as a result of their closeness to humans, whereas people already ate pigs.

98  The transplant market is estimated to be a multi-billion dollar market. The leading drugs used to try to prevent a foreign organ being rejected were also made by Novartis: Montgomery, above note 5 at 87.

99  For further discussion, see Margaret Sommerville, *The Ethical Canary: Science, Society and the Human Spirit* (Toronto: Penguin, 2001) at 89–116; and Lynda Birke & Mike Michael, "The Heart of the Matter: Animal Bodies, Ethics, and Species Boundaries" (1998) 6 Society and Animals 245.

100 This and subsequent details in this paragraph are available online: www.hc-sc. gc.ca/sr-sr/biotech/about-apropos/xeno-eng.php.

101 John Greenwood, "Leading Transgenic Player May Head to Canada: PPL Therapeutics in Negotiations with Potential Partners" *National Post* (19 August 2000) D4.

At the same time, concerns were arising about porcine endogenous retroviruses (PERVs) and their potential to infect humans through xenotransplantation.[102] Further, Britain's *Daily Express* did an exposé about selective publishing of research results, and extensive animal suffering in Imutran's British laboratories.[103] In September 2000, Imutran announced it was moving its operation from the United Kingdom to the United States. Consultations on the subject continued across Canada in 2001, but in 2002 the subject of transgenic pigs disappeared from the Canadian radar screen.

Access to information in order to facilitate debate, including debate about what is happening to animals in biotechnology, emerges as a clear legal issue. Among its many potentially problematic ramifications, biotechnology greatly expands and further institutionalizes the exploitation of animals. However, it has not instigated any additional legal attention to their interests. Peer-review guidelines on the use of transgenic animals produced by the CCAC do not discourage the use of animals in this way, rather they describe transgenic animals as "an extremely powerful tool for the development of disease models."[104] These guidelines have not been updated since 1997. By contrast, the financial implications of biotechnological developments have received considerable attention in intellectual property law.

---

102  PERVs could infect human cells in culture; pig pancreatic islets transplanted into immunosuppressed mice also lead to widespread PERV infection.

103  Several thousand pages of documents leaked to Uncaged Campaigns (an anti-vivisection organization based in the UK) from within Imutran revealed monkeys and wild-caught baboons suffering after receiving transplants of transgenic pig hearts and kidneys. The animals had been observed shivering, unsteady, in spasm, swollen, bruised, and with blood and pus seeping from wounds. Imutran later obtained an injunction prohibiting publication of its internal documents. See three articles by Lucy Johnston & Jonathan Calvert, "Terrible Despair of Animals Cut Up in the Name of Research" *Daily Express* (21 September 2000); "Xenotransplantation: Experimental Organ Transplants on Baboons Could be Putting Human Lives at Risk" *Daily Express* (22 September 2000); and "Xenotransplantation: Imutran Shuts Down Following *Daily Express* Articles" *Daily Express* (28 September 2000); also see discussion by Uncaged Campaigns, online: www.uncaged.co.uk/xeno.htm, and further consideration of the subject online: www.pbs.org/wgbh/pages/frontline/shows/organfarm/rights/controversy.html.

104  Canadian Council on Animal Care, *CCAC Guidelines on Transgenic Animals* (Ottawa: Canadian Council on Animal Care, 1997) at 1, online: www.ccac.ca/Documents/Standards/Guidelines/Transgenic_Animals.pdf.

## 1)  Patenting the Oncomouse

With the support of their corporate partner, DuPont, researchers at Harvard University inserted unnaturally occurring genes into the genome of a mouse in order to predispose the mouse to certain kinds of cancer and, according to some cancer researchers, to make a better tool for them in their work. Harvard then sought a patent on the process, on the mouse, and on all other non-human mammals on which it might impose the same process in future.

Patents had previously been issued in Canada for processes involving "lower life forms," such as microorganisms,[105] for simple organisms, such as a yeast culture capable of digesting by-products of the paper pulp process,[106] and for plants, such as a new variety of soybean,[107] but never for "higher life forms," such as mammals. The Commissioner of Patents rejected the application, as did the Patent Appeal Board and the Federal Court. The Federal Court of Appeal granted an appeal,[108] and the matter went to the Supreme Court. In 2002, the Supreme Court granted the appeal and rejected the patent by a 5:4 majority.[109]

For the patent to issue in Canada, Harvard had to demonstrate that the oncomouse, and all other non-human mammals which it might subject to its process, could be considered "inventions" under the *Patent Act*.[110] Invention is defined in section 2 as "any new and useful art, process, machine, manufacture or composition of matter, or any new and useful improvement in any art, process, machine, manufacture or composition of matter."[111]

Given its many implications, it was a landmark case. For present purposes, it marked a historic occasion because, for the first time, the Supreme Court acknowledged the validity of the animal rights perspective by permitting several animal advocacy organizations to intervene and make an argument from that perspective about why the Court should not entrench the notion that animals are mere things invented in a laboratory.[112]

---

105  *American Cyanamid v Charles E Frost & Co* (1965), 47 CPR 215 (Ex Ct).

106  *Re Application of Abitibi Co* (1982), 62 CPR (2d) 81 (Patent Appeal Board).

107  *Pioneer Hi-Bred v Canada (Commissioner of Patents)*, [1989] 1 SCR 1623.

108  *Harvard College v Canada (Commissioner of Patents)*, [2000] 4 FC 528 (CA).

109  *Harvard College v Canada (Commissioner of Patents)*, 2002 SCC 76 [*Harvard College*].

110  RSC 1985, c P-4.

111  The original *Patent Act* dated from 1869 and the definition of invention had not changed much since that time, see *Harvard College*, above note 109 at para 41.

112  Other intervenors included a coalition of church groups, who had their own ideas about who was the inventor of animal life, as well as a coalition of

In particular, those organizations argued that the idea that animals are machines was an antiquated notion that had lost its factual base; that their legal status as things was undergoing extensive debate in modern times; and that change was imminent. Even if this case was not the place to decide that the legal status of animals had changed, nor was it appropriate to re-entrench that status by finding that animals are "machines" or "manufactures" invented by humans for their own use. In terms of being "compositions of matter," given what modern science knows about the similarities of human and other animal life, there was no logically consistent way of interpreting the term "composition of matter" broadly enough to include all nonhuman animals, and still exclude human animals.[113]

It was the latter concern that troubled the majority.[114] It found that "higher life forms," such as humans and other animals, were not included in the definition of "invention'" in the *Patent Act*. To allow such a patent was a radical departure from the traditional patent regime which would require clear words to that effect by Parliament. It found that the words "machine" and "manufacture" do not imply a conscious, sentient, living creature, and that there were additional reasons for finding that the phrase "composition of matter" does not either. The oncomouse patent had been issued in the United States, Japan, and Europe, so the fact that the Canadian court had the resolve to decide against the international trend was significant.[115]

---

environmental and social justice groups, who had concerns about the global environmental and other implications of redefining life as a manufactured process, subject to ownership by profit-driven corporations. Their factums are available, respectively, online: http://files.efc-canada.net/si/Reproductive%20and%20 Genetic%20Technologies/Harvard_Mouse.pdf, and http://s.cela.ca/files/uploads/ sccfactum.pdf.

113  They further argued that Harvard was in an ironic position since, as several branches of science had already called into question the line that had historically been drawn between humans and the rest of the animal kingdom, whatever may have been left of that line was now further degraded by the very genetic manipulation which Harvard itself was undertaking. Once the lines are blurred by the introduction of various intermediate points, legislators and courts become obliged to rethink what the lines are all about in the first place. They cautioned that the patent would effectively establish a privatized, parallel animal kingdom where different rules apply. A copy of their factum is on file with the author.

114  *Harvard College*, above note 109 at paras 155 and following.

115  For a helpful summary, see Angela Furlanetto, "The Harvard Mouse Case: Developments in the Patentability of Life Forms" *CBA National Intellectual Property Section Newsletter* (June 2003), online: www.cba.org/cba/newsletters/ip-2003/ ip2.aspx.

Neither the majority nor the dissent endorsed the animal rights perspective, but for its first encounter with the argument, the majority made some interesting observations. For example, Bastarache J wrote that the concerns related to animal welfare are more appropriately addressed outside the patent system because by the time a researcher is in a position to file a patent, any harm to the animal resulting from research will already have been done.[116] This is certainly true, although it misapprehended the intervenors' point, which was directed more at the conceptual premise of the patent sought and of the practice, than at their effects.

The minority's treatment of the subject was more normative and dismissive. Justice Binnie wrote that regardless of what position is adopted under patent law, animals have been and will continue to be used in laboratories for scientific research, and that Parliament might address animals' rights as a distinct subject matter. He went on to say that refusing the patent would not prevent Harvard from making and selling the oncomouse, but would deny it its *quid pro quo* for the disclosure of its invention.[117]

Interestingly, the very concerns which most preoccupied the majority in respect of the implications for humans were those which animal rights organizations sought to invoke in respect of animals. Justice Bastarache cited the potential for commodification, commercialization, and objectification of human life, the disturbing aspect of which was not so much the exchange of money as the notion that a subject — a moral agent with autonomy and dignity — could be treated as an instrument for the needs or desires of others without any ethical objections.[118] While he did not go on to explain why those concerns do not extend to other animal species, the question was left hanging, begging to be considered in a future case.

Different concerns occupied the dissenting justices, all of which are discernible from Binnie J's opening paragraph:

> The biotechnology revolution in the 50 years since discovery of the structure of DNA has been fuelled by extraordinary human ingenuity and financed in significant part by private investment. Like most revolutions, it has wide ramifications, and present potential and serious dangers as well as past and future benefits. In this appeal, how-

---

116  *Harvard College*, above note 109 at para 168.

117  *Ibid* at para 100.

118  *Ibid* at para 176, citing Ted Schrecker *et al*, *Ethical Issues Associated with the Patenting of Higher Life Forms* (Ottawa: Intellectual Property Policy Directorate, Industry Canada, 1997) at 62.

ever, we are only dealing with a small corner of the biotechnology controversy. We are asked to determine whether the oncomouse, a genetically modified rodent with heightened susceptibility to cancer, is an invention. The legal issue is a narrow one and does not provide a platform on which to engage in debate over animal rights, or religion, or the arrogance of the human race.[119]

The minority's view ultimately prevailed. The patent application was subsequently amended to omit the "composition of matter" claims and the patent was granted the following year; it remains valid until 2020.[120]

---

119 *Harvard College, ibid* at para 1.
120 Canadian patent 1,341,442 was granted to Harvard College on 7 October 2003, patent number CA 1341442.

# CHAPTER 8

# BEASTS

The squirrel that you kill in jest dies in earnest.

—Henry David Thoreau

Despite the lengthy history of Canadian wildlife laws, there is very little legal writing about them, and what has been written has the same emphasis as the laws themselves: that of resource conservation.[1] In that vein, it has been said that Canadian wildlife laws have gone through three stages of evolution.[2]

The first stage was the "game management era," concerned largely with the animals people hunted and hunting controls. The second stage was the "wildlife management era," characterized by ongoing refinement of hunting controls using a combination of geographic areas, seasons, and limits on the number of animals that could be killed. Habitat protection and management, artificial replenishing of animals, and captive breeding were introduced. The third and current stage is the "sustainable wildlife management era," which reflects continuing changes to the values that Canadians attach to wildlife. International commitments began to affect the content of domestic laws. Laws expanded from a focus on hunted animals to amphibians, reptiles, and other ani-

---

1   For such a review of the history of federal and provincial wildlife laws in Canada and their respective constitutional authorities, see John Donihee, *The Evolution of Wildlife Law in Canada: CIRL Occasional Paper #9* (Calgary: Canadian Institute of Resources Law, May 2000) [Donihee].

2   *Ibid.* The three stages are discussed at 13–17.

mals, as well as the management of habitats and the environment more generally, including, in some cases, addressing species at risk.

This chapter is not focused on conservation, a topic that falls within the realm of environmental law. In this chapter, the relevant laws are considered from the perspective of animals, not as populations, but as individuals who are affected by the activities therein prescribed.[3]

Wild animals living freely are not seen to have an owner, but at common law they were subject to the rule of capture, according to which they could be reduced to the possession of a person who asserted control over them by capturing or killing them.[4] Most jurisdictions have overridden the common law presumption and assumed property interests in wild animals by expressly asserting that wildlife ownership vests in the Crown unless otherwise transferred in accordance with the legislation. Provincial and territorial governments generally have the primary control over wildlife in Canada. Because of provincial ownership of Crown lands, most wildlife habitat is under provincial control. Federal authority generally arises in respect of migratory birds, marine mammals, and some issues relating to trade and endangered species.

As noted, all of these laws have traditionally regarded animals as natural resources. Consistent with that perspective, most of the relevant legislation aims at protecting the human interest in these resources and in allocating it among competing human claims. It seeks to enhance certain animal resources and reduce others, so as to ensure that the preferred resources continue to be available for human use. This is what is meant by the term "wildlife management." Modern wildlife legislation also often includes an administrative system which minimally controls the manner in which wild animals may be held captive, hurt, and killed, whether for human sustenance, profit, or amusement.

Wildlife management is a controversial subject. The idea that people can and should control natural populations has been much criticized,

---

3   For this reason, this chapter will not generally address the important topic of endangered species. Legal protection of wildlife in the environmental context is advocated by Ecojustice (formerly the Sierra Legal Defence Fund), among others, and its website contains useful information on the subject, online: www. ecojustice.ca. Nor does this chapter address fish. This is not to imply that fish have no welfare interests worthy of consideration, or that their capacity for pain is in doubt. Rather, the extensive practice of fishing, both recreational and commercial, is a vast subject unto itself.

4   See discussion in Chapter 3; also: *Young v Hitchens* (1844), 6 QB 606; and RM Allison, "Widlife Ownership in Canada" (1980) 28 Chitty's LJ 47.

and yet the assumption that it is a reliable science underlies these legislative schemes and serves as justification for killing many animals.[5]

Beyond being classified as resources, animals who are the subject of this legislation are labelled more specifically in accordance with their human purpose: "fur-bearers" are the many species of mammals who are killed to supply the fur industry; hunted mammals and birds are called "game," and the total number of individuals who may be killed pursuant to a licence is referred to as the "bag limit." Undesirable animals are referred to as "pests," "vermin," and "nuisances." Such animals are "destroyed" or "culled," implying an objective necessity. As in other areas of animal use, the language obscures the individual animal whose life is affected by the prescribed practices, and it is indicative of the low moral status animals had when the rules governing them were codified.

---

5   Some wildlife management efforts are directed at increasing wildlife populations, whether to enhance hunting or trapping opportunities, or because a population is acknowledged to be at risk. Others are directed at reducing certain populations, whether to increase hunting and trapping opportunities in respect of other animals (such as reducing a wolf population because they kill too many of the caribou people want to kill), or for other reasons, including real or perceived threats to humans, other animals, or the environment, or because they are seen to be a nuisance. Wildlife management is driven by largely political objectives, meaning that its goal is to manipulate a population to the level that some humans would prefer, as distinct from allowing nature to self-regulate. The term "overpopulation" reflects a subjective, value-driven, human preference.

Wildlife populations are affected by many complex interacting factors, both natural and human-caused. When a significant percentage of a given wildlife population is removed from a particular environment in which it has been succeeding, that reduces competition among survivors for existing resources. Since there is more food and shelter to go around, there is often an increase in fecundity and subsequent survival. This process, sometimes called "compensatory mortality," explains why many attempts to reduce large populations of animals not only fail, but are counter-productive. When there is compensatory mortality, healthier animals often produce more young, who in turn survive better, thereby inducing a growth curve that causes the population to exceed what it was before the management initiative was implemented. One way of avoiding this result is to remove so many animals that the population is reduced too much to replenish itself over the next seasons, which can push a species to a point at which its recovery is endangered. A more modern approach recognizes, first, that species become abundant because of a suite of factors, including their compatibility with anthropogenic environmental changes as a function of their overall adaptability, and second, that efforts should be directed toward understanding the role humans play in affecting wildlife populations, and in trying to control human behaviour as well.

While wildlife legislation has evolved and broadened its concerns over the years, it still clearly favours consumptive uses of animals in which the object is to kill them, as compared to non-consumptive activities, such as environmental tourism, observation of living animals, and photography. Minimal aspects of the legislation address ethical issues regarding animals themselves. In recent years, animal protection has been found to be a valid purpose of this legislation, but there is a long way to go before it can accurately be said that wildlife legislation protects animals.

As with all laws, their effects are entirely dependent on the underlying commitment to enforcement. Further, many of the activities which this legislation addresses occur over vast distances in remote areas which cannot be closely monitored. Therefore, the fact that a practice is prohibited or circumscribed does not sufficiently indicate whether or not it occurs. The occasional prohibitions against causing animals "unnecessary suffering" or requiring that they be killed "humanely" must be read not only in terms of the interpretive constraints that have been discussed elsewhere in this book, but also the landscape in which they occur.

As wildlife laws move toward their fourth era of evolution, they will have to continue to incorporate the respect people increasingly express for wildlife and replace the assumption that animals are merely resources to be managed. Perhaps the fourth stage will begin to shift to an era of respectful coexistence.

Part A below reviews issues addressed by provincial legislation, and Part B focuses on those governed by federal legislation.

# A. PROVINCIAL WILDLIFE LEGISLATION

Each province and territory has legislation governing the use, management, and, to some degree, the protection of wildlife within its jurisdiction. The modern trend in wildlife legislation is heavily reliant on broad enabling statutes supported by voluminous regulations, which provide for flexibility and specificity.[6] This section reviews some of the common general features of these laws, highlighting a few of the many specific issues that have attracted legal attention in recent years. The first section looks at issues affecting animals living freely, and the second section focuses on animals in captivity. The relevant statutes are:

---

6    Donihee, above note 1 at 2.

- Alberta: *Wildlife Act*[7]
- British Columbia: *Wildlife Act*[8]
- Manitoba: *Wildlife Act*[9]
- New Brunswick: *Fish and Wildlife Act*[10]
- Newfoundland and Labrador: *Wild Life Act*[11]
- Nova Scotia: *Wildlife Act*[12]
- Northwest Territories: *Wildlife Act*[13]
- Nunavut: *Wildlife Act*[14]
- Prince Edward Island: *Wildlife Conservation Act*[15]
- Quebec: *An Act Respecting the Conservation and Development of Wildlife*[16]
- Ontario: *Fish and Wildlife Conservation Act, 1997*[17]
- Saskatchewan: *Wildlife Act, 1988*[18]
- Yukon: *Wildlife Act*[19]

## 1) Wildlife Living Freely

### a) Administration and Licensing

Provincial wildlife statutes grant broad discretionary powers to provincial ministers to manage wildlife within a province. Ministers may delegate administrative responsibilities to a variety of actors, including departmental staff. Enforcement responsibilities are delegated to wildlife and conservation officers. These officers have the authority and responsibility vested in a peace officer. Other individuals empowered to enforce provincial wildlife law include police officers and other officials. Some provincial regimes require ministers to present regular reports on the administration of the Act to provincial legislature and/or Cabinet.

The Crown generally grants itself immunity from liability for the actions of wildlife, but some regimes create compensation schemes by

---

7   RSA 2000, c W-10 [*Alberta*].
8   RSBC 1996, c 488 [*British Columbia*].
9   CCSM, c W130 [*Manitoba*].
10   SNB 1980, c F-14.1 [*New Brunswick*].
11   RSNL 1990, c W-8 [*Newfoundland and Labrador*].
12   RSNS 1989, c 504 [*Nova Scotia*].
13   RSNWT 1988, c W-4 [*Northwest Territories*].
14   Snu 2003, c 26 [*Nunavut*].
15   RSPEI 1988, c W-4.1 [*Prince Edward Island*].
16   RSQ, c C-61.1 [*Quebec*].
17   SO 1997, c 41 [*Ontario*].
18   SS 1998, c W-13.12 [*Saskatchewan*].
19   RSY 2002, c 229 [*Yukon*].

which the government can provide compensation for damage caused by wildlife in prescribed circumstances.

Licensing regimes are the primary tool used to exercise control over consumptive wildlife activities. It is generally prohibited to hunt or trap most animals without a licence or permit issued by the minister. A licence is also generally required for guides and outfitters, fur and game farms, import, export, and trading activities. Licences are issued for a fee, and conditions can be attached—addressing such things as minimum age,[20] residency,[21] and training requirements. They are issued for limited time periods, and may specify areas, species, hunting methods, and numbers of animals that may be killed. Some jurisdictions exempt Aboriginal persons from licensing requirements and recognize a special Aboriginal right to hunt.

### b)   Enforcement, Offences, and Penalties

Wildlife officers enforce the acts and have the powers of peace officers. Broad enforcement powers generally include the power to enter onto land; demand to see a permit, licence, or identification; inspect weapons; inspect animals; stop vehicles; search without a warrant if there are reasonable grounds to do so; seize property; and make arrests.

Non-compliance with legislation and regulations is generally a summary conviction offence. Limitation periods for instituting prosecutions vary. Penalties include fines and imprisonment, seizure, and forfeiture. Some provinces provide courts with authority to order creative sentencing, including ordering a guilty party to take remedial action, such as paying the cost of habitat remediation or doing anything else necessary to address the harm caused by the offence. In some cases, courts are authorized to prohibit a person convicted of an offence from engaging in activities that could result in the continuation or repetition of the crime.[22] Corporations are generally subject to higher penalties than individuals. Subsequent offences attract higher penalties than first offences. Licences and permits are usually cancelled or suspended upon conviction for a specified period of time.

---

20   Age limits are as low as twelve in some jurisdictions, or even younger with the minister's approval. For example, in Ontario, a twelve-year-old resident can hunt by authority of a hunter apprenticeship safety card: *Hunting*, O Reg 665/98, ss 9 & 10. In Prince Edward Island, a twelve-year-old (or someone even younger, with the minister's permission) may get a junior trapping licence for $5: *Fur Harvesting Regulations*, PEI Reg EC663/04, ss 2(2) & 3.

21   Non-residents are often permitted to hunt pursuant to a different licence.

22   For example: *Saskatchewan*, above note 18, s 76(3); *New Brunswick*, above note 10, s 105.1; and *Yukon*, above note 19, s 169(1).

Some jurisdictions have different categories of offences with different penalties attached. Maximum fines can be fairly low, from several hundred to several thousand dollars, particularly in the eastern half of the country. In western provinces, maximum fines can be in the hundreds of thousands of dollars. Such maximum fines generally apply in the context of offences related to habitat destruction where damages, to the extent they are compensable, could well exceed that figure.

In Nunavut, all offences are subject to a maximum fine of $500,000 and/or up to six months in prison.[23] For a corporation, the fine is between $500,000 and $1 million. In Northwest Territories, for many offences, including but not limited to those involving species at risk, the maximum fine is $250,000 for an individual, and one year in prison. For a corporation, the fine can be up to $1 million. For any contravention for a commercial purpose, the maximum fine increases to $1 million for an individual.[24]

In both of these jurisdictions, subsequent offences entail fines of twice the amount of a first offence. Further, offences are continuing, meaning that each day the offence continues can be seen as a separate offence. Fines are cumulative, meaning a fine imposed for an offence involving more than one member of a species, can be calculated in respect of each one as though it had been the subject of a separate information. Further, if a justice of the peace is satisfied that monetary benefits accrued or could have accrued to a person by way of an offence, the justice of the peace has authority to order an additional fine, in excess of the prescribed maximum fine, equal to the estimated amount of the benefit.[25]

In New Brunswick, fines are very low; however, the law imposes mandatory, if minimal, prison sentences for some offences, such as bartering, buying, or selling hunting rights for land or water; hunting moose, deer, or bear in closed season or by trap or snare, or without a licence or in excess of bag limits; hunting while impaired; selling animal parts without a licence; illegal possession of bear, moose, or deer; killing wildlife with poison; and careless hunting. These offences attract custodial sentences of between seven days and one month, or two months for subsequent offences, in addition to the fine.[26]

---

23  *Nunavut*, above note 14, ss 221–29.
24  *Northwest Territories*, above note 13, s 91.1
25  A similar provision also exists in *British Columbia*, above note 8, s 84; *Alberta*, above note 7, s 96; and *Yukon*, above note 19, s 165.
26  *New Brunswick*, above note 10, ss 104, 105, and Schedule A.

### c) Interests Protected: Human, Animal, Habitat

A review of wildlife legislation across Canada reveals its priorities to be first, the protection of human interests in wildlife consumption, then habitat, and finally the interests of animals themselves.

Nova Scotia expresses these purposes directly. Section 2 describes the purposes of the Act to include: maintaining diversity of species at levels of abundance to meet management objectives; ensuring adequate habitat for established wildlife populations; regulating hunting, fishing, and the possession and sale of wildlife; and providing for the continued renewal of the resource while managing its optimum recreational and economic uses. A specific purpose is to recognize that angling, hunting, and trapping are valued and safe parts of the heritage of the province.

Consistent with that focus, the Act creates a series of offences related to interfering with lawful hunting or fishing and disturbing a hunter. While a person may disturb animals for the purpose of trying to kill them, a person may not do so for the purpose of trying to help them: it is prohibited to disturb animals "with the intention of preventing or impeding lawful hunting or fishing"; it is also an offence to knowingly touch or interfere with any trap set in accordance with the legislation.[27]

Interfering with lawful hunting, trapping, or fishing is also prohibited in other jurisdictions.[28]

Nunavut's lengthy *Wildlife Act*[29] expresses a strong environmental ethic. The purpose of the Act, set out at section 1, is to establish a comprehensive regime for the management of wildlife and habitat in Nunavut, including the conservation, protection, and recovery of species at risk, in a manner that implements provisions of the Nunavut Land Claims Agreement respecting wildlife, habitat, and the rights of Inuit in relation to wildlife and habitat. A list of values, which the Act is intended to uphold, is in section 1(2), and there is a further list of conservation principles in section 1(3). Wildlife is still clearly considered a resource, and the legislation emphasizes the rights of Innu to hunting, trapping, and consumptive wildlife uses; it does however express a greater sense of respect within that context than that which is apparent in other jurisdictions, including listing several offences at sections 68 to 75 under the heading "respect for wildlife."

Section 8 identifies thirteen guiding Inuit principles and concepts that apply under the Act. Included in these are the notions that: people

---

27   *Nova Scotia*, above note 12, ss 38 and 48(4).

28   For example: *Ontario*, above note 17, s 13; *Alberta*, above note 7, s 47; *Northwest Territories*, above note 13, s 83; and *Nunavut*, above note 14, s 60.

29   *Nunavut, ibid*.

are stewards of the environment and must treat all of nature holistic-
ally and with respect, because humans, wildlife and habitat are inter-
connected and each person's actions and intentions towards everything
else have consequences, for good or ill; hunters should only take what
is necessary for their needs and not waste the wildlife they hunt; malice
towards animals is prohibited even though they are harvested for food
and other purposes; hunters should avoid causing wild animals unnecessary suffering when harvesting them; and all wildlife should be
treated respectfully.[30]

Habitat protection is addressed in wildlife legislation in two general ways. First, by protecting the specific abode of wildlife species (such
as dens, dams, or nests) or their habitat through proscriptions against
interference or disturbance. Second, by acquiring lands for habitat protection, designating them as protected, and limiting the activities that
may be conducted there. There are often exceptions, such as for trapping, or when an animal is considered to be causing property damage, and a minister may permit interference as a discretionary matter.
Legislation can create habitat conservation funds for the conservation
of biodiversity, habitat, acquiring land for conservation, or increasing
knowledge of wildlife.

Despite the fact that the Court of Appeal for Ontario determined
that animal protection is a legitimate purpose of wildlife legislation,[31]
most provincial legislation contains relatively few provisions that can
be seen to be protective of the interests of individual animals. Such
provisions include prohibitions against harassing wildlife or disturbing
wildlife in their abode, and prohibitions against particular practices associated with hunting and trapping, like hunting certain species with
dogs, with lights at night, or while they are swimming or captive. Some
legislation requires hunters to kill animals they have wounded, or provides that animals should be killed humanely or without unnecessary
suffering.

### d)  Incentives and Proactive Efforts to Kill Unwanted Wildlife

Wildlife legislation is often used to encourage the killing of individuals
of a particular species that is seen to be too populous or otherwise
undesirable. Legislation may also contain very loose rules, or no rules,

---

30   Section 75, *ibid*, explicitly states that any person harvesting a wild animal shall
respect certain Inuit principles, which essentially reemphasize the guiding
principles set out in s 8.

31   *Ontario Federation of Anglers & Hunters v Ontario (Ministry of Natural Resources)*
(2002), 211 DLR (4th) 741 at para 48 (Ont CA). [*Anglers & Hunters*] This case is
discussed further in Section A(1)(f), below in this chapter.

around the killing of animals of particular species that are seen by some to be undesirable.[32] There are numerous examples in every jurisdiction, a sampling is reviewed here.

Most recently, coyotes have been perceived as nuisances that invade human space, destroy livestock, and endanger the safety of communities. Newfoundland and Labrador offers a $25 "collection fee" for each coyote carcass returned, and establishes no limit on the number of coyotes a person may kill.[33] In 2010, Nova Scotia introduced a $20 coyote "pelt incentive" and made a full-year open season for coyotes,[34] following a coyote attack on a young Nova Scotia woman—the province's first coyote-related human fatality.[35] Ontario has held coyote killing contests in which hunters who kill the most coyotes are awarded prizes including cash, electronics, and hunting gear.[36] These contests take place in apparent violation of provincial law, which makes it is an offence to "hire, employ, or induce another person to hunt for gain" and to "pay or accept a bounty."[37]

In recent years, complaints that the moose population is too high in Newfoundland and Labrador have been the subject of controversy. In June 2011, a class action was certified by motorists hurt in collisions with moose, claiming damages from the provincial government. Some have called for 60,000 moose to be killed in the province.[38] Provincial

---

32  Such acts are controversial. Wildlife populations are the product of a complex interaction of factors, including natural processes and many competing human activities. See further discussion, above note 5, regarding the principle of compensatory mortality. Coyotes provide a good example of it; efforts at artificially reducing their population tend to be counter-productive. By contrast, wolves are more vulnerable to population-reduction efforts.

33  *Wild Life Regulations*, CNLR 1156/96, s 81.

34  Nova Scotia Department of Natural Resources, News Release, "Province Announces Plan to Reduce Aggressive Coyote Behaviour" (22 April 2010), online: www.gov.ns.ca/news/details.asp?id=20100422001.

35  Mary Vallis, "Nova Scotia Now Offering $20 Bounty on Coyotes" *National Post* (22 April 2010), online: http://news.nationalpost.com/2010/04/22/nova-scotia-now-offering-20-bounty-on-coyotes-updated/.

36  According to an official with the Ministry of Natural Resources, there were eight coyote killing contests in the 2011 in Ontario, primarily in the eastern part of the province.

37  *Ontario*, above note 17, ss 11(1)(b) and (e). The penalty provisions in s 102 suggest that offences under s 11 are supposed to be treated seriously; the maximum fine is $100,000 and up to two years in prison, while for most other offences, the maximum fine is $25,000.

38  *George and Bellows v HMTQ in Right of Newfoundland and Labrador*, 2011 01G 0013 CP (SCNLTD); Statement of Claim online: www.chescrosbie.com/library/2011_04_21_Amended_Statemet_of_Claim.pdf. Also see Sue Bailey, "Moose Crash Class Action Lawsuit against Newfoundland Can Proceed" *iPolitics* (28

officials have also claimed that moose are damaging the ecological health of the forest in provincial parks and other areas of the province. The province planned a cull for 2011 and authorized the killing of a significantly higher number of moose, including permission to hunt moose for the first time in Terra Nova and Gros Morne National Parks.[39]

In Prince Edward Island, beavers have been extirpated from the province on several past occasions and the current population was introduced in 1949. The province now hires trappers to kill between seventy-five and one hundred beavers every year, claiming that it must reduce the population to prevent property damage and harm to public roads, trees, and migratory fish runs.[40]

Alberta has historically had few rules governing the hunting of wolves. At various points, the law has allowed unrestricted wolf hunting, no limits on the number of animals that may be killed, trapping, and bounties.[41] Caribou are a threatened species in Alberta, and the province's Woodland Caribou recovery plan calls for a wolf cull with the goal of reducing wolf predation on caribou. The province has been systematically shooting and killing wolves from chartered helicopters since 2005 in some areas.[42]

In British Columbia, the University of Victoria announced plans in 2008 to rid the campus of the estimated 1,600 rabbits living there, claiming they were a nuisance that destroyed vegetation, dug holes and tunnels on the lawns and athletic fields, and were a potential health and safety hazard.[43] Under Schedule C of the *Designation and Exemption Regulation*,[44] rabbits are listed as non-native wildlife species known

---

August 2011), online: ipolitics.ca/2011/06/07/moose-crash-class-action-lawsuit-against-newfoundland-can-proceed/.

39 "Moose Cull Set for National Parks in N.L." *CBC News* (6 April 2011), online: www.cbc.ca/news/canada/newfoundland-labrador/story/2011/04/05/moose-cull-parks-canada-406.html.

40 "P.E.I. Begins Beaver Culling" *CBC News* (12 May 2010), online: www.cbc.ca/news/canada/prince-edward-island/story/2010/05/12/pei-beaver-cull-584.html.

41 Alberta Wilderness Association, "Summary of Wolf Management" (undated), online: http://albertawilderness.ca/issues/wildlife/wolves/management.

42 Frank Landry, "Wolf Cull Continues" *Edmonton Sun* (17 February 2010). A frequent concern in this kind of hunt is the ability of a shooter to accurately target a wolf from the height and motion of a helicopter. Efforts to protect caribou populations are often aimed at protecting the human resource; in other words, wolves are killed because they kill the caribou that humans want to be able to kill.

43 The rabbits first began to appear on campus after pet owners began abandoning unwanted rabbits on campus. See University of Victoria, "Rabbit Management Questions and Answers" (18 July 2011), online: http://communications.uvic.ca/rabbits/qa.php#question9.

44 BC Reg 168/90.

to destroy property or be detrimental to native wildlife. Schedule C species are subject to fewer restrictions regulating their hunting, capture, possession, and killing than other wildlife and they may be captured or killed without a licence. The Ministry of Environment took the position that since the rabbits were Schedule C wildlife residing on private land, the university could control the population as it saw fit, as long as it abided by relevant regulations.[45]

The university began to trap and kill rabbits until the founder of a local animal protection group won an interim injunction, allowing advocates time to acquire permits and undertake a relocation effort.[46] The injunction was later overturned on the basis that the petitioner lacked standing, and the court characterized the dispute as one that lent itself to advocacy and activism, but not to law.[47] The merits of the petitioner's position were never assessed. As of March 2011, fewer than a dozen rabbits remained on campus.

### e)  Hunting, Possession, and Trade in Wildlife

Ministers or their delegates may generally establish limits on the number and species of animals a person may kill and possess pursuant to a licence, open and close dates for seasons in which species can be hunted, the hours and days of the week when hunting is permitted,

---

45  *Cassells v University of Victoria*, 2010 BCSC 1213 at para 10.

46  The university made some efforts to assess the feasibility of a trap, neuter, release, or re-homing program for the rabbits. There were also volunteer efforts to relocate the rabbits to sanctuaries or homes. However, because the rabbits were classified as wildlife, rescue groups were required to obtain permits to lawfully capture, sterilize, and transfer rabbits to sanctuaries or to find homes for them elsewhere. The permitting process was allegedly onerous, expensive, and subject to considerable administrative challenges. See Vancouver Media Co-op, News Release, "Year of the Rabbit Brings New Threats to Rabbits at UVic and in BC" by Roslyn Cassells (8 February 2011), online: http://vancouver.mediacoop. ca/newsrelease/6204.

47  *Cassells v University of Victoria*, above note 45. Local advocates could not afford legal representation and Cassells was self-represented. The British Columbia Supreme Court found that Cassells had not demonstrated that she had a private right or would suffer special damage peculiar to herself, and that she had no legal, equitable, or proprietary interest in the animal that would overlap with the public rights provided in the *Wildlife Act*. The court rejected the argument that the funds her organization raised gave rise to a fiduciary obligation to protect rabbits, or that her reputation as an organizer and politician might suffer if rabbits continued to be trapped or killed. Nor was she found to have public interest standing, as the action was brought against the university as a private entity and did not challenge the validity of provincial legislation or the actions of the Ministry.

and the areas where hunting and trapping may occur. Provinces are frequently divided into multiple geographic zones, sometimes called wildlife management units or areas, with different rules governing different zones.

Hunting and trapping on private property is generally prohibited without the consent of the owner or occupier of the land, and owners may signal their intention to allow it or not by posting signs on their property. However, this rule varies. In some provinces, the absence of signs posted on property does not automatically signal that the owner or occupier consents, and consent must be obtained directly. In other provinces, the onus is on the owner or occupier of the land to post signs prohibiting hunting or trapping activity.

In New Brunswick, a property owner who posts no signs is deemed to consent to hunting, trapping, and snaring on the land, whereas in Manitoba, a hunter or trapper must obtain permission from the owner or occupant of private land, whether or not signs are present on the property. In Saskatchewan, an owner or occupier of private property may prohibit hunting by posting no trespassing signs, but an absence of posted signs does not imply consent to hunting. Hunting on private lands is a common problem in Alberta, resulting in the prosecution of hundreds of hunters every year,[48] however, it can be intimidating for landowners to complain and seek to protect their land, whether for their own safety or that of animals passing by.

Sanctuaries, reserves, parks, or wildlife management areas may have special rules. Animals may be somewhat protected from hunting and trapping, but despite the names given to these areas, the legislation generally still allows the minister to override any prohibition and allow hunting and trapping to take place, subject to special permitting provisions, seasons, and other controls.

The hunting of dozens of species of mammals and birds, including polar bears and other animals whose populations are unofficially thought to be in danger, is usually allowed by way of an array of weapons, generally firearms, crossbows, and bows and arrows. All

---

48   Government of Alberta, "2010–11 Alberta Guide to Trapping Regulations," online: http://www.albertaregulations.ca/trappingregs. Amendments to the *Petty Trespass Act*, RSA 2000, c P-11, in 2004 were designed to address this. Landowners may prohibit entry onto their land by signs or oral notice, but entry on some lands is prohibited without notice. Privately owned lands that are under cultivation, fenced, enclosed by a natural boundary, or enclosed in a way that indicates the landholder's intention to keep people off the premises or animals on the premises, are deemed to be occupied lands; hunters and trappers must seek permission before entering upon them.

jurisdictions prohibit certain hunting practices that pose a threat to human health, safety, and morals. Hunting while intoxicated and hunting within a certain distance of public places, like schools and other buildings, are all generally prohibited. Hunting is often, but not always, prohibited after dark and on Sunday.

Prohibited practices can be permitted with the minister's permission. These can include hunting or killing wildlife (or attempting to do so) by means of poison, drugs, explosives, deleterious substances, or electrical charges, and using aircraft, vehicles, or vessels to chase, pursue, worry, molest, take, hunt, or kill wildlife, or wilfully destroy wildlife habitat.[49]

When it comes to the general prohibition against hunting from vehicles and vessels, the practice varies. For example, some jurisdictions make some exception for persons with disabilities.[50] Alberta's *Wildlife Regulation*[51] prohibits the use of aircraft or helicopter to transport any person to a hunting location; however, wolves may be killed by aircraft as discussed above. Yukon allows wildlife to be hunted from a boat.[52] Nunavut prohibits the use of aircraft for spotting animals, or hunting big game within twelve hours of departing from an aircraft that was chartered for transportation to a hunting location.[53]

The use of dogs is controlled to varying degrees and prohibited for some species, but it is often permitted for others with a licence. Ontario has its own version of the fox hunt that was famously outlawed in Britain, using hounds to hunt coyotes or bobcats instead of foxes.[54] Some jurisdictions allow field trials using dogs, including hunting or killing wildlife with firearms or bows, as well as dog training areas.[55] Dog training and trial areas were prohibited in Ontario in 1997, however, existing facilities, and facilities that were able to establish themselves

---

49  For example, see *Saskatchewan*, above note 18, ss 67 and 70.

50  For example, in *New Brunswick*, above note 10, s 43(2) permits persons who are paraplegic, single or double amputees of the legs, and physically disabled persons authorized pursuant to s 83.1, to hunt from a vehicle that is not in motion. Similarly, see *Saskatchewan*, above note 18, s 26(a).

51  Alta Reg 143/1997, s 124.

52  *Yukon*, above note 19, s 92(3)(a).

53  *Nunavut*, above note 14, s 88.

54  Joanne Laucius, "The Thrill of the Chase, a Fox Hunt Minus the Fox in the Ottawa Valley" *Ottawa Citizen* (27 June 2011).

55  See *Nova Scotia*, above note 12, s 43, and *Dog Hunting and Training Regulations*, NS Reg 209/87.

before the legislation came into effect are exempt, and continue to operate pursuant to regulation.[56]

The purchase, sale, trade, traffic, transport, import, and export of native and non-native (or "exotic") wildlife are regulated by provincial law, but also have federal implications. Trade is an important factor in the consumptive and excessive use of wildlife. Different animal parts are favoured for reasons of status and novelty (heads, antlers, or full bodies for trophies), perceived health benefits (such as bear gall bladders, seal oil, and shark cartilage), and fashion (fur, feathers, tusks, teeth, and skins), and sometimes the sale or possession of these parts is prohibited.

It is very difficult — but not impossible — to change long-standing consumptive practices. One such example is discussed in the next section.

### f)   Spring Bear Hunt

Hunting any animal in the spring is often disfavoured, even by those who engage in consumptive animal practices. Animals are hungry in the spring, babies are born, and mothers need time to nourish the next generation. Hunting bears in the spring has been a contentious subject, in part because of these biological concerns but also because of the particular practices associated with it.

In spring hunts, hungry bears emerging from hibernation are attracted to a specific location by way of bait, such as rotten meat, pastries, or doughnuts. In the early part of the season, the baiting site gives dogs the scent of a bear. The dogs follow the scent and chase down the bear, giving hunters an easy target. Even if the bears escape, the chase depletes precious energy at a time when their reserves are low. In the second part of the season, hunters shoot bears at the baiting stations. Returning to food sites on which they have begun to rely on, the bears are easy targets again and many outfitters use the spring season to guarantee clients the opportunity to shoot a bear.

Baiting also encourages bears, which are usually solitary and roam for great distances, to congregate near the site, which can cause fighting. It discourages bears from relying on natural methods of finding their own food, and habituates them to being around humans, making them more likely to search for food near human dwellings and thereby pose a public risk. The practice takes advantage of bears when they are weak from hibernation and leaves orphaned cubs to die of starvation,

---

56   These are facilities in which dogs are trained to run down captive wildlife. *Ontario*, above note 17, s 35(1) and *Wildlife in Captivity*, O Reg 668/98, ss 28–43.

exposure, and predation after their mothers are shot. Even where it is prohibited to intentionally shoot a female bear with cubs, there is no way of ensuring a bear's gender during spring hunting.[57]

In Ontario, thousands of black bears were killed in spring hunts, not only by residents of the province, but also by Americans whose own states had outlawed the practice. However, opposition to the practice began to mount. In 1999, Ontario responded to sustained public pressure by amending Ontario Regulation 670/98 to abolish the spring open season for black bears.

There were some indications the government saw cancellation of the spring bear hunt as a way of protecting hunting more generally; however, the Ontario Federation of Anglers and Hunters (OFAH) and the Northern Ontario Tourist Outfitters Association (NOTO) saw it differently and commenced an application for judicial review of the regulation, claiming it was *ultra vires* the *Fish and Wildlife Conservation Act*.[58] They sought an interim injunction, claiming the minister had failed to exercise his discretion as the cancelation had come as a directive from the premier. They claimed that the minister considered extraneous factors, such as unethical hunting practices, public opinion, and political expediency. They took the position that animal welfare considerations fell outside the purview of the Act and they alleged that the regulation infringed their rights under sections 2(b) and 7 of the *Charter*,[59] claiming hunting was a form of expression, and that their liberty and security interests were violated.[60]

---

57   Mothers hide their young cubs when they venture out in pursuit of food, so one cannot count on the presence of cubs to reveal the bear's gender. It is also easy to be mistaken, particularly when all bears are dehydrated and have lost much of their body mass after hibernation, and the hunter, who has been waiting for the moment, is filled with adrenaline and wants to shoot the first bear that comes along.

58   *Ontario Federation of Anglers & Hunters v Ontario (Ministry of Natural Resources)* (1999), 43 OR (3d) 760 (SCJ).

59   *Canadian Charter of Rights and Freedoms*, Part I of the *Constitution Act, 1982*, being Schedule B to the *Canada Act 1982* (UK) 1982, c 11 [*Charter*].

60   The Schad Foundation, an organization with a long-standing interest in wildlife conservation, intervened in the case. The Foundation had engaged in extensive lobbying against the spring bear hunt and was seen as instrumental in influencing the Ontario government to cancel it. After the application for an interim injunction was dismissed, a trade association whose members were involved in the business of black bear hunting commenced a civil action against the Crown, the premier, the minister of natural resources, the Schad Foundation, and its chair, Robert Schad, for damages of $40 million. Claims alleged collusion and conspiracy, intentional interference with economic relations, misfeasance of public office, negligence, detrimental reliance, breach of contract, and breach

The application for an interim injunction was rejected. The Superior Court of Justice found that many provisions of the Act embrace ethical and responsible hunting practices, suggesting that the Act incorporates ethical concerns regarding animal welfare, and that it was proper for the minister to take these into account. Further, it was improper for the court to attempt to resolve the public policy inherent in the debate.

As the broader application for judicial review proceeded, OFAH and NOTO attempted to summon the premier and the minister of natural resources to be cross-examined regarding their motivation in amending the regulation. The summonses were upheld by the Divisional Court,[61] but overturned on appeal.[62] In a decision that has become important for the procedural issues arising around cross-examination of ministers as well as for the merits of the case itself, the Court of Appeal found, among other things, that motives are irrelevant in determining the validity of a regulation. It specifically found that concerns regarding animal welfare, including humane and ethical hunting practices, fall squarely within the policy and objectives of the Act.[63] For these reasons, there was no justiciable issue raised as to the validity of the regulation and the application was dismissed.

As these developments came to a conclusion, the province enacted the *Heritage Hunting and Fishing Act, 2002*.[64] It is a short piece of legislation which expresses the importance of recreational hunting and fishing in Ontario's social, cultural, and economic heritage, and that a person has a right to hunt and fish in accordance with the law. The actual legal significance of this legislation and its equivalents in other provinces[65] may be limited, but its symbolic value reflects the adherence to a consumptive ethic that continues to dominate the realm of wildlife management.[66]

---

of fiduciary duty. Most of the claims were struck out for not raising a viable cause of action: *Ontario Black Bear/Ontario Sportsmen & Resources Users Assn v Ontario* (2000), 19 Admin LR (3d) 29 (Ont SCJ). The action did not proceed after that.

61 *Ontario Federation of Anglers & Hunters v Ontario (Ministry of Natural Resources)* (2001), 196 DLR (4th) 367 (Ont SCJ).

62 *Anglers & Hunters*, above note 31.

63 *Ibid* at paras 41–48, citing s 113(1) of *Ontario*, above note 17.

64 SO 2002, c 10.

65 Similar laws have also been passed in British Columbia, Manitoba, and Quebec: *Hunting and Fishing Heritage Act*, SBC 2002, c 79; *The Hunting, Fishing and Trapping Heritage Act*, CCSM H185; and *Quebec*, above note 16, preamble and s 1.3 (added in 2002 by SQ 2002, c 82, ss 1–3).

66 For criticism of right-to-hunt legislation, see Vaughan Black, "Rights Gone Wild" (2005) 54 UNBLJ 3.

Spring bear hunting is still prohibited in Ontario, but it is permitted in other parts of Canada where black bears live, including the western provinces, Quebec, New Brunswick, and Newfoundland and Labrador.

## g) Trapping

Generally, there are three kinds of traps: killing traps, restraining traps, and drowning sets. Killing traps are designed to kill an animal instantly. Restraining traps are designed to hold animals alive until the trapper arrives. Drowning sets are used for semi-aquatic animals. They incorporate leghold and body-gripping devices, and are set underwater, or set so that the animals will be pulled underwater, causing them to drown.

Traps used for certain animals must conform to standards set out in the *Agreement on International Humane Trapping Standards* (AIHTS).[67] Signed by Canada in 1997, AIHTS is an agreement between Canada, Russia, the United States, and the European Union (EU) in response to the 1995 EU decision to ban the import of animals killed with steel-jaw leghold traps. Signing on to AIHTS enabled Canada to export fur to lucrative European markets. To implement the agreement within Canada, provincial legislation tends to specify that only traps that conform with AIHTS standards may be used, and it sometimes specifies a list of traps that may be used for different species.

AIHTS prohibits the use of steel-jaw leghold traps, requires countries to conduct research into humane trapping methods, and sets standards for devices used to trap twelve animals found in Canada: badger, beaver, bobcat, coyote, fisher, lynx, marten, muskrat, otter, raccoon, weasel, and wolf. Other animals are excluded from the agreement.

AIHTS obliges Canada to perform tests on traps. Those that meet the standards set out in the agreement are certified and may be used to trap the twelve listed animals. For traps designed to restrain an animal, testing must show that 80 percent of the animals captured in the trap do not show signs of poor welfare, including self-mutilation, immobility and unresponsiveness, factures, joint dislocation, severance of tendons or ligaments, major abrasion, severe internal or external bleeding, major skeletal muscle degeneration, tooth fracture, eye damage, spinal cord injury, internal organ damage, amputation, and death.

For killing traps, the critical measure is the time lapse between trapping and loss of consciousness or death. At least 80 percent of animals tested must be rendered unconscious and insensible within the time limit, and remain in that state until death. Ermines must be ren-

---

67   Online: www.canadainternational.gc.ca/eu-ue/assets/pdfs/eu25-en.pdf.

dered unconscious within forty-five seconds, two minutes for martens, and five minutes for all other species. Many animals suffer and die in the course of such tests.[68]

AIHTS standards are problematic in several ways. First, the 80 percent threshold means that restraining traps may still cause up to 20 percent of animals to experience severe injury and suffering, and the suffering that is permitted is a fairly high and sometimes subjective standard. Similarly, up to 20 percent of animals trapped in killing traps may not experience unconsciousness or death within the required time frame, and they can remain conscious, alive, and suffering, for prolonged periods. Yet such traps are designated humane. Some animals trapped in Canada are omitted from AIHTS, including foxes and mink. The agreement also gives countries leeway to continue using traps that are classified as humane while conducting research into new trapping methods.

While there is some variation across the country, three kinds of "humane" traps are usually used in Canada: leghold traps, body grip traps, and snares. Unpadded, steel-jaw leghold traps, which have teeth that pierce the flesh of the trapped animal, are generally prohibited, but are permitted in drowning sets. Animals will sometimes chew off their limbs to try to escape. Permitted padded leghold traps have a synthetic material around the jaws of the trap to lessen the pain. They reduce skin breakage, but are otherwise similar to the steel-jaw trap. Offset leghold traps have a space between the jaws so skin and bone breakage is reduced.

A body grip, or "Conibear" trap, consists of two rectangular frames that slam down on an animal's body after he brushes against it. These traps are designed to kill instantly by fatally striking the vertebrae or skull. Because the size of an animal and the manner in which he enters a trap cannot be controlled, non-target animals who are too small or too large get caught and seriously injured. Even when the target animal enters, the metal frames do not always contact vital spots or have sufficient force to kill, and they crush bones, blood vessels, and nerves. These traps are permitted across the country, with some variations as to the size of trap or animals for which they may be set.

---

68   That testing may be done without anesthetic. Researchers from the Alberta Research Council in Vegreville, Alberta, where some of that testing is done, recommended against using anesthesia in experiments since the relationship between anesthetized and unanesthetized animal tests was not found to be predictive: Michelle Hiltz & Laurence D Roy, "Use of Anaesthetized Animals to Test Humaneness of Killing Traps" (Summer 2001) 29:2 Wildlife Society Bulletin 606, online: www.fur.ca/files/Use%20of%20Anaesthetized%20Animals%20to%20Test%20Humaneness%20of%20Killi_ng_.pdf.

Snares are primarily set for canids: wolves, foxes, and coyotes. Both neck and leg snares are used in Canada. They tighten around the animal's neck or limb as she tries to free herself. Most provinces require snares to be fitted with a lock so they cannot be loosened or opened as the animal struggles. As the snare closes, the animal is restrained or strangled. Snares cause prolonged suffering, whether animals are killed by the snare, or until the trapper arrives to kill them. Some provinces permit snares to be placed in trees, which animals hang from until they are killed by the trapper or otherwise die.[69]

Provincial laws vary significantly as to how often restraining traps must be checked, ranging from every one to five days.[70] Traps set in more remote areas may often be checked less frequently. This leaves animals restrained, stressed, often injured and in considerable pain, possibly bleeding, unable to search for food or water, exposed to predators and the elements, with no ability to protect themselves. For killing traps, there is generally no requirement that they be checked regularly (with exceptions of limited effect in British Columbia,[71] Prince Edward Island,[72]

---

69   Cage and deadfall traps are just some of the other types of traps used in Canada. Cage traps were introduced in the 1920s and 1930s because of opposition to steel-jaw leghold traps. The traps contain live or dead bait to attract the animal inside, at which time the door closes. Cage traps are expensive and awkward to transport because of their bulk so they are not often used for trapping. However, they are used in other kinds of wildlife-management initiatives. Deadfall traps also involve the use of bait. The animal is contained or struck by an object that falls when the bait is removed.

70   For example, in Nova Scotia, restraining traps are supposed to be checked every day; in New Brunswick, it is every forty-eight hours; in Northwest Territories it is every seventy-two hours, and in the Yukon, it is every five days: *Fur Harvesting Regulations*, NS Reg 165/87, s 11(9). *Fur Harvesting Regulation*, NB Reg 84-124, s 4; *Trapping Regulations*, NWT Reg 023-92, s 3; *Trapping Regulations*, YOIC 1982/283, s 4.1.

71   Under s 3.05 of the *Wildlife Act Commercial Activities Regulation*, BC Reg 338/82, non-killing traps must be checked every seventy-two hours, except for egg traps for raccoons, which must be checked every twenty-four hours. For traps set on private property with permission, non-killing traps must be checked every twenty-four hours. Killing traps or snares need only be checked every fourteen days.

72   The *Fur Harvesting Regulations*, PEI Reg EC663/04, provides that traps designed to keep animals alive are supposed to be checked at least once per day; snares designed to kill are to be checked every forty-eight hours; body-gripping traps, submarine traps, and underwater snares for beaver must be checked every seventy-two hours. There is no requirement with respect to the time for checking other killing traps.

and Yukon[73]). Animals caught in these traps may be left to suffer indefinitely. No jurisdiction specifies how an animal found alive in a trap must be killed, although some require that animals be killed immediately. Animals are generally clubbed or strangled so as not to spoil their pelts.

In some jurisdictions, it is an offence to interfere with a lawfully set trap, or an animal caught in one, thereby potentially making it an offence for a passerby to try to relieve an animal of her suffering.[74] This seems to include even domesticated pets and other non-target animals who may be caught in a trap. There is no way of ensuring that a device traps only the target species. It is unknown how many non-target animals die as in this manner as there is no duty to report unintended bycatch.

Urban trapping of animals presents different problems. Municipalities tend to be responsible for trapping regulations within city limits, and there are many gaps. Many municipalities do not have any bylaws addressing the subject so the practice sometimes proceeds in an unregulated manner. Where there are bylaws, they often exempt licensed trappers, as well as property owners. An unknown number of both target and non-target animals dies in a wide array of makeshift traps. Provinces themselves have been moving away from trapping as a tactic for the management of urban wildlife because prevention has proved to be a more effective approach.

## 2) Wildlife in Captivity

### a) Hunting Captive Animals

In some jurisdictions, animals may be hunted in confined spaces from which they cannot escape.[75] Quebec and Saskatchewan offer captive hunting pursuant to a licensing regime established by regulation.[76] Both purport to require that animals not be caused unnecessary suffering (Quebec), or that their destruction be accomplished in as humane a manner as possible (Saskatchewan). Manitoba authorizes game bird

---

73   Yukon's *Trapping Regulations*, above note 70, require that quick-killing traps need only be inspected every seven days.

74   *British Columbia*, above note 8, s 46; *Yukon*, above note 19, s 67; and *Northwest Territories*, above note 13, s 49.

75   Beyond the apparent ethical issues, there are concerns that captive game farms breed chronic wasting disease, a form of mad cow disease that affects deer and elk.

76   *Regulation respecting animals in captivity*, RRQ, c C-61.1, r 5; and *Captive Wildlife Regulations*, RRS c W-13.1 Reg 13.

shooting preserves,[77] as well as captive hunting for bison and other wildlife or exotic wildlife pursuant to regulations.[78]

In most jurisdictions, including Ontario, hunting wildlife in captivity is prohibited.[79] The illegality of "penned hunting" was confirmed in *Universal Game Farm Inc v Ontario*.[80] The plaintiffs were the proprietors of an elk farm who allowed customers to purchase individual elk and shoot them within a fenced enclosure. When the Ministry of Natural Resources (MNR) advised the plaintiffs that their activities contravened the Act, they attempted to re-characterize the killing activity as "harvesting." They brought an action against the Crown alleging breach of contract, interference with economic relations, and negligence in relation to money they lost when their business activities were halted. The Superior Court held that regardless of whether the activity was characterized as "hunting" or "harvesting," the activity of shooting captive elk fell squarely within the statutory definition of hunting, and the Court of Appeal affirmed that the activity was "simply a hunt by another name."[81]

Many provinces authorize and regulate game farming, where animals can be raised for food or antlers, though they are not necessarily shot by the consumer at the facility. Game farms are treated more like other agricultural operations and are increasingly run as intensively.[82]

### b) Fur Farms

Trapping alone cannot satisfy all of the need for animals in the fashion industry; therefore, animals are also raised in captivity in fur farms or ranches. In 2009, 1,625,870 foxes and minks were reported killed on fur farms across the country.[83] These are not the only animals raised for fur in intensive operations, but they are the most common.

---

77  *Captive Wild Animal Regulation*, Man Reg 23/98, s 22.

78  *Captive Hunting Regulation*, Man Reg 176/2001.

79  *Ontario*, above note 17, s 41(1)(b). See also *Yukon*, above note 19, s 98.

80  *Universal Game Farm Inc v Ontario* [2007] OJ No 3220 (SCJ).

81  *Universal Game Farm Inc v Ontario*, 2008 ONCA 334 at para 1.

82  For example, in Prince Edward Island, see *Game Farm Regulations*, PEI Reg EC667/90; New Brunswick: *Game Bird Farm Licence Regulation*, NB Reg 2007-75; and Nova Scotia: *Deer Farming and Marketing of Deer Products Regulations*, NS Reg 1/91 and *Game Farming Regulations*, NS Reg 147/96.

83  Between ten and twenty-four foxes and between thirty-six and sixty-five mink are killed to make a fur coat. Statistics Canada surveys mink and fox farms and produces annual estimates of fur farm pelts produced in Canada, as well as provincial estimates of inventories, peltings, and values to aid in determining production value and to identify industry trends. See: Statistics Canada, *Fur Statistics* 2009 (Ottawa: Minister of Industry, October 2010) Table 1-6 at 13.

In fur farms, animals often live in dirty, cramped, barren cages, suspended over their own waste. Foxes live alone in rows of cages, with no den or place to hide. Behavioural studies have referred to farmed foxes as living in a state of continuous fear, and as exhibiting extreme fear in response to humans, characterized by trembling, defecating, and withdrawing to the back of the cage. Foxes are most commonly killed by anal electrocution, which involves an apparatus with electrodes inserted in the rectum and in the mouth. Solitary animals like mink are very stressed living in rows of cages, in the sightline of many other mink. Many have stomach ulcers and show stereotypical behaviours, which are abnormal repetitive behaviours associated with the frustration arising from being unable to perform natural behaviours, like swimming and travelling vast distances. Mink are killed by cervical dislocation, gassing in a killing box, or exhaust gases from gasoline combustion engines.[84]

Similar to other animal uses, industry-produced recommended Codes of Practice touch on some basic care requirements, including provision of adequate and potable food and water and sanitation, endorsing minimal cage sizes with few specific requirements.[85] The Codes recommend that sick animals be treated immediately and destroyed humanely; the humane killing recommended includes anal electrocution, as described above. There is no lawful requirement to follow the Codes' recommendations although compliance would likely provide a defence to any potential charge that might arise under a province's animal welfare legislation, where they help to demonstrate that a person was engaging in a generally accepted practice.[86] However, there is not much indication that these facilities are inspected by anyone with lawful authority to enforce animal welfare legislation in any meaningful way.

The industry is minimally regulated, although some provinces have established licensing regimes and record-keeping requirements. Alberta's *Fur Farms Act*[87] provides for inspection, but does not require it. It contains no requirements addressing the welfare of the confined animals; however, section 14 allows owners to kill any dog found to be terrifying fur-bearing animals by "giving tongue, barking or otherwise."

84   Born Free USA, *Cruelty Uncaged: A Review of Fur Farming in North America* (Sacramento: Born Free USA, 2009) at 3–10.

85   *Recommended Code of Practice for the Care and Handling of Mink* (Ottawa: Agriculture Canada, 1988) and *Recommended Code of Practice for the Care and Handling of Ranched Fox* (Ottawa: Agriculture Canada, 1989).

86   See further discussion in Chapter 4.

87   RSA 2000, c F-30.

British Columbia's *Fur Farm Act*[88] is even less detailed. In Saskatchewan, section 14 of the *Fur Farming Regulations*[89] under the *Animal Products Act*[90] provides that animals must be handled in a humane manner and destroyed in as painless and humane manner as possible, but these terms are undefined and subject to contextual interpretation.

One section of Newfoundland and Labrador's *Wild Life Regulations*[91] addresses fur farms: section 20 provides that animals must be kept in suitable pens or cages to prevent their escape; that fur farms must be kept in a clean and sanitary condition; and that furbearing animals may be kept in a fur farm in a manner that would cause avoidable suffering or injury. In Ontario, the *Fur Farms Act*[92] was repealed in 1997, on the basis that fur farms would be regulated pursuant to the province's new wildlife legislation which was enacted at the time, but no such regulations have been promulgated.

### c)   Captive Wildlife and Zoos

Generally, a person requires a provincial permit to keep wildlife in captivity, although often some species are excluded. Different rules can apply for native species, and non-native or "exotic" species. Regulatory regimes vary across the country, although most of them are enacted by way of regulation pursuant to the jurisdiction's wildlife legislation. Most schemes address such matters as import/export rules, capture of live animals, diseased animals, record keeping, some safety issues in respect of enclosures, and some provisions with respect to maintenance of animals. These can be as minimal as requiring that animals have potable water and adequate food, with access to an outdoor run and shelter.[93]

---

88   RSBC 1996, c 167.
89   RRS, c A-20.2, Reg 6.
90   RSS 1978 (Supp), c A-20.2.
91   CNLR 1156/96.
92   RSO 1990, c F.37.
93   Quebec has a lengthy captive wildlife regulation, but like other jurisdictions, it does not really address the significant welfare issues that captivity presents for animals: *Regulation respecting animals in captivity*, above note 76, ss 20–25. In Saskatchewan, one section noting the maintenance of captive wildlife addresses food and water, sanitary and presentable conditions, clean bathing water, and generally keeping wildlife "in a humane manner": *Captive Wildlife Regulations*, above note 76, s 23. In Prince Edward Island, one subsection authorizes the minster to suspend a zoo's licence if wildlife is kept in unsanitary conditions, without adequate food or water, or otherwise in contravention of a licence condition: *Keeping Wildlife in Captivity Regulations*, PEI Reg EC634/85, s 13(1).

Some regulations address rehabilitation centres and sanctuaries. The terminology and the distinctions can be important. Some rehabilitation centres and sanctuaries work in the best interests of the animals. However, inasmuch as many of these facilities are poorly regulated or not regulated at all, the fact that the owner calls the facility a "sanctuary" is no guarantee of any particular standards of care, or of any efforts to release animals to the wild, where appropriate.

Many roadside zoos exist across the country. These are substandard facilities that typically house animals in poor conditions. Most of them lack the professional animal care staff and the financial resources to provide even minimally adequate care and housing. They often consist of small, ramshackle cages that offer little more than a water bowl, food bowl, and a shelter box for sleeping. Animals in these zoos often become bored and frustrated, exhibiting signs of psychological disturbance, including stereotypical behaviours, like repetitive pacing, circling, and head-swaying; bar-biting; aggression; and self-mutilation.

Bored, frustrated animals showing signs of psychological disturbance are also seen at the more reputable, professionally accredited zoos. Even the strongest standards and the best of facilities keep animals in enclosures that are thousands or even ten of thousands of times smaller than the space the individual would occupy in the wild. Even the best of intentions cannot replicate the conditions to which these animals have been adapted to live or generally accommodate normal social groups, or anything like a normal life.[94]

In the course of breeding efforts, and because of the popularity of babies, many zoos (including those that meet industry guidelines) produce a predictable surplus of animals who end up at auctions, in circuses, as novelty acts, in substandard zoos, and in captive hunting operations. Of approximately 200 zoos in Canada, only twenty-four have been accredited by the Canadian Association of Zoos and Aquariums (CAZA), an industry organization whose standards are self-determined and unenforceable in any event.[95] For all of these reasons,

---

94   The conditions of enclosures that are seen by visitors can be misleading; natural-looking features like trees might be artificial, thereby failing to provide any enrichment to the animals; alternatively, natural trees are sometimes electrified or are on the outside of the enclosure so that the animals will not use them in their normal manner. Animals are often kept in different enclosures behind the scenes when they are not on display, which is most of the time, and these are generally more confining and barren.

95   Canadian Association of Zoos and Aquariums, *CAZA Animal Care and Housing Manual* (1 October 2008), online: www.caza.ca/en/about_caza/accreditation_program/animal_care_standards/.

subjecting animals to the privation inherent in confinement is increasingly contentious.[96]

Ontario is among the worst jurisdictions in Canada when it comes to ensuring the care of captive wildlife. While permits are required to keep most native wildlife in captivity, few basic conditions are attached. They require exhibits to be adequate size to enable animals to exercise natural behaviours and achieve a distance from the public; however, the conditions are undefined, vague, and unenforced. Standards for keeping native wildlife in captivity were developed a decade ago but have yet to be implemented. Ontario has neither regulations nor any proposed standards regarding the keeping of non-native wildlife.[97]

The most comprehensive regulation of zoos is in Alberta, but where agents authorized under the legislation fail or refuse to act to enforce these regulations, they are of no assistance to the animals they purport to protect. This was the issue addressed by the Court of Appeal of Alberta in *Reece v Edmonton (City)*.[98] Two animal protection organizations and a resident of Edmonton brought an application for a declaration that the City of Edmonton, which owns the Valley Zoo, was violating its zoo standards in respect of Lucy, an elephant who has lived alone at the zoo for many years.

The chief justice of Alberta described the province's *Animal Protection Act*,[99] *Wildlife Act*,[100] and *Animal Protection Regulation*[101] as being

---

96   Many reports discussing zoos in Canada and related issues can be found on
     the website of Zoocheck Canada, a national wildlife protection charity, online:
     www.zoocheck.com/reports.html. The claim that zoos are engaged in educa-
     tion or conservation in any meaningful way is dubious. Zoo visitors spend very
     brief times at individual displays where signage is often minimal. The sug-
     gestion that seeing live animals instills respect for them is contraindicated by
     the medium in which the message is delivered, such as by confining them for
     human purposes in the first place. Nor has the lengthy history of zoos had any
     apparent effect on human treatment of animals more generally, as seen through-
     out this book. Breeding programs in zoos are in place mostly for the purpose of
     perpetuating zoo stock, and a small number of closely related animals are bred
     together with no natural selection. Very few zoos or animals are involved in
     programs designed for release to the wild.

97   World Society for the Protection of Animals, *Failing the Grade: A Report on Con-
     ditions in Ontario's Zoos* (Toronto: World Society for the Protection of Animals,
     2005) at iii–iv.

98   *Reece v Edmonton (City)*, 2011 ABCA 238 [*Reece*]. The detailed analysis was
     undertaken by Fraser CJA, in her dissenting reasons at paras 39–199.

99   RSA 2000, c A-41.

100  *Alberta*, above note 7.

101  Alta Reg 203/2005.

designed to protect a "vulnerable group."[102] The *Animal Protection Act* prohibits causing or permitting an animal to be distress.[103] Distress is defined similarly in other jurisdictions to include: being deprived of adequate shelter, ventilation, space, food, water, veterinary care, or reasonable protection from injurious heat or cold; being injured, sick, in pain, or suffering; or being abused or subjected to undue hardship, privation, or neglect.[104] The Act also imposes affirmative duties on owners and persons in charge of animals that correspond with those conditions.[105]

The *Animal Protection Regulation* provides that a person who owns or controls a permitted zoo must comply with the *Government of Alberta Standards for Zoos in Alberta* (GASZA).[106] Section III of GASZA requires that the needs of all animals in the zoo be met with regard to food, water, shelter, space, and health care. Section III(B) requires that animals be maintained in numbers sufficient to meet their social and behavioural needs and that exhibits must be of a size and complexity sufficient to provide for an animal's physical and social needs, and species-typical behaviours and movement. Animals must be protected from injurious cold associated with ambient outdoor conditions or any other weather conditions that are detrimental to their health.

Section III(B)(2) indirectly incorporates certain minimum standards set by the American Zoo and Aquarium Association (AZA),[107] including Standard 2.3.1, which provides that zoos should make every effort to maintain elephants in social groupings, that it is inappropriate to keep highly social female elephants singly, and that institutions should strive to hold no less than three female elephants wherever possible. Standard 2.2.4 provides that institutions must provide an opportunity for each elephant to exercise and interact socially with other elephants.

The applicants relied on extensive affidavit evidence given by four experts.[108] According to the chief justice, the evidence

---

102  *Reece*, above note 98 at para 72.

103  Above note 99, s 2(1).

104  *Ibid*, s 1(2).

105  *Ibid*, s 2.1.

106  Section 2(3) of the regulation, above note 101, and Alberta Sustainable Resource Development, *Government of Alberta Standards for Zoos in Alberta* (Edmonton: Alberta Sustainable Resource Development, 2005).

107  The relevant standards in this case were the Association of Zoos and Aquariums, *American Zoo and Aquarium Association Standards for Elephant Management and Care*, Adopted 21 March 2001; Updated 5 May 2003.

108  One was a veterinarian with approximately thirty years of experience in zoo and wild animal medicine; another was an ecologist with over thirty years

packs a powerful punch. It holds up a mirror for all to see — provided one is prepared to look into the mirror. What it reveals is a disturbing image of the magnitude, gravity and persistence of Lucy's on-going health problems and the severity of the suffering she continues to endure from the conditions in which she has been confined. And it also exposes who is responsible for those conditions and that suffering.[109]

At the same time, the chief justice noted that it would be naïve to assume that problems do not arise from the mere fact of keeping elephants in captivity.[110] She went on to describe many physical and mental ailments from which Lucy suffers, including the health injuries that highly social animals experience when they are held alone as well as arthritis, chronic foot infections, dental problems, and obesity.[111]

The city had refused to allow Lucy to go to an elephant sanctuary in California, claiming she was too sick to move and, that after being alone for so many years, she had become anti-social and could not live with other elephants. The chief justice found that this "smack[ed] of blaming the victim for being held captive in an environment in which she [was being] deprived of the opportunity to develop her normal social skills."[112]

Despite the overwhelming evidence of the extent of Lucy's suffering, and the potential violation of the legislated standards aforementioned, the majority of the court dismissed the application on the basis that it was an abuse of process, finding that the applicants had no standing to effectively seek enforcement of animal welfare legislation. The chief justice's comprehensive reasons make a strong case to the contrary, but

---

experience on the range, habitat, and demography of elephants; another was a veterinarian with twenty-eight years of experience at zoos; and another was an elephant biologist and ethologist with extensive expertise in elephants; *Reece*, above note 98 at paras 108, 111, 115, & 116, Fraser CJA.

109  *Ibid* at para 103.

110  *Ibid*, n 69.

111  The evidence is discussed, *ibid* at paras 103–27. Many of these conditions are common when elephants are required to live in severely confined living spaces with concrete flooring, which is what happens to elephants living in cold climates who are required to spend much of their time indoors. Elephants are normally moving up to twenty hours every day in the wild, covering vast distances. In captivity, they must stand still most of the time. Elephants defecate up to seventeen times a day and urinate almost as frequently. This means that captive elephants are often left to stand in their own waste.

112  *Ibid* at para 126. The sanctuary is well respected and has given refuge to other allegedly anti-social elephants with great success. See Performing Animal Welfare Society, online: www.pawsweb.org/paws_wildlife_sanctuaries_home_page. html.

she was in dissent.[113] Lucy remains at the Valley Zoo, a CAZA-accredited facility, suffering, and alone.

One roadside zoo in Alberta, Guzoo Animal Farm, did lose its licence as a result of the conditions in which it kept animals and its perpetual lack of compliance with zoo standards. After many years of public pressure and documented complaints that animals were kept in filthy conditions in small, overcrowded enclosures, with lack of shelter and shade and rancid water, it lost its licence in 2011.[114]

### d) Marine Mammals in Captivity

While pinnipeds (seals, sea lions, and walruses) and polar bears have their own extensive problems in captivity, this section focuses on cetaceans (whales and dolphins). Cetaceans in particular are well understood to be highly social and intelligent animals who suffer physically and psychologically, and die many years short of their natural lifespans, in the unnatural conditions of captivity. Regardless of how large an enclosure is, it is millions of times smaller than the waters in which the animals it contains have evolved to live, and from which many of them have been captured.[115] Capture itself is a violent, traumatic process. The two remaining facilities in Canada that keep captive cetaceans are the Vancouver Aquarium and Marineland in Niagara Falls, Ontario.[116]

In 2001, the Vancouver Aquarium transferred its sole surviving orca to Sea World, effectively ending its orca display. However, it continues to display beluga whales, dolphins, pinnipeds, and hundreds of

---

113 The chief justice's reasons were possibly the most discerning consideration that has been given to animal interests in Canadian jurisprudence to date. Her analysis addresses the history of animal welfare legislation and its inherent insufficiencies, and it anticipates future developments to better protect the rights of animals. It is further discussed in Chapter 4.

114 See World Society for the Protection of Animals and Zoocheck Canada, *A Review of Guzoo Animal Farm Based on the Alberta Zoo Standards* (2007), online: www.zoocheck.com/Reportpdfs/Guzoo07.pdf; and Kevin Libin, "Animal Rules" *National Post* (8 June 2011) A5.

115 Naomi A Rose, ECM Parsons, & Richard Farinato, *The Case Against Marine Mammals in Captivity*, 4th ed (Washington: The Humane Society of the United States and the World Society for the Protection of Animals, 2009), online: www. wspa-international.org/Images/159_the_case_against_marine_mammals_in_ captivity_english_2009_tcm25-8409.pdf.

116 The West Edmonton Mall used to have a display of four bottlenose dolphins. Each of the two females had two babies and all the babies died shortly after birth. The conditions in the mall were the subject of persistent criticism and the display was eventually phased out, however the dolphins were replaced by sea lions. It continues to display many other animals, including penguins, whose unique needs make them notoriously difficult to maintain in captivity.

other aquatic species. The aquarium is in Stanley Park and is subject to the *Parks Control By-law*,[117] which requires it to refrain from capturing cetaceans from the wild for display purposes. It is supposed to obtain cetaceans from other facilities if they were born in captivity, captured before 1996, or captured because they were injured or in distress and in need of assistance, whether or not they are intended to be released back to the wild.[118] Still, its keeping of cetaceans is very controversial.

Marineland has been the subject of intense local, regional, and international criticism for keeping whales (it currently keeps the largest group of captive belugas in the world as well as orcas), dolphins, and pinnipeds; for its ongoing capture of significant numbers of whales, dolphins, and pinnipeds from the wild; and for providing its terrestrial animals with barren, often overcrowded conditions. In 2004, Marineland commenced a libel action against a small, local advocacy organization and one of its spokespersons. The defendants had distributed correspondence critical of the conditions for animals at Marineland, and indicated the number of cetaceans who had recently died there. The defendants relied on the defences of fair comment and justification. Marineland brought a motion to strike various parts of the defence, but the motion was unsuccessful and the action did not proceed.[119]

While the practice of keeping cetaceans in captivity has come into increasing disfavour, few laws address it and the animals linger in a sort of legal limbo. There is no legislation prohibiting the capture, import, or export of cetaceans from Canada, although permits are required in some cases for some protected species, as discussed in Part B in this chapter. There is no federal legislation governing their welfare or conditions in which they must be kept in captivity. This leaves all aspects of their welfare to the realm of provincial animal welfare legislation, a limited tool even for its intended purposes, and particularly constrained in the context of animals whose needs are so complex and whose size precludes any prospect of seizure. In 2004, the Canadian Council on Animal Care, the peer-review body that purports to oversee

---

117 Section 9(e). The Vancouver Parks and Recreation Board's *Parks Control By-law* is established pursuant to the *Vancouver Charter*, SBC 1953, c 55, online: http://vancouver.ca/parks/info/regs/parkscontrolbylaw.pdf.

118 The bases on which facilities determine whether an animal is in need of rescue or can be released are quite subjective. Evidence has linked dolphins imported from Japanese aquariums into Canada to the now infamous dolphin drives portrayed in the documentary film, *The Cove* (Oceanic Preservation Society, 2009). See Riley Goldstone & Christopher Mackie, "The Vancouver Parks Board and the International Dolphin Trade" (Victoria: Environmental Law Centre, University of Victoria, undated), online: http://vcn.bc.ca/cmeps/images/japan.pdf.

119 *Marineland of Canada v Niagara Action for Animals*, 2004 CanLII 30880 (Ont SCJ).

the use of animals in research in Canada, prepared draft guidelines for the care and maintenance of marine mammals, which to date, have not been finalized.[120]

### e)  Circuses and Travelling Shows

Circuses and travelling shows also present unique legal problems. On the one hand, the impoverished conditions in which circus animals typically live are well documented. Many performing wild animals in circuses and travelling shows touring Canada endure a life characterized by emptiness, deprivation, and brutality. They suffer from extreme confinement, inappropriate social groupings, and harsh, sometimes abusive, training methods.[121]

However, the itinerant nature of circuses frustrates effective enforcement of traditional laws. Federal legislation discussed below sometimes creates permit requirements for protected species that perform in these shows, but these do not establish any requirements concerning their welfare. Provincial wildlife legislation does not generally address travelling shows.[122] Animal welfare legislation applies to varying degree, however, jurisdictional issues create challenges to enforcement. Many animals that appear in Canadian circuses are rented from American corporations. Much of the suffering to which animals are subjected happens either in another jurisdiction (such as capture or training) or is the result of cumulative circumstances over a period of time in which a circus travels through different jurisdictions.[123] Even

---

120  For an analysis of many perceived shortcomings in the draft guidelines, see Correspondence Dr. Toni Frohoff to Director of Guidelines Development, Canadian Council on Animal Care (12 April 2004), online: www.zoocheck.com/ Reportpdfs/CCACFrohoff.pdf.

121  A good summary is provided in Zoocheck Canada, *Performing Prisoners, A Case Against the Use of Wild Animals in Circuses, Traveling Shows and Novelty Acts* (Toronto: Zoocheck Canada, 1998, updated 2006), online: www.zoocheck.com/ Reportpdfs/PrisonersReport2006.pdf [*Performing Prisoners*].

122  Quebec's *Regulation respecting animals in captivity*, above note 76, creates licensing schemes for keeping animals in captivity for the purpose of exhibition (Division XI) and Circuses (Division XI.I, applying to non-residents). These require certain information to be provided as a condition of the licence, addressing such things as the number of animals, locations, dates, terms of insurance, and efforts to prevent escapes, but there are no requirements in respect of the interests of the animals.

123  For example, the "beast wagons" typically used to hold lions and tigers in the circus are enclosures not much larger than their own bodies, in which they eat, sleep, urinate, defecate, travel, and which they never leave, except to perform. Similarly, elephants suffer from the constant loading and unloading from train cars, in which they are tightly chained by the ankle, and from the chains by

where powers of investigation exist, proceeding through all stages of an investigation—examining and potentially seizing the kinds of exotic animals that travel in the circus, laying charges before the circus has moved on, and then prosecuting the offenders—present formidable challenges.

In order to address both the regulatory anomaly of the travelling animal show, as well as the many human health and safety issues posed by keeping wild and exotic animals,[124] many municipalities in Canada have passed bylaws prohibiting keeping certain species within municipal boundaries.[125] They do not prohibit circuses, but they prevent them from bringing the kinds of animals who are known to suffer most from circus life. These bylaws can also apply to individuals who keep dangerous animals as pets or use them in novelty acts.[126]

In Ontario, these prohibitions have been aggressively resisted by the circus industry. When Toronto passed a bylaw prohibiting certain exotic animals in the city, it was challenged by two circuses and the Skydome (as the stadium was then named). The bylaw was upheld by the Divisional Court in 1992, but was overturned by the Court of Appeal the next year.[127] The appellate decision was based on jurisdictional issues that were specific to Toronto, because at the time Toronto was both a city and a municipality, and the court found that the wrong jurisdiction had passed the bylaw. Still, the case had a chilling effect on other municipalities across the province.

However, a decade later, the City of Windsor passed a bylaw that prohibited forms of entertainment involving the use of exotic animals. It was challenged by a circus producer and a trade association for the outdoor amusement industry on numerous grounds, many of which

---

which they are typically held between performances at a given location. However, animals are subjected to those conditions for a matter of days in any one location, making the cumulative impact of a lifestyle difficult to address.

124 Issues in respect of both the diseases that can be passed from animals to people or other animals, as well as the risks of animal escapes, are discussed in *Performing Prisoners*, above note 121.

125 More than 220 British municipalities have passed such bylaws, as have many other municipalities around the world and across Canada. Some countries and states have implemented national prohibitions (full or partial) on exotic animal performances. See list in *Performing Prisoners, ibid* at 25–26.

126 The Toronto bylaw discussed below was initiated after complaints concerning an adult tavern called Jilly's in downtown Toronto in which a 500-pound Siberian tiger named Qadesh was used in one of the performer's acts. During the day, Qadesh was chained in an alley outside the bar across from a school, raising concerns about the safety of the children across the way.

127 *Stadium Corp of Ontario Ltd v Toronto (City)* (1992), 10 OR (3d) 203 (Div Ct), rev'd (1993), 12 OR (3d) 646 (CA) [*Stadium Corp*].

were successful.[128] The bylaw was struck down on the basis that it was passed for an improper purpose; that it discriminated against a particular form of entertainment; that it had been passed in breach of the city's duty of fairness; that it was in pith and substance an attempt to regulate morality and was thus a matter of criminal law; and that it violated the corporations' right to free expression under section 2(b) of the *Charter*.

Much of the court's analysis in *Xentel* was based on its finding that the bylaw was motivated by concern about animal welfare, as opposed to public safety, which would have been a proper purpose. That animal welfare in an improper purpose is an unusual finding, given the variety of other bylaws municipalities pass regarding animals that also share those two purposes. Several of the industry's arguments that Gates J accepted in *Xentel* had been specifically rejected by the Divisional Court in *Stadium Corp*, and not addressed by the Court of Appeal.[129]

The Toronto and Windsor bylaws were substantially different, in that the former prohibited certain species from being kept within the municipality for any purpose, while the latter was addressed to a specific form of entertainment. Given the different bases for the two bylaws, the apparently conflicting decisions, and new municipal legislation that came info effect thereafter, the issue requires further legal consideration before it can be considered settled law in Ontario.[130]

### f)   Liability for Wild Animals in Captivity

Wild animals kept in captivity are considered to be inherently dangerous and liability for damages they cause is strict. This principle was

---

128  *Xentel DM Inc v Windsor (City)* (2004), 243 DLR (4th) 451 (Ont SCJ [*Xentel*]).

129  The Divisional Court in *Stadium Corp*, above note 127, found that the Toronto bylaw was passed both for the purpose of protecting public safety and animal welfare and was within provincial competence as legislation in relation to property and civil rights within the province, and in relation to matters of a local and private nature, within the meaning of ss 92(13) and 92(16) of the *Constitution Act, 1867* (UK), 30 & 31 Vict, c 3, reprinted in RSC 1985, App II, No 5. Further, since the bylaw prohibited keeping exotic animals whether or not cruelty was proven, it did not deal with the same subject matter as the criminal law prohibitions against cruelty to animals, and did not intrude upon any area occupied by Parliament: *Stadium Corp, ibid* at 211.

130  In both *Stadium Corp* and *Xentel*, the bylaw was passed pursuant to the city's authority to prohibit or regulate and license various exhibitions, including circus-riding: *Municipal Act*, RSO 1990, c M.45, s 236(7). That Act has since been repealed and replaced by the *Municipal Act, 2001*, SO 2001, c 25, which gives broad authority to municipalities to pass bylaws in respect of animals at ss 10(2) and 11(3), as well as specific authorities in respect of pounds and other issues.

applied in *Cowles v Balac*,[131] a case arising from an incident in a drive-through safari park in Ontario called African Lion Safari. Various kinds of exotic animals roam freely within several fenced-in sections during the park's visiting hours. When the visiting plaintiffs entered the tiger section, their vehicle was attacked by four tigers. The car windows were lowered at some point and one tiger entered the vehicle and attacked the plaintiffs. Two others bit one of the plaintiffs through the driver window. Both plaintiffs were severely mauled before they escaped. In a lengthy decision, MacFarland J, as she then was, held the facility liable under the law of strict liability, negligence, and occupiers' liability, with no apportionment of liability to either plaintiff, and damages were in the amount $2.5 million. The trial judgment was upheld by a majority of the Court of Appeal.[132]

## B. FEDERAL LEGISLATION

Most issues affecting wildlife are addressed by provincial legislation; however, federal law governs certain animals in certain contexts. Three federal acts are reviewed below: the *Wild Animal and Plant Protection and Regulation of International and Interprovincial Trade Act*,[133] the *Migratory Birds Convention Act, 1994*,[134] and the *Fisheries Act*[135] (in particular, the *Marine Mammal Regulations*[136]).

---

131  2005 CanLII 2038 (Ont SCJ), aff'd (2006), 273 DLR (4th) 596 (Ont CA). For a detailed discussion of the case and of the principles of liability attaching to dangerous animals, see Douglas Christie, "Dog Bites and Tiger Scratches—Liability for Animals that Cause Harm" in Lesli Bisgould, ed, *An Introduction to Animals and the Law* (Toronto: Law Society of Upper Canada, Continuing Legal Education, 2007) at Tab 4.

132  Borins JA, who dissented, would have ordered a new trial on the basis of his finding that the trial judge erred in striking the jury. He agreed that the standard was one of strict liability; however, he stressed that this is not absolute, and he disagreed with the trial judge's finding that it would be contradictory to reduce a plaintiff's damages arising from a defendant's strict liability: *ibid* at paras 203–19.

133  SC 1992, c 52.

134  SC 1994, c 22.

135  RSC 1985, c F-14.

136  SOR/93-56.

## 1) The *Wild Animal and Plant Protection and Regulation of International and Interprovincial Trade Act*

The international trade in animals and plants is a multi-billion dollar enterprise affecting millions of species and individual animals. In 1975, the *Convention on the International Trade in Endangered Species of Wild Fauna and Flora* (CITES) was established to respond to concerns about the risk to populations that the trade posed.[137] Approximately 170 countries, called Parties, have now signed on to CITES, including Canada. CITES regulates the trade of approximately 30,000 species using a system of appendices. Within this regime, animals are referred to as "specimens."

CITES creates a licensing system for the import and export of regulated species. Countries delegate a Management Authority to administer the system and a Scientific Authority gives advice on the status of various species and aspects of trade, which in Canada is the Canadian Wildlife Service. Environment Canada is the lead agency responsible for implementing CITES on behalf of the federal government. Each province and territory also designates a Management Authority and a Scientific Authority, except Alberta.

Appendix I lists species that are rare or endangered, and international trade of these species is generally prohibited for primarily commercial purposes. Exceptions include zoological or scientific research pursuant to permits. These animals may be imported into Canada with a Canadian CITES import permit and a CITES export permit issued by the exporting country. Numerous species of mammals, birds, reptiles, amphibians, fish, and invertebrates are listed on Appendix I, including cetaceans, elephants, big cats (such as the eastern cougar, found in Canada, as well as leopards and tigers), and many primates (including chimpanzees, gorillas, and orangutans).

Appendix II lists species that are not currently rare or endangered, but could become so if trade is not regulated. These animals can be traded for both commercial and non-commercial purposes. The exporting country must issue an exporting permit, but no importing permit is required. Many foxes and wolves are in Appendix II, as well as big cats (such as the Canadian lynx, bobcat, and cougar), bears (black bears, grizzly bears, and polar bears), cetaceans, and ungulates (such as the wood bison).

---

137  The text of the Convention is online: www.cites.org/eng/disc/text.shtml. Environment Canada also provides information about CITES online: www.ec.gc.ca/cites/default.asp?lang=En&n=1BC82E16-1.

Appendix III lists species that are not necessarily endangered, but are managed within the listing nation. Animals imported into Canada must have a CITES export permit issued by the exporting country if the animal is from a listing nation, or a CITES export permit, a CITES certificate of origin, or a CITES re-export certificate if the animal is from another nation. To export an animal from Canada, a CITES export permit is required.

CITES is voluntary and must be implemented domestically. In Canada, it was ratified in 1975 and it is implemented by way of the *Wild Animal and Plant Protection and Regulation of International and Interprovincial Trade Act* (WAPPRIITA).[138] The Act received Royal Assent in 1992 but it did not come into force until regulations took effect in 1996.[139] It addresses international trade and interprovincial transport of certain wild animals and plants and their parts and derivates. It requires that trade statistics be prepared annually by the CITES Management Authority.[140] It authorizes exemptions, allowing both the import and export of species that are listed by CITES, without permits, for noncommercial purposes. These include tourist souvenirs, personal and household effects, and hunting trophies (for black bear hides, skulls and meat, but not organs, as well as the carcass and meat of Sandhill cranes). There is also an exemption for pets under certain conditions.[141]

Many animals listed in the appendices naturally reside in Canada and are hunted and trapped across the country, or appear in and are traded by Canadian zoos, aquariums, and circuses. The claim that CITES protects animals must be understood in its context. As a conservation document, CITES is concerned with populations; it does not in any way address the welfare concerns of individuals.

## 2) The *Migratory Birds Convention Act*

The *Migratory Birds Convention Act* was passed in 1917[142] to ratify and bring into effect the *Migratory Birds Convention*.[143] The Convention was passed, after decades of efforts, and after the millinery trade in bird feathers and parts, and other forms of intensive consumption, brought

---

138 SC 1992, c 52 [WAPPRIITA].
139 *Wild Animal and Plant Trade Regulations*, SOR/96-263.
140 These are available on Environment Canada's website, online: www.ec.gc.ca/cites/default.asp?lang=En&n=18F4AOBC-1.
141 WAPPRIITA, above note 138, ss 14–18.
142 *Migratory Birds Convention Act*, SC 1917, c 18.
143 *Convention for the Protection of Migratory Birds in Canada and the United States of America* (16 August 1916).

many species of migratory birds to or near extinction in the nineteenth century.[144]

The Act was amended several times and then was repealed and replaced in 1994. It binds the Crown and aims to protect the birds identified in the Convention. "Protection areas" can be authorized for migratory birds and their nests and for the control and management of those areas. Neither the Convention nor the Act prevents hunting or other consumptive uses of migratory birds, however, similarly to other regimes, it establishes a licensing system by which it purports to provide some control on hunting practices. Offences under the Act carry strict liability.[145]

Whether or not the Act meaningfully protects migratory birds is a matter of some dispute. In *R v Syncrude Canada Ltd*,[146] approximately 1,600 protected birds were trapped in bitumen on the surface of the defendant's settling bin and all but a few of those birds eventually died. Syncrude was convicted under Alberta's environmental protection legislation, and under section 5.1(1) of the *Migratory Birds Convention Act*, which prohibits persons and vessels from depositing, or permitting to be deposited, substances that are harmful to migratory birds, in waters or areas frequented by migratory birds, or in a place from which the substance may enter such waters or such an area. Syncrude was fined $800,000 and ordered to pay an additional $2.2 million toward research and conservation projects.[147]

By contrast, special regulations passed to enable an international effort between Canada and the United States to intentionally kill several million protected snow geese, by way of baiting and otherwise

---

144 Greta Nilsson & Michael Bean, "Legislation" in *Endangered Species Handbook* (1983; repr, Washington: Animal Welfare Institute, 2005), online: www.endangeredspecieshandbook.org/legislation.php.

145 *R v Chapin* (1979), 95 DLR (3d) 13 (SCC). It was an offence under the regulations to hunt migratory birds within a quarter mile of bait. The Supreme Court found it to be a classic example of a strict liability offence which does not require proof of *mens rea*. The evidence was that a small pile of bait had been deposited in the middle of the road on which the accused had to pass to get to the blind from which she was hunting. The day was windy and the accused claimed she did not see it. Although the Court observed that the regulations were enacted to protect migratory birds from indiscriminate slaughter, and to protect the general public welfare, and although it rejected the need to show *mens rea*, it found that it would have been unreasonable to convict the accused.

146 2010 ABPC 229.

147 Some non-governmental organizations were disappointed in the fine, which they argued was not a significant penalty for an oil sands giant that annually earns billions of dollars: Darcy Henton, "Judge Approves $3M Creative Sentence in Dead Ducks Case" *Edmonton Journal* (23 October 2010).

prohibited practices, was found to be *intra vires* the legislation and otherwise proper.[148]

The Convention and the Act do not encompass all species of migratory birds. Many, including pelicans, cormorants, hawks, and owls, are excluded. At the time the Convention was entered into, these birds were seen as undesirable. Today, some of them still are, cormorants in particular. After being nearly extirpated by hunting and pesticide poisoning, the double-crested cormorant returned to the Great Lakes, where they are now being culled by federal wildlife agents as part of a five-year management plan implemented in 2008.[149] The birds are shot during the nesting season, when they are trying to protect their eggs. The cacophony caused by the shooting and the terrified birds disturbs other species of birds nesting on the island, such as herons, who are supposed to be protected by the Act. The same government agency that kills the birds enforces the Act. Efforts by non-governmental organizations to legally restrain the hunt were temporarily successful but ultimately overturned.[150]

---

148  *Animal Alliance of Canada v Canada (AG)*, [1999] 4 FC 72 (TD). One of the applicants' arguments was in response to the perceived dramatic increase in the snow goose populations in Canada, which was the stated motivation for the initiative. Scientific evidence before the court indicated that the increase was only relative to the time that government agencies began counting these birds in the first place, several decades prior, but that over the much longer history of the species, its population had risen and fallen many times. This was also confirmed by the knowledge of the Dene Nation, one of the applicants. Historical records before the court showed that the birds got their name after naturalists observed what they thought were giant snow banks during their explorations, which turned out, as they got closer, to be giant flocks of white geese, estimated to include as many as one million birds. Documentary evidence suggested that the idea for the initiative originated in American hunting organizations that were becoming concerned about the decreasing interest in hunting and saw a hunt of this magnitude as an opportunity to attract new interest.

149  Although it has not yet recovered to historic population levels, the return is a positive indication of reduced pesticide levels. Cormorants are the only major predator of several damaging, invasive fish species. Angling groups claim that cormorants are responsible for depleting sport fish numbers, destroying shoreline ecosystems, disturbing other colonial water birds, and causing pollution, and they have received government support to reduce their population. The culling takes place on islands near Point Pelee National Park in the western basin of Lake Erie.

150  *Zoocheck Canada Inc v Canada (Parks Canada Agency)*, 2008 FC 540. Records of the applicant reveal that a federal public consultation resulted in a majority of people opposing the cull. They also document the interest, particularly by American anglers and government agencies, to reduce the cormorant population. The presence of voluntary, independent observers who witnessed the cull

## 3) The *Fisheries Act*

Fisheries are a considerable subject in their own right which are gener-ally beyond the scope of this book; however, in the *Fisheries Act*, mar-ine mammals (including cetaceans, narwhals, walruses, and seals) are included in the definition of "fish" in section 1.[151]

Part I of the *Marine Mammal Regulations* establishes several offences in respect of marine mammals which are comparable to other hunting legislation. They prohibit disturbing a marine mammal, except when "fishing" for marine mammals in accordance with the regulations, and further explicitly prohibit moving a live marine mammal from the im-mediate vicinity in which the animal is found; they prohibit attempting to kill a marine mammal except in a manner that is designed to kill the animal quickly; they require a person who kills or wounds a marine mammal to make efforts to retrieve the animal without delay; and they prohibit the waste of edible parts of cetaceans and walruses, but not of seals or narwhals.

Parts II and III provide minimal regulations in respect of fishing for cetaceans and walruses respectively.

Part IV contains the few regulations governing seals. While im-portant legal issues affect all marine mammals, this chapter will close with a discussion of the hunt for harp and hooded seals, a controversy which has likely crossed almost every Canadian mind and has raised a variety of legal issues. It is a good example of the many areas of legal expertise that can be engaged in animal-related conflicts.

### a) The Seal Hunt

The northwest Atlantic harp seals give birth off Canada's east coast from late February until mid-March. Once pups are weaned, female harps join males for the annual mating ritual. They concentrate in large, close groups on the ice to moult the hair and surface layers of skin, then migrate north to summer feeding grounds in Greenland and surrounding areas. The round-trip migration can be more than 3,000

---

in order to document its conditions and effects seems to have been responsible for reducing the number of birds killed in 2011.

151 Throughout this book, the utilitarian manner in which animals are labelled according to the human purpose they fulfill has been noted. Calling mam-mals "fish" is a strange approach in a legal realm that is heavily dependent on scientific premises. If the terminology were only used in the definition in the *Fisheries Act*, above note 135, s 1, it could perhaps be explained as a simplistic, if incorrect, way of incorporating mammals into a fisheries regime; yet refer-ence is made to the act of fishing for marine mammals throughout the *Marine Mammal Regulations*, above note 136.

miles. The time they spend on Canadian shores and ice floes is a matter of several weeks every spring. Hooded seals, who spend roughly the same time in Canada, are less abundant.

For centuries, seals and other pinnipeds[152] have been slaughtered on Canadian shores and ice floes.[153] Seals have been killed for the white furs of newborn babies, their skins, flesh, and for a period, their male genitals. The modern controversy about the extent and nature of the seal hunt, and the fact that it was largely babies just several days old being killed at the time, peaked in 1983. At that time, the European Economic Community instituted a two-year ban on the import of products from harp and hooded seals, which was later extended an additional four years. The commercial hunt appeared to have ended. It continued on a much smaller scale until the East Coast cod fishery collapsed, and it was resurrected in 1996.[154]

The bartering or sale of whitecoats and bluebacks was prohibited,[155] and the federal government, together with the provincial government of Newfoundland, as it then was, began to actively promote the hunt as humane, and to promote seal products (including seal pepperoni, seal

---

152  Walruses were once abundant along the eastern seaboard of North America, but after intensive hunting, they were permanently extirpated by 1800.

153  In the early-nineteenth century, a large-scale commercial fishery began in earnest in Newfoundland. Larger vessels took hunters out to the whelping patches (close concentrations of seals on the ice where mothers give birth and nurse their young). Steal-hulled steamers and longliners came in the twentieth century. Later, airplanes helped to find the herds in more remote places. Seals have also been hunted in parts of Quebec, such as the Magdalene Islands. That region introduced trawl-lines with large, baited hooks, a killing method that was outlawed in the 1960s. The hunt continues there, although seals have been hard to find there in recent years; the Newfoundland hunt remains the largest.

154  At different times, seals have been attributed responsibility for destroying cod stocks or impeding their recovery. Both allegations are unsupported and contra-indicated (seals spend a brief time in Canadian waters and cod is a minor part of their diet; seals also eat cod's predators; further, biological evidence accumulated in the years leading up to the collapse that human over-fishing was seriously threatening cod stocks).

155  "Whitecoats" are defined as harp seals that have not begun to moult their white coats and "bluebacks" are hooded seals that have not moulted their blue coats. To date, it is prohibited to barter or sell them; it is not, however, prohibited to kill them, and seal hunters are permitted to kill seals for their personal use. The whitecoat moult usually begins when an animal is approximately ten days old, so they can be lawfully killed for commercial purposes at that point: *Marine Mammal Regulations*, above note 136, ss 2 and 27.

jerky, seal oil, leather, and fur) around the world. The market for seal products has, however, been slow to develop.[156]

The commercial slaughter of whitecoats and bluebacks continued after it was prohibited. After an inspection of a seal processing factory initiated by the efforts of an independent seal hunt observer in 1996, more than 100 charges were laid against sealers for violating the prohibition. A lengthy series of legal challenges proceeded before sealers were found to have breached the regulations in 2009.[157]

In 2003, the Canadian government announced that the harp seal population had exploded and it introduced an initiative aimed at dramatically reducing the population. For several years in a row, it established a total allowable catch of approximately 350,000 animals. Approximately two million seals were killed between 2003 and 2008. However, beginning in 2009, the number of seals reported killed began to decline again and continued to decline to 38,000 in 2011.

This second decline also has European origins. In May 2009, 550 members of the European Union Parliament voted in favour of a strong prohibition on the seal product trade; this drove pelt prices down and created a strong disincentive to hunt. In February 2011, Canada

---

156 At one point, the carcasses were sold as fox and mink food to the intensive fur operations in the maritime provinces, until high mortality levels among mink were attributed to seal meat and the practice dwindled. Starting in 1996 and for a number of years thereafter, seal penises were a lucrative part of the hunt, used for aphrodisiac purposes although their alleged therapeutic properties were disproved. For many years, including most recently, much of the seals' flesh is discarded and the only real market continues to be in their skin: Proceedings of the Standing Committee on Fisheries and Oceans (15 June 2006), 39th Parl, 1st Sess, Evidence of Ken Jones at 0940.

157 One of the accused challenged the constitutional authority of the regulation while charges against the others were held in abeyance pending the determination. In 2002, the Supreme Court upheld the validity of the regulation: *Ward v Canada (AG)*, 2002 SCC 17. Then, a test case against one of the accused sealers proceeded, testing the defence of officially induced error, in that the actions and inactions of Fisheries and Oceans Canada (DFO) prior to laying charges had led sealers to believe they could continue to hunt those animals despite the regulation; the defence was initially successful: *Canada v Shiner*, 2006 NLTD 93, then overturned on appeal, 2007 NLCA 18; however it gave credence to allegations that seal hunt observers had been making. Thereafter, sealers commenced an application to stay the proceedings on the basis that the delay caused a violation of their rights under s 11(b) of the *Charter*, above note 59; the challenge was dismissed on the basis that the delay had been waived or caused by the defendants themselves: *R v Shiner*, 2008 CanLII 287 (NL Prov Ct). An application for a directed verdict after the Crown's case was entered was dismissed: *R v Barrett*, 2008 CanLII 37892 (NL Prov Ct) and the defendants were found to have breached the regulations in 2009: *R v Barrett*, 2009 CanLII 1122 (NL Prov Ct).

launched a formal dispute at the World Trade Organisation in response to the EU ban. In June 2011, the European Union Parliament adopted a resolution on EU-Canada trade relations, which threatened to block the ratification of CETA[158] should the Canadian government not withdraw its challenge to the ban at the World Trade Organisation. At the time of writing, Canada's dispute is at the panel selection stage.

In the meantime, the hunt continues. Seals may be lawfully killed by any of three methods: by club, *hakapik*,[159] or firearm (rifle or shotgun).[160] Ice floes used to be quite extensive on Canada's eastern shores, and often sealers hunted on those floes, striking seals directly with clubs or *hakapiks*. In recent years, the ice has broken into small pieces, and much of the hunt has shifted to vessels where seals are typically shot from approximately forty to fifty metres away. The conditions can be extremely dangerous for hunters, with high or even gale force winds, ocean swells, low visibility from fog or freezing rain, and very cold temperatures. Both the vessel and the seal target are moving. As a result, some of the animals fall into the water and drown or die from their injuries after they are shot. Others are retrieved by way of a gaffe, an implement with a long handle and a sharp hook at the end. While it is not permitted to kill a seal with a gaffe, there is no prohibition against using a gaffe for dragging.

The *Marine Mammal Regulations* require that a person who shoots or retrieves a seal must palpate the animal's cranium as soon as possible after the animal is shot to confirm that the cranium has been crushed. If it is not crushed, the sealer must immediately strike the seal's head with a club or *hakapik* until it is crushed. It is prohibited to skin a seal until the cranium has been crushed and at least one minute has elapsed after the two auxiliary arteries of the seal, located beneath her flippers, have been severed.[161]

This regulation is the result of documented complaints that, in the perilous weather conditions and in the hurry to kill as many animals as possible, seals have often been skinned alive.[162] Even if this test is

---

158 CETA is the *Canada-European Union Comprehensive Economic and Trade Agreement* currently being negotiated. Information about the agreement is provided by the federal government online: www.international.gc.ca/trade-agreements-accords-commerciaux/agr-acc/eu-ue/can-eu.aspx?view=d.

159 A Norwegian tool, the modern version of which has an iron head with a curved spike several inches long on one side, and a blunt projection on the other. The head is mounted on a long wooden handle.

160 *Marine Mammal Regulations*, above note 136, s 28.

161 *Ibid*, ss 28(3) & (4).

162 Most of the evidence comes from observations undertaken by individuals on behalf of non-governmental organizations; see references at note 168, below

a realistic way of ensuring that a seal is unconscious, and even if it reasonable to expect that sealers can and will do it in the conditions described, the seal has already been shot, then pulled from the ice, through the water, and up into the boat by a sharp implement impaling her face, head, or other body part.

Since the hunt occurs on public land, is supported by public monies, and consumes what are regarded as public resources, the public has a clear entitlement to accurate information about it. The Canadian government has repeatedly defended the hunt as humane, even as one of the most humane hunts in the world,[163] and independent observation is important in light of the inherent challenges to the likelihood of such a claim. However, observation of the hunt has been a persistent challenge. Section 32 of the *Marine Mammal Regulations* creates seal fishery observation licences (SFOL) and section 33 prohibits anyone from coming within one-half nautical mile of a person fishing for seals without one of these licences. The legality of the scheme has been challenged twice.

In *International Fund for Animal Welfare Inc v Canada (Minister of Fisheries and Oceans)*,[164] the plaintiffs sought a declaration that regulations constraining observers contravened their freedom of expression under section 2(b) of the *Charter*. The challenged regulations pertained to restrictions on aircrafts approaching the site of the seal hunt, and requiring the licensing of persons approaching within one-half nautical mile of the site of a seal hunt. The Federal Court of Appeal found that the aircraft approach provision constituted a reasonable limit on the rights of the observers to attend the seal hunt. However, the *locus* limitation went far beyond what was necessary for carrying out the purpose for which it was intended, and violated the *Charter*. The permit procedure was seen to be official discretion at large, with no specified standards at all.[165]

---

in this chapter. Unscrupulous practices associated with killing seals are also discussed in a book written by a Newfoundland sealer: Michael J Dwyer, *Over the Side, Mickey—A Sealer's First Hand Account of the Newfoundland Seal Hunt* (Halifax: Nimbus, 1998).

163  For example: Proceedings of the Standing Committee on Fisheries and Oceans (23 November 2006), 39th Parl, 1st Sess, Testimony of Fabian Manning at 0945.

164  (1988), 35 CRR 359 (FCA).

165  *Ibid* at 374–76. The case was notable for confirming that the right to freedom of expression includes the right to gather the information that forms the basis of that expression.

The government later added standards and conditions to the SFOL.[166] In the second challenge, the plaintiffs moved for an interim injunction to restrain the application of the conditions, again on the basis of their section 2(b) *Charter* rights. They claimed that they had been improperly denied licences, or frustrated in their attempts to exercise those licences for improper and collateral purposes — namely, that the government that often promoted the hunt as the most humane hunt in the world, did not wish images indicating otherwise to be widely and publicly available. The motion was denied.[167] Similar conditions continue to be attached to date, although the distance which observers must keep from sealers has been reduced from twenty-five to ten metres.

Over the years, the seal controversy has been cast as a debate about humane killing, cultural tradition, sustainable use of seals, conservation of other resources, economic necessity, and free trade.[168] However, it is ultimately a political debate grounded in ethics. The abiding question is whether a commercial seal hunt is morally defensible in the twenty-first century.[169] Legal interventions have delimited the scope of some of the issues over the years, but the hunt itself remains lawful.

---

166  The licence was issued for one day only and could only be renewed up to a maximum of two times; the licence holder had to inform the DFO at least one hour before her departure to observe the seal fishery; the licence holder could not approach closer than twenty-five metres from a person conducting a seal fishery; and observation was only permitted within five nautical miles of the area set out in the licence. Each of the conditions made observation difficult. In particular, a sealer who did not appreciate being observed could cause an observer to be in violation of the twenty-five metre condition by intentionally approaching her.

167  *International Fund for Animal Welfare Inc v Canada (AG)* (1998), 157 DLR (4th) 561 (Ont SCJ). The court found that it was too difficult to determine the constitutional issue on an application for interim relief, and that the effects of the injunction would be to make the determination at a preliminary stage that would harm the public interest and restrain the minister from exercising his power under the Act. The case was significant for affirming that the inherent jurisdiction of a provincial superior court includes disputes in respect of the federal government acting pursuant to federal legislation.

168  Many of these issues are considered in International Fund for Animal Welfare, *Canada's Commercial Seal Slaughter 2009* (Ottawa: International Fund for Animal Welfare, 2009). This and many other reports addressing cruelty allegations, scientific, economic, and other issues can be found online: www.ifaw.org/ifaw_canada_english/publications/program_publications/save_baby_seals.php. Organized opposition has been directed exclusively at the commercial hunt and not at Aboriginal hunting for personal use.

169  David M Lavigne & William S Lynn, "Canada's Commercial Seal Hunt: It's More Than a Question of Humane Killing" (2011) 1(1) Journal of Animal Ethics 1.

# CLOSING THOUGHTS

Today's problems cannot be solved by thinking the way we thought when we created them.

— Albert Einstein

What strikes one most about the profound violence to which so many animals are subjected in modern Canadian society is how utterly ordinary it is. That is why anti-cruelty laws have proved unable to diminish that violence in any meaningful way. The word "cruelty," both as the title of criminal offences against animals, and as the general manner in which unacceptable treatment of animals is commonly described, protects the routine practices that are common in a given activity by drawing out for condemnation only singular acts of *extra*ordinary behaviour. If many people find it convenient, enjoyable, or profitable to do things that hurt animals, those things are not legally cruel. So long as causing animals to suffer is not the only object of the act, the fact that they suffer as a result becomes almost entirely irrelevant.

Cruelty connotes a malevolent intention that creates too high and constrained a standard. Many criminal offences could be said to involve cruelty as it is generally understood—breaking in to a person's home, theft of a person's treasured belongings, kidnapping, assault, murder, and so on. Yet there is no additional legal element of "cruelty" to cast an interpretive shadow over those or any other crimes. The term is a legal anachronism that dates from the time the relationship between humans and animals was first codified, a time when animals were seen to be largely irrelevant things which were categorically different from humans.

Similarly, laws that prohibit "unnecessary suffering" or require "humane treatment" fail to protect the interests animals have in living their own lives and in not being made to suffer for human purposes. The former term conveys an objective necessity and corresponding entitlement to hurt animals in accordance with human convenience or preference. The latter term is problematic in two ways: when used as a standard for the treatment of animals, it is bereft of any substance; when used to describe and excuse generally accepted practices in which animals are often severely hurt—practices which would be criminal offences if committed against any human being—it transforms into Orwellian doublespeak.

The problems that have been discussed in this book are ubiquitous. In many cases, vested interests perpetuate activities that have, by any modest ethical standard, lost all credible defences. But that perpetuation depends on societal acceptance of those activities, or at least, of societal willingness to look away and defer to those vested interests to decide right and wrong on the collective behalf. As science has, over time, eroded the categorical distinctions between humans and other animals by revealing our biological kinship, the public attitude has changed. These activities no longer enjoy the lack of scrutiny they once did. The trivialization of animal interests that has long prevailed in law and other social institutions is beginning to yield. Slowly, but undeniably, respect for animals is emerging as a Canadian value.

As it does, the topic of animal law begins its development. This is a sign of considerable progress, indicating that the subject has moved from the stage of ridicule, to debate, and toward adoption, in accordance with the three stages of social movements identified by John Stuart Mill. However, the term "animal law" might not be clear enough. "Human law" would seem to include every possible kind of conflict that two human persons could have, and this would comprise every legal subject under the sun. The term "animal law" is equally vague, potentially including every problem in which animals appear at the centre. A term like "animal rights law" might better identify a body of law in which the *status quo* approach to animals as property is in dispute.

In a democracy, law is expected to change in accordance with changing values. The legal lexicon by which the human-animal relationship is regulated will have to evolve to accommodate modern knowledge and ideas about animals. Law must look back to understand the assumptions that have traditionally impoverished interpretations of statutory language as noted above; otherwise, that language will continue to camouflage the very harms it purports to restrain. However, not only the language which implements these assumptions requires review; where the beliefs on which legal assumptions rest no longer have a factual base, the validity of the assumptions themselves must be re-evaluated, such as the assumption that animals are things with no morally significant interests of their own.

As the law begins to more meaningfully recognize animals as sentient beings, it will have to consider what the morally relevant differences are that justify the negative treatment of some sentient beings, while knowing that treatment would be unacceptable for human beings. It will have to confront the absurdity that while inanimate constructs such as churches, partnerships, trusts, estates, unions, municipalities, and other corporations can advance their interests in law,[1] sentient beings with fundamental interests that are comparable to the very interests the law seeks to protect for humans, are prevented from doing so. It will have to begin to recast some kinds of legal conflicts and consider new ways of resolving others.

Ultimately, in a legal system that seeks to be logically and morally coherent, legal personhood for animals seems an inevitable result. To say that a being is a person is merely to say that the being has morally significant interests, that the principle of equal consideration applies to that being, and that the being is not a thing.[2] However, because of the long-standing nature of the proprietary relationship humans have preferred, the legal shift will take some time. As Professor Stone observed many years ago in his academic inquiry into whether trees should have standing:

> [t]he fact is, that each time there is a movement to confer rights onto some new 'entity,' the proposal is bound to sound odd or frightening or laughable. This is partly because until the rightless thing receives its rights, we cannot see it as anything but a thing for the use of 'us,' those who are holding rights at the time.[3]

---

1   Under international law, states are also recognized as having legal personality. See the discussion in Laurence H Tribe, "Ten Lessons Our Constitutional Experience Can Teach Us About the Puzzle of Animal Rights: The Work of Steven M. Wise" (2001) 7 Animal L 1.

2   Gary L Francione, *Introduction to Animal Rights: Your Child or the Dog?* (Philadelphia: Temple University Press, 2000) at 100–1. For further discussion, see Chapter 2.

3   Christopher D Stone, "Should Trees Have Standing? Toward Legal Rights for Natural Objects" (1972) 45 S Cal L Rev 450 at 453–56.

Personhood might be established by way of direct legal efforts, or it might be the result of an accumulation of indirect initiatives in which the property status of animals is gradually eroded and replaced.[4] For example, American legal scholars have prepared an academic legal brief based on the theoretical case of an individual named Evelyn Hart.[5] Hart is a chimpanzee whose human guardian contested an order dispatching her to a government-funded biomedical research laboratory. The story of Evelyn Hart is a composite; she is intended to personify all great apes who are sold into human commerce. The brief articulates a persuasive argument for great ape personhood based on constitutional and other legal principles.

In a more concrete example, an Austrian shelter housing two chimpanzees filed for bankruptcy in 2007. The animals had been captured as babies in Sierra Leone and smuggled to Austria for use in pharmaceutical experiments. Customs officers intercepted the shipment and turned the animals over to the shelter. Donors were prepared to continue their financial support after the shelter closed, but under Austrian law, only a legal person could receive personal gifts. Advocates commenced a legal proceeding to establish the legal personhood of one of the chimps, named Matthew Hiasl Pan, so that a guardian could be appointed to protect his interests, receive support on his behalf, and ensure that he could not be sold to someone outside of Austria where weaker legal standards applied. The claim was rejected, as novel legal arguments often initially are; in fact, the problem had less novel solutions, such as establishing a foundation to collect the needed financial support. However, the initiative received extensive international attention and debate.[6]

In 2005, an application for a writ of *habeas corpus* was brought on behalf of a lone chimpanzee named Suica, living in a zoo in Brazil.[7] *Hab-*

---

4   See a controversial example, Jessica Berg, "Of Elephants and Embryos: A Proposed Framework for Legal Personhood" (2007) 59 Hastings LJ 369.

5   Lee Hall & Anthony Jon Waters, "From Property to Person: The Case of Evelyn Hart" (2000) 11 Seton Hall Const LJ 1.

6   See William J Cole, "Activists in Austria Want Chimp Declared a 'Person'" *Associated Press* (5 May 2007), online: www.chron.com/news/nation-world/article/ Activists-in-Austria-want-chimp-declared-a-1613850.php; "Austrian Judge: Chimps Aren't People" *Associated Press* (27 September 2007), online: www.usa-today.com/news/offbeat/2007-09-27-chimpanzee_N.htm.

7   In 9th Salvador Criminal Court, Salvador, Bahia, Official Diary for 4 October 2005, Docket Number 833085-3/2005. The decision is available online: www.animallaw.info/nonus/cases/cabrsuicaeng2005.htm. An English translation of the brief filed is available online: www.animallaw.info/nonus/pleadings/pb_pdf/ Habeas%20Corpus%20on%20Behalf%20of%20a%20Chimp%20Rev2.pdf.

*eas corpus* is a legal procedure by which a person can seek relief from unlawful detention. Rather than dismiss the initial application, the Brazilian court found it to be a highly complex issue deserving of discussion and requiring in-depth examination. It sought further information from Suica's advocates, which was to be produced within seventy-two hours; however, in that interim period, Suica was found dead in her cage. The court therefore dismissed the application, but in doing so, it observed that criminal law is not static, that new decisions have to adapt to new times, and that the topic would not die with the writ.[8]

In Canada, no such direct claim for animal personhood has yet been made, but courts have begun to reflect the changing paradigm and have laid the groundwork for a new approach. The cases are few in number to date, but they can be found across the legal spectrum. For example:

- In a variety of cases in the realm of torts, family law, and provincial offences, courts import consideration of an animal's "best interests" and "custody," thereby recognizing the law's interest in protecting a sentient animal for his own sake and not just in his capacity as somebody's property.[9]
- Similarly, in *R v Power*,[10] the Court of Appeal for Ontario confirmed that in criminal offences against animals, the offence is to the animal herself, regardless of whether or not a person has any interest in her.
- In *R v Munroe*,[11] the ten-fold increase in the overall maximum penalty that was implemented in 2008 for crimes against animals was found to be virtually unheard of in criminal law. It reflected Parliament's recognition of widespread concerns that animal cruelty provisions had fallen drastically out of step with current social values and it represented both a fundamental shift in Parliament's approach and a dramatic change to the legislative landscape for these crimes.[12]

---

8   For further discussion, see Deborah Rook, "Should Great Apes Have 'Human Rights'?" [2009] 1 Web JCLI.

9   See discussion in Chapter 5. In a similar spirit, some municipalities have begun to change their terminology and refer to the humans as being "guardians" of animals, rather than "owners": see a By-law for the Licensing and Registration of Dogs and for the Control of Dogs Generally within the City of Windsor, By-law 245/2004, online: www.citywindsor.ca/000024.asp.

10   (2003), 176 CCC (3d) 209.

11   2010 ONCJ 226.

12   *Ibid* at paras 1–3 and 27.

- In *R v Houdek*,[13] the Saskatchewan Court of Queen's Bench contemplated the consequences of dangerous dog proceedings for the dog in issue and expressed that in making the determination of whether or not a dog is dangerous, "the quality of mercy should not be strained."[14]
- In *Ferguson v Birchmount Boarding Kennels Ltd*,[15] Ontario's Divisional Court rejected the categorization of a companion animal as just another consumer product as "incorrect in law."[16]
- In the "oncomouse case,"[17] the Supreme Court recognized the animal rights perspective as a relevant one in Canadian legal discourse.
- In *Reece v Edmonton (City)*,[18] the chief justice of the Alberta Court of Appeal drew upon the growing body of legal scholarship on this topic,[19] and acknowledged both the pressing need for legal progress and the theoretical basis for granting meaningful animal rights. And

---

13  2008 SKQB 434.
14  *Ibid* at para 24.
15  (2006), 79 OR (3d) 681 (SCJ).
16  *Ibid* at paras 20 and 25.
17  *Harvard College v Canada (Commissioner of Patents)*, 2002 SCC 76.
18  2011 ABCA 238.
19  *Ibid* at footnote 24. Fraser CJA relied on what she described as the considerable scholarship in this area that has been generated over the past two decades in both Canada and the United States, including: David Favre & Vivien Tsang, "The Development of Anti-Cruelty Laws During the 1800's" (1993) 1 Detroit College of Law Review 1; Gary Francione, "Animals, Property and Legal Welfarism: Unnecessary Suffering and the Humane Treatment of Animals" (1994) 46:2 Rutgers L Rev 721; Gary Francione, "Animal Rights Theory and Utilitarianism: Relative Normative Guidance" (1997) 3 Animal L 75; Gary Francione, *Rain Without Thunder: The Ideology of the Animal Rights Movement* (Philadelphia: Temple University Press, 1996); Steven Wise, *Rattling the Cage: Toward Legal Rights for Animals* (Cambridge, MA: Perseus, 2000); Elaine L Hughes & Christiane Meyer, "Animal Welfare Law in Canada and Europe" (2000) 6 Animal L 23; FC DeCoste, "Animals and Political Community: Preliminary Reflections Prompted by Bill C-10" (2003) 40:4 Alta L Rev 1057; Lyne Letourneau, "Toward Animal Liberation—The New Anti-Cruelty Provisions in Canada and Their Impact on the Status of Animals" (2003) 40:4 Alta L Rev 1041; Cass R Sunstein & Martha C Nussbaum, eds, *Animal Rights: Current Debates and New Directions* (Oxford: Oxford University Press, 2004); Arlene Kwasniak, *Wildlife Stewardship* (Calgary: Canadian Institute of Resources Law, 2006); Elaine Hughes, *Animal Welfare Law in a Canadian Context*, 3d ed (Edmonton: University of Alberta Faculty of Law, 2006); Cass R Sunstein & Jeff Leslie, "Animal Rights Without Controversy" (2007) 70 Law & Contemp Probs 117; David Favre, "Living Property: A New Status for Animals Within the Legal System" (2010) 93 Marq L Rev 1021; Joan E Schaffner, *An Introduction to Animals and the Law* (Hampshire, UK: Palgrave Macmillan, 2011); and Peter Sankoff & Steven White, eds, *Animal Law in Australasia: A New Dialogue* (Annandale, NSW: The New Federation Press, 2009).

while such progress is being implemented, her reasons provide interim support for a significantly broader interpretation of existing legislation that has animal protection as its aim.

This book has been largely occupied with suffering and exploitation, because those are the characteristics which define the relationships most animals have with humans in Canada. In *Reece*, Fraser CJA found that the evidence revealed a disturbing image of the magnitude, gravity, and persistence of health problems and the severity of the suffering endured by an elephant named Lucy, an animal held captive at Edmonton's Valley Zoo for the benefit of human visitors. The evidence, she found, held up a mirror for all to see—so long as one is prepared to look in it. If one holds up "Fraser's Mirror" high enough, the urgent need for legal change for animals across Canada is patently clear, and the task of Canadian lawyers and lawmakers is to apply the attention, determination, and creativity needed to usher it in.

# GLOSSARY

**animal rights.** A term embodying the idea that animals, as sentient beings, are entitled to not be considered things people own and use for their own purposes, or as means to human ends; the movement to liberate animals from human exploitation.

**animal welfare.** A term embodying the idea that people can own and use animals for their purposes, but that in the course of doing so, animals should be treated humanely and not be subjected to unnecessary suffering; the movement to improve the standards of animal care.

**ankus.** Also called a "bullhook," a long metal rod with a sharp, pointed tip used to dominate elephants and other wild animals by way of pain and fear.

**bag limit.** A term used in hunting to refer to the maximum number of individual animals of a given species that a person may lawfully kill.

**beast wagon.** The bare and cramped cage in which circus animals eat, sleep, urinate, defecate, travel, and generally spend their lives when they are not in the performance ring.

**broiler.** Used in the agricultural context to describe chickens bred specifically for their meat.

**compensatory mortality.** A term that describes the biological phenomenon that sometimes occurs when humans kill a number of wild or free-living animals with the intent of reducing the population of a particular species, which instead results in the return of the population to the same or even greater numbers.

**cruelty.** The title of crimes against animals in the *Criminal Code* and a term commonly used to describe unacceptable human treatment of animals; the term is generally undefined in Canadian law and likely out of date. It connotes a malevolent intent which implies a high standard to be met before harm to an animal is considered a legal wrong. So long as there is some human purpose motivating the act and the harm is not gratuitous, it is not likely to be found to be cruel, however serious the harm to the animal and however trivial the human purpose.

**cull.** An intentional effort to kill a predetermined number of animals for a variety of reasons, whether to reinforce or remove certain characteristics from a group, or to reduce a population of animals, all in accordance with human preference.

**debeak.** A procedure common in intensive agriculture where the nerve-loaded beaks of chickens or other birds are cut off by a hot blade or other methods, often without anaesthetic, in order to reduce the self-mutilation and cannibalism that is seen among stressed and frustrated confined birds.

**dehorn.** A common procedure in intensive agriculture where animals' horns are cut off to prevent them from damaging one another in close confinement and to make them more amenable to human handling and even closer confinement; the process has traditionally involved sawing or otherwise cutting the horns, often without anaesthetic; efforts are underway to develop a caustic paste that prevents the horns from developing.

**de-snood.** A procedure common in intensive agriculture where the snood, or flap of skin that hangs over a turkey's beak, is cut off, often without anaesthetic, to reduce the risk of cannibalism among stressed and frustrated confined birds.

**dissection.** The use of animals or the body parts of animals who have been killed for purposes of research, teaching, or testing.

**domesticated.** Animals that have been specifically bred, generally for hundreds of generations, to bring out particular physical and psychological traits that make them amenable to living with or among humans; having been bred in captivity for several generations does not make an animal domesticated.

**downer**. An animal who, by reason of illness or injury, is so debilitated that she cannot stand up or remain standing; used in the agricultural context, most commonly, but not exclusively, in respect of dairy cows.

**extirpated**. A term used in respect of wildlife, referring to a species that no longer occurs in a particular geographic area; as distinct from "extinct" which means that no member of the species can be found anywhere.

**feral**. A living organism, whether plant or animal, that was domesticated, but now is living freely, untamed, or in the wild.

*hakapik*. A weapon of Norwegian origin used in seal hunting; it consists of an iron or steel hook, sometimes with a hammer head opposite, mounted on a long wooden pole.

**humane**. A term used, though generally undefined in existing Canadian law, in reference to the manner in which animals are supposed to be treated, kept, handled, or killed; the meaning of the term could be seen to vary in accordance with individual perception.

**layer**. A term used in the agricultural context to refer to chickens bred specifically for the purpose of producing eggs.

**moral schizophrenia**. A term coined by American legal scholar Gary Francione to describe humanity's ambivalent relationship with other animals; generally, the conflict between the stated desire not to cause animals any unnecessary pain and suffering, and the support of practices that cause pain and suffering that cannot be regarded as necessary in any normal sense of the word.

**ruminant**. Animals such as cows, goats, sheep, deer, and giraffes, whose stomachs are characteristically divided into four compartments and whose digestion includes a process often referred to as "chewing their cud."

**sentience**. A conscious being's capacity to feel and perceive; in reference to animals, it often refers to the specific ability to feel pain and suffer.

**speciesism**. A term coined by Richard Ryder, though often attributed to Peter Singer, connoting discrimination against animals on the basis of species, suggesting that discriminating on the basis of species is unjustifiable in a manner similar to other forms of discrimination, such as racism and sexism.

**vegan**. A person who refrains from eating any product derived from an animal, distinguished from a vegetarian, who refrains from eating meat but does eat other animal products, such as dairy and eggs; the term vegan connotes diet, however, vegans also often refrain from using any product derived from an animal, such as clothing and furniture.

**vermin.** A derogatory term used to refer to animals that cause or are perceived to cause a problem for people.

**vivisection.** The use of living animals for purposes of research, teaching, or testing.

# TABLE OF CASES

# INDEX

# ABOUT THE AUTHOR

**Lesli Bisgould** has been a litigator in Ontario since 1992. She began in the field of civil litigation and then spent ten years in her own practice in animal rights law, the only practice of its kind in Canada. She has written and lectured widely on the subject of animal rights and the law and is currently an adjunct professor at the University of Toronto's Faculty of Law, where she instructs a seminar entitled "Introduction to Animals and the Law." She has argued at every level of court and deputed at every level of government. In recent years, her full-time work has been in the fields of poverty and human rights law. She is currently the barrister at Legal Aid Ontario's Clinic Resource Office where she assists caseworkers at Ontario's community legal clinics with their appeals. All the opinions expressed in this book are those of the author alone and not those of Legal Aid Ontario or of the University of Toronto.